Media / Reader

Media / Reader

Perspectives on Mass Media

Third Edition

SHIRLEY BIAGI

California State University, Sacramento

Wadsworth Publishing Company
ITP™ An International Thomson Publishing Company

Belmont • Albany • Bonn • Boston • Cincinnati • Detroit • London •
Madrid • Melbourne • Mexico City • New York • Paris • San Francisco •
Singapore • Tokyo • Toronto • Washington

Communications & Media Studies Editor: Todd R. Armstrong
Editorial Assistant: Laura A. Murray
Production Editor: Angela Mann
Interior & Cover Designer: Andrew Ogus
Print Buyer: Barbara Britton
Permissions Editor: Bob Kauser
Copy Editor: Barbara Kimmel
Cover Photograph: Pierre-Yves Goavec
Compositor: Color Type
Printer: Quebecor/Fairfield

Printed in the United States of America
1 2 3 4 5 6 7 8 9 10—02 01 00 99 98 97 96

For more information, contact Wadsworth Publishing Company:

Wadsworth Publishing Company
10 Davis Drive
Belmont, California 94002, USA

International Thomson Publishing Europe
Berkshire House 168-173
High Holborn
London, WC1V 7AA, England

Thomas Nelson Australia
102 Dodds Street
South Melbourne 3205
Victoria, Australia

Nelson Canada
1120 Birchmount Road
Scarborough, Ontario
Canada M1K 5G4

International Thomson Editores
Campos Eliseos 385, Piso 7
Col. Polanco
11560 México D.F. México

International Thomson Publishing GmbH
Königswinterer Strasse 418
53227 Bonn, Germany

International Thomson Publishing Asia
221 Henderson Road
#05-10 Henderson Building
Singapore 0315

International Thomson Publishing Japan
Hirakawacho Kyowa Building, 3F
2-2-1 Hirakawacho
Chiyoda-ku, Tokyo 102, Japan

Library of Congress Cataloging-in-Publication Data

Media/reader: perspectives on mass media / [edited by] Shirley Biagi.
 –3rd, [rev.] ed.
      p.   cm. – (Wadsworth series in mass communication and journalism)
    Includes bibliographical references and index.
    ISBN: 0-534-26598-7
    1. Mass media.   I. Biagi, Shirley.   II. Series.
  P91.25.M374   1995
  302.23–dc20   95-12747

Contents

Preface

This third edition *Media/Reader* introduces several new features. First, there is a new chapter on Technology (Chapter Two), with articles about everything from the electronic electorate to how people say they will and will not use the new technologies. There's even an article in this chapter about a new breed of criminal — the Internet pirate.

Media/Reader, Third Edition, also expands its global outlook, with a separate section on international media and articles on some of the issues common to media in all countries sprinkled throughout. Chapter 11, Public Relations, includes an article on public relations in the United Kingdom, and an article about the practice of "hidden advertising" in Russia is discussed in Chapter 15, Ethical Practices.

Each chapter also reflects my belief that changing technology will be the central focus of any discussion of the media for the next decade. You will find articles about on-line newspapers; on-line magazines; the role of telecommunications companies in the global market; changing methods of TV audience measurement; direct broadcast satellites; and the attempts by media corporations, advertising agencies, and public relations companies to expand their reach overseas.

What are the cultural implications of all this change? You will study, for example, the evolving image of Aunt Jemima and Betty Crocker; learn why your local TV weathercaster may not be your local TV weathercaster; analyze the exploding popcorn exposé; read journalist Molly Ivins' advice about what makes a good journalist; and discover what Stephen King has to say about his fan mail.

The social and economic issues are covered, too, with an analysis of political advertising; a look at portrayals of Native Americans in the movies; a report on advertising to Asian-Americans; a discussion of the U.S. news media's coverage of international conflict; and a review of the role of the traditional TV networks in an era of cable.

These are only some of the highlights. There are 77 selections in this edition of *Media/Reader,* and 51 of them are new additions. *Media/Reader,* divided into 16 chapters, can be used as a stand-alone reader for Introduction to Mass Media and Mass Media and Society courses and for Media Issues seminars. *Media/Reader* also can be used as a companion to any introductory mass media text, including *Media/Impact: An Introduction to Mass Media. Media/Reader* follows the same chapter organization as *Media/Impact.*

Media/Reader is divided into five sections:

Part I   *Overview (Chapters 1 and 2)*
          Understanding Mass Media
          Media in the 21st Century:
             Interactive and On-line

Part II   *The Media Industries
             (Chapters 3–9)*
          Print: The Newspaper Industry
                    The Magazine Industry
                    The Book Publishing
                       Industry
          Audio: The Radio Industry
                    The Recording Industry
          Video: The Television Industry
                    The Movie Industry

Part III *Support Industries
             (Chapters 10 and 11)*
                Advertising
                Public Relations

Part IV   *Issues and Effects
             (Chapters 12–15)*
                Ownership Issues; Press
                   Performance Issues
                Media Effects
                Legal and Regulatory
                   Issues
                Ethical Practices

Part V   *International Media (Chapter 16)*
                Global Media

Part IV has been expanded in this edition to give more attention to media issues and effects, and Part V has been completely updated to give expanded attention to the global media marketplace. Throughout the text are many articles designed to reflect multicultural points of view.

A *Perspective* precedes each article, giving a summary of major points in the form of three or four questions for discussion, which will also help students analyze the content critically. Topical articles are designed to keep readers current with the dynamics of today's media industries and issues. Readings from professional journals and newly issued texts highlight the literature of the media. All the articles were chosen to reflect timely, challenging scholarship, selected for readability and accessibility for today's students. I hope you will find these readings provocative.

Acknowledgments

This text could not have been compiled without each of the voices represented here. Their ongoing and productive analysis, criticism, and praise of the world's media are what make the study of mass media so challenging.

In addition, thanks go to my colleagues at universities and colleges throughout the country who have used the first and second editions and written me to suggest new readings for the text. Reviewers for this edition were James Bolick, Colorado State University; Timothy Meyer, University of Wisconsin-Green Bay; Peter K. Pringle, University of Tennessee at Chattanooga; Linda Steiner, Rutgers University; Robert Woodward, Drake University. Second edition reviewers were Thomas L. Beell, Iowa State University; Richard Campbell, University of Michigan, Ann Arbor; Carolyn Johnson, California State University, Fullerton; Dianne M. Lamb, University of New Mexico; Val Limburg, Washington State University; Daniel G. McDonald, Cornell University; Douglass Starr, Texas A & M

University; and John D. Zelezny, California State University, Fresno.

First edition reviewers were Thomas Beell, Iowa State University; Kenneth Harwood, University of Houston-University Park; Seong Lee, Appalachian State University; and Maclyn McClary, Humboldt State University.

Please send your comments, criticisms, and suggestions to me at California State University, 6000 J Street, Sacramento, California 95819, or you can reach me on-line during the school year at INTERNET:sbiagi@saclink.csus.edu. Thank you.

Shirley Biagi

PART I

Overview

CHAPTER 1
Understanding Mass Media

New Technologies and Today's Culture

In this selection from *The New York Times'* editorial page, futurists Alvin and Heidi Toffler analyze the global rearrangement that is taking place in the world today. As authors of *War and Anti-War: Survival at the Dawn of the 21st Century,* the Tofflers say that the new world will be arranged according to countries that process information and countries that process goods.

Consider:

1. What do Alvin and Heidi Toffler mean when they say that there is now a three-tiered society and the third tier consists of a group of societies that do the world's "knowledge work"? Do you agree? Why? Why not?

2. Why, according to Alvin and Heidi Toffler, are "nations, as such, becoming less important"? Do you agree? Why? Why not?

3. According to Alvin and Heidi Toffler, how will the communications revolution affect (1) agricultural economies; (2) industrial economies; and (3) economies based on information, communications, and technology?

Societies at Hyper-Speed

Alvin Toffler and Heidi Toffler

Why doesn't America know where it is going? U.S. foreign and military policy is swerving like a drunken driver without a map. It shows no clear grasp of our vital short-term national interests — let alone an understanding of the long-term shape of the global system.

We need to start by understanding that the old world map is obsolete — that the global system would be in revolutionary upheaval even if the Soviet Union still existed. We are undergoing the deepest rearrangement of global power since the birth of industrial civilization.

Until very recently, world power was bisected — industrial societies on top, peasant-based societies on the bottom. But the rising importance of goods and services based on sophisticated knowledge and high technology — from computer software and news services to genetically enhanced seeds — has created a third layer, a group of societies that increasingly do the world's economically relevant "knowledge work."

Of course, this transition is not yet clear because nowhere is it complete. Even Japan and the United States, whose economies are the most technically advanced, still have large and politically potent smokestack sectors in which low-skill labor prevails. China, Brazil and India, mainly agrarian, have large industrial economies with pockets of high technology. But these overlaps should not blind us to the powerful forces that are shaping the global system of the [21st] century.

As global competition drives the advanced economies deeper into high-skill, information-intensive production and distribution, they transfer more and more of their unskilled muscle-based jobs to agrarian countries like China or, for that matter, Mexico.

Nations like Japan, the U.S. and Singapore are neither agrarian nor industrial. Their work forces are predominantly white-collar. Societies are media-drenched. Economies rely on complex electronic infrastructures. . . . This digital structure is needed to handle the information that is the most basic raw material of tomorrow's economy. It is to the emerging high-technology nations what roads and ports were to the emerging industrial nations.

But nations, as such, are becoming less important. Powerful transnational businesses are creating information networks that "bypass the nation-state framework," in the words of Riccardo Petrella, director of science and technology forecasting for the European Community.

Regions are also growing in power. Mr. Petrella continues: "By the middle of the [21st] century, such nation-states as Germany, Italy, the United States or Japan will no longer be the most relevant socioeconomic entities and the ultimate political configuration. Instead, areas like Orange County, Calif.; Osaka, Japan; the Lyon region of France, or Germany's Ruhrgebiete will acquire predominant socioeconomic status. The real decision-making powers of the future . . . will be transnational companies in alliance with city-regional governments."

Another type of unit is also growing in importance: thousands of transnational organizations — Greenpeace, for example — are springing up like mushrooms to form a new "civil society."

Add to these components of the new global system world religions like Roman Catholicism and Islam, plus fast-multiplying media networks like CNN that cross (and blur) borders, and it is clear that the world system built around neatly defined nation-states is being replaced by a kind of global computer, with thousands of diverse components plugged into a three-level motherboard.

At one level, agrarian countries are hardly connected to the system, with few links to the outside world other than the countries that serve as markets, and they operate at a leisurely "clock speed." At a second level, industrial nations move faster and are more connected to the global system.

But what we call "third wave" societies —with economies based on information, communications and technology—run at hyper-speeds. And they require an amazing number of connections with the outside world. In 1930 the U.S. was a party to only 34 treaties or agreements with other countries; [in 1993], with the world's most knowledge-intensive economy, it is party to more than 1,000 treaties and tens of thousands of agreements.

This produces an overlooked paradox: a very strange world in which the most powerful and most accelerated countries are the ones most tied down by external commitments, the least free to act independently. This explains why an Aidid in Somalia or a junta in Haiti can run rings around the United States.

These widening differences in the trisected global system also change each nation's list of vital interests. For "first wave," or agricultural, economies, the essentials for survival are land, energy, water for irrigation, cooking oil, food, minimal literacy and markets for cash crops or raw materials. Their natural resources and farm products are their chief salable assets.

States in the second wave, or industrial tier, still rely on cheap manual labor and mass production, with concentrated, integrated national economies. They need high inputs of energy per unit of production. They need bulk raw materials to keep their factories going — iron, steel, cement, timber, petrochemicals and the like. They are the home of a small number of global corporations. They are major producers of pollution and other ecological problems. Above all, they need export markets for their mass-produced products.

Third wave economies, the newest tier of the global system, have sharply different vital interests. Unlike agrarian states, they have no great need for additional territory. Unlike industrial states, they have little need for vast natural resources of their own, as Japan and Singapore demonstrate.

These societies still need energy and food, of course, but they also need knowledge convertible into wealth. They need access to, or control of, world data banks and telecommunications networks. They need markets for products and services that depend on knowledge: financial services, management consulting, software, television programming, banking, economic intelligence and all the technologies on which these things depend.

They need protection against the piracy of intellectual products. And as for ecology, they want the "unspoiled" agrarian countries to protect their jungles, skies and greenery for the "global good" — sometimes even if it stifles development.

When we take all these changes together — differences in the types of units making up the global system, in their connectedness to that system, in their speed and in their vital interests — we arrive at a transformation more revolutionary than anything caused by the end of the cold war.

It is an emerging world in which great powers may decline, tiny states may become shooting stars, nonstates dominate many decisions and advanced technologies and weaponry may turn up in the remotest corners of the planet. This is the arena in which tomorrow's wars — and the efforts to stop those wars — will be fought.

U.S. policy will continue to swerve drunkenly across the globe until its business and political leaders study this road map of tomorrow and develop long-range strategies to advance America's truly vital interests on a trisected planet.

Overcoming Civic Illiteracy

Media play a central role in the way people think about their country. In this excerpt from a speech he delivered at a communications award luncheon, television commentator Bill Moyers says that the media should stimulate public dialogue instead of pandering to the audience with celebrity gossip, tabloid news, and video gadgetry.

Consider:

1. How does Moyers define "civic illiteracy"? the "New News"? Explain.

2. What does Moyers mean when he says that "our public discourse has become the verbal equivalent of mud wrestling"? Do you agree? Why? Why not?

3. According to Moyers, how can responsible journalists, such as those at the *Philadelphia Inquirer,* contribute to the public's understanding of important issues? Why is that contribution so important?

Why Are the Media Important?

Bill Moyers

Americans can turn on a series called "Real Sex" and watch a home strip-tease class; its premiere was HBO's highest-rated documentary for the year.

Or they can flip to NBC News and get "I Witness Video." There they can see a policeman's murder recorded in his cruiser's camcorder, watch it replayed and relived in interviews, complete with ominous music.

Or they can see the video of a pregnant woman plunging from a blazing building's window: they can see it several times, at least once in slow motion.

Yeats was right: "We had fed the heart on fantasies, the heart's grown brutal from the fare." I wonder if "Real Sex" and "I Witness Video" take us deeper into reality or insanity?

Rolling Stone dubs all this the New News.

Straight news—the Old News by Rolling Stone's definition—is "pooped, confused and broke."

In its place a new culture of information is evolving—"a heady concoction, part Hollywood film and TV, part pop music and pop art, mixed with popular culture and celebrity magazines, tabloid telecasts, cable and home video."

Increasingly, says the magazine, the New News is seizing the function of mainstream journalism, sparking conversation and setting the country's social and political agenda.

So it is that we learn first from Bruce Springsteen that jobs aren't coming back.

So it is that inner-city parents who don't subscribe to daily newspapers are taking their children to see "Juice" to educate them about the consequences of street violence; that young people think Bart Simpson's analysis of America more trenchant than that of many newspaper columnists; that we learn just how violent, brutal and desperate society is, not from the establishment press but from Spike Lee, Public Enemy, the Geto Boys and Guns 'n' Roses.

Now even MTV is doing original reporting on [the 1992] political campaign.

Once, newspapers drew people to the public square. They provided a culture of community conversation by activating inquiry on serious public issues.

When the press abandons that function, it no longer stimulates what John Dewey termed "the vital habits" of democracy — "the ability to follow an argument, grasp the point of view of another, expand the boundaries of understanding, debate the alternative purposes that might be pursued."

But I also know that what Dean Joan Konner said recently at the Columbia School of Journalism is true: "There is a civil war in our society today, a conflict between two American cultures, each holding very different values. The adversaries are private profits versus pubic responsibility; personal ambition versus the community good; quantitative measures versus qualitative concerns."

And I sense we're approaching Gettysburg, the moment of truth, the decisive ground for this cultural war — for newspaper publishers especially.

Americans say they no longer trust journalists to tell them the truth about their world. Young people have difficulty finding anything of relevance to their lives in the daily newspaper.

Non-tabloid newspapers are viewed as increasingly elitist, self-important and corrupt on the one hand; on the other, they are increasingly lumped with the tabloids as readers perceive the increasing desperation with which papers are now trying to reach "down market" in order to replace the young readers who are not replacing their elders.

Meanwhile, a study by the Kettering Foundation confirms that our political institutions are fast losing their legitimacy, that increasing numbers of Americans believe they are being dislodged from their rightful place in democracy by politicians, powerful lobbyists and the media — three groups they see as an autonomous political class impervious to the long-term interests of the country and manipulating the democratic discourse so that people are treated only as consumers to be entertained rather than citizens to be engaged.

That our political system is failing to solve the bedrock problems we face is beyond dispute. One reason is that our public discourse has become the verbal equivalent of mud wrestling.

Taken together, these assumptions and developments foreshadow the catastrophe of social and political paralysis: a society that continues to be governed by the same two parties that are driving it into the pits; a society that doesn't understand the link between two students killed in the hallways of a Brooklyn high school and the plea bargain which assures Michael Milken of being able to scrape by on $125 million; a society that every day breaks open its children's piggy banks and steals $1 billion just to pay the daily bills; a society that responds with anger at check-kiting in Congress but doesn't even know that the executive branch has lost track of tens of billions of dollars appropriated for the savings and loan bailout; a society where democracy is constantly thwarted by unaccountable money; a society where more people know George Bush hates broccoli than know that he ordered the invasion of Panama, and more know Marla Maples than Vaclav Havel, and where, by a margin of two to one, people say the government's ability to censor the news during the Persian Gulf war was more important than the media's ability to report it.

What's astonishing about this civic illiteracy — some call it a disease — is that it exists in America just as a series of powerful democratic movements have been toppling autocratic regimes elsewhere in the world.

While people around the globe are clamoring for self-government, survey after survey reports that millions of Americans feel as if they had been locked out of their homes and are unable to regain their rightful place in the operation of democracy. On the other hand, those same millions want to believe that it is still in their power to change America.

Conventional wisdom says people don't want the kind of news that will bring them back to the public square. Well, conventional wisdom is wrong. Just ask *The Philadelphia Inquirer.*

[In the fall of 1991], *The Inquirer* ran a nine-part series that attempted to find a pattern in the economic chaos of the 1980s.

Donald Barlett and James Steele, twice winners of the Pulitzer Prize, spent two years traveling to 50 cities in 16 states and Mexico.

They talked to government officials, corporate managers and workers in lumber mills, factories and department stores. And they amassed a hundred thousand documents.

When they were done they had exposed a money trail that helped readers to understand how rule makers in Washington and deal makers on Wall Street connived to create much of the pain inflicted on American workers and the middle class.

The series was about tax policy, health care, pension rules, corporate debt and the bankruptcy code — all that "stuff" we usually think no one wants to read about.

But it was written crisply and laid out vividly, and when the series appeared so many people thronged the paper's lobby wanting reprints that security guards had to be summoned for crowd control. At last count the number of reprints had reached 400,000.

People want to know what is happening to them and what they can do about it.

Listening to America, you realize that millions of people are not apathetic.

They will respond to a press that stimulates the community without pandering to it, that inspires people to embrace their responsibilities without lecturing or hectoring them, that engages their better natures without sugarcoating ugly realities or patronizing their foibles.

Those of us who are reporters can only hope this generation of publishers understands that what keeps journalism different is something intangible.

For all the talk of price-earnings ratio, bottom line, readouts and restricted stock, what ultimately counts is the soul of the owner.

The test today for capitalism is whether shareholders have souls too.

Who Will Control the World of Information?

In this article from the *Los Angeles Times,* reporter Leslie Helm describes the growing influence in the world economy of companies that control telecommunications. The role of AT&T, says Helm, surpasses the strategic importance of "oil, steel or even computers."

Consider:

1. What advantages does a U.S. telecommunications company, such as AT&T, have over its international competitors? disadvantages?

2. Which services are included in the "package market"? Which country is likely to take the lead in offering these services, and why?

3. Rather than moving from unsophisticated technology to an intermediate technology, as in other industries, Helm says that "in telecommunications it makes sense to put in the latest technology available." Why? Explain.

AT&T: Battling for a Piece of the Global Pie

Leslie Helm

Seventy years ago [in the 1920s], AT&T was a trademark recognized around the world as synonymous with the telephone. Then regulators forced the communications giant to spin off its international operations and focus on building a telephone infrastructure for America.

Today, as AT&T and other U.S. companies move out to take on the world market, they face a bittersweet reality. The once-sleepy telecommunications business has grown to be the world's largest economic sector, with a strategic importance that surpasses that of oil, steel or even computers.

And while U.S. companies were looking inward these past decades, fragments of the old AT&T empire have emerged as leading world players. Alcatel of France is the world's largest supplier of telecommunications equipment — it has a 50% share of the rapidly growing Chinese market — in large part because of the assets it acquired from ITT, the international operation that was broken off from AT&T. NEC Corp., Japan's leading communications and computer company, was once a subsidiary of AT&T's Western Electric.

These companies have strong footholds in the world markets that are growing at an astounding rate in size and importance. Anderson Consulting, which counts most of the world's leading companies as its clients, figures the telecommunications sector will represent a $1.1-trillion industry by the year 2000, about double its current level.

"When you buy a shirt at the store, a computer automatically registers its color, style and size," says Ali Sabeti, chief of telecommunications for the World Bank. But that information is useless, Sabeti says, unless it can be sent over phone lines to the factory in Hong Kong so new shipments will arrive to replenish shelves while the item is still in demand.

"Cheap labor isn't enough to be competitive," Sabeti says. "Countries that don't have access to [telecommunications] networks can't participate in the global economy. They are just left out."

From China to the Czech Republic, from Mexico to the Middle East, nations are responding to this new reality. Advanced landline, mobile and satellite telephone systems are being installed in record numbers. [In 1994], as many as 100 million more phone lines will be connected to the expanding web that is the world telecommunications system.

"One of the major drivers for growth today is the realization of the importance of telecommunications to the economy," says Roger Dorf, president of AT&T's Caribbean and Latin American network systems operations. "People have discovered that there is more of a willingness and ability to pay for [telecommunications] than anybody ever imagined."

In China, which has only one telephone for every 100 people, people are shelling out $1,800 just to get on a two-year waiting list for phone service. That's many times the average annual salary. China wants to quadruple the number of phones it has in service by the end of the [1990s].

India has committed itself to spending $15 billion to modernize its telecommunications sector, although it is more reluctant than China to permit foreign competition. It has plans for a network of hundreds of satellite dishes to bring telecommunications to remote areas.

Industrialized nations such as Britain, Japan and the United States are taking the next giant step forward, making plans for massive investments in new interactive systems that can offer education, video on demand and home shopping as well as wireless telecommunications.

It is hard to judge just how much of a market this telecommunications boom represents to U.S. companies. Only six countries outside the United States have anything approaching open markets: Australia, Britain, Chile, Japan, New Zealand and Sweden.

In France, only France Telecom can offer phone services. And it buys most of its phone equipment from national supplier Alcatel. The same is true of Deutsche Telecom, which has a virtual lock on the German market and buys most of its equipment from German supplier Siemens. Although Japan is nominally open, industry analysts don't expect much of its planned $200-billion-plus investment in a new information superhighway over the next two decades to go to foreign companies.

But freer world markets may be just a matter of time. Anderson Consulting figures that countries representing more than half of the world market have either begun the process of dismantling their old telephone monopolies or have concrete plans to do so in the coming years.

Those that delay too long may find major multinationals choosing to locate their operations in nearby countries where phone services are cheaper and better. Already Britain has become a major communications hub for Europe, and Australia is emerging as a hub for Asia.

Even China, once the epitome of the centrally controlled economy, is beginning to introduce competition of sorts lest it be outflanked by upstarts like Vietnam. The government recently created a new telecommunications company made up of a handful of government ministries to compete with the Ministry of Post and Telecommunications-run phone company.

In Latin America and Europe, countries have begun to privatize their telephone systems to tap private capital and finance ambitious expansion plans. The schemes are working. As monopolies have gone private in Britain, Chile and Mexico, they have sucked money into this rapidly growing sector like air into a vacuum. International financier Alan Bond made a killing recently when he sold his 44% ownership in Chile's national carrier to Telefonica de Espana.

J. P. Morgan and Citibank are each major investors in two new private telephone systems established in Argentina. Mutual funds are pouring billions of dollars of investor money into newly privatized phone companies in places like Mexico and Singapore.

But as with every gold rush, it is the hardware suppliers who make money first. Research firm Dataquest, a technology research firm, estimates that the world market for telecommunications equipment will grow to 184 billion by 1997, up nearly 50% from $125 billion [in 1993].

Alcatel of France and Siemens of Germany are the world leaders in the business of supplying big switches and other sophisticated gear required to make phones work. AT&T comes in a weak third as a world supplier.

With extensive operations around the world and long experience dealing with overseas customers, the large European companies have a distinct advantage. When Alcatel tackles markets in Latin America, it can send employees from its operations in Spain or Portugal who are familiar with the former colonies and speak their languages.

"They have been around a while. They know which buttons to push to influence decisionmakers" says John Dinsdale, associate director for telecommunications at Dataquest.

When the U.S. Justice Department broke up AT&T [in the 1980s], it took away AT&T's last stranglehold on selling telephone equipment, the domestic market. The seven new regional phone-operating companies, once exclusively supplied by Western Electric, sought cheaper suppliers overseas.

Newly emerging companies have also looked overseas for suppliers. McCaw Cellular, the cellular phone giant in the process of being acquired by AT&T, buys almost all of its equipment from the Swedish company Eriksson. AT&T, meanwhile, has faced largely closed markets overseas.

Nevertheless, AT&T and other U.S. companies like Motorola and Northern Telecom are making an aggressive foray into the international market. As recently as seven years ago [in 1987], AT&T had only 100 employees overseas. Today it has 56,000 overseas employees. And it is learning to move fast. When Argentina wanted a cellular company that could quickly establish phone services, it turned to a consortium that included AT&T, GTE and two local companies.

The consortium signed a contract March 28 [1994]. By the end of May [1994], by pulling in 250 engineers from its operations worldwide, AT&T had installed a $250-million cellular system accessible to 22 million potential customers. The system is expected to go into commercial service soon and will offer many Argentines their first access to telephone service.

"We're catching up pretty quickly," says Dorf, the AT&T official for the Caribbean and Latin America.

U.S. companies don't have the advantage of captive markets that European companies like Siemens and Alcatel do. But as markets gradually open, the U.S. companies' experience operating in a competitive rather than a regulated market may give them an important advantage.

"Northern Telecom and AT&T are the product of a deregulated market," says James Long, head of Northern Telecom's international operations. To be competitive, North American companies have been forced to keep adding new features such as 1-800 services, call forwarding and conferencing that are not available in Europe or Japan. Much of this involves writing sophisticated software, an American strength.

U.S. companies will also have an edge in building next-generation broadband networks for video on demand and other applications because of their early investment in this technology. AT&T has won major multibillion-dollar contracts from Pacific Telesis and Bell Atlantic to build such systems.

And after years of watching in frustration as competitors won international contracts with the backing of their governments, U.S. companies are now receiving similar help.

In May [1994], AT&T won a $4-billion deal to build a modern network in Saudi Arabia. Strong support from the Clinton Administration helped to clinch the deal. When Motorola faced obstacles getting fair access to the Japanese market, U.S. trade negotiators intervened, assuring the company a major stake in a market expected to quintuple in seven years [by 2001].

U.S. companies are beginning to reap the harvest of such efforts. Northern Telecom's international sales [in 1993] accounted for a quarter of its sales, up from just 8% four years ago [in 1989]. Motorola has built or is in the process of installing 150 mobile systems in 18 Chinese provinces, establishing itself as a leader in the mobile area, says Tom Hinton, general manager of Motorola's cellular operations in China.

U.S. exports of telecommunications equipment climbed 24% [in 1993] to $9.7 billion, giving the nation a telecommunications trade surplus for the first time in 10 years.

But while equipment sales are where the opportunities are today, in the long term it is the service area that will have the greatest growth. Dataquest sees the services market growing to $680 billion in 1997 from about $500 billion [in 1993].

Most of that growth will come in markets filled with acronyms such as VANs (value added networks), VPNs (virtual private networks) and ISDN (Integrated Synchronous Digital Networks). While the market for POTS (plain old telephone service) is likely to remain flat, the Yankee Group, a Boston-based research firm, expects that new areas involving sophisticated packages of data, voice and video communications to multinationals will more than double [by 1997], making it a $17-billion market.

It is in this package market that America's strength is most apparent. The world's major players have broken up into three teams, each centered around a market-savvy U.S. player. The MCI-British Telecom team has an early start, but AT&T is quickly building up a formidable alliance that could include dozens of large telecommunications players. Sprint's deal with the French and German telephone companies may not go through unless the phone markets are opened up wider in France and Germany.

Among the newer and more aggressive faces in the international arena are America's regional telephone-operating companies. Pacific Telesis has stakes in cellular systems in Japan and Korea, two of the world's fastest-growing markets. Southwestern Bell and France Telecom have major stakes in Telmex, Mexico's successful phone company. Bell Atlantic spent $1 billion for a 42% share of Iusacell, a cellular operator in Mexico.

U.S. West has been among the most aggressive, investing $2.5 billion in cellular, cable and phone systems in Russia, Britain, Hungary, France, Norway and Sweden. The company says its goal is to put together the building blocks for systems that can offer multimedia capabilities including wireless, telephone and entertainment, a goal that it is close to approaching in Britain.

It is a model the company thinks may be appropriate for developing countries as well. The company has proposed to the Indian government a plan that would begin by offering basic telephone service using easily installed cellular base stations. As wire lines are installed, the cellular phone system would be moved farther out to offer services to another population while wire line would take over in its existing area. The idea is to ultimately have a full multimedia system with video service, telephones and wireless.

Experts agree that unlike other industries where it is often reasonable to use cheaper intermediate technology, in telecommunications it makes sense to put in the latest technology available. New digital switches are often the cheapest per subscriber and the easiest to maintain.

"They are going from the 19th Century to the 21st Century," says John Clarke, analyst for the London office of Daiwa Research Institute. "They need top communications services."

"AT&T: Battling for a Piece of the Global Pie," by Leslie Helm, *Los Angeles Times,* July 26, 1994. © 1994 *Los Angeles Times.* Reprinted by permission. Dow//Quest Story ID: 0000346287DC.

Media Influence Is Pervasive and Persuasive

Every day you are affected by the mass media in some way—when you study a textbook for school, when you turn on the radio in your car, when you rent a movie at the video store to watch at home. The collective effects on society of all these media choices are what Ray Newton talks about in this essay.

Consider:

1. In what terms did Harold Lasswell describe the media's roles?

2. Which of the six press systems described in this article best defines the way the mass media actually work in the United States?

3. What roles should the media play in a democratic society?

4. Does the special privilege afforded the press under the First Amendment carry special responsibilities? Explain.

Roles, Rights, and Responsibilities: Whom Should the Media Serve?

Ray Newton
Northern Arizona University

Slightly more than 550 years ago, a German craftsman invented a machine which introduced to the then-civilized world what is now known as mass media. Johannes Gutenberg and his colleagues little realized that moveable type and the printing press would initiate what ultimately became the "communications revolution"—a revolution which has affected virtually everyone throughout the world. . . .

Revolution it has been. It is impossible to tell how many millions of words and pictures have been disseminated in just the past 100 years, let alone since the invention of the printing press. But in that 100 years, we have shifted from the primitive, hand-operated printing presses, which changed little from those of the fifteenth century, to sophisticated, technologically superior systems and devices which permit almost instantaneous transmission of media messages to any locale in the world. Only the most naive among us would say we are not affected by those messages, particularly here in the United States.

From the moment people tumble out of bed in the morning until they crawl under the covers at night, they are in some way subjected to the influences of mass media. The extent and effects of that media influence are examined [here].

Consider this: Just today, some 63 million copies of almost 1,700 daily newspapers are being circulated. Just this week, more than 50 million copies of some 7,500 weekly newspapers will be distributed. Just this month, approximately 10,000 magazine titles will reach the media marketplace. And just this year, some 45,000 new book titles will compete for readers.

The extent of influence of the electronic media is even more difficult to assess. Some 1,450 television stations will send signals to an estimated 98 percent of American households. Additionally, cable television signals will reach an estimated 33 million homes. Radio—who honestly knows the extent of its listenership? Approximately 8,500 stations, AM and FM, are picked up by more than 500 million radio receivers. No one really knows how many radio sets are operative in this country, given the millions of inexpensive transistorized personal receivers that the public uses while jogging, working, or relaxing.

It is also true that no one really knows the extent of the distribution of films. An estimated 400 to 500 feature films are released annually. They are viewed on the big screen in some 21,000 movie theatres across the country by millions of movie-goers (mostly teenagers and young adults). How many millions more watch the same films on VCRs in the privacy of their residences? How many students watch films in classrooms? How many organizations and corporations use films of various types for training?

The above media are the most prominent and publicly conspicuous. Others, though, are so much a part of our lives that we often forget to consider them as mass media—billboards, posters and brochures, matchbook covers, specialty advertising gimmicks such as embossed keychains and golf balls—myriad other forms of messages that compete for our attention and interests.

Media influence is pervasive and persuasive. It surrounds us, engulfs us. Mass media are such an integral part of our educational, social, political, and economic systems today that if they were to disappear, our society would suffer serious consequences.

Developing as they have into perhaps the most significant social influences in the nation today, the media have taken unto themselves—or in some cases, been assigned—several different roles. [Fifty] years ago [in the 1940s], Harold Lasswell, a prominent social scientist, developed the concept in *Communication of Ideas* that media have three major roles in society. The first is surveillance—reporting to society the threats, changes, and dangers to the well-being of the greater community. This function has been popularly labeled as the "watchdog role."

The second role, Lasswell suggests, is the interpretation of current events in the social environment: evaluating and analyzing the impact of contemporary events.

The third role the media play, Lasswell says, is communicating to future generations the social heritage which characterizes that particular culture: media provide a means for transmitting the events of the past to the future. Thus, the media form a unique system whereby values within the social system are perpetuated and give the continuity and consistency which endow a culture with its distinct qualities of identity. Generations ago, this role was often taken by parents and grandparents who transmitted verbally to their children what had happened in the past. Now this transmission of heritage is more often accomplished through some form of media.

The consequences of the roles the media play in our lives are staggering. In fact, it has been speculated that the mass media set the agenda for much of what we do. The media are often telling us what should and should not be important to us socially, culturally, educationally, politically, and economically.

The major events in the nation and the world, about which most of us have strong beliefs and attitudes, undoubtedly have been brought to our awareness, interpreted, and assigned value through media, not personal experience. Nuclear power, AIDS, the energy crisis, the Middle East, famine and drought in Africa, space exploration, education reform, science and religion, minority rights — these and dozens of other topics about which we have vigorous opinions are likely the result of our having been exposed to media transmission of messages.

Sorting out these messages is perhaps one of the most difficult tasks we face. Because of the almost exponential explosion of information, we cannot possibly sift through and assimilate all that surrounds us. We are compelled to let others assess and compress information for us. We are, in a sense, victims of our own inability to handle such large quantities of information without confusion.

We must of necessity let those who are presumably trained and skilled make those decisions about what is important to us — set the agenda, so to speak.

That becomes a critical issue. . . . Can we trust the watchdogs who tell us what has happened or is likely to happen and what the effects of those happenings will be? Have the three roles which Lasswell described been sustained, or have they been misused and corrupted by contemporary media? To be sure, misuse or corruption is not necessarily by design. But is it possible that the media messengers, the information brokers, and the agenda setters have neglected what might possibly be the most critical component of mass media — social responsibility to an audience?

More than [forty] years ago [the 1950s], three noted media scholars and critics examined the development and growth of media in a book called *Four Theories of the Press*. In brief, Theodore Peterson, Fred S. Siebert, and Wilbur Schramm examined the different roles which media seemed to play in several forms of government. They suggested that four dominant press systems were in place: *authoritarian,* where a dictator controls and regulates the press (even though the press might be privately owned) so that the dictatorship will be sustained; *libertarian,* which is in opposition to the authoritarian concept in that it is assumed that the individual rather than the government is superior, and hence, that no governmental control at all is preferable; *Soviet-communist,* where the media are owned and controlled by the government (not necessarily an individual) and are to protect the status quo of the government; and *social responsibility,* where the media are charged with providing the public with meaningful news and information, free from governmental control and yet responsive to societal and sometimes governmental pressures.

A fifth theory of the press was proposed in 1981, when scholar William Hachten suggested a *developmental* model, where the press is viewed as a collaborator with government, especially in Third World and underdeveloped nations, in urging positive social, economic, and political improvements.

In 1983, yet another theory was suggested by Robert G. Picard, when he envisioned a *democratic socialist* system wherein media ownership is public, non-profit, and intended to permit the citizens to debate what they consider important societal concerns.

Still other variants of the above-noted theories exist, and none is totally comprehensive. The theories do, however, point up that differences exist among governments and peoples regarding what they view as the role of media in the social system.

Most Americans would agree that the social responsibility theory is perhaps the ideal toward which the press should aspire, for contained within it is the concept that if the press takes liberties or becomes too excessive in its zeal, the government has the right and responsibility to curb those excesses to protect its citizens. Yet a conflict seems to be growing in the United States between the media and the government, with the frequent complaint that the freedom of the press guaranteed in the First Amendment to the Constitution is being ignored and violated, both legally and ethically.

Ironically, articulate and vocal proponents from both sides of the issue, those who advocate freedom of the press from any governmental restraint and those who support governmental limitations upon alleged abuses by the press (libel, invasion of privacy, and the like), more and more frequently use the media to express their points of view. One of them, Jean Kirkpatrick, in a syndicated column in the *Los Angeles Times* [in May 1987], questioned the right of the media to inquire into the private life of former Democratic presidential candidate Gary Hart and his relationship with Donna Rice. She wrote:

> The fact that no further revelations concerning Hart's sex life followed his withdrawal from the presidential race (although we are told the *Washington Post* has in hand affidavits concerning these matters), tacitly suggests a corollary to the principle: presidential candidates have no right to privacy, but ex-candidates do.

She also notes that public opinion polls indicate that most Americans believe that presidential candidates do in fact have rights to privacy and that they did not approve of the *Miami Herald*'s investigation and consequent stories.

Nationally known columnist Mike Royko of the *Chicago Tribune* discussed the same issue in a recent [1987] column. In an extended anecdote, he tells of telephoning the public relations department at the *New York Times* to ask some personal questions about the top management of the newspaper. Royko reported that he asked the following: "What I want to know is if they are married. And if they have ever been divorced. And if they have been divorced, when did it happen?"

Royko says the woman who answered responded, "I'm not going to give out that information," and she hung up.

Royko continues his anecdote by commenting that he found it ironic that one of the world's major newspapers, which had asked extremely personal questions of presidential candidates — questions about their medical records and psychiatric backgrounds — refused to reveal what, in fact, was a matter of public record about its own executives.

Royko comments that he does not think it unreasonable to ask personal questions about editors of a newspaper which shapes domestic and foreign policy and examines critically the political and public figures of the world. He wrote: ". . . it seems only fair that we should have some insight into the character and judgment and stability of these people."

The point of his anecdote is clear.

A third nationally known writer-columnist looked at the same situation in still another fashion. Ellen Goodman for the *Boston Globe* asked exactly how far the media should go in probing into the personal lives of presidential candidates, citing both the *Miami Herald* stories about Gary Hart and the *New York Times* inquiries of presidential candidates about their private lives. Goodman defends the right of the press to ask any question it wants of candidates — but she also defends the right of the candidates to say, "I do not have to answer that question." She additionally says that the right to ask questions does not belong exclusively to the press; it also belongs to every citizen. But so does the right to say, "I don't have to answer."

She suggests that often the press is on a fishing expedition — and it wants to fish without licenses in private ponds.

Kirkpatrick and Royko and Goodman certainly are not the only respected opinion leaders who have complained about the media's "going too far." They represent a goodly number of respected professional writers and reporters and editors who know down deep the differences between the public's right to know and an individual's right to privacy.

They also represent a substantial number of media professionals who do try to present accurate, balanced, and complete information about significant issues to the public. Among them is Tom Wicker of the *New York Times*.

A recent detailed interview with political columnist Wicker in the Spring 1987 issue of *American Thought Leader* (published by the BB&T Center for Leadership Development at East Carolina University) focuses upon Wicker's observations of the strengths, weaknesses, and influences of mass media as he perceives them today. For several decades, Wicker has covered regional and national political events and has won dozens of awards for his in-depth analysis of what he observes (the interpretive role of the press). During his interview, he responded to a question about ethics and ethical behavior among media practitioners.

No question about it. Journalistic ethics is, I think, a real matter, a real subject, one that at least used to be scanted by the journalism schools. I think they ought to put more emphasis on it; but then again, it is very difficult. I wouldn't want to sit down myself, for example, and try to write a code of ethics for reporters. It is very difficult. . . .

What you have to inculcate in journalists—the editors should, and the journalism schools really should—is a sense of responsibility toward generally sound human values. There are times when journalistic values override what might normally be considered human values. There are other times when they don't. I hear a lot of my colleagues say, "Oh, yes, I'd commit a crime right away in order to inform the public." Then you should say to your colleague right away, "Well, are you prepared to go to jail for doing that?" "Oh, no," he will say, "Why should I go to jail? I am serving the public's right to know." But I don't think you have any right to commit crimes to serve the public's right to know. If you commit a

crime, you commit a crime. There's no way you can go to the judge and plead some extenuating circumstance.

Wicker also comments extensively about the roles the media must play in a democratic nation, and he frequently is critical of what he perceives as abuses which occur through media. Like many of us, he questions whether or not the media are motivated by the social responsibility which has been ascribed to them or by the profit motive and the desire to become power brokers. He decries the influence which television has in shaping public opinion, saying that the networks perhaps have turned their news into trivia and entertainment because of their concern for ratings and profit. Wicker also suggests that the print media have not fulfilled their social responsibility, either. He cites the growth of newspaper chains and the disappearance of local ownership as weaknesses, suggesting the local ownership has more of a stake in a community than do outside owners.

Despite the criticisms of the mass media —and only a few have been noted above—most thoughtful persons will agree that mass media in America in the main do a superior job in reporting the news and informing the public.

Granted, there are those who will claim that the media are controlled by a few—that the content of the media is controlled and manipulated by a cabal of powerful editors and publishers and network executives and station managers. This is simply not true. The competitive nature of the individual reporters and the media themselves mandate against such collusion. The reality is that the tradition and training of most of the professional media personnel in this country are such that they tend to be similar in isolating key ideas and facts. They are taught to put the most critical elements of news—the traditional who, what, when, where, why, and how—at the beginning. Hence, the similarities are not the result of any conspiracy but rather the quest for significant details.

Walter Mears, a Pulitzer Prize-winning newspaperman who is now [in 1987] a vice president with Associated Press, the world's largest news-gathering organization, recently collaborated with John Chancellor, longtime TV anchorman for the NBC news network. In their book, *The News Business,* they talk about the competitive scramble for stories. They describe vividly the daily race to meet deadlines in both print and electronic media, all in an effort to beat the opposition. They analyze how and why newspaper content and news broadcasts often seem similar and yet are distinctly different from one another. And they conclude that the criticism accusing the press of "pack journalism" is simply not true. Rather, they claim that most professional news personnel have as both short- and long-range goals the objective of beating the competition and having more and better information and details than anyone else. The ultimate result of this objective, of course, is increased circulation or better ratings — which translates into more money for the ownership. . . .

It is not coincidental that the First Amendment to the Constitution is the one which focuses upon freedoms of speech and of the press. Those freedoms, if seriously contemplated and responsibly practiced by media personnel in relationship to the roles, rights, and responsibilities of their profession, define the obligation of the media to the public.

Thomas Jefferson, a primary architect of the Constitution, was certainly aware of the significance of the document and the consequent First Amendment and the power it gave to the press. He addressed this very issue when he wrote in a letter in 1787, "The basis of our government being the opinion of the people, the very first objective should be to keep that right; and were it left to me to decide whether we should have a government without newspapers, or newspapers without a government, I should not hesitate a moment to prefer the latter."

Jefferson, of course, had no way of knowing that newspapers, then the dominant medium, would evolve and expand into what they are today. He certainly had no idea of the likelihood of development of electronic media which would evolve some 140 years later. But he did have the wisdom and the insight to recognize that despite all the flaws and warts and wrinkles, the press (now more broadly defined as the mass media) should and would become the most significant and influential force in the nation. What remains is for the mass media to continue evaluating and assessing their social obligations with respect to their roles, rights, and responsibilities.

"Roles, Rights, and Responsibilities: Whom Should the Media Serve?" by Ray Newton, *National Forum,* Vol. LXVIII, No. 4, Fall 1987, pp. 2–4. Used with permission of *National Forum.*

CHAPTER 2

Media in the 21st Century: Interactive and On-line

Tomorrow's Electronic Electorate

In this article from *The Futurist* magazine, James Snider, a university fellow of political science at Northwestern University, explains how advances in information technology can transform the societies that adopt those changes. The ability to spread information quickly can enhance democracy, according to Snider, and today's technology promises to deliver information even more quickly than in the past.

Consider:

1. What does Snider mean by the term *direct democracy*? How does direct democracy change the political process?

2. What are the "qualitative changes" that Snider sees emerging from the new information technology?

3. What are some of the changes Snider foresees for the electoral process? Do you think they would work? Why? Why not?

Information Technology Brings Democracy On-line

Tomorrow's Electronic Electorate

James Snider

Over the last 200 years, new information technologies have significantly transformed the possibilities and practice of democracy. For example, the early-nineteenth-century invention of the penny press for printing newspapers made the acquisition of political information by the masses both convenient and affordable. This, in turn, greatly facilitated the extension of suffrage during that period. Later, the advent of television weakened the traditional political-party system and led to the growing influence of the media in elections.

Over the next 20 years [the first two decades of the 21st century], many experts believe that information technology may change more than it has over the last 200 years. If they are right, we can expect major changes in the democratic system of government.

Problems with Democracy

[Today], it is hard to imagine that such a large democracy as the United States, with its 250 million citizens, could survive if information technologies such as books, magazines, newspapers, radio, and television suddenly vanished. Indeed, until the last few hundred years the most-respected political thinkers uniformly agreed that only small-scale democracy was possible, in part because of communication limitations. Aristotle argued in the fourth century B.C. that democracy could not work in a country larger than a small city-state such as Athens. One reason was that in a democracy all citizens should be able to assemble at one place to hear a speaker. Thus, the range of the human voice limited a democracy's size. As late as the mid-eighteenth century, political thinkers of the stature of Montesquieu and Rousseau continued to echo this conventional wisdom and argue against the possibility of large-scale democracy.

After the birth of the United States — a huge democracy by historical standards — such arguments were discredited. But as evidence mounts that America's democratic system is moving farther away from the democratic ideal, it is easy to wonder if the pre-modern thinkers weren't on to something. According to a widely quoted study by the Kettering Foundation entitled *Citizens and Politics: A View from Main Street America*, "Americans are both frustrated and downright angry about the state of the current political system. They do not believe they are living in a democracy now. They don't believe that 'We the people' actually rule. What is more, people do not believe this system is able to solve the pressing problems they face."

Perhaps the early political thinkers simply got the maximum democratic size wrong. Instead of it being 5,000, or 20,000, or even 100,000, maybe it is 250 million. Convinced that large-scale democracy was impossible, the early political thinkers surely would have had little trouble identifying at least part of America's main governmental problem — its growing size and complexity.

Over the last 200 years, America's population has grown from 3 million to 250 million. At the same time, the size and complexity of government has grown exponentially. In 1831, there were only 11,491 federal employees; today [in 1994], there are millions. As government grows larger and more complex, it is harder to keep it accountable. And as the proportion of citizens to representatives increases (thus decreasing the odds of any individual citizen making a difference), citizens have even less incentive to try and keep it accountable. The development of mass media such as newspapers and television has helped to alleviate these problems. The maximum range of a politician's message is no longer the hundreds or thousands within the physical range of the voice, but the tens of millions who can watch television. Similarly, the mass media usually offer better and more convenient political news than could word of mouth.

Unfortunately, the technology and institutions of democracy are no longer keeping up with its growth. America continues to have democratic ideals, but not an informed and engaged electorate able to act upon those ideals. The result is a government that neither knows nor implements the public's will. The savings-and-loan scandal [of the early 1990s] is a notorious example: If the government had regulated banks in the public interest, taxpayers would have saved hundreds of billions of dollars.

There are, of course, non-technology-based approaches to solving our democratic woes; for example, we might instill a better sense of civic duty in schools, or overhaul campaign-finance laws in order to minimize the influence of special-interest groups. A more fundamental approach might be to use a new information technology to transcend the inherent historic limitations of democracy. In moving from today's Industrial Age democracy to tomorrow's Information Age democracy, both direct and mediated democracy can and should be enhanced.

Direct Democracy

Most of the literature on the democratic significance of new information technology has focused on its ability to enhance direct participation by citizens in the political process. For the many people who have lost confidence in the ability of both elected representatives and the media to act in their interest, direct democracy, such as the ballot referendum or the town meeting, offers an appealing alternative.

Clearly, the new technology facilitates new forms of voting and thus direct participation. For example, instead of physically going to the polls, people could vote from their homes. With more-convenient and less-expensive voting, people could be expected to vote more frequently and on more issues. Ballot referendums and polls could proliferate.

Another benefit of the new technology is improved access to the deliberations of public bodies. Already, cable television's C-SPAN channel gives us coverage of the U.S. House and Senate chambers and many congressional hearings. Similarly, the California Channel provides coverage of the California House and Senate chambers and legislative hearings. At a local level, many public-access cable television channels cover city council and school board meetings. In the future, coverage of such meetings at local, state, and national levels is likely to expand dramatically, thus making government deliberations much more accessible to the average person. New technology also facilitates previously impractical forms of democratic deliberation. With the electronic town meeting via television, computer, or some synthesis of both, citizens are offered direct contact with public officials, unmediated by journalists. The idea is to force politicians and the media to talk to the public about important issues that might otherwise escape the political agenda. Combined with televoting, the electronic town meeting offers a potentially significant improvement on the ballot referendum or tradi-

tional telephone poll, both of which are poor at fostering deliberation and thus lead to uninformed voting.

Government records could also be made more accessible. The cumbersome procedures necessary to gain access to information under the federal Freedom of Information Act or the local public records laws could be replaced by instantaneous computerized access. Information that is an expensive nightmare to get from government today would thus become available, inexpensively and conveniently, with a few keystrokes. Congress' recent passage of the Government Printing Office (GPO) Electronic Information Access Enhancement Act, which provides Internet access to GPO documents, is a major step in this direction.

Mediated Democracy

As the many critics of direct democracy have argued, the average person does not have the time, ability, or inclination to become an expert on issues and candidates. Direct democracy, which inevitably leads to information overload can, at best, only be a minor palliative to the political information problem. What people want are trustworthy information sources that will do the hard work of gathering and digesting political information for them. This is already a function of the media, but only in a primitive form. The greatest potential of new information technology to improve democracy lies in its ability to enhance mediated democracy.

The importance of today's passive mass media is likely to diminish greatly over the coming decades. Passive media may be replaced by a new type of interactive multimedia, characterized by highly specialized media outlets often described as "information agents."

For example, a typical city [in 1994] has one dominant newspaper. This newspaper achieves its dominance largely because of huge economies of scale associated with its distribution system. In the future, the reporters who work for such newspapers are likely to become independent information entrepreneurs, selling their information wares directly to the public over the telecommunications network. Part person and part computer program, these information agents will gather and digest information, then disseminate it to their clients just as high-priced consultants do today. Accordingly, their customized advice will be short and clear and allow for as much background and explanatory information as desired.

A vast literature exists criticizing our current mass media. While there is no guarantee that the media of the future will cure all these ills (and avoid creating new ones), the potential for more competitive, diverse, and customized media in the future is good cause for hope.

The new media could lead to some important qualitative changes in politics. In the past, the growing influence of mass media in the political process has led candidates to rely increasingly on media-based self-promotion (as opposed to the political parties) to get themselves elected. The new media, while continuing to weaken the political parties, could nevertheless greatly diminish the utility of candidate self-promotion.

The reasoning is that voters in the future will increasingly get their political information from the impartial information agents, not from the candidates directly. If that turns out to be the case, then not only will traditional candidate self-promotion become obsolete, but so will the power of lobbyists and special interests who derive their power from the ability to fund candidates' media campaigns. A candidate could spend huge sums taking out television ads, but it would do no good if the voter has come to rely on agents for political information.

In many respects, this argument merely extends to the political realm what many have argued is likely to be an effect of interactive multimedia in the commercial realm — the making of advertising, especially unrequested advertising, much less effective, if not completely useless.

Citizens in Action

An important new form of mediated democracy facilitated by new information technology has average citizens, not specialized information agents, doing the mediation.

This approach entails bringing together a random sample of voters to deliberate on issues and candidates. They, in effect, do the hard work of democracy that the rest of us don't have the time or motivation to do. Curiously, this is a form of mediated democracy widely used in ancient Athens more than 2,000 years ago and has continued, in a vastly restricted fashion, in the American jury system. New information technology facilitates its expansion in historically new ways.

Many variations on this idea have been proposed. In one of the three 1992 presidential debates, the Gallup Poll randomly selected 200 Americans to serve as the audience. In the 1992 U.S. Senate race in Pennsylvania, a small, random group of citizens were convened as a citizen jury to interview and evaluate the candidates. A more rigorous form of citizen-mediated democracy has been proposed by political scientist Jim Fishkin in his book *Democracy and Deliberation*. In what Fishkin calls a "deliberative opinion poll," a scientifically representative microcosm of American citizens deliberates on issues and candidates with the purpose of finding out what the public would think if it had the motivation and resources for informed decision making.

If we accept the assumption of modern polling techniques that a group as small as 500 people can be an accurate barometer of the public sentiment, then such an approach preserves the essence of the democratic ideal while substantially solving the problem of the individual voter's low motivation and inadequate resources. Members of the sample would know that their voice has disproportionate weight (maybe by as much as 500,000 Americans) and that they are getting otherwise inconceivable access to special resources, such as one-on-one contact with candidates and leading experts.

Public Policy Recommendations

New public policies are necessary to facilitate the new forms of democracy made possible by emerging information technology. To make sure that we don't disintegrate into a nation of information haves and have-nots, it will be necessary to ensure universal access to the coming information highway.

More important are the less obvious political institutions made possible by new information technology. For example, the new technology will make possible new ways to publicly finance elections. Instead of money going to candidates, money could be given directly to the voters. Instead of tens of millions of dollars in communication vouchers being given to presidential candidates to spend on 30-second television ads, money could be given directly to citizens to spend on information about presidential candidates. Such voter-based vouchers are far more democratic than candidate-based vouchers but have never been practical before.

Similarly, new laws and policies need to be developed to maximize the social utility of information agents. A special class of information agent—the electoral agent—could be given special treatment much like nonprofit organizations, which receive privileges such as tax exemptions and reduced postal rates. As with nonprofits, electoral agents could provide a public good that would otherwise be underproduced. If mass-media advertising becomes obsolete and thus no longer able to subsidize "free TV" or cheap newspapers (the traditional media for election

information), then the need for electoral agents could become even more acute than it is today.

The obligations for electoral agents could include: (1) No funding from candidates or candidate proxies (that is, no financial conflicts of interest), (2) a complete public record of all contact with candidates or their proxies (for example, a video if a personal contact and an electronic letter if a text-based contact), (3) agent computer systems that facilitate candidate rebuttals of any agent assertion (the candidate could ask for a "rebuttal button" to appear on the screen when the challenged assertion appears), and finally (4) information structured to help voters make decisions between candidates (for example, a news format would not qualify). In return for meeting these obligations, electoral agents would be entitled to receive the voter information vouchers as well as significantly reduced liability for libel.

The First Amendment needs to be reinterpreted. Too often today it only protects the rights of information producers, not consumers. If the media become even more important in the political process, it is vital that the public have the right to know as much about the media as they do about politicians, lobbyists, and government agencies. The White House Correspondents Association already requires members to disclose their major financial interests, including investments, speaking fees, and perks. Similarly, new technology facilitates enhanced rights of rebuttal and rights to diverse information sources.

The traditional right-to-know laws that pertain to government information also need to be rewritten. In many states, the public-records laws and the open-meeting laws were conceived when the photocopier and audiotape recorder were the most-advanced forms of information technology. These laws need to be brought into the present and made to anticipate the future so that public access to government and candidate information can be improved. Even if the public doesn't avail itself of this information, it is absolutely necessary for the effective functioning of the emerging media.

Perhaps the party system could be abolished as well. Already the growth of television over the last few decades [of the twentieth century] has seriously diminished the power of the parties. This trend toward weakened parties is likely to continue as a result of the emerging information infrastructure and the new agent-based media it engenders. A logical implication is to institutionalize the growing powers of the media over the nominating system. For example, an electoral agents' association could set dates and criteria for nominations — something the media currently do in a much less democratic way with so-called "hidden" nominations. The hidden nomination is the process, most pronounced in presidential primaries, whereby the media anoint a handful of candidates as serious contenders.

More generally, the practical realities limiting nominating systems can be rethought in light of new information technology. The current [1994] nominating systems in the United States are based on certain assumptions about communications and transportation requirements. As the information infrastructure changes, so do the possibilities for creating nominating systems that will attract and select the best candidates. Theoretically elegant but heretofore impractical voting systems could come into widespread use. Instead of starting with an initial pool of five to 10 candidates preselected by political parties or mass-media pundits, it might be practical with computer voting to start with hundreds or thousands of candidates and have the public do the selecting. With the advent of relatively inexpensive and convenient home voting, we could also have three or four nominating rounds instead of the two customary today. And the new media rather than the parties could be given control of the basic nominating system protocols.

Modern civilization requires a large and complex government because the private sector alone simply cannot provide many vital services such as defense and environmental protection. It is unfortunate that its immensity has made the government so unaccountable to its citizens and their general welfare. But new information technology, combined with forward-thinking public policies, can help bring the democratic ideal much closer to reality.

"Information Technology Brings Democracy On-line: Tomorrow's Electronic Electorate" by James Snider, *The Futurist,* September 1, 1994, Bethesda, Maryland. Reprinted by permission of the World Futurist Society.

Consumers Go On-line

In this short study of technology and consumers, *The New York Times* reports that consumers say they care more about the information they can gather using new information technologies than the products they can buy or the games they can play. Consumers also worry about the potential misuse of the information that is gathered through the use of new information technology.

Consider:

1. According to the poll, for what purpose are consumers most likely to use the new information technology?

2. According to the poll, for what purpose are consumers least likely to use the new information technology?

3. Answer the questions in the box marked "Reacting to Interactive Choices." How do your answers compare to the answers of the people polled?

Few Plan to Shop Electronically

Poll Shows More Interest in Other National Information System Aspects

The New York Times

Americans show a high interest in the educational and communications aspects of the emerging national information system, but not in the interactive entertainment and home-shopping features that have attracted the most investment from businesses, it was noted in a new national poll released [in October 1994].

The poll, conducted by Louis Harris and Associates in cooperation with the newsletter Privacy & American Business, also indicated a growing concern among consumers about the potential abuse of personal information gleaned from households by advertisers and other interactive-service providers.

But after they were informed of possible ways to safeguard their privacy in the electronic world, the number of adult Americans who said they were "most interested" in using interactive services doubled — to 20 percent of the respondents.

"That translates to 38.2 million adults, a dandy audience for interactive service people to enroll," said Alan F. Westin, a professor of law and government at Columbia University and publisher of Privacy & American Business, the co-sponsor of the poll.

Interactive services is the term commonly used to describe new technologies that allow

Reacting to Interactive Choices

How interested Americans are in various emerging interactive services that are available using new technologies that combine cable television, telephone and computer network wiring, based on a telephone survey conducted by Louis Harris and Associates in cooperation with the Privacy & American Business newsletter.[*]

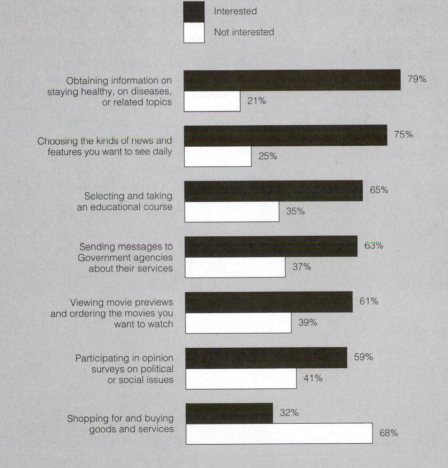

Interested

Not interested

Obtaining information on staying healthy, on diseases, or related topics
79%
21%

Choosing the kinds of news and features you want to see daily
75%
25%

Selecting and taking an educational course
65%
35%

Sending messages to Government agencies about their services
63%
37%

Viewing movie previews and ordering the movies you want to watch
61%
39%

Participating in opinion surveys on political or social issues
59%
41%

Shopping for and buying goods and services
32%
68%

[*]The survey of 1,000 adults in the continental United States was done in July and has a margin of sampling error of plus or minus 3 percentage points.

Source: Adapted from data collected by Louis Harris and Associates in cooperation with Privacy & American Business newsletter.

people to use cable television, telephones and computer networks to request consumer information, order movies on demand and shop for products electronically.

Meanwhile, in a separate but related Harris poll . . . the level of citizens' distrust of government and institutions reached the highest level since the annual poll was first taken in 1978. This survey also indicated that for the first time a majority of Americans agree that technology is "out of control."

Reflecting the broader distrust of government, big business and institutions, more than three-fourths of the people responding to the interactive-technology survey said they wanted privacy safeguards built into any interactive system before they would be comfortable using it. Most expressed a desire to control the types of products and services being offered, to be able to review and perhaps edit the information that firms could gather about viewing and buying habits, and to be able to place restrictions on the use of that information.

Only 32 percent reported any interest in shopping for products and services electronically — the lowest level of interest among 14 specific interactive services described to the 1,000 adults who responded to the telephone survey in July [1994].

"The problem with polls is that consumers are being asked to understand and judge something they've never seen or encountered before," said Gary Arlen, president of Arlen Research Inc., a research company based in Bethesda, Md., who was not involved in the poll but was told of the results.

"Field tests of interactive services show that consumers are slow to adopt much of it. When they find something they like, though, they bring it into viewing habits fairly quickly."

"Few Plan to Shop Electronically: Poll Shows More Interest in Other National Information System Aspects," Peter H. Lewis, *The New York Times,* reprinted in *The Sacramento Bee,* October 12, 1994, p. F-20. © 1994 by The New York Times Company. Reprinted by permission.

Transforming the Definition of News

In this article from the city magazine *Minneapolis-St. Paul CityBusiness,* reporter Sandra Earley describes how broadcast stations and newspapers are using technology to solicit information from their viewers and readers. This represents an increasing effort by news organizations to market their newsgathering as a service to customers beyond their regular audience.

Consider:

1. List three ways that print and broadcast companies in Minneapolis are expanding the market for the news they gather. Are media companies in your city using similar techniques? What are they?

2. Larry Werner of the Minneapolis *Star Tribune* says that the general philosophy is that the newspaper is "in the information business, not the paper business." How does this philosophy change the role of the newspaper as a business?

3. Do you agree with the prediction that newspapers "might turn into little more than printed menus for information that's on-line"? Why? Why not?

Technology Changes How Media Deliver News

Sandra Earley

Wayne Studes sat last week [in May 1994] with a bricksized, wireless keypad in his hands under the strong lights of a WCCO-TV [Minneapolis] studio.

With about 40 others, Studes was participating in one of the station's twice-weekly community meetings. He was there to watch a Dimension segment produced for the 10 P.M. news, vote his feelings on the story using the keypad, note the results tabulated and flashed on a screen by a computer and then discuss the story and the conclusions with host Don Shelby.

As he punched in numbers, Studes became part of a trend among the Twin Cities news media — television, print and radio alike — to connect with their audiences via electronic technology, showing their concern for what their audiences need and think and further positioning themselves as a place to go for attractive, necessary information, whatever the form.

And it's an effort that Studes, a computer software design analyst by profession, applauds.

"It's the wave of the future," he said. "If they're only jumping in now, they're behind the game."

Here's some of what's going on these days in the local media:

- WCCO-TV (Channel 4) has also installed kiosks in Best Buy stores around the community where viewers can videotape a message to the station or talk to it by computer. In the near future, WCCO plans to let home computer users log into its newsroom computer to read scripts, through a service it plans to call "Interact 4."

- Several times a month, KSTP-TV (Channel 5) asks viewers to call in and record reactions to its news stories using a voice-mail service called Cityline Inc., owned and operated, as the station is, by Hubbard Broadcasting Inc.

  Before the town meeting with President Clinton in April [1994], KSTP used the voice-mail system to screen potential audience members. About 4,000 people called in possible questions, and the hundred who asked the best ones were selected to meet with Clinton.

- The Star Tribune now gets 500,000 calls monthly to its 2 1/2-year-old audiotext service. Readers dial numbers provided in the paper and can hear pre-recorded information on everything from stock quotations and capsule movie reviews to news updates since the paper went to press.

  The newspaper also sells readers a service that after a phone call will fax them information such as corporate earnings reports, reviews of new automobiles and summaries of amenities in Twin Cities suburbs. The faxes cost $2 to $3 each.

- The Saint Paul Pioneer Press started a similar audiotext service in April at a projected cost of under $100,000 annually. In addition to movie reviews and stock quotations,

"The Line" has featured bird calls and frog choruses, introduced by its nature columnist Anne Brataas. The newspaper also is experimenting with faxed information.

- At the weekly Shakopee Valley News, readers can call an audiotext system for notices of deaths and funerals since the paper came out. Other small area papers have interactive personal classified ads, voice mail for letters to the editor and addresses on the Internet for contacting the paper and its writers.

- Minnesota Public Radio (MPR), Twin Cities Public Television and three other local public broadcasters recently received $150,000 from the Corporation for Public Broadcasting, in cooperation with U.S. West, to set up a community-wide computer networking service designed to provide the public with access to education and on-line information.

- KARE-TV (Channel 11) has offered its Weather Line featuring updated weather information, for a number of years. It receives about 35,000 calls each month.

All the effort is primarily to make viewers, listeners and readers feel warm and happy about the media outlets and also to accustom the audiences further to turning to the stations and papers for information in any form.

"It's all for the viewers' benefit," said Debbie Berg, WCCO's director of community relations who organized the keypad sessions. "People seem to enjoy the technology — it's more fun. And the discussions do get heated."

At the Star Tribune, Larry Werner, the business editor who also oversees the audiotext service, said, "It's all part of the overall strategy to deepen our relationship with our customers. We don't need lots more customers, so we said, 'Let's solidify the relationship.' "

At the newspaper, the audiotext service also has the effect of adding space to the paper without the $500,000 in annual cost required to add pages in fact. When audiotext was instituted, the paper stopped printing some 4,000 stock listings and asked readers to call in for them. The cost, Werner said, is about equivalent to a column of editorial space per day.

Audiotext has also, in essence, extended deadlines. With it, the paper can print a phone number adjacent to, say, a story on whether the pope will visit Denver or the Twin Cities. Then an editor gets up early the next morning, checks the wire services for updated information and records the results of the overnight decision for the audiotext service.

"The general philosophy is that we're in the information business, not the paper business," Werner said.

That philosophy could also mean that the new technologies will become a profit center for the paper.

The Star Tribune's fax service currently earns a small profit beyond its cost, according to Bob Schaffer, the newspaper's new products leader, "but not enough to retire on." Sales are hampered, he said, because only 1 percent to 2 percent of American homes have fax machines.

Still, Schaffer is searching for other more profitable, electronic ways to sell information gathered by the newspaper. "Like all metropolitan newspapers, we're looking at what our options might be," he said.

The Pioneer Press has sold advertising on one of its audiotext recordings, according to Ken Doctor, managing editor. Burger Brothers Outdoor Outfitters, a sporting goods retailer based in Bloomington, bought time on a fishing interview conducted by outdoor columnist Chris Niskanen.

"We're experimenting with the advertisers," Doctor said. "We think it gives added value to their print ads."

Compared with some other newspapers around the county, the local dailies and weeklies and their experiments are relatively low-tech.

Both the Chicago Tribune and the San Jose Mercury News have spots on America Online (AOL). Not only can readers use AOL to scan stories and classifieds from daily papers, they can also examine back issues and talk to the papers' staffs and to other readers via chat sessions and electronic bulletin boards.

Too much access, especially to newsroom computer information as planned with Interact 4 at WCCO, worries some journalists.

"There is all sorts of information in our system," said Gary Hill, managing editor in KSTP's newsroom. "Unless you're sure of security, I'd be worried about publicizing how to get into the system."

At smaller newspapers, using voice mail to collect letters to the editor and similar information from the public causes other worries.

First, there's the burden of transcribing the calls from the voice mail. The task can weigh heavily on small neighborhood and suburban papers. Then there's the question of crank and prank calls.

And then, simply, there are the media types who can't cope with too much technology. Linda Falkman, executive director of the

Cartoon by Doug Borgstedt from *Editor and Publisher*. Reprinted by permission of Doug Borgstedt.

Minnesota Newspaper Association, tells of holding a new technology seminar where a pair of 60ish publishers became very upset.

"They had just gotten Macs in their offices, and they didn't want to think about electronic news," she remembered.

Industry predictions for the foggy future suggest that newspapers might turn into little more than printed menus for information that's on-line. Or that everyone will carry small, flat electronic units that can call up the newspaper whenever it is wanted.

Whatever the truth, the old publishers with their new Macs had better get ready. As Falkman said, "Electronic news is here, whether you like it or not."

PERSPECTIVE 2-4

Magazine Readers Talk Back

Jennifer Wolff, in an article from the *Columbia Journalism Review,* describes the rewards and hazards for magazines that have invited their readers to talk back to the magazines on-line. This means that readers are given an on-line address for the magazine, to which readers can immediately send complaints and compliments; editors can use the same system to communicate with their readers.

Consider:

1. List two advantages that magazines gain from going on-line. List two disadvantages. Discuss.

2. Wolff describes a specific situation, when the editor of *Time* went on-line to discuss the controversial O. J. Simpson cover photo. Why did the editor feel that it was important to go on-line to handle the controversy? Do you agree that it was a good idea? Why? Why not?

3. Do you agree that a magazine's on-line access can improve journalistic accountability? Why? Why not?

Opening Up Online: What Happens When the Public Comes at You from Cyberspace

Jennifer Wolff

It was a small moment in history. At 6:57 P.M. on Wednesday, June 22, [1994] managing editor Jim Gaines of *Time* addressed a group of irate computer users who had been pounding their keyboards in protest because the magazine had darkened a mug shot of O.J. Simpson for the cover of that week's issue, making him look more guilty, more sinister, more black. "To the extent that this caused offense to anyone, I obviously regret it," Gaines said, emphasizing that any racial overtones were surely unintended. "I'll be a little more careful about

doing portraiture or photo illustration on a very tight deadline, which was the case here."

This wasn't the first time Gaines made himself accountable to the public, but it was the first time he or any other journalist of comparable stature had done so in cyberspace. Two days after the darkened cover appeared it was a top news story around the country and under attack from the NAACP. But it was the "vivid and insistent" outpouring online, Gaines said, that made him decide not to wait five more days for the next "To Our Readers" column in *Time*.

So he took his white flag and waved it across a message board of America Online (AOL), an online service that claims over a million subscribers (and supplies *Time*'s own service, *Time* Online). His explanation was important for its own sake, but also for where he first made it. Gaines and journalists at all levels around the country are increasingly making themselves accessible electronically for give-and-take with a growing segment of their public.

Cyberspace, particularly the Internet — a worldwide network of interlinked computers reachable by some 25 million users, including subscribers to commercial systems like AOL, Prodigy, and CompuServe — has proved an invaluable resource for journalists, providing boundless access to obscure information and research, unique story ideas, and the sources to flesh them out. Message boards and e-mail have long been integral facets of this technology. Increasingly, they are fostering an unusual symbiosis: readers have unprecedented access to reporters and editors, and journalists enjoy the rare opportunity to learn with lightning speed what their audience is thinking on a variety of issues. At last count some 300 publications had some degree of availability online, or were planning to, and the popularity of these ventures is often measured by their level of interactivity.

Enthusiasts hail these developments as the Second Coming of journalism, a chink in the thick wall that has largely separated the media from their audience. But critics, even some who embrace the new information age, have some legitimate concerns, not least of which is that journalists can't possibly do their jobs *and* answer every piece of e-mail. Nor can they partake in every message board exchange, particularly those that serve as dumping grounds for keystroke-happy zealots. And no one can be sure who the people behind the screen really are, or if what they're saying is true. (Yet when Gaines posted his mea culpa about *Time*'s cover, none of the newspapers that picked up his quote called *Time* to confirm that it was in fact Gaines who had posted it.)

There's another issue. The population of cyberspace is expected to double in [1995], but at this point just one-third of American households own computers; far fewer have modems or know how to use them. While the efficiency of electronic feedback can be constructive — or destructive — for some journalists, the opinions delivered through the medium aren't yet likely to represent the country at large.

About one-fifth of *Time*'s New York news staff have AOL accounts, and many use the message boards to some degree. Associate editor Sophfronia Scott-Gregory had already been online discussing the possible racial implications of the Simpson case when she read in *The New York Times* that *Time* had intentionally altered the mug shot. "Did anyone do comparison shopping at their local newsstands?" Gregory posted for all to see at 12:24 P.M. on Tuesday, June 21, [1994]. "Our cover, though we used the same photo, is markedly different from *Newsweek*'s . . . our(s) is credited as a 'photo illustration' because an artist darkened it and did other things to it for a more dramatic effect. *Newsweek* ran the straight photo credited to the AP."

In the next day-and-a-half accusations of racism, commercialism, and cultural insensitivity flooded *Time* Online's message boards, and not just from average users. "We took a boring photo and made it more interesting looking, more sinister . . . that was misleading, no matter how we try to explain it," wrote *Time* associate editor Mike Lemonick. Added writer Chris Farley, "Darkened skin should not be used to symbolize tragedy and violence." Gregory posted again: "It never occurred to me that we would do such a thing on purpose. I was surprised and confused to find out that we did."

Gaines admits that initially he didn't like to see staff members posting negative comments about the cover, and "thought they shouldn't do it and told them not to." Eventually, however, he "realized they shouldn't be constrained from stating their opinion, that the First Amendment rests on it."

After three days of dodging calls from media reporters, Gaines took to the message boards himself. "I didn't want to let them hang there thinking *Time* was idiotic for what we did, but that we had understandable motives, even if they were wrongheaded," he says.

Gaines had another purpose, one that transformed a forum devoted to the voice of the people into one of equal service to his magazine. If he responded to press inquiries, he says, "I was concerned I wouldn't be quoted accurately," but he assumed that if he offered an official response in writing online, he would be. "The longer we said nothing," he adds, "the longer we looked like we were stonewalling, which surely was not the intention."

The angry tones continued after Gaines posted, but with an occasional smattering of good will. "I am comforted that the 'darkening' was not racially motivated and [Gaines's reply] illustrates what *Time* or *Newsweek* go through on a weekly basis deciding what to place on their covers," wrote one AOL user. Wrote another: "I am impressed that various *Time* employees have joined in . . . impressed more than anything at [their] flat-out honesty." One hopeful response: "This forum enables ordinary Americans to give some input to the writers and editors of the nation's most influential publications. Perhaps we too can help shape public opinion."

Few if any mandates exist to regulate what any journalist discusses online. But what distinguishes reporters' posts from their letters and phone conversations is that they are inherently public. That's why some media institutions are concerned with issues such as libel, and with whether First Amendment and contractual protections extend to what any individual reporter composes in a piece of e-mail or on a message board, which can be read by thousands and thousands of users.

Gaines's post touched on another issue. Debate has centered on who owns words posted in electronic forums, and how accountable the people are behind them. Some online services issue "You Own Your Own Words" disclaimers suggesting that authors can challenge unauthorized use of their messages in other mediums. But that isn't a legal guarantee; it's an unenforceable ethic promulgated with two principles in mind: users should take responsibility both for what they write and for online material they may be tempted to disseminate elsewhere.

Journalistic assumption, however, argues that since these forums are public, they are therefore public record. Gaines wanted his quote picked up, and it was, by *The New York Times, The Washington Post,* and others. Says Michael Godwin, counsel for the Electronic Frontier Foundation (EFF), a cyberspace civil liberties watchdog group: "Gaines took a very traditional journalist's view; you show up in a public forum, you say it and it's out there. It was a clash between the journalism ethic and the not-always-articulated ethic that has developed on a number of online systems." Not every user wants his post used without permission. And even though common sense warns journalists not to take at face value anything they find online, that is, of course, exactly what some did with Gaines's post.

Not everyone at *Time* considers this electronic brush with the public worthwhile. "I don't believe in this interface bullshit," snorts the art critic Robert Hughes. "It's a giant waste of time that takes away from what writers are supposed to do, which is read and write and experience the world. I'm an elitist; I value my time. You're not going to catch me going online apologizing because I was cruel to an artist."

As for culling valuable information online, many still prefer the street. "As an investigative reporter, it's rare that I get a letter from a reader who has direct knowledge about a subject I've investigated or am interested in investigating," says associate editor Richard Behar of *Time*. "If I went online I'd probably miss a lot of the things I'd find if I were out pounding the pavement."

There's also that question of how well on-line culture represents the world at large. Poor people aren't as likely to show up on-line. Computer users, rich or poor, are technically savvier than the average American, and as a rule better educated. It could smack of elitism if journalists took electronic correspondence more seriously than letters or phone calls.

Then again, maybe it's the other way around. At a luncheon of the American Society of Magazine Editors, *Vanity Fair*'s editor in chief, Graydon Carter, told his colleagues, "We pride ourselves that our articles tell you as much as you need to know." Carter doesn't expect his staff to venture online. For readers with further questions or opinions about a certain piece, he suggests, "That's what cocktail parties are for."

Well, many journalists counter, that's a problem, because too often cocktail parties and similarly narrow, homogeneous forums are the places where reporters and editors get story ideas. While working at *New York* magazine, Jon Carroll, now a columnist for the *San Francisco Chronicle,* remembers editorial meetings at which Clay Felker, then *New York*'s editor, would "reach into his pocket and bring out pieces of paper and say, 'Here's a story,' because someone at a party mentioned it." Cyberspace, say Carroll and others, is less limited than its critics contend, and far broader than the circles in which many journalists travel. There are even users who are poor, he says — they use university or corporate accounts or the mailroom computer — and he adds that the online community is growing more ethnically diverse.

Such broad access can be invaluable, some journalists think. "The absence of contact with people who are after all our customers has gotten in the way of our understanding of what it is we really need," says

Bill Mitchell, director of electronic publishing for the *San Jose Mercury News.*

Time's executive editor, Dick Duncan, has a similar view. Last winter [in 1993] he spent hours investigating a challenge made by two users who, in a message board entitled TIME'S ANTI-GUN BIAS, accused the magazine of not delivering the entire truth about NRA opposition to the "cop killer bullet" bill passed in 1986. Duncan's research revealed they were half right: *Time* had neglected to report the little-publicized fact that the NRA had abandoned its opposition once legislators reworded the bill to exclude certain forms of standard ammunition.

The New York Times also closely monitors its message boards, available on AOL. As a result, and in small steps, the newspaper is trying not only to become more accountable, but also more sensitive to readers. Recently a religious Republican complained that media use of the phrase "religious right" unfairly associated him with people like Jerry Falwell or Pat Buchanan. "It prompted a discussion among staff members, and we might try to think about how we approach this issue in the future," says Andrew Rosenthal, managing editor of the *Times*' Washington bureau. "These message boards are valuable because when entering the electronic world you make a commitment not just to present your product, but to establish a two-way street of communication."

For some, this mode of communication has become an integral part of their job. In a column about Whitewater coverage, *New York* magazine's media critic, Jon Katz, reproached the Washington press corps for acting as morality police when investigating the lives and behavior of politicians, a practice he felt was damaging to the political process. Afterwards he was invited to attend a computer chat with several Washington journalists who took issue with his stance, and they raised points Katz had not previously considered. "I realized I was too rigid in saying that journalists should get out of this area," admits

Katz, who since [May 1993] has put his e-mail address at the end of each column, and has received some 5,500 correspondences. "I concluded that I should have defined more broadly and less absolutely the circumstances surrounding the issue."

When the electronic aftermath of a column on blacks and Jews led Katz to plug into a national bulletin board service of some 600 black professionals, he was quickly aware that "I had actually never spoken to that many African-Americans in my life and it really opened my eyes to their issues." In his piece Katz raised several questions about race that he thought the media should address. But he said his online experience made him realize that he was directing his message exclusively to whites, thus excluding African-American concerns. "This dramatically improved my ability to write about media coverage on this subject," Katz says.

Could seriously heeding online feedback undercut a journalist's confidence, and perhaps even stifle one's voice, tone, and sense of irony? Online journalists insist they are trained to filter information, and thus don't take every gripe to heart, just those that indicate they could have done a better job. This connection to public opinion "stops us from becoming Moses on the mountaintop hurling tablets down at the masses," says Katz, adding that many pieces of angry but well-informed e-mail have led him to re-evaluate his work.

That is not every journalist's experience, however. Many who try it find certain aspects of electronic communication more frustrating than enlightening. "I thought we'd get an interesting cross-section of discussion on various topics and it got overwhelmed with anti-gun-control people," bemoans Bruce Dold, an editorial board member of the *Chicago Tribune,* available on AOL as Chicago Online. "They were fixed in their ways and didn't want to debate the subject. I stopped responding."

U.S. News & World Report columnist John Leo, whose "Dear John Leo" message board appears in the magazine's forum on CompuServe, wishes he had something to respond to. "I don't deduce anything from the flow of conversation, which is chaotic and disorganized and sometimes irritating. So little of what's written there is addressed to me," Leo complains. Topic drift, as such things are known, is a common occurrence online, and may even yield more interesting material than the topic itself. But wading through this irrelevance can be maddening for journalists on deadline. Recently the discussion in Leo's area turned to alcoholism. Leo's contribution to the exchange seemed ancillary, as users appeared more interested in exploring their own battles with the disease or those of people they knew. Often, he said "It's like if I said the world was flat no one would contest me but instead start talking about maps and earth and dirt and nothing that had to do with what I've written."

And online critiques of specific stories aren't always appreciated. "A danger of going online is that you're bombarded with opinions and you think it's the whole world and it's very easy to be influenced," says Debra Rosenberg, a reporter in *Newsweek*'s Boston bureau. Rosenberg took some nasty swipes in the media conference of The Well, a Sausalito, California-based bulletin board service, for a May 16, [1994,] cover story, "Men, Women & Computers," that she had helped research. The exchange lasted nearly a month, her critics alleging that the coverage was "poorly researched," "uninformed," and "sexist" in its stereotyping of women as computer-phobes. "These weren't specific complaints, like 'you said X and that's not really right,' " Rosenberg says. "Nothing they said was really helpful."

Another concern about interactivity is that online journalists may begin to regard other users of the Internet as more important than ordinary readers. "We need to avoid the sanctification of online communication as somehow being more holy than any other kind of communication," says Denise Caruso, an authority on media technology.

Then there is the problem of sheer volume. When reporter Adam Bauman of the *Los Angeles Times* wrote about hackers illegally storing pornographic images in the computers at Lawrence Livermore National Laboratory, a nuclear weapons research facility — a clear security breach, he said — he received over 5,000 pieces of angry e-mail, and had to change his e-mail address. But his editors wanted to understand the controversy surrounding his piece better, so he posted it in The Well and in alt.media-coverage in Usenet, home to some 6,000 newsgroups that serve as forums on as many issues. Between the lines of the many vituperative responses, Bauman thought he found a lesson for the future. He concluded that editors had cut too much essential information when the story was bumped from the business section to the front page, and readers were left confused. As for comments that he did a lousy reporting job and had sensationalized the situation at Livermore, he observed: "People are beginning to respond to what traditionally was a one-way medium. How that ultimately shapes coverage is yet to be defined, but at this point you can't let it dictate what you do."

It is obviously too early to tell how journalists will fare in cyberspace. The technology is still too new to them, and most reporters haven't mastered it. Few, so far, feel any obligation to use it at all. Concerns about time constraints, user accountability, and getting too close to members of the cyber community are valid ones. But there can clearly be benefits, too, and they go well beyond supplementing traditional reporting tools with electronic ones. They include a heightening of journalistic accountability and the opportunity to know better the needs of the people journalism serves, notions too often overlooked in the world of paper and ink.

Are These On-line Criminals?

About 25 million people today use the Internet, an international web of on-line communications. A few of these people steal copyrighted software and then use the Internet to distribute it. According to *Los Angeles Times* reporter Adam S. Bauman, these pirates are attracted by the danger of the game. Individual software manufacturers can sacrifice millions of dollars in lost income, however, when their products are distributed illegally on "the net."

Consider:

1. Describe the steps in the process that software pirate Jenny used to acquire and distribute "TIE Fighter." Explain the difficulties that face law enforcement agencies who try to stop the process.

2. Define the difference between a "releasing group" and a "courier group."

3. What are the long-range consequences to the computer software industry of the activities of these software pirates?

The Pirates of the Internet

Adam S. Bauman

In the early hours of July 6, [1994,] Jenny, head of a software piracy ring based in the Pacific Northwest, paced impatiently in front of a rack of high-speed personal computers, waiting for the phone call that would make her a superstar in the pirate underground.

It would come from an employee of LucasArts Entertainment Co. in San Rafael, who for $300 would supply Jenny's pirate group with one of the most anticipated games of summer: "TIE Fighter," based on the "Star Wars" movie trilogy and priced at about $60 per copy.

At LucasArts, the employee attached a small cellular modem to the back of his PC — a technique that would keep any record of the call off the company telephone bill — and dialed. Within a few minutes, the program had arrived in Jenny's computer, lacking only the code keys that would make it possible to play the game without an owner's manual.

Jenny then dialed into the Internet, the global computer network, and after taking several deliberate electronic detours she connected with a small computer in Moscow. There, a programming whiz who goes by the name "Skipjack" quickly cracked the codes and sent the program back across the Internet to "Waves of Warez," a Seattle bulletin board popular with software pirates.

Within 24 hours, "TIE Fighter" would be available to thousands of software pirates in major cities around the world — days before its official release date of July 20 [1994].

Welcome to the underside of the Internet, where stealing software has become highly sophisticated and hotly competitive — pursued more for thrills than for money. It's a world where pirate groups build alliances, undertake mergers and sometimes launch all-out battles against rivals.

And, contrary to common stereotypes, it is populated not only by nerdy teenage misfits, but by a curious cross-section of computer enthusiasts looking for some dangerous fun.

Jenny, for example, is a woman whose hobbies include motorcycles and collecting rare birds. The head of a big East Coast–based ring is a commercial airline pilot. Another group leader is a junior studying chemical engineering at Carnegie Mellon University in Pittsburgh, Pa. Yet another is a grandmother, leader of an elite group called Nokturnal Trading Alliance.

Their activities are, of course, illegal, potential felonies in many cases. And to most denizens of cyberspace, who use the Internet for scientific research, legitimate commerce and legal forms of entertainment, the pirates are common vandals at best.

Still, a number of pirates agreed to allow a reporter to observe their operations — both in person and via computer techniques that make it possible to monitor computer activities remotely — on the condition that their real names not be used.

The economic impact of the pirates' activities is difficult to measure. Electronic software theft via the Internet and other on-line services accounts for about one-third of the $2.2 billion lost in the United States [in 1993] as a result of piracy, according to the Business Software Alliance, a trade group. Pirates who mass-produce CD-ROM and floppy disks with stolen software pose a much bigger problem.

But Internet software theft is growing rapidly, along with the global network itself. Even major, mainstream software programs — like the new version of IBM's OS/2 operating system — are now routinely obtainable for free on the Internet.

And the pirates' activities have other consequences as well. They sometimes invade and effectively disable computers being used for scientific research, for example. And many in the information technology industries fear that software theft and other illegal activities are giving the Internet a bad name just when it is gaining unprecedented popularity.

Yet stopping the pirates turns out to be a very difficult task. Law enforcement agencies, software companies and even indignant individuals are stepping up efforts to hunt down electronic lawbreakers, but new methods of stealing and distributing stolen software are developed every day.

By design, the Internet lacks any central administrative authority, and security procedures aimed at thwarting pirates could interfere with the philosophy of free and open communications that is integral to the network. Some suggest the thievery won't be stopped until "bounty hunters" are recruited from the pirates' ranks and paid to hunt their former cohorts.

It may be small comfort to the victims, but most of the pirates interviewed for this story insisted they were not in it for the money.

"It was just for the thrill of getting free software or logging onto pirate bulletin boards that normal people don't know about," said Mike from Seattle, who says he has never earned a dime in his role as a "courier" for a pirate group.

During the interview, conducted in a tidy suburban home that he shares with friends, Mike uploaded a new program —

"Lode Runner for Windows" by Sierra Games — to the Internet from his custom-built computer. He then typed e-mail messages to other couriers notifying them of the new game and instructing them to copy it to various pirate sites around the world.

There appear to be about 20 major groups dedicated to software piracy, a lengthy *Times* investigation has found, with names such as Razor 1911, Tristar Red Sector Inc. (TRSi), Pirates With Attitude (PWA), Revolutionizing International Piracy (RIP), Legend, Malice and Anti Lamers Foundation (ALF). The groups vary in size from 20 to 100 members, and most have a similar hierarchy: group leaders, senior staff, regional coordinators, couriers and members.

The groups divide into two broad types: releasing groups, which arrange for software to be supplied and transferred to local computer bulletin board systems, and courier groups, which have a worldwide network of members who quickly transfer software from local bulletin boards to the Internet for instantaneous worldwide distribution.

Operators generally pay a pirate group a "donation" of $50 to $200 per month to carry that group's software on their bulletin boards. The more successful groups boast as many as several dozen affiliated bulletin boards.

The logistics of coordinating these far-flung networks are daunting, but the pirates are resourceful. One crucial communications method is the Internet Relay Chat (IRC) system, a kind of citizens' band of cyberspace that connects thousands of computer users in 21 countries. A particular series of channels, known as "warez" channels, are used both for conversation between software pirates and the on-line trading of freshly stolen software.

But the IRC has its limits, and even computer hackers sometimes need to talk with each other.

One method they have developed involves a "beige box," or custom-built telephone. The pirate travels a distance from his or her home and taps into the exterior wiring of an apart-ment building or house to arrange a conference call, possibly involving 20 people or more in several countries, via an AT&T Alliance Teleconference operator.

The pirate controls the conference call from a pay phone. But at the end of the month, the person whose line was tapped receives the bill — which can run well into five figures.

Several leaders of software pirating groups also described a method to avoid charges that involve a special computer program, a pay phone and a recordable greeting card that contains a small computer memory. The electronic sounds a quarter makes when dropped in a pay phone are recorded on the memory chip, then are played back into the phone in lieu of depositing money.

Despite the seeming ease with which many pirates stay one step ahead of law enforcement, there are plenty of risks — especially for those who work in the computer industry.

On Aug. 3, [1994,] Cupertino-based Symantec Corp., best known for its line of Norton Utility software backup and security products, discovered an employee in its Baton Rouge, La., facility running a pirate site on a company computer.

A Symantec source says the company took the unusual step of packing the offending computer inside a chilled and shielded container and flying it to corporate headquarters in Cupertino for laboratory analysis. The employee — who the source said was motivated by "the thrill of being a part of the pirate scene" — was fired.

[In October 1993], Dr. William L. Sebok, an astronomer at the University of Maryland, announced he had shut down a large pirate site that contained more than 500 megabytes of stolen software — enough to fill half a dozen personal computer hard disks. The site had been running on a laboratory computer used for processing images from the recent collision of Jupiter and the Shoemaker-Levy comet. The illegal use was detected [in October

1993] when processing on the computer inexplicably slowed to a crawl.

Maryland officials tried to trace the thieves back through the Internet, but met with little success: Many of the pirates were found to have used computer accounts belonging to university students in Switzerland, Spain and Slovenia who were unaware their accounts were being used for illicit purposes.

Still, Sebok says the time he spent tracking the pirates was well justified.

"I figured by shutting their site down, I would create a stir for [the pirates] that would be worth it for me. I didn't want to see the cockroaches tunneling through our computer system any more," he said.

Law enforcement officials have grown more vigilant about computer crime of all types. A group of special FBI agents now cruises the Internet, and many local and state law enforcement agencies have been training investigators to root out computer crime. But software piracy — especially involving games — takes a back seat to credit card theft and other more destructive crimes.

Dr. Gene Spafford, an associate professor at Purdue University and a computer security expert, says software manufacturers and trade groups like the Software Publishers Assn. may have to resort to frontier justice to stem the tide of illicit software being transferred over the Internet.

"Some of these same guys who are out pirating right now could very easily turn in the rival groups for a buck or more, and they'll be very willing to do so," Spafford said. He expects to see bounty hunters who get paid based on damages recovered or convictions of software pirating groups.

"We are already seeing private detective agencies investigating computer break-ins, because the local law enforcement agencies aren't equipped," he added.

Robert Roden, general counsel at Lucas-Arts, said the growth of the Internet has made it much easier for people to steal and distribute games around the world. Usually a company sends out cease and desist letters to pirates if it can find them, but that has become harder, Roden said.

"If they're stealing 'TIE Fighter' because they love the game, the irony in all of it is that they're harming the thing they love," Roden added. "They're making it more difficult for software companies to make these products and survive in the market."

But the pirates aren't much impressed with that argument. On July 14, [1994,] a 20-year-old pirate nicknamed Drizzit took a morning drive from his home in the San Fernando Valley to the Babbage's computer retail store at the Glendale Galleria. He wanted to check if LucasArts' "TIE Fighter" game had come in yet.

Glancing inside, Drizzit could see the game had not arrived. On a shelf near the front of the store stood empty "TIE Fighter" boxes, gaily decorated with ribbons that said "coming soon."

Drizzit recalls laughing at the sight of those empty boxes. "The funny thing was," he later told a reporter, "I'd been playing that game for the last seven days. I'd downloaded it off the Internet, I didn't have to pay for it, I was up to the sixth mission and it worked great."

PART II
The Media Industries

CHAPTER 3: PRINT MEDIA

The Newspaper Industry

Newspapers Adapt to the Video Era

Mediaweek's Michael Katz says that the newspaper industry has a promising future, even in the face of growing competition for their audience from many other information sources. The ability to continue to attract advertisers is the biggest necessary ingredient in a newspaper's success.

Consider:

1. According to Katz, what are some of the major factors that affect the cost of doing business for newspapers?

2. What advantages do newspapers have over other media? Explain.

3. According to Katz, how are newspapers attempting to maintain the size of their audience? Why is this important for newspapers' long-term survival?

Newspapers: Is the Nation's First Mass Medium Built to Last?

Michael Katz

Are newspapers obsolete? That depends on how you define newspapers or how in the future newspapers redefine themselves. An overview of today's newspaper industry must examine both the short and long term.

Short term, the industry's outlook is surprisingly strong. The only downside . . . looks to be the near-certainty, after several years of overproduction, of newsprint rate increases [the cost of paper], estimated by various analysts at between 15% and 20%. All other indicators, though, are bright.

To start, newspapers, like their auto industry brethren, have helped themselves in both the long and short term by cutting operating costs — what Brown Brothers analyst Maryann Winter calls "wages, head counts and administrative expenses" — during the 1989-90 recession, then keeping them down even as the economy recovered and revenues rebounded.

Will the rebound continue? Most forecasters say yes. Circulation, after dropping for several years, has evened out and is expected to hold firm. Circulation prices, meanwhile, have crept steadily upward. And with the national economy now steaming forward, advertising revenues have followed suit. "We're projecting that, on average, earnings growth will reach 25% [in 1994]," says John Morton, a media analyst with Washington, D.C.–based

Lynch, Jones & Ryan. "It'll be difficult to match that in '95, but it should be another strong year."

Robert Garrett, president of New York–based AdMedia, a print media investment bank, agrees, though he cautions that some areas will grow more sharply than others. "Retail display advertising," he points out, "has grown at a slower rate than classified."

Nicholas Cannistraro, senior vice president/chief marketing officer of the Newspaper Association of America (NAA), concurs: "Classifieds will be leading the parade in the three traditional categories." Classified, he says, is up some 9% so far [in 1994], with national ads up 6% and retail up 4%.

Classified tends to rise and fall with the economy: thus [1993's] linage surge. The slower growth of local retail advertisers like Kmart, Sears and Walgreen, on the other hand, reflects what Cannistraro calls "structural changes that have been at work for four or five years"; namely, the relentless spread of mega-retailers like Wal-Mart, whose advertising-to-sales ratios are much lower than those of smaller competitors. "Retail will be OK," says Cannistraro, "but nobody expects to see explosive growth for the foreseeable future."

That leaves the industry's greatest unknown — the putative return of national advertising, the crucial big-ticket categories like automotive and airlines that had all but abandoned daily newspapers. Slowly, like prodigal sons, these categories have begun coming home. "The more targeted TV becomes," says Larry Wynn, V.P./advertising at *The Miami Herald*, "the greater newspapers' ability to become the mass medium again." One of the hottest national ad growth rates Wynn has seen this year, for instance, has come from phone companies eager to describe their programs in greater detail than, as he puts it, "just seeing Candice Bergen tell you the same message over and over."

The Newspaper National Network is being formed by the NAA to help convince national advertisers beset by splintered broadcast markets to return to newspapers — and service them better once they do. . . . "All indications are that the concept has been well-received by potential advertisers." This, though, isn't quite news. "That's a fond hope, one that the industry's been maintaining for years," says Morton dubiously. "It hasn't happened."

Lest this one gloomy note mar an otherwise rosy picture, bear in mind that, as Winter puts it, "newspaper companies are not just newspaper companies." In fact, they are often sprawling media conglomerates that also operate magazines and TV and radio stations — all booming of late. "When you put it all together," says Winter, "you get earnings-per-share growth for newspaper companies in 1995 in the 12–13% range, whereas Standard & Poor's earnings are just going to be up 9%. Newspaper stocks are selling like we're going into a recession."

This leads to what Winter calls "this longer-term nonsense." Undervalued newspaper company stocks may reflect an undercurrent of doubt about whether the industry will do what it takes to flourish in the interactive age. "Circulation, except for Sundays, has declined," says Garrett. "More and more, people are getting their information other ways. Newspapers need to look at what they want to be when they grow up."

That's starting to happen. Papers from *The New York Times,* which tiptoed into the digital era earlier [in 1994] via America Online, to the *San Jose Mercury News*, whose online news service remains the industry standard, have begun exploring how their essential product — in-depth reporting and analysis on a scale still unapproached by the broadcast media — can be leveraged into new forms.

The trend should continue. "At this point," says Charles Wrubel, a senior advisor at AdMedia and former president of the Suburban Newspaper Association, "newspapers still have the resources to gather information more quickly and less expensively than new media." The question is how effectively they can package the info for an increasingly post-literate populace. "In their traditional form," says Wrubel, "newspapers have become much more imaginative in providing niche sections, coded stock products and the like."

The fact that *The Chicago Tribune* still dominates its market hasn't kept the paper from starting [a regular] section called Kid News written by and for children, with an eye toward the next generation of *Tribune* subscribers. "The threat of new competition is growing all the time," says the *Miami Herald*'s Wynn, whose ad team is preparing a host of new initiatives for the next few years. "We just don't think doing business as usual will bring in the revenue our company needs."

Is this future-minded activity impacting today's numbers? Not yet — but today isn't really the point. "As young people who've been trained to use electronic data retrieval start coming of age," says Morton, "it will make these services more in demand. But that's probably 10 years away." For the time being, says Morton, "it's difficult to beat the economics of newsprint. It's still very cheap and very easy to use."

The bottom line? The newspaper industry should enjoy an economically healthy grace period in which to adapt its product to the next century's new media demands. All of us who love 24-point headlines and smudged fingertips hope the industry will use it wisely.

Reporter Molly Ivins' Prescription for Journalists

After nearly 25 years as a journalist, syndicated columnist Molly Ivins has some strong feelings about what makes a good reporter; but one of the interesting things about this excerpt is that Ivins wrote it when she was just beginning her career. As a political commentator on Texas politics, Ivins has earned a reputation for plain speaking. She is no less candid in her expectations for her profession.

Consider:

1. Do you agree with Ivins that "it helps, anything and everything, if the people know"? Why? Why not?

2. List five characteristics that Ivins says are essential for a good reporter to possess. Explain why each quality is important.

3. What are the dangers, according to Ivins, of Establishment journalism? How can journalists overcome this temptation?

How to Be a Good Reporter

Molly Ivins

Best get yourself straight early on about why you're in this business. Not for the money, we trust. Some people are in it because it's so seldom boring, which I regard as an acceptable excuse. This next part is extremely sticky because it's a damn sight simpler to criticize other people's ideas than it is to set forth your own. One is never in so much danger of making an ass of one's self as when one is engaged in saying, "This I believe . . ."

Having adequately prefaced my credo, I'm ready to fire. I believe that ignorance is the root of all evil. And that no one knows the truth. I believe that the people is not dumb. Ignorant, bigoted, and mean-minded, maybe, but not stupid. I just think it helps, anything and everything, if the people know. Know what the hell is going on. What they do about it once they know is not my problem.

The discerning reader will have noticed several pitfalls in the preceding paragraph. For example, the people pit. I have meditated on the people pit and have come to the conclusion that it has always been there and always will be. Reporters are constrained to think of readers and viewers and listeners abstractly, a great, gray blob, out there. But what amazes me is the ubiquitous reportorial attitude which holds that the masses *out* there are the masses *down* there. Every newspaper I've ever worked on has had a Mythical Average Reader. In Minneapolis, our MAR was the retarded wife of a North Dakota farmer. In Houston, I am told, the MAR is an Aggie sophomore.

Any good teacher will tell you that aiming at the lowest common denominator is poor practice. In communicating anything, you do better if you aim slightly above the heads of your audience. If you make them stretch a little, they respond better. If you keep aiming at the dumb ones, you never challenge them and you bore the hell out of the bright ones. You also commit the grievous and pernicious error of thinking that the people is dumb. One of the most horrific results is that the people start to think so themselves. . . .

You know and I know that it's not easy to get the truth into newspapers—so much of it is not family fare. But you can't have been in this business for a year without learning at least the basics of all the gimmicks there are for getting the stuff through. The curve ball, the slideroo, the old put-it-in-the-17th-graf trick. Tell your editor the opposition will have the story in its next edition. Show 'em where *The New York Times,* or better yet, the *Dallas Morning News,* has already done this story. If you haven't got enough points with management to pull off a strong story on your own, give it to one of your colleagues. Find another angle on it. Localize the hell out of it. Disguise it as a feature.

Or, you can use the Janis Joplin–Zarko Franks take-another-little-chunk-of-their-ass-out technique. The inimitable Zarko, the Chronk's city editor, was grousing one day about all these g.d. kids he's got working for him who want to tell the Truth allatime, fer Chrissakes. "I tell 'em," said Zark, "you can't tell the *truth,* honey, this is a *daily newspaper.*

Every day these kids wanna write *War and Peace.* I tell 'em, look, baby, today you just tell the readers a little bit of the truth. That's all we got room for. Then tomorrow you go back and you pick up another little piece of the truth. And the day after that, another piece. You'll get it all eventually, but you ain't never gonna get none of it if you shoot for the whole wad every day. . . ."

Whatever you do, don't give up. Because all you can do once you've given up is bitch. I've known some great bitchers in my time. With some it's a passion, with others an art. With all of them, it is a dissipation of the energy they should be putting into reporting. I know, I know, the reason why newspeople bitch so much is because they've got a lot to bitch about. It's still a waste of time. Think Pollyanna. Read George Bernard Shaw or go listen to Ralph Yarborough. Anything but full-time bitching. . . .

Reporters need to be people people. It helps if you're an extrovert, but it's not necessary. I have frequently been amazed, when taking a colleague along to a meeting of radicals or blacks, to find my colleague actually afraid of such people. I find it absurd and wrong when reporters are ill at ease with people, just plain people, who happen not to be like them. There are reporters who simply can't deal with anyone who's not white, college-educated, middle class. I'm not sure whether that's sad or funny, but I know it doesn't make for good journalism. I don't know how you learn to relate to people—listen to them, I suppose. Spend enough time around very different kinds of people so that they don't strike you as odd. Maybe read some of the *I'm O.K., You're O.K.* genre of interpersonal relations. Dale Carnegie, anyone? . . .

One of the happy side effects of doing a lot of reading is that it will improve your writing, which needs it. Would you like to know why people don't read newspapers anymore? Because newspapers are boring. Dull. Tedious. Unreadable. No fun. I don't need your excuses: I read both Houston papers every day and I'd rather listen to local television news myself.

An editor once told me, "Adjectives and adverbs are dangerous words." There went half the English language. "Facts," Norman Mailer said to Judge Julius Hoffman, "mean nothing, sir, without their nuance." Nuances, I grant you, are very damned hard to get by the copy desk. Every desk has someone on it who is convinced that both *whispered* and *screamed* mean the same thing as *said*. I dare say, we have all seen our fair share of murmurs, croaks, rasps, shouts, and gasps bite the dust, not to mention all the adjectives and adverbs of our lives. Nevertheless, recalling previous pits, you will be neither cynical, discouraged, or bitchy about this. Right? Right. You will try. And try again. And again. And you will smile. Because it's so much healthier than crying or throwing up.

Be comforted, good writing is the wave of the future. *The New York Times* gets more readable every day: it's hard to find a pure-fact pyramid story in a good paper anymore. They throw in little hints now about what the facts mean. If you do get discouraged about trying to bring a little humanity into your writing in the face of constant desk opposition, think of yourself as part of the anti-anomie brigade. Fight alienation. Get on John Donne's side. There are too damn many lonely people in the world who just can't handle it, who are afraid of other people, who don't understand what's going on, who fear change. It doesn't help them to get a newspaper plopped on their front stoops every day that reduces the whole rich, human, comic, tragic, absurd, exasperating, and exciting parade of one day's events into a dehydrated lifeless set of unrelated facts. We keep writing about events as though they were pictures on a wall, something we could stand off and look at, when in fact they are the stuff of our lives. The news gets sanitized, homogenized, pasteurized, dehumanized, and wrapped in cellophane. No wonder people forget they're human. Fight it. Use adjectives.

Which brings us to the serious pitfall. That is, taking one's self seriously. In a way, I'm afraid to broach this one, since there's no shortage of cynics to remind us that the product only costs 10 cents and most people use it to wrap their fish.

How easily we come to accept the power, such as it is, that we carry around with us. I imagine most of you have had the experience, on an investigation, of walking up to some crook and saying, "I'm Joe Smith from the *Daily Hallelujah*" and watching the poor beggar start to sweat. Now there's a power trip. So is watching a pol, as you whip out your notebook, shift out of his normal style, get glassy-eyed, take on a fake heartiness, and say, "Well now Joe, let me tell you about my stand on that issue. . . ." The mayor calls you by your first name. So does the superintendent of schools and the head of the black power movement in town. Not to mention the bartender at the Press Club. You're in with the big people, all right. . . .

Look, we know the movers and the shakers because they make news and that's what we write about. But watch your ass, reporter, or you'll wind up like most of your brethren — a power groupie. Power is an insidious commodity. It's fascinating. Once you get into who's doing what to whom for why, it's as addictive as smack. And it works the same way: you need more and more of it and you produce less and less. You start to identify with your sources and then you're gone. You spend so much time with those people that you can't imagine the city being run in any other way. "That's the way it always has been and that's the way it always will be, baby." That's why it's called Establishment journalism. You concentrate on the people at the top, the people with power; you watch, you study how they make their moves, you get fascinated by it, and pretty soon you can't see anything else — just the top, just the power. And the others, the people, the readers, matter so little that you don't even bother to let them know what's going on. You start to think like the people you cover. . . .

There are ways to kick the habit. . . .

Cultivate clerks and secretaries. They haven't got as big a stake as their bosses in covering up what's going on. . . . Go look at Johnny Coward's foot and eye and chest. Don't listen to the president of Armco tell you about ship channel pollution: go look at the ship channel.

Do not go to press conferences. An abomination. A manipulative device. Stop letting sources get away with lies because they hold high positions and titles. The *Chronicle* ran a front-page story not long ago about some astronaut blasting the government for cutting back the space program. The astronaut was quoted as saying that 80 percent of the federal budget went for welfare programs. Don't let him get away with that just because he's an astronaut. Right after that quote, the *Chronicle* should have run the actual percentage of the budget that goes for welfare pro-

grams. There's no excuse for spreading misinformation just because it comes from someone in a high place.

I am told that a Houston editor is fond of reminding his reporters, "This is not a crusading newspaper." I think that's too bad myself, but I could live with it. Us crusaders screw up with alarming frequency, too. Don Rottenberg, late of the *Chicago Journalism Review,* declared in his farewell article, "There are still places where people think the function of the media is to provide information." I'd settle for that. And I don't think you should settle for anything less.

"How to Be a Good Reporter," by Molly Ivins. Excerpted from *Molly Ivins Can't Say That, Can She?,* New York: Random House, 1991, pp. 233–241. Copyright © 1991 by Molly Ivins. Used with permission of Random House, Inc.

Uncovering Black Press Heritage

Most of the readings in this text discuss contemporary media developments. In contrast, this article is important for the historical perspective it offers on the role of the black press in the United States, about which little has been written until recently. In this article, written especially for *Media/Reader*, journalism historian Frankie Hutton describes the values that under-scored the development of the black press in this country. Hutton also has compiled a valuable list, which follows this reading, of historical black newspapers that have survived for scholars to examine today.

Consider:

1. What evidence is there in Hutton's article to support her contention the "editors of color supported the ideals of democracy"? Explain.

2. According to Hutton, what are the two reasons that African-American editors were willing to embrace democratic ideology?

3. Explain the special value of black newspapers for nineteenth century readers.

The Ideological Origins of the Black Press in America

Frankie Hutton

". . . Questions we discuss involve the Honor of the country as much as the prospects of the Blacks."
    Samuel R. Ward, *The Aliened American*,
    April 9, 1853

The hopeful, humanitarian spirit of the early black press in America has been a continued source of wonder for me as I've read and studied the columns of these little known weeklies and monthlies for a number of years. This article explores the ideals of the first black newspapers in America. Remarkably, there was no lurid, hateful tone in the editorial commentary of these newspapers during the pre-Civil War period. This is true even though the publications were led by men of color, some of whom, like Frederick Douglass, had been fugitive slaves and had a right to be riled.

Of the twenty-five or so black newspapers begun between 1827 and 1860, fewer than twenty of that group are now extant for study. Little has been noted in journalism histories of the first decades of weeklies such as *Free-dom's Journal,* begun in New York City in 1827 by Samuel Cornish and John Russwurm, and *The North Star,* Frederick Douglass' first paper, begun twenty years later in Rochester. Even less is known about the ideological foundations of the newspapers comprising this fledgling but important ethnic press. It is clear, however, that the black press was begun during a difficult and unethical period in American journalism, described by a respected historian, Frank Luther Mott, as the "dark ages" of the profession.[1] Contemporary journalism historians Michael and Edwin Emery concluded that some newspapers during this time were known to lower standards and "sacrifice truth if it would bring in more customers."[2]

John Brown Russwurm, 1799–1851

Photo courtesy of Moorland-Springarn Research Center, Howard University.

We know that the black press was far outside the mainstream of establishment journalism of the pre-Civil War period. The first years of this era were dominated by newspapers that were politically partisan and steeped with vile innuendos, the profit motive, and a number of peccadillos. Although they had little clout in the overall profession, black editors used their newspapers to note the irresponsible practices of some of the establishment newspapers during the antebellum (pre-Civil War) years. *Freedom's Journal,* for instance, charged in 1828 that blacks had been "daily slandered."[3]

It was probably the unnecessarily vile attacks on personal character and the ridicule of blacks in some white-owned newspapers that prompted the black editor of *The Mirror of Liberty,* David Ruggles, to write in 1838, "The greedy appetite of scandal and abuse shall never be satisfied in the columns of this Journal."[4] Headed by Thomas Hamilton in New York City, *The Weekly Anglo-African* noted likewise in 1859 that "nothing was so common at that time as attempts of Republican journals to write down people of color."[5]

Despite the slander and ridicule of blacks by the establishment press, editors of color continued to support the ideals of democracy. The first black newspapers in the United States were begun by editors who believed in the same ideals that spawned the American Revolution and were embedded in the Constitution. When the editors of *Freedom's Journal* boasted in 1828, "We shall ever regard the Constitution of the United States as our polar star,"[6] they bespoke the sentiments of later black newspapers of the pre-Civil War period. Those precepts of liberty for all, domestic tranquility, and promotion of the general welfare were, surprisingly, ever-present themes in both the editorial commentary of black editors and in their overall strivings for responsible journalistic practices. From its beginning, *Freedom's Journal* gave editorial support to the democratic values held dear by America's founding fathers, although blacks, like women and Native Americans, were among those pushed far outside the framework of establishment journalism.

Financially fledgling black newspapers embraced the ideals of democracy and were intent on responsible practices, even though they were at the bottom rung of the profession. This is not, however, a paradox of press history; there were two apparent reasons for the editors' concern with these themes. First, the ideals of republicanism appear to have been strategically pushed in the columns of black newspapers as a reminder that blacks, most of whom were in slavery, were well aware of the inconsistencies in America's democratic experiment. Second, black editors espoused press responsibility as an aspect of promoting domestic tranquility and the general welfare

of all Americans. Their papers were published in accordance with these principles even as establishment, white-owned newspapers typically overlooked good news from black communities and often reported the activities of people of color with a spiteful, racist tinge.

When they espoused and practiced truth, fairness, and responsibility in reporting, (pre-Civil War) black editors must have thought these could become self-fulfilling prophecies. The hope of black editors was that establishment newspapers would stop derogatory reporting and false comment about people of color; they set out to show by example that this was unacceptable journalism. In 1837, when Samuel Cornish chided editors of some establishment newspapers, he charged that

Samuel E. Cornish, 1795–1858

Photo courtesy of Moorland-Springarn Research Center, Howard University.

The first black newspaper published in the United States.

Photo courtesy of the Library of Congress.

they had "no conscience at all — that principle is lost and forgotten in their eager pursuit of money."[7] An editorial in *Mirror of the Times,* San Francisco's first black weekly, echoed a similar message in 1857 when it charged that "avarice" was the root cause of the "flagrant wrongs" against people of color in America.[8]

Antebellum black newspapers were no editorial weaklings, but their columns clearly were not militantly focused. The themes of education, morality, temperance, and the abolition of slavery were the editorial fare, all topics befitting uplift, mid-nineteenth century social reform, and the spirit of democratic republicanism. As editor of *The Rights of All* in 1829, Samuel Cornish made it clear that his newspaper was democratic and humanitarian in spirit, and did not focus solely on matters

of concern to blacks. Cornish said he was "interested in the general improvement of society," and pledged his newspaper and abilities as an editor "to the general benefit of society."[9] Given the editors' interest in the ideals of democracy, it is not surprising that black newspapers during this period were also generally supportive of women's rights. News and information about women's constructive community activities, some of their provocative views, as well as literature and poetry, were part and parcel of black newspapers.

As people of color continued to be ostracized socially, politically, and economically throughout the decades leading to the Civil War, black editors seemed determined to use their newspapers and journals in a sort of moral suasion. Their aim was to work toward acceptance and full citizenship for their people. The editors thought this was a reasonable goal, in keeping with the tenets of American democracy. In 1837, Samuel Cornish, then associated with his fourth pre-Civil War, New York City newspaper, *The Colored American,* wrote, "Many would gladly rob us of the endeared name, 'Americans.'" This was a birthright, however, that Cornish felt belonged emphatically as much to blacks as to whites, one he felt blacks would "never yield."[10]

Over the years, Cornish's democratic idealism was echoed by other black editors, including William Howard Day, who began *The Aliened American,* the only extant pre-Civil War black weekly published in Cleveland. Day, Samuel Ringgold Ward, and J. W. C. Pennington, as an editorial committee, explained in an April 1853 missive their belief in the United States Constitution: "We claim for all and especially for all Americans, equal justice before American law; and are willing to stand or fall by its just application, under the Constitution of our common country."[11]

The idealism that was characteristic of antebellum black editors and their associates

Frederick Douglass, 1817–1895

Photo courtesy of the Library of Congress.

hinged on the belief that the nation's democratic ideals, such as liberty and equality, could eventually become realities for people of color. Belief in republicanism and in the ideals of the Revolution had indeed been contagious and, through several generations, had never left the minds and hearts of politically astute, upwardly mobile blacks. During the early years of the black press, editors were intent on reaching reform-minded whites with their newspapers. Mostly, however, they geared their columns to a black middle class that was characterized by attempts to move up in America through stable family relationships, respectability, and organizations of uplift. As agenda-setters, black editors addressed their papers to a middle class that pursued an idealistic quest for the mainstream of the country their people had helped to build.

Despite their own financial and personal hardships, the editors worked diligently to circulate their small publications through widely placed agents and a small prepaid annual subscription rate of $1.50 to $3. Although there are no reliable figures, it appears that most of the early newspapers were published in the Northeast irregularly and had circulations of 1,000 to 3,000. Frederick Douglass' first two weeklies, *The North Star* and *Frederick Douglass' Paper,* were the longest running of the pre-Civil War black newspapers.

As a reform-minded humanitarian and the premiere black editor of his time, Douglass' journalistic career embodied democratic idealism. And even though he became immensely frustrated by America's racism and the continued growth of slavery, he clung

Frederick Douglass' newspaper, first published in 1847.

Photo courtesy of the Library of Congress.

stubbornly to democratic ideals for what he and other black editors thought were good, practical reasons. Where democratic idealism was concerned, Douglass' rationale was foolproof: He explained that blacks had "grown up" with the country and had done back-breaking labor to help develop it. He reasoned further, "We have watered your soil with our tears, nourished it with our blood, tilled it with our hard hands. Why should we not stay here?"[12]

Of course, the merits of black editors' messages of democratic idealism and optimism about correcting the plight of blacks in America during these early years are debatable. It could be argued that their idealism got in the way of real progress of the race and that the editorial fare of antebellum black newspapers should have been replete with vivid descriptions of the horrors of slavery and militancy for the cause of abolition. The black press also might have been more attuned to the poverty of free blacks in America. It also could be argued that, for the black elite, the intelligentsia of the race, belief in and optimism about the ideals of democracy did much to preempt some of the African cultural and ancestral forms that were kept and held dear, especially by the lower classes of blacks.

Indeed, as the black press revealed its preoccupation with the ideals of democracy, it also kept alive the hopeful spirit necessary for the survival and continued socialization of an already resilient group of would-be black Americans. It is clear, then, that the first

List of Pre-Civil War Black Newspapers and Journals

Dates	Title	Place	Editor(s)
1827–1829	Freedom's Journal	(New York City)	Samuel Cornish/ John Russwurm
1829	Rights of All	(New York City)	Samuel Cornish
1837	The Weekly Advocate	(New York City)	Samuel Cornish/ Philip Bell
1837–1841	The Colored American	(New York City)	Samuel Cornish/Philip Bell/Charles B. Ray
1838–1839	The National Reformer	(Philadelphia)	William Whipper
1838–1840	The Mirror of Liberty	(New York City)	David Ruggles
1843–1847	The Mystery	(Pittsburgh)	Martin Delany
1842	The Northern Star and Freeman's Advocate	(Albany, New York)	Stephen Myers
1846–1848	The Ram's Horn	(New York City)	Van Rensallear/ Frederick Douglass
1852–1856	The Aliened American	(Cleveland, Ohio)	William Howard Day/ W. J. C. Pennington

black editors in America set a hopeful agenda for people of color based on the illusive ideals of democracy.

End Notes

1. Frank Luther Mott, *American Journalism, A History, 1690–1960,* 3d ed. (New York: Macmillan, 1962), 172.
2. Edwin Emery and Michael Emery, *The Press and America: An Interpretive History of the Mass Media,* 5th ed. (Englewood Cliffs, N.J.: Prentice-Hall, 1984), 181.
3. *Freedom's Journal* (New York), April 25, 1828.
4. *The Mirror of Liberty* (New York), August 1838, 1.
5. *The Weekly Anglo-African* (New York), September 3, 1859.
6. *Freedom's Journal* (New York), April 25, 1828.
7. *The Weekly Advocate* (New York), January 14, 1837.
8. *Mirror of the Times* (San Francisco), December 12, 1857.
9. *The Rights of All* (New York), May 29, 1829.
10. *The Colored American* (New York), March 4, 1837.
11. *The Aliened American* (Cleveland), April 9, 1853.
12. John W. Blassingame, ed., *The Frederick Douglass Papers, Series One, Volume 2, 1847–54* (New Haven, Conn.: Yale University Press, 1982), 304.

"The Ideological Origins of the Black Press in America," by Frankie Hutton, © 1992 by Frankie Hutton. Article written for this text.

List of Pre-Civil War Black Newspapers and Journals *(continued)*

Dates	Title	Place	Editor(s)
1852–1960	The Christian Recorder*	(Philadelphia)	Japez P. Campbell
1855	The Mirror of the Times	(San Francisco)	Mifflin W. Gibbs/ J. H. Townsend
1847–1851	The North Star	(Rochester, New York)	Frederick Douglass
1851–1859	Frederick Douglass' Paper	(Rochester, New York)	Frederick Douglass
1859–1860	Douglass' Monthly	(Rochester, New York)	Frederick Douglass
1859–	The Weekly Anglo-African	(New York City)	Thomas Hamilton
1859–1861	The Anglo-African Magazine	(New York City)	Thomas Hamilton

*Though religiously affiliated, *The Christian Recorder,* originally edited by The Reverend Campbell and published from 1852 until 1960 as the official organ of the African Methodist Church, was also consulted.

"The Ideological Origins of the Black Press in America," by Frankie Hutton, © 1992 by Frankie Hutton. Article written expressly for the text.

The Newspaper Owner as Media Entrepreneur

As a result of concentration of media ownership—when large corporations buy up small media companies—a local newspaper is one of the few places that individuals can enter the media business as owners. The following article describes the challenges that faced Julie Ardery and Bill Bishop when they decided to buy the *Bastrop County Times*. It is an important case study in the difficulties of first-time media ownership.

Consider:

1. Why does Bill Bishop say that the business of newspaper publishing has been taken out of the small-time, independent publisher's control?

2. What stories can a small-town newspaper cover differently from a larger newspaper?

3. What personal price must a small-town publisher be willing to pay, according to Bishop?

4. Do you agree with Bishop that the future winners in the newspaper business will be "the fellows who understand cash flow, marketing, and demographics"? Why? Why not?

Owning Your Own Weekly

A Warning from Smithville

Bill Bishop

Slip a few beers into many a metropolitan reporter and he'll tell you he wants nothing more from life than his own smalltown weekly newspaper. No more editors, no more rush to meet the daily deadline, no more stuffy assignments. That conversation's good for another round (until the dreamer gets stuck with the tab).

It was my dream, too. So in the summer of 1983 my wife, Julie Ardery, and I bought the *Bastrop County Times*—a 3,000-circulation fact of life in Smithville, Texas, since 1892. During the next four years we published one of the better small weeklies in the state. We conducted an investigative series that changed a major state agency; we printed a short story, long reviews and editorials; we sponsored an ugly dog contest; we won awards for our news writing and features and for community service. We had fun and we made money.

But in August 1987 we sold the paper to our competitor in a town 12 miles away, and it was not exhaustion that convinced us to sell; we'd expected the long hours. What we didn't count on was a new rural economy that takes the business of newspapering out of the small-time independent publisher's control.

Before we get into the business end of things, this introduction to rural newspaper publishing should carry a warning: weekly newspapering can be hazardous to your health. The terrors of small-business owner-ship are compounded by the pressures of news reporting. And everything is so, well, close up. A lost ad account isn't just a prob-lem for somebody on the third floor. It means you have to skip paying yourself to cover the next printing bill. And imagine finishing your editorial excoriating Ed Meese only to meet him a half hour later, coming down a grocery aisle between the Little Debbie snack cakes and the Folgers coffee. There ain't no place to hide.

And even if there were, there wouldn't be time. In 1976 I worked at the *Mountain Eagle,* an award-winning weekly in the coal-fields of eastern Kentucky. The paper was, and is, Tom and Pat Gish, a brilliant pair of journalists who passed the burnout stage of weekly newspapering sometime in the mid-1960s. Though he had done the heart by-pass routine several years before I arrived in Whitesburg, Tom still spent every Tuesday night (production night at most weeklies) at the newspaper office until dawn. He would sit ashen-faced at his desk, reading copy or tap-ping out an editorial. Then, about midnight, he would collapse on one of those narrow, nylon cots you get at K-Mart. Someone would throw a dust-covered blanket over the famous editor, and he would snore as we pasted up headlines and finished the grocery ad.

Pat was tougher, though I suspect the last time she felt well-rested was sometime during the Eisenhower administration. She would proof all the copy and finish the layout while the rest of us were club-handed with fatigue,

and, as the sun came up, hustle off to her 9-to-5 job running a rural housing authority. I once asked Jim Branscome, who contributed articles on the Tennessee Valley Authority to the *Eagle,* if he would ever consider buying a weekly. "Naw," muttered Branscome, now a McGraw-Hill editor. "I think I'd rather go to prison." At least in prison you have a chance of parole.

By 1982, the memory of Tom snoozing away on that little aluminum cot had waned and the romance of the weekly returned. Julie and I had started and then sold a small news-letter, so we had some money to shop with. We felt that we had something to say and that, through a weekly newspaper, we might get it said. Moreover, we wanted to measure an American community; the weekly seemed a subtle and accurate thermometer. For the better part of a year we looked for just the right paper.

There are nearly 8,000 publications in this country that come out less often than daily and at least weekly, according to the National Newspaper Association, and each is occasionally for sale. If you have lots of money, you look for three things: the ideal paper is in a growing market, lacks signifi-cant competition, and has a gross income of nearly $500,000. Few papers of these stan-dards ever come up for sale, and when they do, they'll cost $900,000, minimum, with a good third of that required in a cash down payment.

Got $300,000, plus enough in the bank to operate the paper through the first three months? Neither did we, so we found our-selves considering Smithville's newspaper, even though it violated two of the three cardi-nal rules: Smithville, located 50 miles east of Austin, is the smallest town in a county with three newspapers (competition writ large) and the *Bastrop County Times* was grossing only $160,000. We bought the *County Times* because it was for sale at a price we could afford and because we liked the town. Our decision to put $40,000 down on the paper was made over a Shiner beer at Charlie's Bar-b-que, a Main Street establishment that serves sausage and brisket sliced onto butcher paper, garnished with a package of saltines. We'd wanted romance. Well, this was it.

During the month before our move to Smithville, Julie and I had a chance to think about what kind of paper the *County Times* would be. Weekly newspaper editors become famous when they are assaulted or their headquarters are torched. The Gishes, in fact, received national recognition for their work after a policeman paid a teenager 50 bucks to burn down the *Mountain Eagle* office (bad things happen to smalltown publishers when they are critical of the local constabulary). That's a high price to pay for fame. Julie and I decided our move to Smithville was to be no exercise in self-immolation. We wanted a tough newspaper, but we wanted to survive.

At the same time, we believed that a weekly can achieve a style and form denied metropolitan dailies. They can become living, breathing creatures, complete with charms and foibles. The grand small papers, it seems, are built on human eccentricity. The Gishes brought an intensity to the *Mountain Eagle*; Sam Ragan's poetry imbues the Southern Pines, North Carolina, *Pilot*; the *Hungry Horse News* (Columbia Falls, Montana) is a weekly exhibit of Brian Kennedy's photography, and the *Vineyard Gazette* (Martha's Vineyard, Massachusetts) still rings with the elegance and clear thinking of its late publisher, Henry Beetle Hough. Our goal at the *County Times,* we decided, was to orchestrate a true community newspaper with a chorus of photos, art, and stories from a panorama of local contributors.

Before we get too far astray, hard-news enthusiasts should know that a weekly can contain — and readers enjoy — as much enterprising journalism as you can dish out. The weekly deadline demands that stories be written in a more explanatory way, since readers may pick up the paper at any time over the week between publications. But you'll find the same range and depth of stories in a rural county as in Metropolis.

News stories in a weekly can have substantial impact: our continuing reports on a regional power agency led to a $385,000 investigation by a former U.S. attorney. But crusading editors soon meet the test of the grocery aisle. Knowing the subjects of your reporting — taking pictures of their kids in school and their parents in the nursing home — makes you more understanding, and, I believe, fairer.

News gathering, while hard work, was the predictable part of our experience. What we'd hoped for, but could never have foreseen, was the vibrancy of Bastrop County's residents. We built up a corps of columnists, ranging from Homer (a former country music singer who divulged the county's night life) to Doris Laake (a proper Lutheran widow from the hamlet of Paige).

Doris turned out to be our best reporter, a fearless chronicler of her town's activities. When a person fell from a ladder, twisting an ankle, Doris was ready with the hospital report; an attack of bees was good for a headline; she enumerated the losses, down to the last sausage link, when fire took a smokehouse. She was also the first reporter to write about what became, in 1985, the most active oil play in the state. But Doris' first love was disaster. I remember when the state police called to ask about the gray-haired woman with the Polaroid who'd crossed their yellow barriers to snap a close-up of an automobile wreck. I could only imagine the police, slack-jawed, as they watched Doris bend over the carnage, her camera spitting out its little photo-squares.

We had an imaginative layout artist. For several weeks she changed the job titles in the staff box to fit her fancy. One week we became characters from "Star Trek," and for New Year's week we were all highballs. For a while, the *County Times'* staff box became the best read part of the paper.

Two fine artists in the county contributed

editorial cartoons. One charged $25; the other expected two six-packs.

And then there was the Bird Lady, Melissa Bishop (no relation). Melissa was, and is, bird crazy. She ministers to sick birds, runs what appears to be a bird orphanage, and studies birds constantly, hiding under a pile of leaves or standing mannequin-still in the middle of a field. We met her one day on a country road as she walked her geese, and asked if she would write about birds for the paper. She did, and her "Bird Lady" column became an instant hit. (Particularly popular was the account of the Bird Lady's Thanksgiving Day ritual — serving her turkeys a cake in the shape of a pilgrim.)

In four years of running the paper, we published pictures of every unusual edible item grown, caught, or created in Bastrop County. There were eggs big enough to be a hen's worst nightmare, catfish of biblical proportion, two-handed pears, and turnips so large they would set a smile on the face of the grimmest Bohemian farmer. Our philosophical justification for this weekly horn of plenty was that we wanted people not only to read the paper, but to *be* the paper. Everyone was a potential contributor.

We wanted each issue to be a surprise. We ran an April Fool's page every year (some readers are still upset that Ferdinand and Imelda Marcos are moving to nearby Kirtley).

The bottom-line result of this combination of hard news, editorials, features, and a cornucopia of contributors was a 33 percent increase in subscribers in the first three years to more than 4,000. Revenues also jumped, from the $160,000 in the year before we bought the paper to $285,000 in 1986, a 78 percent increase.

What seemed a successful business venture, however, produced an intolerable way of life. There was always too much work and not enough money. Stories were dashed out Tuesday afternoons, between taking classified ads and fixing a typesetting machine.

Even when the paper was finished the job wasn't over. One morning, having been up until 3 A.M., putting the paper to bed, we were living the life of the righteous — drinking coffee, trading gossip — when word came from the press; the computer-generated list of our 2,000 mail subscribers was off center. The machine that sliced and pasted each address label was tirelessly separating city from state, first name from last. It was a disaster, and we spent our only off-day of the week (and every Glue Stic in Smithville) cutting and pasting those 2,000 labels by hand.

"You want your own voice, at least that's how I started 20 years ago," says Kentucky weekly publisher Albert Smith, in words that make more sense now than before we put out our first edition. "I had had it with writing for these people, had it writing for dull editors, had it with unresponsive, insensitive pieces about serious topics. I would do my own thing. So you start, and the first thing you find out is that you are preoccupied with just economic survival, and your voice begins to croak or fall mute in your desperate sweat to produce the paper, to get enough ads to pay the bills."

By early 1987 we were croaking. Every bit of creativity, the fun of the job, came *after* the full-time chore of putting out a paper. And there was never a break. Even our infrequent three-day-weekend vacations became traumatic. We returned one Monday morning to learn that an employee had taken the company car (a ten-year-old Pontiac station wagon) on a shopping trip with his family. The car had caught fire on the road and the driver had steered the smoldering heap into the parking lot of a restaurant holding a grand-opening celebration. The restaurant owner was on the phone first thing that Monday threatening us with a lawsuit. In 1983, we would have laughed; three years later it stopped us as cold as an oar in a set of wagon wheels.

We learned in 1987 why the day of the independent smalltown weekly is passing.

By early that year we had survived the

collapse of the Texas economy (*i.e.,* oil and real estate), but we didn't know if we could withstand prosperity in Bastrop County. Developers had announced that a large shopping center would open in Bastrop, the county seat 12 miles west of Smithville and the hometown of our large, twice-a-week competitor, the *Bastrop Advertiser.* The center would house a Wal-Mart department store and an H.E.B. grocery, both, at that time, big advertisers in small Texas newspapers.

Normally, this would have been good news. But we weren't in Bastrop, and we had seen that having a Wal-Mart in the area wasn't necessarily a good thing. For the uninitiated, Wal-Mart is the prodigy of a Bentonville, Arkansas, genius named Sam Walton. Walton realized that chain marketers had ignored small towns, so he began opening huge department stores in rural areas, first in Rogers, Arkansas, and now in 23 other states. In Texas, these stores are enormously popular. Families will spend the afternoon or evening at a Wal-Mart, checking the bargains, meeting friends, and, most of all, buying Mr. Walton's goods. Rural people have made Sam Walton the richest man in America.

Two Wal-Marts had already opened near Smithville; we had learned the effect these stores had on the local economy — and our newspaper. A new Wal-Mart takes away business from nearly every store on Main Street. In the two towns near us, Giddings and La Grange, several businesses closed. The rest saw their profits slip away.

Even though many merchants in Giddings and La Grange advertised with the *County Times,* the Wal-Mart did not. Moreover, since our regular customers, the ones still in business, were short of cash, they cut back on their advertising — or, as one soon finds out in the newspaper business, they just didn't pay.

What would happen, we asked ourselves, when the new stores opened in the Bastrop shopping center? Would they advertise with us? How many of our old Bastrop customers

would still have the cash to spend with the *County Times?* And if we didn't get the new accounts, would we begin losing subscribers? Our content was good, we knew, but people buy newspapers also to see ads. What would happen if those ads weren't in the *County Times?*

We were, indeed, in Smith's "desperate sweat."

Press associations make several recommendations for how small newspapers can attract chain advertisers, and we tried them all. We cut our ad rates, showed off our healthy circulation in a market that would be served by their stores, and bragged about our growth and the quality of the paper. We did not get one written answer to our inquiries. When I would call the main corporate office, I would get vague admonitions that "we normally only advertise in the hometown paper."

Bad news. It seemed we were finally going to pay for violating Rule One: we'd bought a paper in the wrong town. The only business solution was to combine with our adversary in Bastrop and present a united front to the chains. We approached the owners of that paper about merging the two enterprises; they preferred to buy us out. In May we agreed on a price, $440,000. Selling was the only realistic thing to do. The dream was over.

As I look back, it is clear that we had experienced, in less than a year, the economic forces that have shaped newspaper ownership over the last generation: mass merchandisers consolidate advertising dollars and seek the biggest and cheapest print medium. The preferred medium becomes the monopoly newspaper. Smaller publications are bought up or go out of business. The monopoly becomes so profitable it can only be purchased by a corporation with access to huge amounts of capital. Hello, Mr. Neuharth.

We saw that this same process had shifted to rural towns. Mass merchandisers have invaded the countryside. Fifteen years ago, few small towns had a McDonald's; now they have the Golden Arches and a Hardee's and a Burger King and a Long John Silver's.

The cost for rural papers in growing small towns has increased as smaller newspaper chains, excluded from the cities by the Gannetts and Knight-Ridders, bid up the prices for the remaining independent print franchises. Singly, but inexorably, independent newspapers fall to the chains. The combination of the *County Times* and its new sister paper in Bastrop will go on the block some day for well over a million dollars. Only a chain will be able to swing that kind of deal.

Moreover, those weekly newspaper publishers who remain in the trade are finding that the invasion of chain merchandisers has changed their way of doing business. Advertising decisions once made at the front counter of a newspaper office are now fashioned at corporate headquarters. The flick of an MBA's pen in Dallas or Bentonville can put a healthy paper on the rocks overnight.

Indeed, two months after we sold our paper, the chain-owned grocery that opened in the new shopping center changed from run-of-paper ads to preprinted inserts. The result: most small newspapers in Texas lost between $10,000 and $40,000 of pure profit. To save money, many Texas weeklies did the only thing they could to compensate for the lost revenues; they laid off reporters. This is not an isolated story. Several years ago, K-Mart dropped its newspaper advertising in several Midwestern states. The impact on small weeklies was "devastating," according to one publisher. Meanwhile, Wal-Mart has begun to move away from print advertising, shaving 10 to 15 percent off its advertising budget for community newspapers each year.

The winners in this game will be the sharp-pencil boys, the fellows who understand cash flow, marketing, and demographics. Those spending the long hours required to produce a great newspaper will be honored by their readers, but not by the gang at corporate headquarters.

This was not the kind of business we had bargained for when we came to Texas. Nor, I suspect, is it the stuff of a newsroom dreamer's fantasy. It is, however, the way the wind is blowing out here in the sticks. If you don't believe it, just wet a finger.

"Owning Your Own Weekly," by Bill Bishop, *Washington Journalism Review* (now *American Journalism Review*) Vol. 10, May 1988. Used with permission of *Washington Journalism Review*.

CHAPTER 4
The Magazine Industry

Magazines Go On-line

"The electronic newsstand in cyberspace" is what reporter Elizabeth Sanger calls the new efforts by magazine publishers to communicate with their readers. This electronic newsstand takes many forms — from expanded on-line coverage of issues discussed in the magazine to debates on current hot topics. All are attempts to maintain and expand each magazine's audience.

Consider:

1. Describe three new features of electronic publishing. Have you tried any of these services? If not, do they interest you? Why? Why not?

2. What are the advantages and disadvantages of electronic publishing for publishers?

3. How do you think electronic publishing will affect the long-term economics of the magazine business?

Magazines Going Beyond the Page

Elizabeth Sanger

[In] February [1994], *U.S. News & World Report* devoted eight pages to the various health care plans being debated in Congress. Readers who craved more could turn on their computers and read the plans in full from the magazine's library online.

[The August 1994] *Self* includes articles on violence and gun control and invites readers to debate the topics on The Well, a small but widely known electronic service based in the San Francisco Bay area.

Each month, the *Yoga Journal* makes its table of contents and a sampling of current stories available electronically, hoping to attract new subscribers. In the past year, swept up in the fascination of the much-hyped information highway, hundreds of consumer magazines have joined the electronic newsstand in cyberspace.

Many are finding a receptive audience. *Time* magazine has logged more than 2.5 million visitors to its America Online site and expects to pass 3 million when it hits the one-year mark in September [1994]. Jon Katz, media columnist for *New York* magazine, has received nearly 5,000 pieces of electronic mail in three months. The Electronic Newsstand, which features magazines' current tables of contents, a sample of articles and subscription offers, was launched [in 1993] with eight titles. Now it boasts 150.

"It's amazing how crowded it's gotten," *Time* spokesman Robert Pondiscio said. "We were in Montana, off on a prairie by ourselves, a year ago. Now it's like being on I-95."

About 200 magazines are available online in some form for computer users who connect to information services, and more than 100 magazines have produced multimedia CD-ROMs, said James Guthrie, executive vice president of marketing development for the Magazine Publishers of America.

Magazines generally have been quicker than newspapers to embrace the emerging technologies because they have national audiences and are specialized. People interested in home decorating, fitness or O.J. Simpson can connect and converse, even if they live across the country or around the world.

But profits are harder to come by. While magazines concede they haven't made much, if any, money from electronic publishing, they still aren't willing to ignore it, for fear they will be shut out of the next hot market.

"We're keeping our finger in the pool, but I don't see anything emerging as a monstrous business for a number of years," said Fred Drasner, president of *U.S. News*, which has a presence on CompuServe. "I still think people are more comfortable reading in print than on a terminal."

Reading a magazine electronically is more expensive and cumbersome than in print; it involves phone bills and fees to information services. But electronic publishing is well-suited for searching databases of back issues, opening up communication between readers and writers, providing new information and sponsoring live forums with reporters or newsmakers.

"It's so new there are no rules about how to put things online," explained *Self*'s interactive editor, Cassandra Markham Nelson. *Self,* aimed at women 18 to 40, uses computer services to complement what's inside the magazine. It holds discussion groups stemming from articles and solicits feedback to its 11 e-mail addresses on topics such as nutrition, beauty and polls.

So far, most information services don't include photos or graphics on the same screen with text and don't have the feel of magazines. Many are upgrading, however, and new services with greater capabilities are starting.

But another big problem is how to run advertisements. Merrill Lynch and Compaq computer placed ads on *Time* Online and Saab advertises in *U.S. News*'s area, but computer users have to seek them out. Magazines are figuring out how to price them.

Times Mirror Magazines, owned by the same company that owns *Newsday,* thinks electronic classified advertising would be an "obvious fit" with its titles if they go online. *Skiing* and *Ski Magazine* could display ads for mountain lodgings available the following week, which could be booked with a few keystrokes. *Yachting* magazine could offer charters. Print magazines, by contrast, are prepared months before they appear.

Currently, [in 1994,] most commercial information services give magazines about 15 percent of the revenues derived from the time spent in their area of the service. Fed up with meager returns, some magazine groups, such as Time Inc. and Times Mirror Co., are considering starting their own services and bypassing CompuServe, America Online, Prodigy and the like. Ziff-Davis Publishing, the leading computer magazine publisher, is starting an electronic service for its titles and others called Interchange, and will let participating magazines price their own services.

All this doesn't really matter, though, if readers don't use computers. Trying to entice its subscribers to be computer literate, *Self* devotes a page to interactive news. It reprints e-mail in the letters section and foresees the day when it will reprint online discussions in the magazine.

Online magazines have made conventional letters to the editor outmoded. Reader feedback is immediate. When a reporter or editor responds, everyone else can eavesdrop.

"It brings us closer to our readers. They get to peek inside behind the curtain," said Kathy Bushkin, director of editorial administration for *U.S. News.*

Katz said that including his e-mail address in his columns has been "a phenomenal success on many levels. I have a personal relationship with hundreds of readers. To me, it's the most exciting thing I do."

Every Tuesday evening, *Time* holds a live news conference via computer. Guests have included New York City Mayor Rudolph Giuliani, Federal Communications Commission Chairman Reed Hundt and the Rev. Billy Graham. Participants ask questions and chat with other audience members.

Despite all the cyberspace hoopla, some mainstream magazines still are found only on the corner newsstand. But probably not for long.

"The technology and knowledge are accelerating so quickly, no serious magazine publisher will risk not gaining knowledge in this area, even as an investment expense," Guthrie said.

Times Mirror Magazines' 12 sporting and leisure titles are expected to plunge online in six to 12 months [, in 1995]. "We're spending an enormous amount of time and energy figuring out the best strategy," said Jay Moses, the business' vice president of multimedia. "We don't see this as a race to get up first, but an opportunity to build a very sound foundation we can leverage into a lot of emerging technologies."

Moses is concerned that by choosing a commercial online service, its magazines will be accessible only to those subscribers, not all computer users. "We want to put information out there so anybody can access it, like on a newsstand," he said.

John Mack Carter, editor in chief of *Good Housekeeping,* said that if the magazine goes online, the staff must work to support the service, which could take several hours a day. "It isn't just a case of throwing the switch," Carter said. "You have to be prepared to devote assets and people to expand the material in the magazine. I don't see the return to support that kind of investment."

Still, the Hearst Corp., *Good Housekeeping*'s owner, is developing a multimedia service devoted to the home, expected to launch within a year. HomeNet will cull information from *Good Housekeeping, House Beautiful, Country Living* and *Popular Mechanics* for online services, CD-ROMs and TV.

Many publications are expected to sign deals. . . . *Newsweek,* which encourages e-mail letters to the editor and produces quarterly CD-ROMs, [launched] on Prodigy in the fall [of 1994]. Time Inc. will bring seven or eight of its titles to computer services. Sources say *Sports Illustrated, Fortune* and *People* will appear on CompuServe. *Travel & Leisure, Elle, Woman's Day* and *Entertainment Weekly* will join America Online.

While many are sorting out what to make of the new technology, the magazine of the future is at hand. In September [1994], 12 publications are getting together to produce *Magatzine,* the first magazine that will exist only in cyberspace, with no print counterpart.

Get ready to log on.

"Magazines Going Beyond the Page," by Elizabeth Sanger, *Newsday,* August 15, 1994. Reprinted by permission of Los Angeles Times Syndicate International. Dow//Quest Story ID: 0000351178DC.

How Magazines Work

Before radio and television, magazines were the best way to reach a large audience quickly; even the largest metropolitan newspapers circulated only in the regions where they originated. So magazines became the nation's educators and entertainers. Today, the magazine industry earns $23 billion a year. This Perspective concentrates on the structure of magazine publication.

Consider:

1. What are the three general categories of magazines and who are their audiences?

2. Why are magazines considered a targeted medium?

3. What is the proportion of advertising to copy in most consumer magazines?

4. What is the advantage of regional editions for large-circulation magazines?

Understanding Magazines

Shirley Biagi
California State University, Sacramento

Turn-of-the-century American muckraker Ida Tarbell, known for her exposure of the Standard Oil Company as a monopoly, began her writing career as a free-lancer, submitting articles purely on speculation to magazines in America while she paid her way through Europe. In Paris, American editor S. S. McClure ran up the eighty steps to Tarbell's apartment one day and knocked on her door. Her writing impressed him, he said, and would she write for his new magazine, *McClure's,* when she returned to the United States?

McClure's disheveled, disorganized manner made Tarbell doubt that he would ever start the magazine, yet she agreed to consider the idea. Tarbell grew even more doubtful about her future when, as McClure was leaving her apartment, he asked for a forty-dollar loan. She gave him the money, which she had been saving for a vacation.

Tarbell's doubts were misplaced, however, because for twenty-one years *McClure's* magazine was the very successful showcase for Tarbell, as well as Lincoln Steffens and Rudyard Kipling. And McClure returned the forty dollars.

Editors are as diverse as their magazines. Writer Dorothy Parker claimed that *New Yorker* magazine editor Harold Ross had a "profound ignorance." He admitted he could not spell and once asked a colleague whether Moby Dick in the novel was the man or the whale. Yet, he attracted and published the writings of Dorothy Parker, Robert Benchley, James Thurber, Janet Flanner, and H. L. Mencken.

In *The Powers That Be,* author David Halberstam called *Time* founding editor Henry Luce "a curiously artless man, graceless and brusque and lonely, rude inevitably even to those whose favors and good will he coveted; he could only be what he was, he could never be facile or slick, though on frequent occasions his magazines were."

Esquire founding editor Arnold Gingrich liked to wake at dawn to fish in the trout stream near his home. Then he dressed in natty tweeds for work, where he arrived early so he could practice his violin. *Esquire* published Hemingway, Fitzgerald, and Steinbeck under his direction.

American magazines celebrated their 250th birthday in 1991. They have evolved from their polemical beginnings in 1741 with Ben Franklin's *General Magazine* and Andrew Bradford's *American Magazine* to the general interest magazines born in the 1930s, such as *Life* and *Look,* to today's proliferation of specialized publications, such as *International Musician* and *Dairy Herd Management.*

According to *Magazine Industry Market Place,* more than 350 magazines are created in the United States each year. Of these, only ten percent will survive the marketplace, which indicates the competitiveness of the magazine business.

Company, Trade, and Consumer Magazines

Magazines can be divided into three categories — company publications, trade publications, and consumer publications.

Company publications are produced by a specific company or industry mainly for its employees, stockholders, and customers. Trade publications are produced by businesses for professional retailers, manufacturers, and technical experts in a particular industry. Consumer publications are all those popularly marketed at newsstands, in supermarkets, and bookstores.

Employees of the Underwood Company, for example, may read *The Red Devil,* a company publication that emphasizes food products and the history of food, while your grocer reads the trade publication *Progressive Grocer* to learn how to create a more attractive canned meat display, and you read the consumer publication *Family Circle* to learn how to use minced ham to stretch your food budget. Clearly each magazine has a different audience, which in turn dictates the magazine's content.

How Magazines Are Organized

Magazines, small and large, follow a predictable pattern of organization. The larger the magazine, the more elaborate the staff.

Overseeing both the business and the writing on a magazine is the publisher, who owns the publication. The publisher may sometimes also be the editor, but more often these functions are separate.

The business side must organize subscriptions, advertising, marketing, and production of the magazine. The editorial side worries about what goes inside the magazine and how the magazine looks.

Most magazines, except for those concerned with personalities (*People*) and news (*Time* and *Newsweek*), have a three-to-four month lead time from final copy to publication. So, editors celebrate Christmas in August or September and get ready for the Fourth of July in the winter.

Magazine editors use charts to track future magazines and their status in production. An editor of a monthly magazine may have three issues going at once, so each of these issues is assigned to an associate editor.

A magazine's size each month is decided by the size of the issue at the same time the year before and the number of advertisements sold for each issue. A consumer magazine usually runs about forty percent ads and sixty percent copy.

How Magazines Are Published

Most of today's magazines are published using computers. With desktop publishing, copy can be organized on-screen and then sent to computer typesetters to prepare the magazine for publication. Large-circulation national magazines that publish regional editions can send articles by satellite to printing plants sprinkled throughout the country, where regional copy and ads are inserted for each area. A national magazine that sells ads to Arizona advertisers who want to reach primarily the Arizona market, for example, can insert copy on Arizona subjects in its Southwest edition to cater to that audience and those advertisers.

Using market research, most magazine publishers target their audiences carefully — by sex, income, education, even zip code. In a magazine without advertising, the articles must entertain and inform the audience so the readers will return to the magazine. The articles in magazines that carry advertising must complement the ads.

Magazine staffs supervise cover design, organize and copyedit articles, select artwork and styles and sizes of type, and meet deadlines. Into all of this must fit the audience, for whom all magazines are created. This audience can be as specific as people who raise goats (*Dairy Herd Management*) or as broad as people who watch television (*TV Guide*).

Because magazines are delivered directly to subscribers, they are a very *targeted* medium. Their audiences are much easier to define than the audience for a TV program, for example. This makes magazines very efficient for advertisers. For example, the magazines owned by the Hearst Corporation (including *Good Housekeeping, Cosmopolitan,* and *Popular Mechanics*) earned more than $1 billion in 1993 (the last year for which figures are available). In an era saturated with visual media, the success of major magazine publishing firms like Hearst reaffirms the continuing power of print.

"Understanding Magazines," by Shirley Biagi. Adapted from *How to Write and Sell Magazine Articles,* 2nd ed., Englewood Cliffs, N.J.: Prentice-Hall, 1989. Used with permission of Shirley Biagi.

Finding Teenage Readers

Magazines are the most targeted medium available to advertisers. Because magazine publishers know more about their audiences than in other media industries, companies that advertise in magazines are relatively certain that their messages will reach the intended target audience. Teenagers represent a very lucrative potential audience for advertisers, but today's teenagers are reading fewer magazines than their parents did. In this article from *The Wall Street Journal,* reporter Meg Cox describes how some new magazines are designing their messages to attract teen readers.

Consider:

1. **Why is the teenage audience such an attractive market for magazine publishers, according to Cox?**

2. **What makes teenagers "slippery customers"?**

3. **List three elements common to all the new magazines mentioned. Which magazines do you think will succeed? Which magazines do you think will fail? Explain.**

New Magazines for New Cliques of Teens

Meg Cox

American teenagers spend nearly $90 billion a year, and magazine publishers hope they'll spend even more.

Arriving on newsstands [in March 1994] is *Mouth2Mouth,* a hip new magazine, funded by Time Warner Inc. and aimed at the MTV generation. It follows by just a few months the launch of two competitors, *Tell* and *Quake.*

The new magazines enter a field that already includes *Seventeen* — the leader — *YM, Sassy* and *Teen,* plus a host of specialized magazines like *YSB* (Young Sisters and Brothers), aimed at black teens, and *Young Scholar,* for nerds.

As baby boomers' children reach adolescence, the teen market is expanding. In 1992, for the first time in 17 years, the population of teenagers increased, says Peter Zollo, president of Teenage Research Unlimited of Northbrook, Ill. Mr. Zollo says there are about 28.5 million Americans between the ages of 12 and 19.

For advertisers, this age group is particularly attractive because, as teenagers explore their own identities, they experiment with new brands of consumer products. "Teenagers don't just buy more magazines every year, they buy more of everything, and advertisers have woken up to that," says Valerie Muller, media director for DeWitt Media Inc.

Attractive as they are to advertisers, teenagers are slippery customers. Over the years, teens have become a whole lot more sophisticated, some would say cynical, and are put off by the old Pollyanna platitudes. Both *Sassy* and *YM* have helped turn the whole genre cheekier (*Sassy*'s idea of a service piece is "How to Drink in College Without Puking Every Night"), but there is a fine line to walk. *Mademoiselle* recently dumped an editor the magazine thought had alienated readers by going too kinky.

Advertisers get skittish when magazines are too edgy and dark, but they also want their ads in a context considered trendy by teens.

If trendiness is the yardstick, then *Mouth2Mouth* stands tallest among the latest batch of competitors. Described by its founders as a cross between *Mad* and *Vanity Fair,* the magazine is loaded with pop-culture celebrities and marked by an offbeat sense of humor. In the first issue, for example, Amy Fisher, convicted of shooting her lover's wife, gives advice on sex. Each issue will end with a photo of an actual teenager's room, a sort of Dewar's profile for the Beavis and Butthead set.

"We want the magazine to be as outspoken, gutsy and loud as teenagers are," says editor in chief Angela Janklow Harrington, 29 years old, who has spent much of her career writing for *Vanity Fair.* "I want it to be celebrity-driven but not an insult to the reader's intelligence. It's about lifestyle, not 62 different ways to twirl your hair."

What sets *M2M* apart is its goal of appealing to both males and females, a strategy that *YSB* is also trying but that has rarely worked with magazines for this age group. "Nobody has ever successfully created a dual audience for teen magazines, because there is

a huge maturity gap between 16-year-old boys and girls of the same age," says New York City-based magazine consultant Martin Walker. "Most of the magazines are aimed at girls, partly because they are seen as the bigger spenders, and these magazines make most of their money on fashion and cosmetics ads."

But Ms. Harrington says she believes this generation is different. "Everybody in this generation watches MTV and wears the same grunge clothes," she says. "I think they're more mature and media-inundated; the media has demystified sexual differences for them."

In its first issue last summer [1993], *Quake* tried to position itself for a dual audience, but has already redirected itself more to girls. A fashion spread in the premiere issue on what to wear on a first date featured both sexes, but the second issue, out [in February 1994], carries a piece on "Prom Style" showing 12 outfits for girls and only two for boys.

Tell has been squarely aimed at girls from the start, with articles like "Girls Talk Sex" and "Why Can't I Be a Model?"

It's still too early to predict whether boys will buy a magazine, however hip, that carries lipstick and nail polish ads, but many of the early reviews for *Mouth2Mouth* have been raves.

Mouth2Mouth starts out with extra pull not just because its editor, Ms. Harrington, has Hollywood connections and a famous father (literary agent Morton Janklow), but because it is published by deep-pocketed Time Warner. Developed by the company's Ventures division, which also publishes the very slick *Vibe* and *Martha Stewart Living, M2M* has already gotten the green light for a second issue, due in August [1994].

But most of the competitors also have deep pockets and a strong commitment from their publishers. *Quake,* jointly published by Welsh Publishing Group and Cowles Magazines, has decided to publish six times a year. *Tell,* published by Hachette Filipacchi in partnership with NBC, has agreed to go quarterly [in 1994] and then evaluate circulation.

But none of these new titles will have an easy time, given the competitiveness of the established teen magazines. In fact, the rivalry is about to intensify between the two giants of the teen genre, *Seventeen* and *YM*.

Seventeen, owned by K-III Communications Corp. has a circulation of 1.85 million, but the irreverent *YM* is yapping at its heels as never before. *YM* now has circulation of 1.8 million, up 90% over the past three years [since 1991]. *Seventeen* has a brand new editor, Caroline Miller, and *YM* will appoint a new one in the next few weeks.

Still, the newcomers believe there's room in the expanding teen market for new voices. "There has been an idea that the adult market is segmented, but teens are one big mass market," says Webb Howell, publisher of *Young Scholar.* "We believe that there are lots of niches in this market, and that some kids care about more than Luke Perry and 90210."

"New Magazines for New Cliques of Teens," by Meg Cox, *The Wall Street Journal,* March 14, 1994, p. B-1. Reprinted by permission of *The Wall Street Journal,* © 1994, Dow Jones & Company, Inc. All Rights Reserved Worldwide.

Targeting a Lucrative Audience

Like other media, magazines must compete for their audience; and most magazines have been losing. But magazines are very much affected by social trends, and the recent upward trend in the number of marriages is pushing up the circulation of bridal magazines. Brides are an identifiable audience segment that is very attractive for advertisers because they are also very likely to spend money quickly on the products the magazines offer.

Consider:

1. Why, according to reporter Deirdre Carmody, has the bridal market proved to be "relatively recession-proof"? How does that affect bridal magazines?

2. Define "polybagging." What are its advantages for the magazine industry?

3. Describe three innovations in bridal magazine marketing and the new markets they are targeting. Do you think they will be successful? Why? Why not?

Bridal Magazines Find Cupid Is Recession-Proof

Deirdre Carmody

After years in which cohabitation seemed more compelling than commitment, wedding bells are again ringing throughout the land. And so are cash registers in bridal markets and at bridal magazines. . . .

For years, the bridal market consisted of two magazines. Cahners Publishing's *Modern Bride* led the field until the late 1970s, when Condé Nast's *Bride's* overtook it. It was more coexistence than competition.

"We sort of had a very comfortable position as a very strong, profitable No. 2 in a two-book field," said Howard Friedberg, vice president and group publisher of the Cahners Bridal Group. "Then, with the addition of new national publications like *Bridal Guide* and *Elegant Bride,* plus the popping up of regional publications, the newsstand became very crowded."

Crowded Newsstands

There is a huge appetite out there, however, for pages and pages of pictures of wedding gowns and answers to endless questions about how to discourage children from attending a wedding (hold it at night), how to remind your bridesmaids without seeming pushy that it is customary for them to give the bride a shower (subtly, in a phone call to your maid of honor) and whether you have to invite your hated first cousin (no).

[In 1982], there were about a million marriages a year, according to research by these magazines. [In 1992 there were] 2.3 million. And once again, the bridal market has proved to be relatively recession-proof because of its "once in a lifetime" mystique.

"Traditional values are now very strong in this country — home, family, romance," Mr. Friedberg said. "Weddings are taking place in a relatively traditional way, and that is good for the bridal market."

Other factors, too. Engagements, which used to average eight months, are now more likely to be 12 to 16 months — all the more conducive to plan an elaborate wedding — average cost: $16,000 and climbing, Mr. Friedberg said — followed by an extensive honeymoon. People are getting married at an older age, with brides around 25 to 26 years old and grooms a few years older, which means they have more money to spend.

The bridal books are trying to play all of this to their advantage. Several include supplements in a plastic bag with each issue. *Modern Bride* has included a fashion supplement, a shower organizer and a wedding gift planner with recent issues.

"Polybagging is the hot thing now," said William F. Bondlow, publisher of *Bridal Guide.* "With our March–April [1992] issue, we included a groom's supplement for the first time. We also took the honeymoon section out of our regular issue and published a honeymoon guide as a supplement."

Then, to make sure no one missed out on all this vital information, *Bridal Guide* sent 50,000 reprints of the groom's supplement to 250 formal-wear retailers and 100,000 copies of the honeymoon guides to 700 American Express agents.

"When Mr. and Mrs. To Be around the country walk into a travel agent wanting to know the most romantic place to honeymoon, we will have the information for them," Mr. Bondlow said.

Publishing Schedule

At *Bridal Guide,* which is published by Globe Communications, Mr. Bondlow said its ad pages were up 17 percent for its May–June [1992] issue from a year earlier. The number of advertisers [went] from 251 for the first three [1991] issues to 405 [in 1992]. He attributes part of this increase to the fact that *Bride's, Modern Bride,* and *Elegant Bride* all come out on the same every-other-month schedule — February–March, April–May and so on. All three battle for readers on the same month.

Bridal Guide, however, comes out on an alternate schedule — January–February, March–April — so that it appears on the newsstand when the other three publications have been there for a month.

"I think to be effective you have to have something different," said Jane Novatt, who does media planning for Novatt Advertising and places ads in *Bridal Guide* for Krups coffee makers and kitchen appliances. "*Bridal Guide* is trying to add ad pages while not trying to become another book like the other two; they feel they have a secure place for off months."

Bride's tried another kind of gamble. After changing its name to appeal to the home-furnishings market as well as the traditional bride's market, it split the magazine into three parts: the first and largest section devoted to the wedding, the second to the honeymoon and the third to furnishing the new home.

"Advertisers love it," said Elliot Marion, *Bride's* publisher.

Bride's and Your New Home has another distinction. Its 1990 February–March issue was entered in the Guinness Book of Records as "the weightiest book ever," at 1,024 pages. That record no longer stands, however. *Bride's* surpassed itself with its February–March 1991 issue, which weighed in with 1,046 pages.

CHAPTER 5

The Book Publishing Industry

Technology and the Printed Word

The introduction of any new technology always leads to speculation that the old technology will disappear. America's first book was published in 1744. Three hundred fifty years later, the widespread use of CD-ROM storage systems presented a challenge to the old technology. Perspectives 1 and 2 offer different points of view on the future of the book. The first is an article by D. T. Max that appeared in *The Atlantic Monthly* ("The End of the Book?"); the second is a commentary by E. Annie Proulx ("Software Will Never Replace Fanciful, Portable, Bendable Books"), whose novel, *The Shipping News*, won the Pulitzer Prize for fiction in 1994.

Consider:

1. Do you agree that there is "something special about the book that would ensure that no technical innovation could ever supplant it"? Why? Why not?

2. According to D. T. Max, what are the three principal arguments in favor of the "classic 1990s cybervisionarism"?

3. What advantages does multimedia offer over the book, according to D. T. Max? Disadvantages?

4. "The so-called information age is really the age of information lost," says computer pioneer Ted Nelson in D. T. Max's article. What does Nelson mean when he says this? Do you agree? Why? Why not?

5. According to E. Annie Proulx, why will the book survive the introduction of new technologies? Do you agree? Explain.

The End of the Book?

D. T. Max

We'll teach you about multimedia before
your kids have to.
    Billboard on Route 101 near Silicon Valley

An office-party atmosphere pervaded the headquarters of *Wired* magazine, the newly created oracle of the computer-literate generation. *Wired* is housed on the third floor of a flat, low brick building with plain-pine interiors in an industrial section of San Francisco south of Market Street. The area is known as Multimedia Gulch, for the scores of small companies working in the neighborhood which mix sound, video, and text into experimental interactive multimedia computer products that they hope will one day sell millions of copies. *Wired* is not an ordinary computer magazine; it promises the faithful reader not mere computing power—something available from a grown-up computer magazine like *Macworld,* which happens to be across the street—but, more important, hipness, the same sense of being ahead of the curve that once attached to a new Bob Dylan album or Richard Brautigan book.

The weekday afternoon I was there, hero sandwiches lay on the table, the magazine's pet gray parrot was hanging outside its cage, and young men and women with sophisticated eyewear sat rapt before their computer screens. The reference folders and layout paraphernalia common to magazine editorial departments were scattered around. The ringing of the phones was constant. When I had first called *Wired*'s co-founder, Louis Rossetto, in the summer of 1993, I got through to him immediately, and he had, if anything, too much time to speculate about the shape of things to come. Several months later I had to go through a secretary and a publicist for my interview, and once I arrived, I was made to wait while more urgent calls were put through. What happened in the interim is that the information highway became a hot subject. Rossetto was now every media journalist's and Hollywood agent's first call.

What I wanted from Louis Rossetto was his opinion on whether the rise of the computer culture that his magazine covered would end with the elimination by CD-ROMs and networked computer databases of the hardcover, the paperback, and the world of libraries and literate culture that had grown up alongside them. Was print on its way out? And if it was, what would happen to the publishers who had for generations put out books, and to the writers who had written them? Or was there something special about the book that would ensure that no technical innovation could ever supplant it? Would the book resist the CD-ROM and the Internet just as it has resisted radio, television, and the movies?

Finally I was taken into the sunlit confines of his office. Bookshelves ran along one wall. A forty-five-year-old career journalist with shoulder-grazing gray hair, Rossetto is a late convert to computers. He spent much of the 1980s in Europe, and gives off a mild sense of disengagement—there is a touch of the sixties about him, as there is about much else in the Gulch. Now he set out his vision of a fast-changing computerized, paperless, nearly book-free society, and did so with a certainty that would frighten even someone whose sense of equilibrium, unlike mine, did not involve visits to bookstores or the belief that last year's laptop is basically good enough. "The changes going on in the world now are literally a revolution in progress, a revolution that makes political revolution seem like a game," Rossetto, who recently sold a minority interest in his magazine to Condé Nast, said. "It will revolutionize how people work, how they communicate, and how they entertain themselves, and it is the biggest engine for change in our world today. We're looking at the end of a twenty- or thirty- or forty-year process, from the invention of tubes to transistors to fiber-optic and cable to the development of cable networks, until we've reached critical mass today."

I asked if there was no downside, no tradeoff for all that information in the world that was to come. "It doesn't keep me up at night, I admit," he said. "Written information is a relatively new phenomenon. Depositing it and being able to reference it centuries later is not common human experience. In some ways what is happening with on-line is a return to our earlier oral tradition. In other ways, it is utterly new, a direct connection of minds. Humans have always been isolated, and now we're starting to see electronic connections generating an intellectual organism of their own, literally a quantum leap beyond our experience with consciousness."

This is classic 1990s cybervisionarism, repeated up and down the halls of *Wired* and echoed throughout the Bay area, and it derives directly from the teenage-male personalities of the hackers who created the computer industry: cyberspace will be like a better kind of school.

There are three principal articles of faith behind this vision. (1) The classroom will be huge: the linking of information worldwide will cause a democratic explosion in the accessibility of knowledge. (2) The classroom will be messy: the sense of information as an orderly and retrievable quantity will decline, and you won't necessarily be able to find what you're looking for in cyberspace at any given time. (3) There will be no teachers: the "controllers of information"—censors, editors, and studio executives—will disappear, and the gates of public discourse will swing open before everyone who can get on-line. Anyone can publish; anyone can read what is published; anyone can comment on what he or she has read. Rossetto had been delineating his vision for twenty minutes, but suddenly it was time to go. An assistant popped in to pull him into an editorial meeting. "I have a pretty cynical view of most of the American media," Rossetto said before leaving (read: "You'll get this wrong. You'll be hostile"). "Their jobs are at stake, because their businesses are threatened. Take *Time* magazine. What function would it have in the modern world?"

One look at *Wired* suggests a gap between message and messenger. *Wired* looks more radical than it is. It cheerleads and debunks its subjects using editorial formulas that came in with the nineteenth-century magazines—a fictional takeoff on Microsoft, written by Douglas Coupland, the author of *Generation X,* a classic star cover on Laurie Anderson, "America's multimediatrix"— rather than harnessing any global back-and-forth among literate minds. Although *Wired* communicates extensively by E-mail with its readers, conducts forums, and makes back issues available on-line, its much-repeated goal of creating a magazine—currently [in 1994] called *HotWired*—that is especially designed to exist electronically remains fuzzy. For the moment this is no open democracy, and *Wired* is no computer screen—its bright graphics would make a fashion magazine envious. *Wired* celebrates what doesn't yet exist by exploiting a format that does: it's as if a scribe copied out a manuscript extolling the beauty that would one day be print.

The Limitations of the Book

Overhyped or not, interactive multimedia do hold vast potential for the companies that in the next decades back the right products in the right formats. Multimedia are not new— a child's pop-up book is one example, and an illustrated pre-Gutenberg Bible is another. But interactive multimedia as envisioned by the computer industry (especially if television cables or telephone wires are reconfigured to accommodate two-way high-quality video digital transmissions—technologies that may be in place on a national scale sometime around the millennium) have great potential, because they would persuade consumers to bring software into their homes as they brought it into their offices in the 1980s. Who wouldn't want a screen that accessed all currently existing forms of information, from mail to movies, and did so with great convenience and flexibility?

Even if this vision is only partly realized, the book, the newspaper, and the video will be hard-pressed to maintain their place in our culture. Look at the book without sentiment and its limitations are evident: books can excite the imagination, but they can't literally make you see and hear. "What is the use of a book without pictures or conversations?" Lewis Carroll's Alice grouses, before tumbling down the rabbit hole into the more absorbing precincts of Wonderland, in one of the favorite texts of hackers. Interactive multimedia designers, with their brew of sights, sounds, and words, believe that they could keep Alice (her age puts her very much in their target group) above-ground and interested. Or a multimedia designer could expand the book's plot line, giving the reader the choice of whether Alice goes down the hole or decides to stick around and read alongside her sister on the riverbank. The reader could hear Alice's voice, or ask her questions about herself, the answers to which are only implicit in the book.

When something intrigues the readers of a printed book, they have to wrestle with an index and then, perhaps, go to a library to find out more about the subject; they can't just hit a search button to log on to a database attached to the book and read something else on the same subject, as they can on a computer. "I decided books were obsolete thirty-four years ago," says Ted Nelson, an early computer hacker who coined the word "hypertext" in the early sixties to describe how knowledge would be accessed if all information were available simultaneously. "I have thousands of books and I love them. It's only intertwining I want more of."

But such intertwining — a vast linkage of electronic text across databases worldwide — would inevitably push the printed word to the margins and replace it with sleeker, more efficient text conveyers. It is not the viability of text itself that is in question. On the contrary, whether paper gives way to the computer screen or not, there is little question that words as the cornerstone of communication are safe. *Littera scripta manet,* an anonymous Roman wrote; "The written word endures." This is a comforting quotation — typically if erroneously attributed to the poet Horace — that writers about multimedia are fond of using. In fact, words are multiplying wildly. In the world of computers they are a bargain compared with images: cheap to transport and easy to store. Probably more words are put out in a week by the 20 million people who use the loosely strung computer

networks that constitute the Internet than are published by all major American publishing companies in a year. There's a "Poetry Corner" and bulletin boards where new novels get posted constantly. In a recent announcement a nonprofit organization called Project Gutenberg, run out of a university in Illinois, presented as its mysteriously precise goal "To Give Away One Trillion E[lectronic] Text Files [of classic books] by December 21, 2001." When I mentioned the scope of fiction on the Internet to the novelist John Updike, he said lightly, "I imagine most of that stuff on the information highway is roadkill anyway." And of course he is right. But his is a minority opinion outside the circles of tastemakers.

Vaporware Intimidation

Text and books are not, however, joined at the hip — words don't need print. "Books on paper are a medium unto themselves," Louis Rossetto says, "and my sense is that anything that is stand-alone is a dead end." But even to Rossetto a world completely without books seems unlikely. One view is that the book will become the equivalent of the horse after the invention of the automobile or the phonograph record after the arrival of the compact disc — a thing for eccentrics, hobbyists, and historians. It will not disappear, but it will become obsolete. Multimedia programmers themselves disagree sharply on whether this will come to pass in five years, ten years, or never. One question is whether there is money to be made in the production of multimedia. Another is how good multimedia products will ever be, for by industry admission they are not very good now. The great majority of the 3,000 multimedia products launched [in 1993] were little more than rudimentary efforts. "I think that there are fewer than thirty titles with good, solid, deep information out there," Rick Fischer, the director of product development at Sony Electronic

Publishing, says. "The majority of titles are kind of pseudo-multimedia. People are still learning how to do this." Besides, computer companies are not as excited by books as they are by games, which represent an ever-increasing share of the market. Sony, for example, has backed an interactive game version of its movie *Bram Stoker's Dracula*—Harker races against rats, wolves, and flaming torches to slay the Prince of Darkness—rather than the book *Dracula,* 300 pages of print that could be augmented with perhaps a moving illustration or two.

Publishers are terrified. They have read a thousand times that one day we will play games, shop, watch movies, read books, and do research all on our computer or television screens. Computer companies are skillful at bluffing one another, forever claiming that they are nearly ready to release a hot new product, which is in truth barely in prototype. This kind of nonproduct has the nickname "vaporware" within the industry. But publishers, unfamiliar with computer culture, believe the hype. In [1993] *Publishers Weekly* ran six major stories on how CD-ROM and the Internet will remake publishing. The comments of Laurence Kirshbaum, the president of Warner Books, a subsidiary of Time Warner, were not untypical: "I don't know if there's the smell of crisis in the air, but there should be. Publishers should be sleeping badly these days. They have to be prepared to compete with software giants like [Microsoft's chairman] Bill Gates." Publishers are most of all afraid of doing nothing—as hardback publishers did when they ignored the paperback explosion of the 1960s and 1970s. So they are rushing to form electronic-publishing divisions and to find partners in the software business. "Eighteen months ago no one was talking about multimedia and CD-ROMs seriously, and now everyone is deeply involved and deeply conscious of them," says Alberto Vitale, the chairman of the normally cautious Random House, Inc., which has signed a co-venture deal with Broderbund, a leading children's software

developer in Novato, California, to create children's interactive multimedia. Putting Dr. Seuss on CD-ROM is one of their first efforts. The Palo Alto "media kitchen" owned by Viacom, where the company's film, television, and book divisions cooperate—at least theoretically—on interactive-multimedia research, is designing new travel guides: why actually go to San Francisco when by 1995 you will be able to take a virtual walking tour on a Frommer CD-ROM? Interest has even percolated into the last redoubt of traditional publishing, the firm of Alfred A. Knopf. Since its inception Knopf has placed great emphasis on the book as handsome object. But Knopf's president attended the first International Illustrated Book and New Media Publishing Market fair, held earlier [in 1994], which was designed to introduce multimedia's various content providers to one another. (The fact that the fair was in Cannes probably did not hurt attendance.)

Behind the stampede into electronic publishing is doubtless a widespread feeling among those in conventional publishing that the industry is in dire, if ill-defined, trouble. A decade-long trend among major publishers toward publishing fewer trade books recently had an impact on four imprints in just two months, most notably a near-total cutback of Harcourt, Brace's trade department (the publishers of T. S. Eliot, Virginia Woolf, and Alice Walker) and the closing of Ticknor & Fields adult books, a Houghton Mifflin imprint (which included William Gass and Robert Stone among its authors). Aggressive marketing has allowed publishers to sell more copies of their top titles, creating the illusion of pink-cheeked health in some years. But after decades of competition from radio, television, movies, videos, and Americans' increasingly long workdays, it is hard to imagine how the publishers of mainstream fiction and nonfiction in book form will ever again publish as many titles as they did in the past; after all, popular fiction magazines never recovered from the advent of radio serials. Giants like Doubleday and Putnam publish perhaps a third as many hardcover books as they did ten years ago [in 1984], and McGraw-Hill, once the publisher of Vladimir Nabokov and hundreds of other authors, is out of the new-trade-book business altogether. Recently Random House sent a glass-is-half-full letter to book review editors, letting them know that the company would be making their jobs easier by publishing fewer books. According to a 1993 survey by Dataquest, a San Jose information-technology market-research firm, most employees in the multimedia-content industry come from traditional print backgrounds. And the extremely rudimentary employment statistics that exist for the publishing industry show a decline since the late 1980s in New York–based publishing jobs, though it is hardly enough of one to confirm a sea change in publishing fortunes, or to suggest that Armageddon is around the corner. [In 1993] nearly 50,000 new titles destined for bookstores were published, and total consumer-reference CD-ROM software sales amounted to only about three percent of trade-book sales.

Besides, the computer industry acknowledges that what most readers think of as books — that is, novels and nonfiction text — gain nothing from being on screen; the appeal of the product depends on the quality of the prose and the research, neither of which is enhanced by current screens. Whether you scroll down a screen or turn a page to read *The Bridges of Madison County* makes a great deal of difference in the quality of the reading experience. "I just don't personally believe in reading novels on a computer screen," says Olaf Olafsson, the president of Sony Electronic Publishing and the author of *Absolution,* a novel published in March [1994] by Pantheon Books. He says that he would never want to see his own work on a computer: "There's a lot of content that's now being delivered on paper that's fine on paper." The book has great advantages over the computer: it's light and it's cheap. That it

has changed little in 400 years suggests an uncommonly apt design. John Updike says, "It seems to me the book has not just aesthetic values — the charming little clothy box of the thing, the smell of the glue, even the print, which has its own beauty. But there's something about the sensation of ink on paper that is in some sense a thing, a phenomenon rather than an epiphenomenon. I can't break the association of electric trash with the computer screen. Words on the screen give the sense of being just another passing electronic wriggle." You can drop a book in the bathtub, dry it out on the radiator, and still read it. You can put it in the attic, pull it out 200 years later, and probably decipher the words. You can curl up in bed with it or get suntan lotion on it. These are definitely not possibilities suggested by the computer. A well-thumbed paperback copy of John Grisham blowing in a beach breeze represents a technological stronghold the computer may never invade.

A Solution in Search of a Problem

Lovers of literature (and schlock) may not see much change, then, but that doesn't mean publishers are in for an easy ride. Novels, nonfiction, and belles lettres are a prestige sideshow for publishers — they amount to only a few billion dollars in a roughly $18 billion book industry. Take dictionaries and encyclopedias, which are in effect databases in book form. The hand cannot match a computer chip in accessing given references, which constitutes the primary function of such works. [In 1993] the 1989 edition of the *Oxford English Dictionary,* the flagship publication of the 400-year-old university press, sold four times as many copies in a new CD-ROM version as in its traditional twenty-volume book form. The company has said that the next print edition, due in a decade, may well be the last. At an October, 1993, celebration at the New York Public Library in honor of the publication of the fifth edition of the *Columbia Encyclopedia* in both book form and (a year hence) on CD-ROM, one guest speaker commented that the next edition, whenever it was ready, might well not have a paper counterpart. There was barely an objection from the audience.

Publishers are divided over the fate of so-called "soft reference titles" — cookbooks and how-to-books — and children's books. These are huge markets, and the question is whether electronic books will capture them or expand on them. "My generation may be the last . . . to have a strong visceral affection for books," Janet Wikler, a former director of advanced media at Harper-Collins, told *Publishers Weekly* [in 1993].

What publishers have not stopped to consider is whether consumers like CD-ROMs in the first place — or how comfortable they will ever be with networked, digitalized, downloaded books when they become available. It may be a question of technical proficiency: how many families possess the sophistication to use Microsoft's new CD-ROM Musical Instruments — a charming visual and audio tour of the instruments of the world which is perfect for six-year-olds? The product requires either a multimedia computer or "a Multimedia PC upgrade kit, which includes CD-ROM drive (with CD-DA outputs, sustained 150K/second transfer rate and a maximum seek time of 1 second while using no more than 40% of the CPU's processing power)." Electronic encyclopedias have all but driven print encyclopedias out of the market in large part because they are "bundled" — sold at a deep discount to computer-hardware manufacturers to be included free when the consumer buys a CD-ROM drive. This is roughly like giving the consumer a book if he will only buy a lamp. "Traditional publishers may be a Luddite elite, but software publishers are arrogant sheep," says Michael Mellin, a multimedia executive who until last year was the publisher of Random House's electronic-publishing division. "One thing publishers

don't realize is that there hasn't been a comparable kick in sales of CD-ROM multimedia titles given the rise in the number of CD-ROM drives installed." In other words, books on CD-ROM don't sell — at least not yet. A study of the industry [in 1993] found that of those people who had bought a CD-ROM drive, fewer than half had returned to the computer store to buy new discs. Compare this with the way the compact-disc player caught on in the mid-1980s. Interactive multimedia may turn out to be the biggest bust since the paperless office. One former industry executive describes multimedia as "a solution in search of a problem, doing what other things do already, only slightly less well."

Publishers derive their impressions of the awesome potential of multimedia from products like Microsoft's much publicized Encarta CD-ROM, a magnificent encyclopedia with text drawn from Funk & Wagnall's twenty-nine-volume encyclopedia and augmented by hundreds of video and audio clips. Alice would have fun with this: she could listen to bird calls and African drums, or experiment with changing the moon's orbit. (She could also click on Bill Gates's name and hear his nasal assurance that Microsoft "has never wavered from the vision" of a personal computer "on every desk and in every home." This was not part of Funk & Wagnall's original text.) But having been five years in development, employing a hundred people at its peak, and reportedly costing Microsoft well upward of $5 million, Encarta may be something of a Potemkin Village, meant for credulous competitors to marvel at. The company has dropped the price from $395 to $139 to try to get consumers to buy it.

The Limitations of the Computer

Paper has limitations, but the computer may have more. As a physical object, it is hardly comforting. "Who'd want to go to bed with a Powerbook?" John Baker, a vice president at

Broderbund, asks. And even if the laptop goes on shrinking, its screen, whose components represent nearly all the machine's cost, remains at best a chore to read. At the Xerox Palo Alto Research Center (where the receptionist's cubicle still houses an IBM Selectric typewriter) is a display room with half a dozen prototype six-million-pixel AMLCD screens. The quiet hum of the room, the bright white lighting, the clean, flat antiseptic surfaces, give the impression of an aspirin commercial. "It was clear to us that no reader was going to read a book off any of the current screens for more than ten minutes," says Malcolm Thompson, the chief technologist. "We hoped to change that." A large annotated poster on the wall illustrates point for point the screen's superiority to paper, as in an old-fashioned magazine ad. This flat panel display is indeed better than commercial screens, but it is neither as flexible nor as mobile as a book, and it still depends on fickle battery power. A twentysomething software marketer who began as an editorial assistant in book publishing points out, "A book requires one good eye, one good light source, and one good finger."

Lost in Cyberspace

In the heart of official Washington, D.C., down the street from the capitol and at the same intersection as the Supreme Court and the Library of Congress, stands an incongruous statue of Puck, whom the *Oxford Companion to English Literature,* soon to be issued on CD-ROM, defines as "a goblin," and whom Microsoft Encarta passes over in favor of "puck," which it defines solely as a mouse-like device with crosshairs printed on it, used in engineering applications. The 1930s building next to the statue is the Folger Shakespeare Library. Two flights below the reading room, designed in the style of a Tudor banquet hall, next to which librarians and scholars click quietly on laptops and log on to the Internet's

Shakespeare reference group for the latest scholarly chatter, is a locked bank gate. Behind it is what librarians call a "short-title catalogue vault"—in other words, a very-rare-book room. This main room—there is another—is rectangular, carpeted in red, and kept permanently at 68 degrees. Sprinkler valves are interspersed among eight evenly spaced shelves of books dating from 1475 to 1640 and lit by harsh institutional light. Of these books 180 are the only copies of their titles left in the world: you can spot them by the small blue slips reading "Unique" which modestly poke out from their tops. At the end of the room is a long shelf on which stacks of oversize volumes rest on their sides: these are nearly a third of the surviving First Folio editions of the plays of William Shakespeare. When the First Folios were printed, in the 1620s, printing was still an inexact art. Each page had to be checked by hand, and the volumes are full of mistakes: backward type, ill-cut pages, and variant lines. Several copies lack the 1602 tragedy *Troilus and Cressida,* owing to a copyright dispute. And yet, 370 years after they came off the printing press, you can still pull down these books and read them. The pages are often lightly cockled and foxed, because the folio was printed on mid-priced rag paper, but the type is still bright and the volume falls open easily. You can balance it on your lap and run your finger along the page to feel the paper grain in that sensuous gesture known to centuries of book readers: here is knowledge.

In 1620 Francis Bacon ranked printing, along with gunpowder and the compass, as one of the three inventions that had "changed the appearance and state of the whole world." Indeed, the existence of multiple identical copies of texts that are nearly indelibly recorded, permanently retrievable, and widely decipherable has determined so much of modern history that what the world would be like without printing can only be guessed at. More books likely came into existence in the fifty years after the Gutenberg Bible than in the millennium that preceded it. "Printing was a huge change for Western culture," says Paul Saffo, who studies the effect of technology on society at the Institute for the Future, in Menlo Park (where the receptionist also uses an IBM Selectric). "The dominant intellectual skill before the age of print was the art of memory." And now we may be going back.

For the question may not be whether, given enough time, CD-ROMs and the Internet can replace books, but whether they should. Ours is a culture that has made a fetish of impermanence. Paperbacks disintegrate, Polaroids fade, video images wear out. Perhaps the first novel ever written specifically to be read on a computer and to take advantage of the concept of hypertext — the structuring of written passages to allow the reader to take different paths through the story — was Rob Swigart's *Portal,* published in 1986 and designed for the Apple Macintosh, among other computers of its day. The Apple Macintosh was superseded months later by the more sophisticated Macintosh SE, which, according to Swigart, could not run his hypertext novel. Over time people threw out their old computers (fewer and fewer new programs could be run on them), and so *Portal* became for the most part unreadable. A similar fate will befall literary works of the future if they are committed not to paper but to transitional technology like diskettes, CD-ROMs, and Unix tapes — candidates, with eight-track tapes, Betamax, and the Apple Macintosh, for rapid obscurity.

"It's not clear, with fifty incompatible standards around, what will survive," says Ted Nelson, the computer pioneer, who has grown disenchanted with the forces commercializing the Internet. "The so-called information age is really the age of information lost." Software companies don't care — early moviemakers didn't worry that they were filming on volatile stock. In a graphic dramatization of this mad dash to obsolescence, in 1992 the author William Gibson, who coined the term "cyberspace," created an autobiographical story on computer disc called "Agrippa." "Agrippa" is encoded to erase itself entirely as the purchaser plays the story. Only thirty-five copies were printed, and those who bought it left it intact. One copy was somehow pirated and sent out onto the Internet, where anyone could copy it. Many users did, but who and where is not consistently indexed, nor are the copies permanent — the Internet is anarchic. "The original disc is already almost obsolete on Macintoshes," says Kevin Begos, the publisher of "Agrippa." "Within four or five years [by 1999] it will get very hard to find a machine that will run it." Collectors will soon find Gibson's story gone before they can destroy it themselves.

Software Will Never Replace Fanciful, Portable, Bendable Books

E. Annie Proulx

Every other week someone says that books are dead or dying, that just around the corner is the black hour when they will be curiosities like stereopticon slides or milk stools—probably the same thing they said when radio was invented, when television flickered its way into our living rooms.

To some the phrase means sluggish book sales in the recent and lingering recession, to others it means that the old gray novel ain't what it used to be.

Not a few associate the obliteration of distinguished literary houses and imprints in the age of the corporate takeover as synonymous with the inevitable disappearance of books.

The hearse followers mournfully announce that no one reads these days, can't read, won't read. It doesn't strike them as peculiar that there is a fierce scramble among corporate interests to buy the publishing houses that put out these dying books.

It's possible that the premature obituaries merely cover our confusion about the clouded direction of change in the culture.

As the big publishers try for best sellers at the expense of serious books, it is increasingly the small publishers and university presses that are finding and publishing the books of interesting new writers.

Books once rather scornfully considered grist for the small publisher's mill are catching the reading public's interest.

Among the new books published last year were important works of fiction from Arab Americans, African Americans, Chinese Americans, Mexican Americans, Caribbean Americans, American Indians and others.

The so-called gay and lesbian novel is beginning to escape the genre closet and stand on bookstore shelves alongside traditional works.

Book groups, an old idea, are everywhere. Books are moving into motel and hotel rooms, where a year ago one could find only a single title in a black binding. Now thousands of copies of Joel Conarroe's "Six American Poets" engage travelers in lonely rooms across the continent.

There are guidebooks to used bookshops, and a few imaginative independent booksellers thrive in the shadow of ever-increasing numbers of super stores.

Those who say the book is moribund often cite the computer as the asp on the mat. But the electronic highway is for bulletin boards on esoteric subjects, reference works, lists and news—timely, utilitarian information, efficiently pulled through the wires.

Nobody is going to sit down and read a novel on a twitchy little screen. Ever.

In a curious way the computer emphasizes the unique virtues of the book.

The book is small, lightweight and durable and can be stuffed in a coat pocket, read in the waiting room, on the plane. What are planes but flying reading rooms?

Books give aesthetic and tactile pleasure, from the dust-jacket art to the binding, paper, typography and text design, from the moment of purchase until the last page is turned.

Books speak even when they stand unopened on the shelf.

If you would know women or men, look at their books, not their software.

Listening to the Printed Word

The $1.3 billion market for books on tape has created an industry that did not even exist ten years ago. Audio books are expanding the audience for authors and creating a new source of revenue to publishers. For readers, audio books are making books even more portable and accessible. The economic implications for publishers and authors are significant.

Consider:

1. What advantages do audio books have over the printed versions? Disadvantages?

2. How do publishers respond to the criticism that audio books are replacing the audience for printed books? Do you agree? Disagree? Explain.

3. Have you ever listened to an audio book? If so, explain what you liked or disliked about the experience.

Audio Books: Books to Go

Busy schedules, a lack of leisure time and traffic tie-ups have driven readers crazy.

In the past few years, however, commuters by the tens of thousands have flattened their snarls, tuned out rush-hour gridlock and gone full speed into books on tape.

So have cyclists, walkers and hobbyists of all sorts — anyone who has an ear for words.

The audio-book industry is delighted. The audio business, according to Audio Publishers Association President George Hodgkins, is booming — having generated $1.3 billion in sales and rentals in 1993, a 40 percent leap from 1992.

And it should boom some more: Sales and rentals of spoken-word, children's, foreign-language, fiction, nonfiction, self-help, inspirational and business-oriented tapes were up 16.8 percent through the first six months of 1994, Hodgkins said from his Los Angeles office. The association projects sales and rentals of $3 billion by 1997, with most of the profits in rentals.

"Where few people are willing to plunk down as much as $40 for an audio book, renting it for as little as $1 a day (the industry standard) is the low-cost alternative," said Terry Lipelt, vice president of Rezound International. The audio-book distributor, based in Minneapolis, supplies almost 3,000 video-rental outlets nationwide, including Meijer and Kroger stores in Columbus.

"Once people get started on audio books,

they're hooked," said Flo Gibson, one of the stars of the industry, who narrates books for Audio Book Contractors. The company does a brisk phone- and mail-order business out of Washington, D.C.

"A lot of our customers are desperate for something on a car trip and need something to listen to — as of yesterday," Gibson said. "Most of them are drivers, but also we have a lot of painters, upholsterers and people whose hands are busy when their minds are not. Audio books add an extra dimension to their lives."

Hundreds of new audio products and old-time classics are available each month.

In central Ohio, listeners can buy or rent the likes of Shakespeare, Terry McMillan or Stephen King at bookstores and many food chains, and by phone, or borrow them free from libraries.

Nationwide, nearly 140 stores rent or sell only to the audiotape customer. Five bookstores in Ohio deal only in audio books; one is in Columbus: Audio Books Buffs at 787 Bethel Rd. (326-1100).

Since it opened in June 1993, the store is doing well enough that owner Jenny David wants to open a store in northeast Columbus in June [1995]. Books by Tom Clancy and Stephen Covey, and James Redfield's *The Celestine Prophecy,* were the hottest rentals [in mid-September 1994].

Rezound International spokeswoman Christine McConnell said the audio-book industry could eclipse the video-rental boom of the 1980s.

"Only 17 to 20 percent of Americans are aware of the concept of audio books," McConnell said. "That figure should take off."

More outlets are likely, too: According to a survey of grocers by *Supermarket News,* 70 percent plan to merchandise audio books before the end of this year.

"There's a big opportunity for growth," David said, "especially if more people knew what audio books are."

Many Columbus drivers know because David advertised Audio Book Buffs on a billboard along Rt. 315, where traffic can grind to a near standstill during rush hours or as cars trickle past small accidents.

Audio books aren't just for people stuck in traffic, David is quick to say. Forty-six percent of audio-book users listen to tapes on the road, but most use them while cleaning, exercising or doing handwork that requires no headwork.

Audio products are as diverse as their users and, as an added lure, often are narrated by actors and celebrities.

For $10 to $20, car-grounded Earthlings can equip themselves with complete or abridged copies of books in the popular Star Trek series, Erica Jong's *Fear of Fifty* or Robert James Waller's *The Bridges of Madison County;* or a boxed set of Timothy Zahn's *Star Wars* novels ($59).

Audio Partners offers titles by Isak Dinesen, Walt Whitman, Mark Twain and Anais Nin, with the voices of Robert Redford, Isaac Asimov, Julie Harris and Hal Holbrook. Dove's latest include Sidney Sheldon's just-out [in 1994] *Nothing Lasts Forever* and Alan Rachins' *Nixon: A Life,* read by the authors; and Dale Brown's *Storming Heaven,* read by television regular Robert Foxworth.

Time Warner Audio offers books by Douglas Adams, Bebe Moore Campbell and Joanna Cole, while Simon & Schuster Audio has Winston Groom's *Forrest Gump,* Tom Clancy's *Clear and Present Danger* and Anne Rice's erotica, *The Claiming of Sleeping Beauty.*

Some publishers shorten books (Garry Wills abridged his *Certain Trumpets* to $4^{1}/_{2}$ hours for Simon & Schuster), but others present them whole — for listeners who want it all.

Books on Tape is one of several companies that record only full-length readings; it has 2,500 titles. Rentals run typically in the $15-to-$20 range — about what one would pay retail for an abridged recording. Tape sets are sold for about $8 a cassette. (John Grisham's eight-cassette *The Pelican Brief,* for example, sells for $64; a rental costs $17.50 for 30 days).

Spoken-word recordings have been around at least since Dylan Thomas recorded his best-selling *A Child's Christmas in Wales* in 1952, and audio books have been mainstays for the blind for at least 40 years.

The industry has been bullish on audio, though, since Waldenbooks decided in 1983 to routinely carry books on tape. To compete with the giant retailer, other chains and independents followed suit — setting the stage for the '90s boom.

Industry officials reject comments that audio books might discourage people from reading. They say the genre can promote books, genuine books, when listeners find they enjoy particular writers and want to search out their books.

"It's different from reading. It's not replacing it," said Jenny Frost, vice president of Bantam Doubleday Dell Audio in New York City. "People who buy books are going to continue to buy books. What we can do is bring new people to that author."

Who's Narrating

Some actors have built second careers out of the audio-book genre.

In the past seven years [since 1987], Darren McGavin has recorded 19 John D. MacDonald mysteries for Random House Audio. (His most recent: [1993's] *A Tan and Sandy Silence.*)

The McGavin-MacDonald series has been re-released by Random House in its budget-friendly Price-Less line for $8.99 each. The packaging is smaller, but two tapes still hold three hours.

McGavin also has recorded Robert Ludlum's *The Bourne Identity* and *The Bourne Supremacy* for BDD, and James Michener's *Space* for Random House.

Flo Gibson recently recorded her 630th book for Audio Book Contractors, which specializes in unabridged classics.

"Listening to a book, no matter how good it is, is still just the third-best way to appreciate a book," she said in her well-modulated voice. "Ideally, you should read the printed

Top Rentals

As listed in the September [1994] issue of Rezound's *In/Audio* magazine:

1. *The Client* by John Grisham (BDD, read by Blair Brown)

2. *Disclosure* by Michael Crichton (Random House, John Lithgow)

3. *Like Water for Chocolate* by Laura Esquivel (BDD, Yareli Arizmendi)

4. *Schindler's List* by Thomas Keneally (Simon & Schuster, Ben Kingsley)

5. *Pleading Guilty* by Scott Turow (Simon & Schuster, Stacy Keach)

6. *Gone but Not Forgotten* by Philip Margolin (BDD, Margaret Whitton)

7. *The Pelican Brief* by John Grisham (BDD, Anthony Heald)

8. *Without Remorse* by Tom Clancy (Random House, David Dukes)

9. *A Time To Kill* by John Grisham (BDD, Michael Beck)

10. *Clear and Present Danger* by Tom Clancy (Simon & Schuster, Michael Pritchard)

word and read it in a leisurely fashion. The second-best way is for someone who loves you to read aloud to you or for you to read to them.

"It's a sad thing that families aren't reading to their children the way they used to. Fathers and mothers come home from work too tired to read to their children."

Gibson was a radio actress for 25 years before she retired to raise a family. Back in "the voice business" for the past 19 years, she is happy to be "deeply immersed in the great works," she said.

"What we do with recorded books is help teach the art of listening and the art of concentration. Our books re-sensitize ears to the sounds of birds, rustling leaves, the art of silence — and, of course, the spoken word."

"Audio Books: Books to Go," by George Myers, Jr., *Columbus Dispatch,* September 27, 1994. Reprinted by permission of *The Columbus Dispatch.* Dow//Quest ID: 0000365641DC.

African-American Romance Novels

The traditional romance novel is taking on a new hue, according to Edith Updike, as publishers introduce specialty collections targeted at specific audiences. In this article from *New York Newsday,* Updike describes a new line of books featuring African-American heroes and heroines.

Consider:

1. Why is the romance novel market so valuable for publishers, according to Updike?

2. Why would a publisher want to introduce a collection of romance novels targeted at a specific ethnic group?

3. According to Updike, why have publishers of romance novels been so slow to realize the value of the African-American audience?

Publishers of Romance Novels Add Color to Their Lines

Edith Updike

Regina Moxey is in love with romance. The Indianapolis mother of three found *Love Everlasting* at a local bookstore earlier [in 1994], and "was delighted to read a story I could relate to in terms of people who looked like me, African-Americans." But still, love is hard to find. "I'm trying to find other works of yours," she told the author, "along with other African-American romance writers, with no luck so far."

Moxey just got lucky. [In July 1994], Zebra Books launched a brand new line of romance novels exclusively for heroes and heroines of color. Zebra and its new multicultural line will be in the spotlight [in July 1994] as New York fills with incurable romantics attending the Romance Writers of America's national conference.

Authors and agents say that for years, publishers and editors of romance novels have said or implied, "We don't print black romances because they don't sell because blacks don't read."

But the success of black authors, magazines and a few maverick publishers is making the major publishers think again. There's money to be made in this neglected market. Zebra's way was paved by a couple of small, independent, sometimes unlikely, publishers.

Letitia Peoples spent more than 30 years working for the federal government—and reading romance novels. After retiring in 1990, she founded Odyssey Books for the express purpose of publishing multicultural romances—the kind of books she wanted to read and couldn't find.

"There were no books like that on the market," the 54-year-old entrepreneur said. "First I thought about writing one, but then I realized that even if I did write one, nobody would publish it."

Sandra Kitt, a well-known African-American author of romance novels, began writing about both black and white couples 11 years ago [in 1983]. "I didn't think I was doing anything special, just writing stories," she said. "Lo and behold, one day I realized the books being turned down were the ones with black characters."

Peoples published 11 books in four years, with great success. But Odyssey's distribution and production were limited by its size. Denise Little, a buyer for Barnes & Noble from 1990–93, said Odyssey books "did very well, but we had to be very conservative with orders."

Now, in a classic food-chain scenario, Odyssey may be edged out by bigger fish. Monica Harris, the editor of Zebra's new ethnic line, Arabesque, said, "This line couldn't have been started without people like her taking a lot of the risk."

Peoples said, "I knew that they would be watching, and that if it was successful they would jump on the bandwagon." It's the same thing Walter Zacharius, chairman of medium-sized Zebra, says about the really big houses. "When it grows, they'll all get in it," he said. "Years ago, the big publishers didn't even want to get into the romance market."

Romance novels account for nearly 50 percent of mass market paperback sales. In 1992, readers spent $885 million on 177 million romance books. Harlequin alone puts out 62 new titles each month, almost 750 a year.

Romance readers are insatiable. Many spend more than $1,000 a year on books, purchasing as many as 30 paperbacks a month.

"Romance readers are the sanest cult members I ever met," said Rob Cohen, a veteran literary agent at Richard Curtis Associates also penning a book for Zebra. "They read everything they can get their hands on."

Industry insiders estimate that a third of romance readers are non-white. They read "white" romances, but they're eager for more diversity. "Dear Ms. Kitt," one reader recently wrote to the author whose *Serenade* inaugurated the Arabesque imprint. "It's good to know that we have some of our sisters writing about black romance . . . I'm very grateful to you."

"I wanted to [start an ethnic line] for a long time," Zacharius said. "People told me 'You're crazy. Blacks don't read.' But I watched the growth of the black magazines and noticed a lot of black and Hispanic readers."

Zacharius said the two inaugural Arabesques have been so well received that he's increased print runs from 65,000 to more than 100,000. When Arabesque gets a foothold, they'll go to four titles a month. "I think it's a very big market," he said. "For now, maybe $100 million, but when it really explodes, $500 million at least."

Why have publishers been so slow to exploit this market? One explanation may lie in the publishing's lily-whiteness. Kitt said, "They don't know anything about the black community, so they worried, 'How do we market this?' and were making it a big problem."

Harlequin publishes the occasional ethnic story, but has no ethnic line. "We didn't want to designate it by color because that's not what the books are about," said Katherine Orr, director of publicity. She estimated the number of Harlequins with non-white heroines is growing by 3 percent to 5 percent a year.

There remain some racist assumptions. Ethnic romance is presumed to appeal mostly to members of the ethnic group. "I've been reading white romances for years and had no trouble empathizing with the protagonists," Cohen said. "It's a strange form of prejudice to assume that a mainstream audience will not be able to overcome this hurdle of imagination."

And some think the author should be of the ethnic group, even though black writers write white romances. Publicity is one factor, but editors also want authenticity, not characters who are "black for no reason," as Harris put it.

"As an African-American, I had to adapt to a white society," Kitt said. "But I don't think it necessarily works the other way. If you're going to write about another culture, it has to be something you've lived or experienced."

"Publishers of Romance Novels Add Color to Their Lines," by Edith Updike, *New York Newsday,* July 25, 1994. Reprinted by permission of Edith Updike. Dow//Quest Story ID: 0000343581DC.

PERSPECTIVE 5-5

Writers in the Public Eye

The public's perception of a writer's life often differs quite a bit from reality. When someone writes horror stories, like author Stephen King does, people sometimes believe he is what he writes. In this essay from *The New York Times Book Review,* King describes some of the inconveniences of being a celebrity.

Consider:

1. How do most of the letter-writers Stephen King describes view his life?

2. What does King's essay tell you about the life of a celebrity author?

3. From what King says, what is his primary motivation to write?

"Ever Et Raw Meat?" and Other Weird Questions

Stephen King

It seems to me that, in the minds of readers, writers actually exist to serve two purposes, and the more important may not be the writing of books and stories. The primary function of writers, it seems, is to answer readers' questions. These fall into three categories. The third is the one that fascinates me most, but I'll identify the other two first.

The One-of-a-Kind Questions: Each day's mail brings a few of these. Often they reflect the writer's field of interest—history, horror, romance, the American West, outer space, big business. The only thing they have in common is their uniqueness. Novelists are frequently asked where they get their ideas (see category No. 2), but writers must wonder where this relentless curiosity, these really strange questions, come from.

There was, for instance, the young woman who wrote to me from a penal institution in Minnesota. She informed me she was a kleptomaniac. She further informed me that I was her favorite writer, and she had stolen every one of my books she could get her hands on. "But after I stole *Different Seasons* from the library and read it, I felt moved to send it back," she wrote. "Do you think this means you wrote this one the best?" After due consideration, I decided that reform on the part of the reader has nothing to do with artistic merit. I came close to writing back to find out if she had stolen *Misery* yet, but decided I ought to just keep my mouth shut.

From Bill V. in North Carolina: "I see you have a beard. Are you morbid of razors?"

From Carol K. in Hawaii: "Will you soon write of pimples or some other facial blemish?"

From Don G., no address (and a blurry postmark): "Why do you keep up this disgusting mother worship when anyone with any sense knows a MAN has no use to his mother once he is weened?"

From Raymond R. in Mississippi: "Ever et raw meat?" (It's the laconic ones like this that really get me.)

I have been asked if I beat my children and/or my wife. I have been asked to parties in places I have never been and hope never to go. I was once asked to give away the bride at a wedding, and one young woman sent me an ounce of pot, with the attached question: "This is where I get my inspiration—where do you get yours?" Actually, mine usually comes in envelopes—the kind through which you can view your name and address printed by a computer—that arrive at the end of every month.

My favorite question of this type, from Anchorage, asked simply: "How could you write such a why?" Unsigned. If E. E. Cummings were still alive, I'd try to find out if he'd moved to the Big North.

The Old Standards: These are the questions writers dream of answering when they are collecting rejection slips, and the ones they tire of quickest once they start to publish. In other words, they are the questions that come up without fail in every dull interview the writer has ever given or will ever give. I'll enumerate a few of them:

Where do you get your ideas? (I get mine in Utica.)

How do you get an agent? (Sell your soul to the Devil.)

Do you have to know somebody to get published? (Yes; in fact, it helps to grovel, toady and be willing to perform twisted acts of sexual depravity at a moment's notice, and in public if necessary.)

How do you start a novel? (I usually start by writing the number 1 in the upper right-hand corner of a clean sheet of paper.)

How do you write best sellers? (Same way you get an agent.)

How do you sell your book to the movies? (Tell them they don't want it.)

What time of day do you write? (It doesn't matter; if I don't keep busy enough, the time inevitably comes.)

Do you ever run out of ideas? (Does a bear defecate in the woods?)

Who is your favorite writer? (Anyone who writes stories I would have written had I thought of them first.)

There are others, but they're pretty boring, so let us march on.

The Real Weirdies: Here I am, bopping down the street, on my morning walk, when some guy pulls over in this pickup truck or just happens to walk by and says, "Hi, Steve! Writing any good books lately?" I have an answer for this; I've developed it over the years out of pure necessity. I say, "I'm taking some time off." I say that even if I'm working like mad, thundering down the homestretch on a book. The reason *why* I say this is because no other answer seems to fit. Believe me, I know. In the course of the trial and error that has finally resulted in "I'm taking some time off," I have discarded about 500 other answers.

Having an answer for "You writing any good books lately?" is a good thing, but I'd be lying if I said it solves the problem of *what the question means.* It is this inability on my part to make sense of this odd query, which reminds me of that Zen riddle — "Why is a mouse when it runs?" — that leaves me feeling mentally shaken and impotent. You see, it isn't just *one* question; it is a *bundle* of questions, cunningly wrapped up in one package. It's like that old favorite, "Are you still beating your wife?"

If I answer in the affirmative, it means I may have written — how many books? two? four? — (all of them good) in the last — how long? Well, how long is "lately"? It could mean I wrote maybe three good books just last week, or maybe two *on this very walk up to Bangor International Airport and back!* On the other hand, if I say no, what does *that* mean? I wrote three or four *bad* books in the last "lately" (surely "lately" can be no longer than a month, six weeks at the outside)?

Or here I am, signing books at the Betts' Bookstore or B. Dalton's in the local consumer factory (nicknamed "the mall"). This is something I do twice a year, and it serves much the same purpose as those little bundles of twigs religious people in the Middle Ages used to braid into whips and flagellate themselves with. During the course of this exercise in madness and self-abnegation, at least a dozen people will approach the little coffee table where I sit behind a barrier of books and ask brightly, "Don't you wish you had a rubber stamp?"

I have an answer to this one, too, an answer that has been developed over the years in a trial-and-error method similar to "I'm taking some time off." The answer to the rubber-stamp question is: "No, I don't mind."

Never mind if I really do or don't (this time it's my own motivations I want to skip over, you'll notice); the question is, Why does such an illogical query occur to so many people? My signature is actually stamped on the covers of several of my books, but people seem just as eager to get these signed, as those that aren't so stamped. Would these questioners stand in line for the privilege of watching me slam a rubber stamp down on the title page of *The Shining* or *Pet Sematary?* I don't think they would.

If you still don't sense something peculiar in these questions, this one might help convince you. I'm sitting in the cafe around the corner from my house, grabbing a little lunch by myself and reading a book (reading at the table is one of the few bad habits acquired in my youth that I have nobly resisted giving up) until a customer or maybe even a waitress sidles up and asks, "How come you're not reading one of your own books?"

This hasn't happened just once, or even occasionally; it happens *a lot.* The computer-generated answer to this question usually gains a chuckle, although it is nothing but the pure logical and apparent truth. "I know how they all come out," I say. End of exchange. Back to lunch, with only a pause to wonder why people assume you want to read what you wrote, rewrote, and read again following the obligatory editorial conference and yet again during the process of correcting the mistakes that a good copy editor always prods, screaming, from their hiding places (I once heard a crime writer suggest that God could have used a copy editor, and while I find the notion slightly blasphemous, I tend to agree).

And then people sometimes ask in that chatty, let's-strike-up-a-conversation way people have, "How long does it take you to write a book?" Perfectly reasonable question — at least until you try to answer it and discover there *is* no answer. This time the computer-generated answer is a total falsehood, but at least it serves the purpose of advancing the conversation to some more discussable topic. "Usually about nine months," I say, "the same length of time it takes to make a baby." This satisfies everyone but me.

I know that nine months is just an average, and probably a fictional one at that. It ignores *The Running Man* (published under the name Richard Bachman), which was written in four days during a snowy February vacation when I was teaching high school. It also ignores *It* and . . . *The Tommyknockers*. *It* is over 1,000 pages long and took four years to write. *The Tommyknockers* is 400 pages shorter but took five years to write.

Do I mind these questions? Yes . . . and no. Anyone minds questions that have no real answers and thus expose the fellow being questioned to be not a real doctor but a sort of witch doctor. But no one — at least no one with a modicum of simple human kindness — resents questions from people who honestly want answers. And now and then someone will ask a really interesting question, like, Do you write in the nude? The answer — not generated by computer — is: I don't think I ever have, but if it works, I'm willing to try it.

" 'Ever Et Raw Meat?' and Other Weird Questions," by Stephen King, *The New York Times Book Review,* December 6, 1987, p. 7. Used with permission of the author's agent, Kirby McCauley Ltd.

The Radio Industry

The Rise of Spanish-Language Radio

Spanish-language radio is one of the fastest growing radio formats in the country. Nowhere has this format been more successful than in Los Angeles, where KLAX became the number one station in the market in 1993 and continues today to be the Los Angeles market leader. In this story from the *Los Angeles Times,* reporter Jonathan Widran describes the popularity of the station's top disc jockey, Juan Carlos Hidalgo.

Consider:

1. Like many radio stations, KLAX combines the features of different radio formats to create its own distinct programming. Describe the format that has made KLAX successful.

2. Why do you think a station like KLAX would enjoy such success in a market such as Los Angeles?

3. How does the success of KLAX reflect the ability of radio to target specific audience segments? Explain.

L.A.'s Top DJ: He's Not Stern

Jonathan Widran

"Buenos dias, Los Angeles!" Taking his cue from Robin Williams' charismatic character in "Good Morning, Vietnam," KLAX-FM (97.9) morning drive-time deejay Juan Carlos Hidalgo awakens the city's Latino community at 5 A.M. with an amusing take on this greeting, which sets the humorous tone he takes with listeners for the next five hours.

"People don't want to hear about problems and bad news first thing in the morning," Hidalgo, 27, says in explaining his light-hearted approach. "We make them feel better about the things they face every day by simply making them laugh."

The only one, it seems, who isn't amused by Hidalgo these days is Howard Stern, whose syndicated show on KLSX-FM (97.1) was edged by KLAX in the . . . quarterly Arbitron ratings for winter '93. Hidalgo attracted 6.5% of the audience to Stern's 6.3%.

This upset, which sent shock waves through the local radio market and the disbelieving Stern camp—just as happened three months earlier when KLAX itself had surged to the top of the ratings among stations — proved once and for all that KLAX's combination of personalities with *ranchera* (country) and *banda* (wind instrument-oriented) music has made it

L.A.'s most-listened-to spot on the radio dial.

Though never imagining such quick and resounding success for his show, which debuted last Aug. 3, [1992,] Hidalgo attributes his lofty numbers to the casual and amusing approach he takes in relating to his listeners. And, in clear contrast to the raciness that seems to be Stern's bread and butter, Hidalgo attracts many people by keeping his humor squeaky clean.

"The first thing we do is have fun on our show, but we stay away from dirty jokes," he says. "People like us because we appeal to everybody in the house. We don't focus on any special age, so everyone from kids to seniors can enjoy listening to us. We talk to everybody like they are our friends, and everything we do is positive, nothing is negative."

The laughter comes from the natural, unassuming and seemingly unrehearsed way that Hidalgo and his sidekick, known only as "El Peladillo," take on the ordinary, everyday topics. They pride themselves on their disarming nonseriousness and unpredictability.

Variations abound on a daily basis, but a typical Hidalgo show begins by relating to the 5 A.M. attitude of his listeners, doing mock grunts and groans about not wanting to get up while Peladillo tries to wake him.

Off and running, the 5 o'clock hour features news, "done in a humorous way, of course," followed at 6 by amusing recipes, "talking to folks like we are chefs and this is what they must cook and eat each day, which is another joke." Between 7 and 8 A.M. come funny horoscopes ("Churroscopos"), their trademark "Happy Birthday Joke" (where they call the birthday person a la Rick Dees and "Candid Phone"), and a kids' song at 7:30, after which they discuss youth-oriented topics and give away prizes.

In between the fun during later hours are traffic reports by Jorge Jarrin and three live on-air dedications per hour.

"While I feel our station's overall success is due to the Hispanic community responding to the music and format, Juan Carlos does well because he is extremely good at communicating with listeners," says General Sales Manager Jack McVeigh. "His being able to portray his own personality and relate to the public with something enjoyable helps set the tone for our entire day."

Hidalgo's own rise in radio parallels the explosive story of his station. Feeling that his native Mexico wasn't about to offer him any meaningful opportunities, he immigrated to Southern California in 1985 and lived at first with a friend in Oxnard. While working on a farm picking strawberries ("not speaking English, it was the only job I could get at the time"), he heard a radio ad for the International Broadcasting School in Ventura, and decided to enroll.

Upon completing his courses in 1987, he began his first stint as a deejay at Oxnard's tiny KTRO, where he did the graveyard shift for three months before switching to drive time, where he garnered the station's highest ratings ever.

From there, it was up the coast in 1990 to San Francisco as morning man and program director at KOFY-AM, where Hidalgo worked similar magic. His ability to lift the station from a .7 rating to a 2.7 in a matter of months attracted the interest of Alfredo Rodriguez, who was in the process of creating KLAX and is currently its general manager.

Despite his Midas touch over the Spanish-speaking airwaves, Hidalgo tempers his optimism with caution when asked about maintaining his throne.

"I thought I'd do well here, but nothing this big," he says. "Being first is not easy. I have a big responsibility and we have to work that much harder. And you can't get too excited because the nature of radio is always up and down."

"L.A.'s Top DJ: He's Not Stern," by Jonathan Widran, *Los Angeles Times,* June 10, 1993, p. F-1.

Radio Tries to Find Itself

Today's radio industry is driven by formats — standardized playlists of specific types of music targeted to attract specific audiences. Top 40 radio began as the original radio format, with hits derived from *Billboard* magazine's list of Top 40 best-selling singles. Today's music, and today's radio, are much more complicated.

Consider:

1. Why is radio, according to David Browne, having a "midlife crisis"?

2. Explain why Browne says that today's FM dial is "sliced and diced into as many different music formats as there are shredded vegetables at a salad bar." What effect does this have on the audience?

3. Do you agree with Browne that "pop radio's power and signal grow a little dimmer every day"? Why? Why not?

Pop Radio Suffers a Midlife Crisis

David Browne

As Wilson Phillips' "You're in Love" booms through the control room of Z100, you would think the New York-area radio station was doing everything right. At its Secaucus, N.J., headquarters, the "morning zoo" disk jockeys Gary Bryan and Ross Brittain are bustling around making prank phone calls to executives and rattling off traffic and news updates. Every so often, Mr. Bryan scans the music log — a computerized list of songs he must play every hour — and grabs a pile of tape cartridges, each containing a current hit. Those marked with blue dots indicate songs that, in the words of the show's producer, Mike Opelka, are "really happening." For a Top 40 station, one that plays the pop hits of the moment, life doesn't get any more normal.

But at Z100, officially known as WHTZ-FM, and many other pop radio stations around the country, things are seriously out of tune. Z100 had been No. 1 in its market from 1987 through the summer of 1989, three times earning a competition-squelching 6.2 share (percentage of the listening audience, based on Arbitron data). By the spring, Z100 was lingering at 3.6, lagging behind stations specializing in oldies (WCBS, with a 5.2 share), dance pop (WRKS, with 5.1), soft rock (WLTW, with 4.8) and six others.

Z100's sinking ratings are an indication of the dire circumstances of Top 40 radio, which, when it was the only game in town, used to determine what was a hit record. Top 40 has experienced slumps before, but now must compete with formats that specifically appeal to fans of rock oldies or hip-hop or hard rock. This fragmented audience, combined with the increasing role of MTV and the aging of the baby boomers, is taking its toll on old-fashioned Top 40. The national Arbitron/Billboard share for the format went from 14.4 percent in the spring of 1990 to 11.9 percent in the winter of 1991.

And it's not just Top 40. No longer the sole backbone of the music business, pop radio as a whole is having a midlife crisis. Unsure of whether to grab teenagers or baby boomers, station owners have switched formats faster than listeners can switch stations; [in 1991] alone, 1,050 stations — roughly one-tenth of all commercial stations — changed formats, lurching from Top 40 (Paula Abdul) to Adult Contemporary (Gloria Estefan), from hard rock (Guns 'n' Roses) to Classic Rock (the Doors). As station playlists focus narrowly on one type of music fan, and as stations become more attuned to advertisers than listeners, the result is a significant change in what we hear and where we hear it.

Granted, Top 40 is still instrumental in making hit singles. "Unless radio brings it home, it won't be a hit," says John Boulos, a vice president of promotion and field operations at Virgin Records. But as Steve Kingston, Z100's vice president of programming, says, "The rules have changed — it's a whole new ball game."

Much of the conundrum is radio's own fault. In the '60s, it was possible to hear the Rolling Stones, the Supremes, the Monkees and Aretha Franklin on one Top 40 station in an hour. In [1992], with the expansion of the FM band that began in the early '70s, those acts would probably be found on separate stations. The FM dial is sliced and diced into as many different music formats as there are shredded vegetables at a salad bar.

Top 40 — or CHR, Contemporary Hit Radio — blares hits from *Billboard*'s singles chart. For the latest in synthesized dance pop, rap and club beats, there's UC (Urban Contemporary). For primarily white rock-and-roll, there's AOR (Album-Oriented Rock). For mellow soft rock AC (Adult Contemporary).

If you're not yet confused, each has subdivisions (like Adult Urban Contemporary, which features upscale black performers like Luther Vandross, or Classic Rock, an offshoot of AOR). There are formats so new they have not yet developed acronyms — alternative-rock stations that dare to play bands (Depeche Mode, the La's) with members under the age of 40.

This fragmentation and segregation has done wonders for advertisers, who love niche marketing. It has also alienated people who would sooner watch MTV than turn the radio dial in search of music they like.

In the record business, radio is both tolerated because it helps sell records and scorned because it is too static and formulaic. Record companies have been stung by the lack of "back announcing" on radio, the practice of telling listeners what songs they just heard. (A sign of discontent: "When You Play It, Say it!" stickers pasted on new albums as forceful reminders to careless disk jockeys.) In fact, it is increasingly common for record companies to forgo radio initially and introduce a song on MTV.

The very idea of a mass-appeal station — one that would attract a wide class and age range with something for everyone — has been lost. Given the cultural fragmentation of the country itself, maybe it was inevitable. In the '60s the weekly WABC-AM Top 40 show "Cousin Brucie's Saturday Night Dance Party" had a 25 share in New York and reached an audience between the ages of 10 and 60. In the [1990s], a Top 40 station would be lucky to get a 5 share with an audience aged 18 to 24.

Possibly the decline is a backlash against rap or the pulsating dance music of groups like C&C Music Factory and Tara Kemp. "Top 40 has become a real balancing act," says Mr. Brittain of Z100. "In '83, there was Michael Jackson, the songs from 'Flashdance,' Cyndi Lauper—all these mass-appeal artists who crossed boundaries. Now it's difficult to play rap without the adults saying, 'Goodby!' And you can't play the softer pop without the kids saying, 'Too wimpy!' It's a problem."

Demographics

Wanted: Young Single Female

Top 40 used to be simple—the hits just kept on coming. When the baby boomers came of age (and took the lion's share of buying power with them), radio began singing the tune of pinpoint demographics.

The result? Too much dance pop. Not enough dance pop. Too much Led Zeppelin. Not nearly enough Led Zeppelin. Everyone complains about radio except the advertising community. In that demographic-dominated world, keeping listeners apart is precisely the plan. Music is a tool to reach a specific consumer, preferably age 25 to 54 and female, advertisers' ideal consumer.

If you listen to a particular station, the radio world already has you pegged. According to the Radio Advertising Bureau, Top 40 listeners—those who tune in to KISS-FM in Los Angeles or WBBM in Chicago, for example—are 18- to 34-year-olds who buy CD players, drink Coors Light beer and drive a Toyota Celica. Album-Oriented Rock and Classic Rock stations (WNEW in New York, WYSP in Philadelphia) are targeted at 25- to 35-year-olds who drink Corona beer, buy audio components and drive a Toyota MR2. Those who listen to soft rock on Adult Contemporary stations (WBZ-FM in Boston, KOST-FM in Los Angeles) are 24 to 44 years old, gulp Miller High Life, buy TV sets and drive a Toyota Corolla.

"You have to sell specifics—the whole idea of 'wide' is gone," says Warren Potash, the president of the Radio Advertising Bureau. "The only one who wants to reach everybody is the census."

Pushing Product

All the Hits, All the Time

To reach these specific demographics, radio stations must make sure they are playing exactly the right songs at exactly the right time, reducing playlists to a science. Program directors gauge phone requests, conduct phone surveys, scan the *Billboard* charts, study the playlists of competing stations and listen to relentless pitches from radio promotion executives at record companies. Although dozens of singles are released each week, only three or four (at most) are added to the average Top 40 station.

Shady characters have long been a part of the music promotion business, and they still lurk in the shadows. Flogging performers like Vanilla Ice and Wilson Phillips through independent promoters—hired guns who, in exchange for large salaries, pitch records to stations—continues unabated despite the Justice Department's most recent payola investigation. (The case ran aground when charges brought in Los Angeles were dismissed [in 1991] against the leading promoter, Joseph Isgro, and other industry figures.) Independent promotion is not illegal, but payola is.

One former executive at a major record label (who insists on anonymity) says her company's radio promotion department would routinely entice program directors and other personnel with vacations in the Bahamas and prostitutes. "People in radio promotion have unbelievable expense accounts that they don't have to justify," she says. "There was an attitude of 'Whatever it takes. . . .' "

Labels spend an average of $70,000 on independent promotion for high-priority albums, according to a survey by a Los Angeles accounting firm. The promoters' influence means that banal songs are often added to radio playlists.

Once songs are selected, many stations use a computer to group them into hourly music blocks; the computer insures that the same artist isn't played twice in a row and that certain cuts are played regularly. The big hits, called "powers," are played about every two hours. In a technique called "day parting," hit and easy-on-the-ears pop are played in the morning, ballads in the afternoon and hard rockers later in the day and into the night. Mr. Kingston of Z100 says there is no other way for radio stations to compete for narrow demographics. "The alternative is to put a box of records in the studio with the deejays," he says. "But the business is too sophisticated these days for the primitive ways of the past to work."

Mr. Bryan, the Z100 deejay, agrees, but with reservations. "Programming is too research driven," he says. "There's too much money at stake for people to make decisions based on gut feelings."

Competition

The Video Takeover

Research, among other things, dictates that Top 40 stations play catch-up with video. "MTV is the single most important factor on your side," says Mark Di Dia, general manager of the record company Def American. "You still need radio, but if MTV's on your side, it's the equivalent of 100 radio stations playing your song."

The Top 10 success of the Divinyls' "I Touch Myself" provides a textbook example. Until [1992], the Australian band had never had a hit and was regarded as a cult rock act—a hard sell to Urban Contemporary stations. So John Boulos of Virgin

Records developed a multitiered approach to convince Top 40 radio to add the song.

In the process that Mr. Boulos calls "a relay race," Virgin first established the song at college and alternative-rock stations and sent its provocative video to MTV. The network immediately took to the clip. It was six weeks before "I Touch Myself" was shipped to pop radio, at which time program directors had no choice but to play the song.

"We set it up so that, when it went to pop radio, everything was ready," says Mr. Boulos. The tab for making "I Touch Myself" a hit, he says: more than $500,000 spent on making a video, independent promotion and air fare for Mr. Boulos and others to visit radio stations around the country plus the use of most of Virgin's 25-person radio promotion staff. The payoff: 500,000 albums sold.

Adults Only

Nothing but Love Songs

The power of the baby boomers is reflected in the Adult Contemporary formats, which have grabbed the largest slice of the pop radio pie. These playlists—the perfect way to reach 25- to 50-year-old listeners — program pleasant, mid-tempo soft pop, from Chicago to Londonbeat. Unlike Top 40 announcers, Adult Contemporary disk jockeys are calm and mild-mannered, and the general mood is as reassuring as a phone message from a good friend. "We play songs you can sing along to but not get depressed over," says Robert Dunphy, vice president of programming at WNSR-FM, a New York Adult Contemporary station.

But there are many different kinds of adults. Basic easy-listening Adult Contemporary relies on Barry Manilow, Kenny Rogers and other relative old-timers of the genre. For a slightly "hipper" alternative, there is Hot AC (also called Mix), which favors a younger, more rhythmic generation: Phil

Collins, Sting, Mariah Carey, even Billy Idol. Other specializations include Lite (heavy on love songs), Beautiful Music (instrumental selections à la Muzak) and light jazz-fusion. Adult Contemporary stations are so numerous, in fact, that the format leads in overall ratings even though any one station may not be No. 1 in its market.

"AC does better when times are economically shaky," says Mr. Dunphy. "People don't know where the country's headed, so they're looking for a safe haven."

WNSR and other Adult Contemporary outlets may be in for some competition over the male component of the demographic. Several stations around the country have switched to the latest variation on the format — Rock AC, essentially singer-songwriters and country-rockers of the 60's and 70's like Jackson Browne. "Instead of just playing the Eagles' 'Desperado,'" says Mr. Dunphy, "they'll go deeper into the album and play, say, 'Tequila Sunrise.'" He adds, not at all facetiously, "It's a variation with a lot of promise."

What's Missing?

Between Rock and a Hard Place

Wonder where brash, new, innovative rock-and-roll fits into this bleak scenario? You're not alone. Since the advertising world's targeted age group is 25 and up, rock stations tend to dwell in the past — the Rolling Stones, Jethro Tull, Crosby, Stills and Nash and other baby-boomer war horses. According to *Broadcasting* magazine, the number of Classic Rock outlets went up 160 percent — to 240 stations — from 1989 to 1990.

Nor is new rock welcome on Top 40 stations, whose audience favors electronic dance-pop and rap. Stations are therefore often reluctant to add guitar-based rock bands to their playlist. Current albums by Van Halen and Skid Row have both hit No. 1 without the

benefit of a Top 40 single. Even an eagerly awaited single like Guns 'n' Roses' "You Could Be Mine," a thundering rocker from the band's long overdue "Use Your Illusion II" album, has not been immediately embraced by Top 40 stations.

If any new rock band could have attained a foothold on either Album-Oriented Rock or Top 40, it should have been the Black Crowes, the Atlanta boogie-rockers who sound like the illegitimate sons of the Rolling Stones and Humble Pie. Nonetheless, pop radio turned a deaf ear to all four singles from their first album, "Shake Your Money Maker." As a result, their label, Def American, opted to promote the band through touring and MTV. It worked: the album sold two million copies with hardly any radio air play. Only now is the band's third single, "Hard to Handle," which was released [in fall 1991], receiving consistent air play.

"It's a sad state of affairs," says Mr. Di Dia of Def American. "If people are buying it and radio isn't playing it, something's wrong. . . ."

Pop radio's acceptance of R.E.M.'s brooding folk-rock single, "Losing My Religion," could be a harbinger of things to come. Or, says Ken Barnes, the editor of the trade magazine *Radio and Records,* "it could also be the last hurrah" for rock on Top 40.

Forecast

Increasingly Cloudy

There is no denying the continued appeal of Top 40 radio, nor the exhilarating feeling of hearing a favorite oldie or a compelling new single boom over the airwaves. "Radio is a comforting and comfortable medium," says Mr. Barnes. "It attempts to communicate one-on-one."

There is no denying that pop radio still has a few tricks up its sleeve. [In 1991,] it would have been unimaginable that the Top

40 hits would include "Losing My Religion," E.M.F.'s "Unbelievable" or the Extreme's Beatlesque ballad "More Than Words." But that's just what happened. It might be rash to expect a return to Top 40's most recent golden era of 1983 to 1985, but such loosening up does mean that listeners will be able to hear a little variety — or at least something other than the thump-thump of a drum machine — on their local stations. In radioland, this is considered progress.

Yet even Mr. Barnes says he believes that, in the '90s, pop radio will continue to fragment, reflecting the aging of the baby boomers, their continued spending power and their outright disdain for beat-heavy pop.

Says Sean Ross, radio editor of *Billboard:* "The days when 'American Pie' came out on Monday and everyone was talking about it by Friday are gone. But I believe it can happen again."

The Z100 crew hopes so, too, but it's easier said than programmed. Gary Bryan says it has been his dream to invite a bunch of legendary black '50s disk jockeys in and let them play their favorite 45's from that period. "You know, it might be fun to return to that sense of anarchy," he muses, turning to his co-host. "Ross, will anarchy *ever* happen here?"

"Nope," says Mr. Brittain, chuckling and shaking his head. "*Highly* doubtful." Case closed.

Outside the confines of the Z100 studios, though, the situation is not such a laughing matter. Lost in a morass of generation gaps and market research, pop radio's power and signal grow a little dimmer every day.

Orson Welles' "War of the Worlds"

On October 30, 1938, Orson Welles' *Mercury Theater on the Air* broadcast over CBS a dramatization of an H. G. Wells story about an invasion from Mars. Although the announcer in New York interrupted three times to emphasize that it was a dramatization, many listeners believed it was a news story; some distraught people fled into the streets in terror. The uproar resulted in a reexamination of the responsibility of broadcasters to their audience.

Perspective 6-3 consists of several excerpts from the program, and Perspective 6-4 is a commentary by well-known columnist Dorothy Thompson about the implications of the audience's reaction. The column appeared on November 2, 1938, in the *New York Herald Tribune*. (Remember that Thompson's commentary was written against the backdrop of impending war in Europe.)

Consider:

1. Which events described in the script do you think would most frighten an audience?

2. Do you agree with Dorothy Thompson that the event proves how easy it is to start a "mass delusion"?

3. How is Thompson's commentary a criticism of the use of propaganda techniques? What evidence does she use to support her assertion?

4. Is it possible today for the media to create what Thompson calls "mass prejudices and mass divisions and schisms"? Why? Why not?

War of the Worlds

Orson Welles

ANNOUNCER
Ladies and gentlemen, here is the latest bulletin from the Intercontinental Radio News, Toronto, Canada: Professor Morse of Macmillan University reports observing a total of three explosions on the planet Mars, between the hours of 7:45 P.M. and 9:20 P.M., eastern standard time. This confirms earlier reports received from American observatories. Now, nearer home, comes a special announcement from Trenton, New Jersey. It is reported that at 8:50 P.M. a huge, flaming object, believed to be a meteorite, fell on a farm in the neighborhood of Grovers Mill, New Jersey, twenty-two miles from Trenton. The flash in the sky was visible within a radius of

several hundred miles and the noise of the impact was heard as far north as Elizabeth.

We have dispatched a special mobile unit to the scene, and we will have our commentator, Mr. Phillips, give you a word description as soon as he can reach there from Princeton. In the meantime, we take you to the Hotel Martinet in Brooklyn, where Bobby Millette and his orchestra are offering a program of dance music. (SWING BAND FOR 20 SECONDS . . . THEN CUT)

ANNOUNCER
We take you now to Grovers Mill, New Jersey. (CROWD NOISES . . . POLICE SIRENS)

PHILLIPS
Ladies and gentlemen, this is Carl Phillips again, at the Wilmuth farm, Grovers Mill, New Jersey. Professor Pierson and myself made the eleven miles from Princeton in ten minutes. Well, I . . . hardly know where to begin, to paint for you a word picture of the strange scene before my eyes, like something out of a modern Arabian Nights. Well, I just got here. I haven't had a chance to look around yet. I guess that's *it.* Yes, I guess that's the . . . *thing,* directly in front of me, half buried in a vast pit. Must have struck with terrific force. The ground is covered with splinters of a tree it must have struck on the way down. What I can see of the . . . object itself doesn't look very much like a meteor, at least not the meteors I've seen. It looks more like a huge cylinder. It has a diameter of . . . what would you say, Professor Pierson? . . .

ANNOUNCER
Ladies and gentlemen, I have a grave announcement to make. Incredible as it may seem, both the observations of science and the evidence of our eyes lead to the inescapable assumption that those strange beings who landed in the Jersey farmlands tonight are the vanguard of an invading army from the planet Mars. The battle which took

place tonight at Grovers Mill has ended in one of the most startling defeats ever suffered by an army in modern times; seven thousand men armed with rifles and machine guns pitted against a single fighting machine of the invaders from Mars. One hundred and twenty known survivors. The rest strewn over the battle area from Grovers Mill to Plainsboro crushed and trampled to death under the metal feet of the monster, or burned to cinders by its heat-ray. The monster is now in control of the middle section of New Jersey and has effectively cut the state through its center. Communication lines are down from Pennsylvania to the Atlantic Ocean. Railroad tracks are torn and service from New York to Philadelphia discontinued except routing some of the trains through Allentown and Phoenixville. Highways to the north, south, and west are clogged with frantic human traffic. Police and army reserves are unable to control the mad flight. By morning the fugitives will have swelled Philadelphia, Camden and Trenton, it is estimated, to twice their normal population.

At this time martial law prevails throughout New Jersey and eastern Pennsylvania. We take you now to Washington for a special broadcast on the National Emergency . . . the Secretary of the Interior . . . [pause]

ANNOUNCER
I'm speaking from the roof of Broadcasting Building, New York City. The bells you hear are ringing to warn the people to evacuate the city as the Martians approach. Estimated in last two hours three million people have moved out along the roads to the north, Hutchison River Parkway still kept open for motor traffic. Avoid bridges to Long Island . . . hopelessly jammed. All communication with Jersey shore closed ten minutes ago. No more defenses. Our army wiped out . . . artillery, air force, everything wiped out. This may be the last broadcast. We'll stay here to the end. . . . People are holding service below us . . . in the cathedral. (VOICES SINGING HYMN)

Now I look down the harbor. All manner of boats, overloaded with fleeing population, pulling out from docks. (SOUND OF BOAT WHISTLES)

Streets are all jammed. Noise in crowds like New Year's Eve in city. Wait a minute. . . . Enemy now in sight above the Palisades. Five great machines. First one is crossing river. I can see it from here, wading the Hudson like a man wading through a brook. . . . A bulletin's handed me. . . . Martian cylinders are falling all over the country. One outside Buffalo, one in Chicago, St. Louis . . . seem to be timed and spaced. . . . Now the first machine reaches the shore. He stands watching, looking over the city. His steel, cowlish head is even with the skyscrapers. He waits for the others. They rise like a line of new towers on the city's west side. . . . Now they're lifting their metal hands. This is the end now. Smoke comes out . . . black smoke, drifting over the city. People in the streets see it now. They're running towards the East River . . . thousands of them, dropping in like rats. Now the smoke's spreading faster. It's reached Times Square. People trying to run away from it, but it's no use. They're falling like flies. Now the smoke's crossing Sixth Avenue . . . Fifth Avenue . . . 100 yards away . . . it's fifty feet. . . .

War of the Worlds, by Orson Welles, as broadcast on the CBS radio network, October 30, 1938.

Mr. Welles and Mass Delusion

Dorothy Thompson

All unwittingly, Mr. Orson Welles and the *Mercury Theater on the Air* have made one of the most fascinating and important demonstrations of all time. They have proved that a few effective voices, accompanied by sound effects, can so convince masses of people of a totally unreasonable, completely fantastic proposition as to create nationwide panic.

They have demonstrated more potently than any argument, demonstrated beyond question of a doubt, the appalling dangers and enormous effectiveness of popular and theatrical demagoguery.

They have cast a brilliant and cruel light upon the failure of popular education.

They have shown up the incredible stupidity, lack of nerve and ignorance of thousands.

They have proved how easy it is to start a mass delusion.

They have uncovered the primeval fears lying under the thinnest surface of the so-called civilized man.

They have shown that man, when the victim of his own gullibility, turns to the government to protect him against his own errors of judgment.

The newspapers are correct in playing up this story over every other news event in the world. It is the story of the century.

And far from blaming Mr. Orson Welles, he ought to be given a Congressional medal and a national prize for having made the most amazing and important contribution to the social sciences. For Mr. Orson Welles and his theater have made a greater contribution to an understanding of Hitlerism, Mussolinism, Stalinism, anti-Semitism and all the other terrorisms of our times than all the words about them that have been written by reasonable men. They have made the *reductio ad absurdum* of mass manias. They have thrown more light on recent events in Europe leading to the Munich pact than everything that has been said on the subject by all the journalists and commentators.

Hitler managed to scare all Europe to its knees a month ago, but he at least had an army and an air force to back up his shrieking words.

But Mr. Welles scared thousands into demoralization with nothing at all.

That historic hour on the air was an act of unconscious genius, performed by the very innocence of intelligence.

Nothing whatever about the dramatization of the "War of the Worlds" was in the least credible, no matter at what point the hearer might have tuned in. The entire verisimilitude was in the names of a few specific places. Monsters were depicted of a type that nobody has ever seen, equipped with "rays" entirely fantastic; they were described as "straddling the Pulaski Skyway" and throughout the broadcast they were referred to as Martians, men from another planet.

A twist of the dial would have established for anybody that the national catastrophe was not being noted on any other station. A second of logic would have dispelled any terror. A notice that the broadcast came from a non-existent agency would have awakened skepticism.

A reference to the radio program would have established that the "War of the Worlds" was announced in advance.

The time element was obviously lunatic.

Listeners were told that "within two hours three million people have moved out of New York" — an obvious impossibility for the most disciplined army moving exactly as planned, and a double fallacy because only a few minutes before, the news of the arrival of the monster had been announced.

And of course it was not even a planned hoax. Nobody was more surprised at the result than Mr. Welles. The public was told at the beginning, at the end and during the course of the drama that it *was* a drama.

But eyewitnesses presented themselves; the report became second hand, third hand, fourth hand, and became more and more credible, so that nurses and doctors and National Guardsmen rushed to defense.

When the truth became known the reaction was also significant. The deceived were furious and of course demanded that the state protect them, demonstrating that they were incapable of relying on their own judgment.

Again there was a complete failure of logic. For if the deceived had thought about it they would realize that the greatest organizers of mass hysterias and mass delusions today are states using the radio to excite terrors, incite hatreds, inflame masses, win mass support for policies, create idolatries, abolish reason and maintain themselves in power.

The immediate moral is apparent if the whole incident is viewed in reason: no political body must ever, under any circumstances, obtain a monopoly of radio.

The second moral is that our popular and universal education is failing to train reason and logic, even in the educated.

The third is that the popularization of science has led to gullibility and new superstitions, rather than to skepticism and the really scientific attitude of mind.

The fourth is that the power of mass suggestion is the most potent force today and that the political demagogue is more powerful than all the other economic forces.

For, mind you, Mr. Welles was managing an obscure program, competing with one of the most popular entertainments on the air!

The conclusion is that the radio must not be used to create mass prejudices and mass divisions and schisms, either by private individuals or by government or its agencies, or its officials, or its opponents.

If people can be frightened out of their wits by mythical men from Mars, they can be frightened into fanaticism by the fear of Reds, or convinced that America is in the hands of sixty families, or aroused to revenge against any minority, or terrorized into subservience to leadership because of any imaginable menace.

The technique of modern mass politics calling itself democracy is to create a fear — a fear of economic royalists, or of Reds, or of Jews, or of starvation, or of an outside enemy — and exploit that fear into obtaining subservience in return for protection.

I wrote in this column a short time ago that the new warfare was waged by propaganda, the outcome depending on which side could first frighten the other to death.

The British people were frightened into obedience to a policy a few weeks ago by a radio speech and by digging a few trenches in Hyde Park, and afterward led to hysterical jubilation over a catastrophic defeat for their democracy.

But Mr. Welles went all the politicians one better. He made the scare to end scares, the menace to end menaces, the unreason to end unreason, the perfect demonstration that the danger is not from Mars but from the theatrical demagogue.

"Mr. Welles and Mass Delusion," by Dorothy Thompson, *New York Herald Tribune,* November 2, 1938.

The Importance of Radio as an Advertising Medium

Like magazines, radio can target an audience according to demographics such as interests, income, and age. The programming you choose defines you as an audience for an advertiser. To Charles D. Peebler, chief executive officer of a major advertising agency, radio is a very important part of the marketing mix.

Consider:

1. According to Peebler, what are radio's advantages for advertisers?

2. Why would Peebler's agency advise *The New York Times* to advertise on radio?

3. Which specific audiences does Peebler define that radio can deliver?

Radio's Unique Ability to Target and Deliver Specific Audience Segments

Charles D. Peebler

I am CEO of the only major advertising agency in America that commits nearly 15 per cent of the advertising funds placed in its trust to radio. For the most part, the rest of the top shops award radio anywhere from 5 to 10 per cent of the media spending pie. In fact, Bozell, Jacobs, Kenyon & Eckhardt, according to published and accurate reports appearing in the trade press . . . was this nation's Number 1 buyer of radio time, not just on a percentage basis, but in actual dollar volume as well.

Why should that be? Have we discovered the ultimate marketing and media mix? I would love to say "yes," but it wouldn't be true. Do we know something that all other agencies don't know? I hope so, but I don't think it has anything to do with the way we evaluate radio. I believe we assess radio's value in a manner not dissimilar to most other agencies. What then accounts for our obvious faith in the medium? Radio attracts and reaches its publics . . . all of them, young and old, men and women . . . by getting close to them . . . by delivering the programming and the values that each targeted audience segment wants to hear. So it's only natural that our buyers relate to radio's exceptional ability to get close to the customer. I'm a member of a small and vanishing breed of advertising executives who grew up "watching" radio. You heard me right. For those of you too young to remember [and sometimes I wish I were], we didn't merely listen to it on the radio . . . we watched it on the radio. Radio brought us soap operas and westerns, action and drama, comedy and variety, mystery and history, ballads and boogie.

Which of us watched it on the radio . . . and how many of us watched at the same time . . . depended on the appeal of the program. They didn't call it targeting back then, and markets weren't segments, but the objectives were the same . . . and believe me, they knew how to reach their audience. Radio brought to us entertainment, information and amusement. We brought it to our imagination. It was a pretty good trade-off then . . . and it's a pretty good trade-off now.

Newspaper Clients

In case you were not aware, one of our clients of whom we are most proud is *The New York Times*. In addition, we also represent, with equal pride, the *Minneapolis Star-Tribune* and the *Omaha World Herald*. But we'll turn to *The Times* to help me make my point. It's easy for us, you might say, to demonstrate our belief in radio by putting millions of Chrysler dollars into broadcast. After all, with a budget the size of Chrysler's, they're important players everywhere. But that certainly couldn't and wouldn't be true with *The New York Times*.

Their target market is too educated and the income level too high. In other words, radio is a terrible advertising medium for *The New York Times* . . . right? Wrong! Radio is, in fact, a great buy for *The New York Times*. It helps us reach precisely the audience we must: younger, better educated and high or higher income. We fine tune our demographics with the same care with which the New York Philharmonic's first violinist tunes his Stradivarius . . . and then we orchestrate the campaign.

By the way, I'd be remiss if I didn't point out that we not only try to buy radio creatively, we try to be creative on the radio.

Ringing the Cash Register

If there is one common thread among our heavy radio clients, it is that they are action-oriented. When they advertise, they expect something to happen — now — at the counter and at the cash register. Perhaps that's another reason why we buy radio at double and even triple the rate of the overall U.S. agency community.

Ten Bozell, Jacobs, Kenyon & Eckhardt clients spent over $1 million each in radio. . . . Number 1 and Chrysler had cars to sell . . . and they wanted action. American Airlines was close behind. They had seats to fill. And you better believe they wanted sales action, too . . . and like Chrysler, they relied on radio to help them get it.

Our Number 3 radio user, American Stores, lives in a totally different world. But they coexist in the same medium, and for many of the same cash register reasons. Where else can they tailor advertising to reach women 18 to 34? Then tailor it again to reach more women 35 to 49? And finally, custom fit it once again for ages 49 to 54? And just as important, they can actually afford to make different commercials appealing to each separate age group. Whether you're American Stores or Zale's Fine Jewelers, you talk to the millions of women in today's workforce, many of whom can be reached most effectively in their cars as they commute to and from the job.

Or, if you're Greyhound or McDonald's, we know how important it is for you to reach blacks, Hispanics and other minorities . . . or young adults, or seniors. Radio helps us find them and reach them, affordably and frequently.

CHAPTER 7
The Recording Industry

Name That Tune

People surveyed for this report from *American Demographics* were asked to choose whether they liked 20 different types of music. This information is important because it is different from surveys that show the sales of recording or radio station formats. The people who answered the survey questions didn't have to buy recordings or listen to the radio, so the study probably is a wider reflection of public taste than most other measurements.

Consider:

1. How are people's preferences for certain types of music affected by their age group, according to the study?

2. What is the most popular type of music? According to the survey, what are the characteristics of the audience for this music?

3. What do the survey results reveal about how people's ethnicity and gender affect their choice of music?

Name That Tune: Americans Reveal Their Favorite Types of Music

Nicholas Zill and John Robinson

What kind of music do you like? Ask the public that question, and you'll get differences in opinion that are just as divisive as those on abortion, gun control, or school prayer. Music tastes vary strongly by age, education, race, and gender, according to the 1992 Survey of Public Participation in the Arts. The survey, conducted for the National Endowment for the Arts (NEA) by the Census Bureau, provides vital new audience information to broadcasters and other businesses that buy, sell, or entertain with music.

The NEA survey asked adults whether they liked 20 different kinds of music, from grand opera to bluegrass. The resulting portrait differs in some interesting ways from other measures of musical popularity, such as a tally of record sales or a count of radio station formats. A major advantage of the survey is that everyone gets to vote, whether or not they buy records or listen to the radio. This approach describes the distinctive demographic profiles of each kind of music, but it also reveals a significant potential market among "crossover audiences" seeking more musical variety.

Country Is Most-Liked

More than half of adults say they like country/western music, placing it just ahead of mood/easy-listening music. Yet America's most popular form of music ranks second in record sales. Third place goes to rock, the leader in record sales. Blues or rhythm and blues is fourth, followed by gospel or hymns.

The top-five musical genres are liked by about 40 to 50 percent of the adult population, or between 72 and 96 million people. Yet the division between country-music fans and other forms of music represents the deepest of the many gulfs that define America's musical topography. Country audiences have a distinct demographic profile, and they tend not to cross over into other types of music.

The NEA survey also reveals a surprisingly large and growing audience for jazz and classical, the more high-brow and demanding music that doesn't sell many recordings. Each is liked by about one-third of U.S. adults, or more than 60 million people. Yet classical recordings represented just 4 percent of the total dollar volume of prerecorded music sales in 1993, according to the Recording Industry Association of America, while jazz recordings accounted for about 3 percent.

At the bottom of the popularity rankings are two radically different types of music, opera and rap. Opera is liked by just 13 percent of the adult population, rap is liked by 12 percent, and there is virtually no overlap between the two groups of fans. These may seem like small fractions, but each represents an audience of more than 22 million potential radio listeners, TV watchers, ticket holders, and record buyers. Nor do these rap numbers reflect teenagers under age 18, who were not included in the survey.

People may like many kinds of music, but almost everyone has a favorite. When asked to name the one type of music they like best, respondents again choose country over all others. Country/western music emerges as the top choice of 21 percent of adults, followed by rock (14 percent), gospel/hymns (9 percent), mood/easy listening (9 percent), classical (6 percent), and jazz (5 percent). Interestingly, these proportions for classical and jazz

music as top favorites are close to their shares of total record sales. Although one-third of adults say they like classical and jazz artists, much smaller numbers buy their recordings.

Rock's Generation Gap

Another demographic borderline in music preferences shows up in the age of rock music fans. Seven in ten young adults (aged 18 to 24) say they like rock, compared with only 7 percent of adults aged 75 and older. In the words of demographer Otis Dudley Duncan, that is not a generation gap: it is a cohort chasm.

Rock music is age-bound in other ways, too. Most adults who came of age during and after the 1950s are still fond of the music, and their parents still don't like it. Younger adults are also fond of jazz, blues, reggae, rap, and New-Age music. Older generations prefer easy listening, big-band music, Broadway tunes and operettas, classical, opera, and country/western. Some "older" kinds of music could eventually lose their audience if they do not find a way to attract younger fans, although some are making strides in this direction.

Yet another demographic divider shows up in opinions about classical music. Nearly two-thirds of adults who have been to graduate school like classical, compared with one-fourth of adults with no college education. But more schooling is also associated with greater appreciation for almost all other forms of music, including rock.

The major exception to the rule about education and music appreciation is country/western. The more educated the American, the less likely he or she is to enjoy country music. Most Americans (57 percent) whose education stops with a high school diploma like country, compared with 42 percent of college graduates. This difference is relatively small, however, and country is the seventh most popular music form among college grads.

Race is another musical divider. Not surprisingly, African Americans are considerably more likely than others to like music rooted in black culture, such as jazz, blues, rhythm and blues, soul, and rap. Yet blacks are less enthusiastic than whites about two other forms of music that have been strongly influenced by black composers and performers, namely big band and rock. Perhaps blacks see these two types of music as having been "taken over" by whites, despite the seminal roles of musicians like Duke Ellington, Count Basie, Chuck Berry, and Jimi Hendrix.

African Americans are much less interested in music that has its origin in white cultures. Blacks are only half as likely as whites to say they like classical music or Broadway show tunes, and only one-third as likely as whites to like country/western music. Yet black Americans have been major contributors to virtually all forms of music, from the country ballads of Charley Pride to the classical recitals of Jessye Norman. Also, the vast majority of fans for several types of "black" music are, in fact, white. Seven in ten adults who like jazz are white, as are 73 percent of those who like blues or rhythm and blues. Overall, whites may be less likely than blacks to appreciate jazz and blues — but non-Hispanic whites make up 78 percent of American adults.

Men and women have relatively minor differences in musical tastes. Yet certain stereotypes about music and the sexes may contain a grain of truth. Women prefer music that is gentler and more lyrical, while men tend to like their tunes fast and loud. Women have a greater preference for easy-listening music, show tunes, opera, and classical music, while men more strongly prefer rock, jazz, rhythm and blues, bluegrass, and rap. The sexes are about equal in their liking for country, folk, and big-band music.

Blues Explosion

Musical tastes are like other public tastes, and the popularity of each type of music changes over time. These changes are apparent when comparing the new survey with responses to similar questions asked for the National Endowment for the Arts in 1982 and 1985.

The most evident trend in America's musical tastes is a hefty increase in the popularity of blues, rhythm and blues, and soul music. The proportion of adults who like these forms of music has grown from about one-fourth of adults in 1982 and 1985 to around four-tenths in 1992.*

Another sizable change is a nine-point rise in the percentage of adults who like rock, from 35 percent in 1982 to 44 percent in 1992. Much of this growth is due to the number of people exposed to rock in their younger years. This process is likely to continue for several decades, until rock fans dominate the adult population.

The popularity of jazz, classical music, show tunes, and even opera has also increased significantly. This is clear evidence that young people's musical tastes evolve as they grow older. Comparisons across surveys within specific birth-year groups show that baby boomers are becoming distinctly more positive about classical music and jazz as they move from their 30s to their 40s. Yet the current generation of young adults may not follow this pattern. Due to changing trends in public education, baby busters had less exposure than boomers to music-appreciation classes in school. As a result, there is no guarantee that baby busters will undergo a similar transformation when they reach middle age.

The most puzzling trend in music preferences is a six-point decline in the percentage of adults who say they like country/western music. This seems to contradict recording-industry figures showing marked increases in sales of country music over the last five years. Sales of country recordings have grown almost threefold, from 7 percent of the

---

*The assessment of this change must remain somewhat imprecise because blues and soul were covered by a single question in 1982 and 1985 but by two questions in 1992.

total dollar volume of prerecorded music sales in 1989 to nearly 18 percent in 1993. How can the NEA data show a decline in popularity?

Some of the shrinkage in the proportion of adults who like country music could be attributed to the increase in average educational attainment over the last decade, because of the negative correlation between education levels and the preference for country. And even while the percentage of adults who say they like country has declined over the last decade, the absolute number of country fans has increased from 95 million to 96 million because of overall population growth.

The number of people who like country music is so large that a small increase in the number of recordings each fan purchases per year would produce a huge increase in sales. More spending by country fans could easily overwhelm the slight decline in share. This may explain most of the gap, because recording-industry data show that the middle-aged are a growing segment of the market for recorded music. Older buyers are considerably more likely than young adults or teenagers to be country-music fans.

Musical Variety

The NEA survey also raises an interesting question: why aren't there more musical variety shows? The data show that most Americans like several different kinds of music, but broadcasting has been moving toward increased market segmentation. Most radio stations play only a single form of music; a few stations play different music in different time slots. By narrowing their musical offerings, broadcasters hope to deliver an audience with known and desirable demographic characteristics to advertisers.

An unfortunate consequence of this trend is that people have fewer opportunities to broaden their musical horizons. Teenagers watch MTV, while senior citizens watch

reruns of the "Lawrence Welk Show," and each group has minimal exposure to the music of the other. To compound this problem, relatively few children today take music-appreciation classes. The result is that many young people are growing up unaware of America's rich musical legacy.

Once upon a time, Ed Sullivan managed to bring Elvis Presley and Isaac Stern together on the same top-rated television show. Today, the logic of market segmentation makes such a program all but impossible to support commercially. Yet the data show that average Americans appreciate many forms of music. Advertiser assumptions about musical tastes may be wrong.

There are now signs that the public is ready for an end to musical segregation. Music fans in their 20s are passionate about hard rockers like Pearl Jam and Soundgarden — but they are also partially responsible for the comeback of aging crooners like Tony Bennett and Frank Sinatra. Paul Simon, Peter Gabriel, and other stars have made their mark in the 1990s with multi-platinum recordings that mix rock with African and Latin rhythms. Earlier [in 1994], blues [singer] B. B. King even played at the grand opening of the Hard Rock Cafe in Beijing.

The NEA data give broadcasters and other businesses a rare opportunity to re-evaluate their assumptions. By serving the same diet of music to audiences over and over again, businesses may be trying to exploit group differences that are no longer significant. Americans' musical preferences are full of cohort chasms, but many listeners will cross over them whenever someone builds a bridge.

Blank Future for Cassette Tapes?

It took less than five years for the CD to replace the audiocassette tape as the most popular format for recorded music. In this article from the *Washington Post,* Paul Farhi says that some industry experts claim the audiocassette tape could even disappear.

Consider:

1. What are the consequences for *consumers* when technological changes, such as the replacement of cassette tapes by CDs, happen so fast?

2. What are the consequences for the *recording industry* when technological changes (like the replacement of cassette tapes by CDs) happen so fast?

3. Farhi says the rise of the CD offers a "window on the larger trend toward digitalization." Explain.

Compact Discs' Surging Popularity Could Hasten the Older Technology's Demise

Paul Farhi

Its first victim was the vinyl record, which disappeared from store shelves in about the time it takes to play the latest Top 40 hit. And now, the compact disc is doing a number on another old standard — the audiocassette tape.

Yes, the cassette — cheap, convenient, formerly ubiquitous — is slowly but surely making its way to the endangered species list thanks to the surging popularity of those shiny little discs with the crystal-clear sound.

With a swiftness that has surprised even people in the recording industry, the CD has shot past the cassette in unit sales and is far outrunning it in dollar volume. Cassette sales peaked five years ago [in 1989], and have dropped 25 percent since. Tape's inexorable decline — down another 4 percent in the first half of 1994 — has prompted some companies to stop releasing recordings on cassette.

"I guess it was bound to happen," said Kevin Stander, owner of Record & Tape

Traders, an eight-store chain in the Baltimore area. "CDs sound better, they're more durable, they're better quality." The chain now [in 1994] derives about 75 percent of its sales from CDs, up from about half [in 1992], prompting Stander to give some thought to changing his stores' increasingly anachronistic name.

As recently as 1989, prerecorded cassettes outsold CDs by more than 2 to 1, according to the Recording Industry Association of America [RIAA], a Washington-based group that represents manufacturers. (The vast majority of cassettes are sold with music already on them and are never used by the consumer for recording.) Just three years ago [in 1991], says the RIAA, the cassette was still hanging on as the most popular form of prerecorded media.

No more. Recording companies shipped nearly twice the number of discs as prerecorded tapes during the first half of 1994. In dollar terms, it isn't close — CDs represent a market nearly three times as large as cassettes, owing to both greater unit sales and relatively higher prices (the average list price of a CD was $11.92 vs. $8.34 for a tape in the first six months of [1994]).

The rise of the CD, and fall of the tape, offers a window on the larger trend toward digitalization, a shift to the technology of converting sound, images and text into the language understood by computers.

Much of electronic communications — telephone calls, television shows, movies, music — is moving toward digital media, which can store and manipulate information far more efficiently than its precursor, the analog technology used in records and most tapes.

For music buyers, digitalization has meant vastly superior sound quality. CD units use a laser to "read" electronic digits stored on a disc and a microprocessor to translate these numerical codes into sound. The result is sound free of the hiss and noise of conventional records and tapes.

At the same time, falling prices for CD players and discs have spurred an ever-broader market, putting CD players into an estimated 50 percent of all U.S. homes. Sophisticated CD hardware [in 1994] generally sells for less than $200 — down from more than $1,000 a decade [earlier] — and the price differential between discs and tapes has narrowed to about $3.60 from $4.56 two years ago, [in 1992].

What's more, said Jay Berman, chairman of the RIAA, home CD units offer superior convenience to tape players because CD players can be programmed to play as many as seven discs consecutively and to skip to selected recordings.

But people in the recording industry say cassettes won't suffer the same fate as vinyl — at least not as quickly — for two reasons: tapes are portable and enable consumers to make their own recordings.

Although the cassette market is in decline, it still represents an important part of the recording industry's sales, said Pete Jones, president of BMG Distribution, a unit of Bertelsmann AG, which owns the RCA and Arista record labels.

"The question is, is the glass half empty or half full?" Jones said. "It's clear many consumers continue to want cassettes. . . . There's still a huge demand for a portable [format]" — one that can be carried from a car stereo to a personal stereo to a boombox.

Well, give it time. Sales of car CD players and portable units such as Sony Corp.'s Discman personal stereo are booming as prices fall, indicating that many consumers are consigning their old tape players to the closet. Factory sales of portable CD hardware will climb to more than 14 million units in [1994], three times the level of 1991, according to estimates by the Electronic Industries Association.

Meanwhile, in a further assault on the portable market, two new portable digital formats are being touted, Philips Electronics' Digital Compact Cassette tapes and Sony's Mini-Disc.

Though neither has yet to capture much consumer interest — some say they have canceled each other out — Sony's Paul Smith remains confident.

Within five years [, by 1999], predicted Smith, chairman of Sony's music distribution arm, Mini-Disc sales will outstrip conventional tapes.

"The future," he said, "is in digital."

PERSPECTIVE 7-3

Electronic Composers

As synthesizers replace traditional instruments, music has gone digital. Reproducing the sounds of an entire orchestra with one keyboard is affordable for even the amateur musician. In this article from *Business Week,* the authors describe the potential of digital sound.

Consider:

1. How have synthesizers changed the economics of the music business?

2. What musical benefits do music systems like the Kurzweil 250 offer for musicians and composers?

3. What are the benefits of MIDI?

4. Do you agree that musicians are being given unprecedented creative tools or will all the music eventually sound the same? Explain.

Music Is Alive with the Sound of High Tech

Terri Thompson,
Carlo Wolff, and Dan Cook

In the 1960s composer Walter Carlos created a sensation with a recording he called *Switched-On Bach*. Using one of the first music synthesizers, devices that electronically mimic a variety of musical instruments, Carlos spent months creating sounds, recording the music bit by bit, and editing together thousands of snippets of tape. The result: a top-selling album of electronically produced classical compositions that sounded as if they were played on a harpsichord—sort of.

From Bach to rock, musical technology has changed since then. Carlos still flouts convention: He's had a sex-change operation and now is called Wendy. But electronic music is no longer the stuff of the avant-garde. These days, anyone capable of playing a keyboard instrument can be a one-man band. For only hundreds of dollars, today's electronic instruments will respond with sounds respectably close to those of a concert grand piano, a whole orchestra, a vast choir, or just about anything that the player can dream up.

Sax and Violins

With a technique called digital sampling, the sound of a car door slamming or a dog barking can be turned into music that can be played at any pitch. These sounds are captured and stored as numerical values on floppy disks; to clone sounds, the sampler merely recalculates the numerical values. Flip a switch and you can "sample" patches of existing recordings. If you don't like it as a violin, punch a key and it's a saxophone. If you want to see it as sheet music, print it with a personal computer.

Artists from Stevie Wonder to French composer-conductor Pierre Boulez are embracing the new technology. Instead of practicing in soundproof rooms or copying sheet music a note at a time, musicians wearing headphones are sitting at music workstations that look more like a control panel at NASA than musical instruments. Indeed, the new technology is revolutionizing the way music is played, composed, studied—and enjoyed.

Even New York's Juilliard School, the most respected conservatory in the U.S. and a bastion of classicism, has embraced high tech. It opened its first electronic studio in 1987 thanks to donations of synthesizers and music editing equipment from Yamaha International Corp., a leading producer of new music technology. "It's the wave of the future," says Dean Bruce MacCombie. "Better to get involved with it than to pretend it doesn't exist."

It exists, all right. . . . That's because the plunging cost of the computer power needed to make electronic systems work means they are affordable to more people. At the same time, escalating labor and material costs have

caused prices for acoustic pianos to nearly double over the past five years. . . .

[In 1987] an estimated 25 million people in the U.S. played keyboard instruments. And thanks to the new musical technology, predicts Robert Moog, the first to use a keyboard rather than knobs and dials on a synthesizer in the early 1960s, "musical activity on the part of amateurs will increase."

Despite the pioneering developments in the U.S., it took the Japanese to make the market sing. Composer Larry Fast, who has been creating synthesizer music [since the 1960s], remembers working on a synthesizer that used a mainframe computer and cost $2 million when he was a researcher at AT&T Bell Laboratories in Murray Hill, N.J., in the 1970s. But in 1983, Yamaha swept into the U.S. with its DX7. The portable keyboard did everything the monster at Bell Labs could— and sold for $2,000. [In 1987], for a mere $400, "you can get a Yamaha synthesizer with features that were lacking in the DX7," says Fast. And other foreign manufacturers, including Casio, Akai, Roland, and Korg, now dominate the market along with Yamaha.

Steinway Sound

The U.S. is not completely out of the picture, however. Although Moog's original company folded in 1977, he has joined forces with Raymond C. Kurzweil, a computer scientist and entrepreneur, who has put his small, Waltham (Mass.) company, Kurzweil Music Systems Inc., at the forefront of electronic music. While many developers of electronic instruments concentrated on adding new sounds to composers' vocabularies, Kurzweil set out to reproduce faithfully the sound of traditional instruments and the response of high-quality piano keyboards.

In 1983, Kurzweil introduced its prototype of the Kurzweil 250. Instead of using analog circuits, like those in the first electronic synthesizers, this new generation of musical instrument has gone digital. To create the sound of, say, a key on a Steinway piano, it simply calls from its computer memory the sound of that note and reproduces it through speakers. To all but the most discerning, the sound is very close to the real thing.

But that system — and similar ones from the Ensoniq, E-mu Systems, Lowrey Electronics, Oberheim Electronics, Sequential Circuits, and Yamaha — can do far more. They sound just as good mimicking a violin, a flute, or a massive chorus. And they can do all those things at once. A musician can "layer" sounds on top of one another, so a single keystroke can simultaneously produce the same note sounded by a guitar, piano, or a full string section. Or, with a so-called sequencer function, the musician can play a part on one instrument and store it, then add another part while the first part is being played back, and so on, gradually creating a full orchestra.

But it's not just the individual instruments that are driving the revolution in music. It is an industry standard known as MIDI, short for Musical Instrument Digital Interface. While companies trying to automate factories still can't agree on protocols that will let their dissimilar equipment communicate, in 1983 music makers agreed on MIDI. It allows a musician to hook up synthesizers, electronic drums, and organs to a single keyboard and connect the entire system to a personal computer, regardless of the manufacturer. MIDI is the conduit through which all the signals pass from one instrument to another.

That way, all the information can be stored in digital form in the computer's memory, rather than on recording tape. So the composer can manipulate it in ways that were unheard of a few years ago. Play a tune on the keyboard, and the written notes appear on the computer screen. Change a note on the screen, and the computer plays back the corrected version. Don't like the tempo? Have the computer change it. Or alter the key, or change the violin part to a flute. Nor does the composer have to be adept at the keyboard. A saxophone player, for example, can hook up a so-called "wind-controller" and play music into the system, then tell the composer to play it back through the synthesizer. Or MIDI can turn the sound from the saxophone into an entire orchestra.

Miami Heist?

Professional musicians quickly saw the potential in linking instruments to computers. Since the MIDI standard was introduced, sales of computer hardware and software based on MIDI have shot up to about $500 million, and the market is expected to double . . . . The latest generation of personal computers from Apple, Atari, Commodore, and IBM accommodates the technology. Many brands of musical software are available for $50 to $500. And the five top manufacturers of synthesizers are building MIDI into all but their lowest-priced instruments.

Such changes are not without controversy. The biggest battle centers around the so-called digital sampling technology. These devices are so adept at stealing others' sounds — even styles and human voices — that composers soon will have at their disposal unlimited electronic "sidemen" stored on computer chips. Put Beverly Sills singing a high C into the memory, for instance, and a digital sampler can play it back as a high D, or any other note. Hit two keys at once, and you hear two Beverly Sills. Play a few notes in sequence, and you have Sills singing a melody she never sang before.

Professional musicians have taken the issue to court. David Earl Johnson, a struggling percussionist, is suing the producers of *Miami Vice,* claiming the theme music of the popular TV show rips off his conga sound. Johnson says that the composer of the score with the pulsating beat had sampled his conga playing at a recording session and later used his sound without compensating him.

To protect his latest record album, Frank Zappa has taken the precaution of copyrighting against sampling.

Now that entire orchestras can be replaced by synthesizers, some worry that thousands of musicians may be put out of work. Others fear that music as an artistic endeavor will stagnate as the new crop of musicians become ever more dependent on technology.

Most, though, believe new technology is giving musicians unprecedented creative tools. After all, what past composer could invent new instruments at will, make music from any sound, and hear their compositions just seconds after they were written?

"We want to revolutionize music making," says Jeffrey G. Gusman, R&D manager at Yamaha Communications Center Inc. in New York. "We are supplying the artist with the tools he needs." Even Bruce A. Stevens, president of venerable piano maker Steinway & Sons, believes "there is a world of opportunity for the use of computers" in music. Nor does he expect it to put him out of business. He is convinced that after musicians learn how to play an electronic keyboard, they'll want to upgrade to a fine acoustic piano.

No one is happier with the new wind blowing through music than Wendy Carlos. It will lead to "a lot of alternative styles," she says. "This is the first time I've felt I haven't needed to apologize for producing electronic music."

"Music Is Alive with the Sound of High Tech," by Terri Thompson, Carlo Wolff, and Dan Cook, *Business Week,* No. 3023, October 26, 1987. Copyright © 1987 by McGraw-Hill, Inc. Used with special permission of *Business Week.*

The Cost of Sound

The recording industry includes not only all the recording artists but also all the employees of recording studios that produce the sounds you hear. This article describes the relationship between recording company profits and the recording studio business.

Consider:

1. What major factors have affected recording studio profits recently ?

2. How does changing technology affect the costs?

3. What is "organic recording"? Do you agree that it may be the trend for future music? Why? Why not?

The Beat Goes On, But It Costs Lots More

William K. Knoedelseder, Jr.

When a singer goes into a recording studio to cut an album, the money for the session is usually paid by a record[ing] company in the form of an advance against the artist's royalties on the eventual sale of the record[ing].

The success of the studio business, therefore, is tied directly to the performance of the record[ing] industry at large. In [the 1980s], that has meant hard times for studio operators.

For example, according to the Recording Industry Association of America, the major record companies released 4,170 new albums in 1978. The following year, as the record industry began to feel the effects of declining sales, only 3,575 new albums were released.

In 1980, the number fell to 3,000. By 1984, with the record industry in a full-blown depression, the number had dropped to 2,170.

In 1985, the number of new releases started inching upward again as the record industry began recovering from its slump.

The problem is, the recovery has been fueled largely by the sale of older records reissued on compact disks — records that don't require additional time at the recording studio. . . .

Making matters worse for the studios, belt-tightening by the record companies has reduced the average recording budget for an album from about $125,000 a few years ago to between $80,000 and $100,000 [in 1988], according to studio operators.

And with home studios siphoning off recording time, studio operators estimate that their share of an average album's recording budget has fallen to between 50 and 60 percent.

In 1967, the Beatles' classic album "Sgt. Pepper's Lonely Hearts Club Band" was recorded using what was then state-of-the-art studio technology: a four-track tape-recording machine. That meant that four different elements — vocals, guitars, drums and piano — were recorded separately and then combined on a single half-inch tape.

In the [following] 21 years, technological advances in sound recording have made four-track recording seem almost as primitive as, well, chiseling in stone.

[In 1988], the state of the art is 48-track recording. For music lovers, the advances have meant better-sounding records; for studio operators, they've meant huge expenses. A 24-track recorder — considered the minimum for professional recording — can cost $25,000 to $90,000. A 32-track digital recorder costs about $140,000.

One studio operator estimates that to keep up with technology and remain competitive, a studio must completely upgrade its equipment "every 2½ or three years — consoles, tape machines, new mikes, the whole schmear."

When Chris Stone opened his famous Record Plant studio in 1968, "fully equipped, including construction, right down to the floor tile, it cost $75,000," he said. "Today, [in 1988,] that same room would cost $1.5 million."

[In 1988, after] a five-year onslaught of computerized pop music — what one sound engineer described as "two skinny English kids, a synthesizer and a drum machine" — studio operators say they are witnessing a backlash.

"Right now, the cutting edge is live music; some of the new young bands are looking down on synthesized sound," said one veteran recorder, adding with a chuckle: "They actually think they've discovered something new; they're calling it 'organic recording.'"

"The Beat Goes On, But It Costs Lots More," by William K. Knoedelseder, Jr. From "Memo: Recording Studios," *Los Angeles Times,* July 4, 1988. © 1988 *Los Angeles Times.* Used with permission of *Los Angeles Times.*

The Television Industry

PERSPECTIVE 8-1

The Big Three Networks

In the 1980s, as cable television began to capture a growing portion of the audience, and the networks' share of viewers declined, several observers predicted the end of network television. Why would people watch network TV when cable offered so many other choices? But in the 1990s, network television responded to the competition, and the networks' share stabilized. This article, from the *Boston Globe,* details the strategy the networks used to stay ahead.

Consider:

1. Describe three strategies the networks are using to maintain their audience share.

2. Why is program distribution so important to the networks?

3. Explain the effect of 1995 FCC rules allowing the networks to produce and syndicate more of their own programming.

The Established TV Networks Move Fast to Lock Up the Choice Channels

Frederic M. Biddle

Fast: What spins most often on TV these days? The "Wheel of Fortune"? . . . [not] for long. Before year's end [1994] a nationwide TV channel shuffle will spin dials fast enough to daze even Vanna White and Robert Shapiro—not to mention millions of viewers.

Variety magazine estimates that up to 40 percent of the nation's 94 million television households will soon be forced to change channels to locate their favorite shows— or will discover new shows on their old favorite channels.

As chaotic as it all may seem to viewers, network executives say the shuffle is crucial to their organizations' long-term survival. As new networks try to crowd onto the broadcast dial, the big three and upstart Fox Inc. are scrambling to lock up the choice channels in as many markets as possible.

In Boston, for example, CBS will soon abandon WHDH-TV (Ch. 7) in favor of WBZ-TV (Ch. 4). The reason: CBS signed a deal with, 'BZ's owner, Group W Television, to secure affiliations with several other big-city Group W stations. That one move has set off [changes] in Boston broadcasting as NBC seeks a new Boston affiliate and WHDH seeks a new network.

Despite the peerless hype of cable television's place on the information superhighway, the reaffiliation deals are the latest proof that network TV is alive and kicking. Last season [in 1993] ABC, CBS and NBC stanched a decade-long loss of audience to cable, with their combined audience share holding at 61 percent. Although that showing is partly attributable to one-time blockbusters like [the 1993] Winter Olympic Games, it reminded everyone in the industry that network television remains the best way — the only way — to consistently deliver audiences in tens of millions night after night.

The reaffiliation deals also illustrate the television industry's rediscovery of the value of channels 2–13. With more broadcast power than the higher-numbered UHF stations, the 2–13 VHF channels remain the key to reaching and retaining huge audiences.

To be sure, UHF channels come in just as clearly as VHF channels — for the two-thirds of Americans who have cable TV. But non-cable viewers often need rabbit-ears antennas to tune in to stations on the sometimes-fuzzy UHF band. Many don't bother. A network's move from UHF to VHF can mean a 1 or 2 percent increase in audience share in a given market, a critical margin in the hyper-competitive TV world.

It is this logic that inspired Fox Inc., the 8-year-old network that was born [in 1986] on UHF, to raid affiliates of enemy networks in May [1994]. Fox swiped 12 VHF channels from the big three networks, including eight from CBS. The stations were owned or in the process of being acquired by New World Communications Inc.; Fox snagged them by investing $500 million in New World.

Fueling competition is the fact that Fox and the big three networks aren't the only contenders for the federally limited number of television stations.

Paramount Communications Inc. and Time Warner Inc. have announced plans to go on the air as the fifth and sixth broadcast television networks. . . . Thus far neither has secured enough affiliates to make a go of it — but their efforts are driving everyone to keep dealing.*

It's like "fitting a square peg into a round-hole," says Jonathan Klein, president of Westinghouse Broadcasting Inc.'s Group W Television unit. "What's changed is having the same . . . number of VHF stations available, but more networks — Fox — and down the horizon, Paramount and Time Warner."

Indeed, Fox's May raid begat rebound affiliation deals by CBS and ABC, which suddenly looked at key cities and found themselves either without affiliated stations or facing the threat of losing affiliates. (Federal Communications Commission rules will require New World to sell some of its stations such as WSBK-V (Ch. 38) in Boston; thus not all channels now under New World control will move to Fox.)

Both CBS and ABC wooed E. Scripps Co. [In June 1994] ABC won that round, announcing a 10-year agreement guaranteeing that five Scripps stations, including current ABC affiliates in Detroit and Cleveland, will stick with the network. So desperate was ABC that it abandoned VHF stations in several smaller markets in return for the sworn allegiance of Scripps' Detroit and Cleveland VHF properties.

CBS ended up cutting its deal: with Group W, signing the 10-year agreement that jolted Boston TV.

"What the networks obviously in all three cases clearly were able to do was secure distribution," Anthony Malara, CBS's chief of affiliate relations, says of the deals with New World, Group W and Scripps.

CBS, which already owned stations in the four largest markets, nailed down long-term affiliation in San Francisco and Boston, the fifth- and sixth-largest markets. And by allying itself with Group W without purchasing the broadcast group outright, CBS sidestepped federal regulations forbidding a network from owning television stations reaching more than 25 percent of TV households. Collectively, stations owned by CBS and Group W cover nearly a third of U.S. television householders.

Similarly, Fox's agreement with New World enables that network to effectively control more television stations than it could legally own.

But the deal-making involves syndication as well as distribution, with syndication creating a big incentive for organizations like Group W to get cozy with a network.

Group W and New World are both up-and-coming syndicators of shows such as the recently canceled "Vicki!" talk show (Group W) and Channel 38's new late-night soap "Valley of the Dolls" (New World).

Beginning in November 1995 FCC rules will allow the networks to produce and syndicate reruns of more of their own programming, a move that's sure to shut out many syndicators who don't have an "in" with the networks.

What effect the affiliation deals will have beyond the bottom lines and strategic positions of the networks is disputed.

While the dealmakers insist the impact on viewers will be minimal—"It's no watershed," says Group W's Klein—there will be an adjustment period that could mean falling ratings.

CBS has said it plans to spend millions to reeducate TV viewers who will blink when they suddenly see the famous CBS eye on new channels. Robert A. Iger, ABC Network Television Group president, told TV critics in Hollywood [in July 1994]: "When a network switches stations in a marketplace, it creates a confusion that takes a pretty long time to recover from."

In many affected markets, advertisers are trying to figure out which stations they should buy time on, considering that some stations are due to switch affiliations in mid-season [1994-95]. "Estimating ratings points will be a real challenge," said Rosemary Bell, executive vice president of media services for Pro Media in Needham, "because new viewers are going to have to look to find out where their favorite programs are, and that leads to sampling of new shows."

The scramble for stations might also make it that much harder for Paramount and Time Warner to realize their network dreams. "There's going to be no good place for a fifth network to go," says Gary Arlen, president of Arlen Communications Inc., an industry consultant. In Boston, for example, Time Warner has affiliated with WLVI-TV (Ch. 56), a UHF station, and Paramount has yet to announce a Boston affiliate.

Of course, if Networks 5 and 6 do succeed, there are ramifications for ABC, NBC and CBS that airwave piracy won't solve.

"The three networks are inevitably going to have to change as a result of the fragmentation of the TV audience," Arlen says — all the more if audiences resume their defection to cable TV. "What will happen when shows on the broadcast networks start getting 1 ratings? Would CBS be able to run such a show against 'Roseanne'?"

*Note: Paramout and Time Warner each launched new networks in 1995.

"Feeding Frenzy: The Established TV Networks Move Fast to Lock Up the Choice Channels," by Frederic M. Biddle, *Boston Globe,* July 24, 1994. Reprinted courtesy of *The Boston Globe.* Dow//Quest Story ID: 0000350356DC.

Keeping Track

The A. C. Nielsen Company is the only company in the United States that provides ratings — a report on the share of audience each station delivers — to television stations and advertising agencies. Accurate ratings are important because they determine how much advertising agencies will charge advertisers to reach a specific audience. Recently, broadcasters have charged that the ratings are seriously flawed. This article from *The Wall Street Journal* describes the networks' challenge to Nielsen, which may lead to some changes in the way ratings information is gathered in the future.

Consider:

1. Describe the major points of criticism from broadcasters and advertising agencies about the methods the A. C. Nielsen Company uses to gather audience information.

2. How does the A. C. Nielsen Company respond to the criticism?

3. What role will the passive people meter play in changing the information that is gathered? Do you think it will work? Why? Why not?

If Measuring TV Audiences Is Inaccurate Today, Critics Ask, What Happens When Things Get Really Complicated?

Thomas R. King

It's 1999, a little before 8 P.M., and the multimedia, interactive big-screen television in the Smith house has just been turned on. The Smiths are a "Nielsen family," one of a few thousand nationwide whose tastes in programming still dictate which shows get renewed and how billions of advertising dollars are spent.

But unlike Nielsen families of the mid-1990s, who had to keep track of their choices by laboriously pushing buttons or making entries in a viewing diary, the Smiths need do nothing but vegetate in front of the set. They have a "passive people meter," which has a sensor buried inside that takes "pictures" of all those watching. If Junior stays tuned for all of "The Brides of Beverly Hills, 90210," the system knows. If Dad leaves during a commercial of "The Tonight Show Starring Martin Lawrence," the system notes that, too.

The TV-ratings gurus at A. C. Nielsen Co. say this may be one of the main ways to track viewing in the future. Nielsen's critics, however, argue that the concept has serious flaws. They say that it raises alarming privacy issues that will keep consumers from accepting it, and that it falls far short of what will be needed to track viewing as the audience splinters among new kinds of viewing choices in the 500-channel age.

The search for a more reliable ratings system is a serious quest. Advertisers buy more than $30 billion of television time annually based on Nielsen's national and local ratings. They, along with TV stations and ad agencies, have criticized Nielsen's methods for years, but now their complaints are reaching a feverish pitch. Their longtime worries —that Nielsen has faulty sampling methods and flawed recruitment procedures that produce defective data that doesn't accurately report who's watching TV—are now being replaced with what may be a far more dire concern:

If Nielsen can't accurately track TV viewing today, its critics ask, how will it be able to keep pace as the nature of television changes rapidly tomorrow?

Nielsen rejects the premise of the criticism. "Our data isn't perfect and probably never will be," says John Dimling, president and chief operating officer at Nielsen Media Research U.S.A., the New York-based unit that runs the company's ratings operation. "But it's better than any commercial data that's available, and we're working to make it better and better." As for the 500-channel future, he adds, "certainly the technology will change, but not the fundamentals" of audience measurement.

Nielsen's harshest critics say the multimedia age may enable other companies to provide better audience information. The builders of the information superhighway promise technology that will report exactly who watched what programs when. Supersmart set-top boxes might be able to spit out information that could be used to produce a complete census of precisely who watched what—not simply a sample of the audience, as Nielsen has done for so long.

But executives of Nielsen, a unit of Dun & Bradstreet Corp. of Westport, Conn., say they fully expect to be the principal assessors of TV audiences well into the future. Their current system is already compatible with the superhighway, they claim, pointing to Nielsen's tracking of a Time Warner Inc. 150-channel Quantum system in New York. That system is a "near video-on-demand" service in which subscribers can "access" movies and special-events programs—and Nielsen meters connected to set-top boxes record each request as it's made.

That doesn't mean Nielsen won't have to make some adjustments. Mr. Dimling says the company is making significant improvements in its current methodology. Over the next several months [in the fall of 1994], it will expand the number of households it uses for national ratings by 25%, to 5,000. It says it has also improved training of Nielsen families to get more accurate data from them.

For the customers that buy its information, Nielsen is investing heavily in a state-of-the-art system to deliver ratings data faster and in more detail. Mr. Dimling also says Nielsen is "sharing information" with an assortment of companies that are designing tomorrow's program pipelines, with an eye toward hooking up to viewers' set-top boxes or other equipment.

Still, many industry officials are skeptical of Nielsen's promises. Nicholas Schiavone, vice president of media and marketing research at General Electric Co.'s NBC television unit, says: "I hate to invoke my mother here, but she used to say to me, 'Actions speak louder than words. And you know, Nick, talk is cheap.'"

The problem, Mr. Schiavone says, is that Nielsen has been doing business the same way for decades. And since Britain's AGB Television Research, its only competitor, folded its U.S. operations in 1988, Nielsen has had a monopoly on the business and little incentive to make improvements.

In 1989, the Committee on Nationwide Television Audience Measurement, or Contam, whose members include the three major TV networks and the National Association of Broadcasters, concluded in a study that the company's "people meter" was producing seriously flawed data. The committee said the people meter, which requires each viewer to press some buttons when he or she starts or stops watching television, demanded too much effort to be accurate.

But Nielsen, members of Contam say, didn't bat an eyelash. "Nothing of significance or substance has changed," says NBC's Mr. Schiavone, who also serves as Contam's current chairman. "There was no midcourse correction on their part, and we have the same measure we had [in 1989]. There's one difference: The TV environment is much more complex now than it was in 1989, and it's only going to get more so."

Nielsen executives are betting that the information highway's developers—perhaps ventures between cable-TV companies and telephone companies or engineers of two-way cable systems—won't elect to plunge into the business of audience measurement. Beware the hype, they say; there may be so few people hooked up for many years that it would be hard to get a legitimate sample just from the superhighway. In which case, who would measure homes that choose to stay off the superhighway? And even if every home is wired, what about TV sets that aren't wired within those homes?

Nielsen executives see other basic problems if huge cable-telephone-studio ventures try to create a measuring service. "Why would advertisers and their agencies want to have audience data supplied to them by the very same companies who are selling the time?" Mr. Dimling asks. "I think there is an implied conflict of interest in that arrangement."

Nielsen believes the cable-telephone ventures will instead be a provider of data

to Nielsen, which in turn will crunch the numbers and come up with the census. This would make manipulation of data by program providers less likely, Mr. Dimling argues. Nielsen, he says, is uniquely positioned to decipher information from multiple sources and present it to its customers in a meaningful way.

For now, the many companies scrambling to design the television set-top boxes say they aren't interested in getting into audience measurement—but suggest that their expertise might help Nielsen do a better job. "Our boxes are going to give Nielsen a vastly improved tool set," says Geoff Roman, vice president of technology and business development at General Instrument Corp. of Chicago, a leading maker of cable-converter boxes. "But I wouldn't see us as a competitor to them."

Nielsen may face new competition anyway. Contam executives, undaunted by Nielsen's snub in 1989, are returning with another effort. They recently hired Statistical Research Inc., a research company in Westfield, N.J., to run a "laboratory" that . . . will test a ratings system the networks believe will produce more accurate data. Contam says the lab will be open to Nielsen and hopes the research giant will adopt some of the techniques it tests. Though Contam officials say they know it will be costly and complicated to start a rival system, they add that they're prepared to do so if Nielsen doesn't adopt some of the strategies they plan to showcase.

At least publicly, Nielsen doesn't profess to be concerned about such threats. Instead, it prefers to talk about the passive people meter, created to tell more about who is watching television, the aspect of audience measurement that Nielsen regards as something akin to the Holy Grail.

The passive people meter, which Nielsen [planned] to test in a small market at the end of [1994], has an imaging system that takes digitized "photographs" of all those watching.

The meter's memory is programmed to recognize the faces of everyone in a household and to record what each person watches.

Many media executives, however, say the passive meter will be sunk by privacy concerns. Critics say consumers won't go for a system that takes pictures of them in their bedrooms — where, statistics show, Americans do a significant amount of TV viewing.

"Could they get 4,000 homes to sign up to try it?" Mr. Schiavone asks. "Probably. But what you'd end up with is a sample of exhibitionists. I'm simply saying they're not representative." Calling the passive people meter "a Faustian bargain, a deal with the devil," he adds: "Nielsen just doesn't seem to understand that this is a measurement system that amounts to a wholesale invasion of privacy."

Nielsen says the critics are overreacting. "Any kind of Big Brother intrusion is really far beyond the passive meter's capability or purpose," Mr. Dimling says. "The only information collected and transmitted is that 'person No. 1' is watching television." Mr. Dimling says the passive meter represents an advance because it eliminates the effort Nielsen families now must make to record what they watch.

The information gathered and reported by the passive people meter will be completely different from the data Nielsen currently reports. Because of the continuous nature of the meter's data—it tracks images of the viewers on a second-by-second basis—Nielsen says it will finally be possible to see whether viewers stay in the room or turn the channel when, say, "Seinfeld" goes to a commercial break.

Nielsen says the passive meter will represent a particular advance in tracking viewing by children and teenagers, who have been the most difficult to measure because they aren't as reliable as adults in filling out diaries or working the traditional people meter. What's more, Nielsen says, the passive meter should erase any lingering concerns on the part of broadcasters that "button-pushing fatigue" from the traditional people meter skews ratings.

Says Mr. Dimling, "It doesn't require that people in the sample wear a badge, a wristwatch or wrap an antenna around their head."

"If Measuring TV Audiences Is Inaccurate Today, Critics Ask, What Happens When Things Get Really Complicated?" by Thomas R. King, *The Wall Street Journal,* September 9, 1994. Reprinted by permission of *The Wall Street Journal,* © 1994 Dow Jones & Company, Inc. All Rights Reserved Worldwide. Dow//Quest Story ID: 0000301897WJ.

Satellite Weather Network

When you watch the local weather on TV, you probably assume that the weathercaster is reporting from your local TV station. This article shows how one enterprising company has standardized the weather format for delivery to many stations at once from a central location in Jackson, Mississippi.

Consider:

1. Do you agree that TV weathercasters "enjoy a level of trust and dependence others in the public eye don't"? Why is the issue of trust important?

2. This centralized delivery of weather reports could establish a precedent for the delivery of other elements of your local newscast. Which other elements of news could be adapted to a similar central delivery system?

3. What are the economic implications for local broadcasters and for local television reporters if parts of the newscast are produced outside of the local market?

You May Not Know Your Weatherman Is in Jackson, Miss.

Dave Barber, the local weatherman for WTLW-TV in Lima, Ohio, nods and smiles into the camera as news anchors Brad Schultz and Lisa Kroehler chat about celebrating the first anniversary of their station's newscast.

"I'm looking forward to the cake and ice cream after work, Brad and Lisa," says Mr. Barber before launching into his nightly weather report. It's going to be cloudy in Lima, with scattered showers, he says.

But Mr. Barber won't be needing his raincoat. And he won't be eating any of that cake and ice cream, either. For Mr. Barber is about

700 miles away, under the clear skies of Jackson, Miss. Jackson, of all places, is home to National Weather Network Inc., a tiny company with a big lesson in TV reality for viewers scattered around the country: Your trusty local weatherman may be an illusion.

Lima to Panama City

Seven days a week, NWN's dozen or so employees beam customized, localized weather reports to about 50 TV stations, reaching, the company says, some 18 million households. After signing off with Brad and Lisa in Lima, for instance, Mr. Barber moves on to Panama City, Fla., and many other places. Satellite technology and up-to-the-minute data from the National Weather Service make these feats possible.

Most viewers haven't the foggiest notion what's going on. And NWN isn't about to clear it up for them.

"Hopefully, not too many of our viewers will read this," Mr. Barber says. "I imagine they might feel kind of funny knowing we're not there."

Disappointed is more like it.

"I feel deceived," says Susan Jones, a banker in Rome, Ga., upon learning that her local meteorologist, Chris Dahlquist, is two states away. In Tulsa, Clara Nipper, a massage therapist, is taken aback when told that her favorite broadcaster, Brian Sleeth ("He does this little smile that you have to see to believe") doesn't live and work in Oklahoma. "I'm shocked," she says after soaking it in.

A Special Relationship

Some viewers simply shrug when informed that Mr. Barber and his cohorts aren't where they seem to be. But many others feel a personal attachment to their weatherman. It is like "a patient/doctor relationship," explains Bruce Northcott, president of a media consulting firm in Marion, Iowa. TV weatherpeople, it seems, enjoy a level of trust and dependence others in the public eye don't. "It could be the weathercaster who saves your life," says Robert Henson, author of a history on weather broadcasting. "How often does the sportscaster do that?"

NWN's 39-year-old founder and owner Edward St. Pe plays down the proximity issue. He says his weathermen never directly state that they are anywhere in particular. But they never say they are in Jackson, Miss.

"As long as the information is accurate and serving the public, it doesn't matter," says Mr. St. Pe, an energetic weatherman-turned-entrepreneur who has the blue eyes, tanned face and blow-dried look of a TV weatherguy. He keeps his hand in by doing a few of the broadcasts himself. "The world has been shrunk down so much by satellite, people expect this kind of thing to be happening."

But not Sheri Rose, who watches Mr. Barber on a Memphis station and was more than a little surprised one day when she took a trip to the other side of Tennessee and flipped on a TV set. "I turned to my sister and said, 'Hey look. There's Dave Barber. He's in Nashville, too.' "

Even competing weathercasters have been fooled. Mr. Barber recalls being invited to lunch one day by a fellow meteorologist in another state. "I said he's got an awful long drive," Mr. Barber jokes. Says Joe Lauria, chief meteorologist for KOSA in Odessa, Texas: "If I didn't know about them through the business, odds are I wouldn't know they were 1,000 miles away."

By providing its own on-camera talent and by penetrating so many markets since it started up on TV in 1991, NWN is a true pioneer. It is not to be confused with the Weather Channel, on cable television, which produces national and regional forecasts from Atlanta. NWN's services appeal to small stations that can't afford their own in-house weather operations.

Verisimilitude in NWN reports occasionally goes awry, as when one of the network's trained meteorologists gets the name of a town wrong. Just the other day, Mr. Barber committed the cardinal sin of calling Celina, Ohio, "Ce-LEEN-a" instead of "Ce-LINE-a." "That's bad," he admits. "When you mispronounce a town, it doesn't look like you're doing it locally."

Another problem: the weather itself. Ms. Kroehler, the news anchor in Lima (pronounced LIME-a), recalls Mr. Barber's telling viewers that they could "expect rain" at just the moment she could "hear rain pelting the roof of the building."

But mishaps actually are rare.

Placing Weather Patterns

NWN reports are produced in a small building that is sandwiched between Interstate 55 and an industrial park in Jackson. Each day, in a cramped studio jammed with TV cameras and computer equipment, meteorologists hastily draw up map after map to reflect the day's weather patterns as reported by the National Weather Service. With a rapid-fire series of keystrokes and movements of a computer pen, they place brightly colored clouds, suns, lightning bolts and raindrops here and there.

Showtime comes twice a day — at 6:30 A.M. and 5 P.M., when the company beams its programming to an orbiting satellite. Local stations retrieve the reports and run them at their convenience. They either splice them into newscasts or run them as stand-alone

pieces between regular shows. The making of each "feed" — an hour of "local" weather reports — is an extraordinary display of improvisation and split-second timing.

One afternoon, Mr. Barber, wearing a blazer and tie and standing in front of a bright blue screen, begins with the forecast for New Jersey. On monitors to his right and left, he can see weather maps that flash up behind him on the home screen, and he points out various cloud patterns and temperature readings. Finally, he nods goodbye to the camera.

Seconds later, after a deep breath and a rub of the eyes, he says hello to viewers in Memphis, then to Hampton Roads, Va.; Daytona Beach, Fla.; Seattle; Corpus Christi, Texas, and so on. For more than 30 minutes, and with no script, he stands before the camera, smoothly moving from one location to the next, not once stumbling over a word or

"And for all of us here at the six-o'clock news — and don't forget we'll be appearing Saturday night at Mr. Fun — make it a good one!"

forgetting where he is supposed to be. Then, Mr. Dahlquist takes over where Mr. Barber leaves off.

Getting Personal

Segments frequently run no longer than 30 seconds. But the reports that are spliced into full newscasts can be tricky. Local anchors often ask NWN forecasters for some customized banter as a lead-in to the weather. Mr. Barber's crack about the cake and ice cream was prompted by a fax message he had received from Ms. Kroehler.

NWN's weathermen (they all are men) cater to local interests in other ways as well, making sure to mention special festivals and local landmarks whenever possible. Mr. Barber once wore a Syracuse University "Orangemen" sweat shirt and hat in promotional programming for WSYT. And, in November [1994], Georgia's CNWG is actually bringing Mr. Dahlquist to Rome for a public appearance.

The extra effort earns NWN forecasters a loyal following. Ms. Rose, despite her surprise at learning Mr. Barber's whereabouts, is still quite fond of him. "He's so friendly and upbeat," she says. "You feel like you know him."

Marcia Richards, another fan of Mr. Barber's Memphis reports, says she appreciates his accuracy. "In Memphis, none of them ever get it right," she says. "Sometimes his forecast is closer to the truth."

An Alternative to Cable

In 1994, several companies introduced a new method of television home delivery—direct broadcast satellites (DBS). This article, from the *Baltimore Sun,* describes how the arrival of DBS is challenging cable delivery in one metropolitan area.

Consider:

1. What are the implications for cable providers if DBS is successful?

2. What are the advantages that DBS offers over cable? Disadvantages?

3. How does Congress' role in media regulation affect the economics of program delivery?

Cable Gets Big Competitor in Little Satellite Dish

Michael Dresser

Vincent Mazza has a new "toy." He was the first on his block to get one. It's small, but he really, really likes it. Now his neighbors are getting them too.

And that's grim news for the beleaguered cable television industry.

The gizmo in the driveway of Mr. Mazza's Davidsonville home is a Direct broadcast satellite (DBS) receiver—the hottest new consumer electronics product to reach the marketplace since the VCR. With it, a viewer can bring in cable TV programs without paying a dime to the local cable TV monopoly.

"It's going to blow cable away because they're not the only kid on the block any more," said Walter Frazier, president of Stanbury Decker Systems Specialists, a Linthicum satellite dealer that has more than 1,200 customers on a waiting list to buy the dishes when they go on sale in Maryland late [September] or in early October [1994].

Mr. Frazier is hardly a neutral observer, but even cable partisans admit that times are tough.

While the cable industry sweats under the burdens of price regulation and a public image even politicians don't envy, all facets of the satellite TV business are booming at its expense.

And if the aerial assault wasn't enough, the telephone industry has launched a ground offensive with its plans to offer video services over its phone lines.

Satellite TV is nothing new, but until [1994] bringing in a signal has required a bulky C-band dish measuring at least 7½ feet across. Such dishes have become commonplace in the rural areas and atop the taverns of America, but their spread in metropolitan residential areas has been limited by their cost and conspicuousness.

Mr. Mazza's dish measures a mere 18 inches across, about the size of a pizza pan. Unlike traditional satellite dishes, it is "very unobtrusive," the retired chemical engineer said. In fact, it's not all that much bigger than a cable television node.

So far, there are only a handful of 18-inch DBS dishes in Maryland. Mr. Mazza ordered his from a dealer in Roanoke, Va., because he didn't want to wait until the devices go on sale here.

If Maryland consumers follow the pattern of other markets where DBS has rolled out, Mr. Mazza might have sidestepped a stampede.

From Albuquerque to Roanoke, consumer electronics retailers are reporting a buying frenzy worthy of the Mighty Morphin Power Rangers action figures.

Con Maloney, owner of Cowboy Maloney's Electric City in Jackson, Miss., witnessed the birth of the phenomenon because his market was among the first to receive DBS dishes back in June [1994].

"This thing started out on opening day with 200 people outside of our store and it's been burning bright ever since," he said.

Mr. Maloney said he had been surprised to find that consumers were buying more of the $899 dishes, which support two television sets, than the $699 models, which support one. While those prices aren't cheap, they compare favorably with those of 7$\frac{1}{2}$-foot C-band dishes, which start at about $2,500.

Cable Customers Switch

Most ominously for the cable industry, Mr. Maloney and other retailers say they've had stronger-than-expected sales among customers who are currently cable subscribers.

"We're expecting that over the next three to five years [from 1995 to 1999,] 60 percent of our customers will come from cabled areas," said Stan Hubbard, chief operating officer of Hubbard Broadcasting Co., managing partner in a venture called USSB, one of the two DBS programming providers.

If Mr. Hubbard's projections of 10 million to 15 million DBS customers by the end of the [1990s] come true, that works out to a loss of 6 million to 9 million current or potential cable customers over the next 5$\frac{1}{2}$ years [,by the year 2000].

Those numbers represent 10 percent to 15 percent of the cable business' current subscriber base of about 60 million — a fact that has not escaped cable industry officials.

"It's definitely of competitive concern to us," said Stephen R. Effros, president of the Cable Telecommunications Association.

But Mr. Effros dismissed predictions that DBS would cut heavily into the cable industry's franchise. He complained that it had been marketed in a deceptive manner, that it had no potential for interactivity, that there were hidden costs and that the system was highly susceptible to "rain fade" — a loss or degradation of reception during stormy weather.

"It's entirely a buyer-beware market," he said.

But Mr. Effros would have a hard time convincing Mr. Mazza, who said the programming, pictures and sound are all superior to cable. When his neighbors — who also happen to be his sons — saw the laser-disc quality video and heard the CD-quality sound, they ordered their own DBS systems, Mr. Mazza said.

The number of dishes sold is merely a leading indicator of DBS's acceptance. Ultimately, it will live or die by programming. And there it has great strengths — plus one glaring weakness.

No Local Broadcast

Unlike cable, DBS won't bring in your local broadcast stations, at least no time soon. So say goodbye to Sally Thorner and Marty Bass unless you're prepared to spend about $10 a month to keep basic "lifeline" cable service or rely on an antenna.

The larger provider, GM Hughes Electronic's DirecTV, started out with 40-50 channels, including most of the familiar offerings, in an expanded basic cable package — CNN, MTV, the Discovery Channel, the Disney Channel.

Tom Bracken, a spokesman for DirecTV, said the company's offerings will expand to 150 channels by October [1994], including 40–50 channels of pay-per-view movies priced at $2.99, 30–40 channels of sports, and 30 channels of CD-quality music. The cost will be $21.95 a month.

USSB has a much smaller offering of 20 channels, but it has carved out a niche by negotiating exclusive rights to offer the most popular premium movie channels: HBO, Showtime and Cinemax. Its packages, designed to complement rather than compete with DirecTV's, run from $7.95 to $34.95.

If DBS ends up saving you money or improving your service, you can thank a group that seldom gets thanked much: Congress.

The key change that made DBS possible was enacted over President George Bush's veto in the 1992 Cable Act, a law best known for reimposing price regulation on cable operators. One provision of that act was a requirement that cable programmers offer their shows to satellite broadcasters on an equal basis with cable networks.

That step was "the single most important thing in the success of DBS," said August Grant, professor of mass communications at the University of Texas. "People don't want music videos. They want their MTV."

With such programming on their team, satellite investors felt emboldened to move ahead with a technology that had been viewed as a dangerous gamble because of start-up costs estimated at $500 million to $1 billion. In December 1993, with Hubbard hitching a ride, GM Hughes launched its first

satellite, followed by a second [in 1994]. Another six to eight licensees are waiting in the wings.

But DBS is limited by the laws of people and physics.

Like other forms of satellite TV, DBS needs a clear sight line to the south. So if you live in a garden apartment with a north-facing deck or a house in the woods, you probably have no choice but cable.

Meanwhile, according to Columbia attorney Michael Nagle, about 30 percent of the nation's households are covered by homeowners' association covenants. Many of these include absolute bans on satellite dishes written in the days when the standard size was about 14 feet, said Mr. Nagle, a specialist in such cases.

Mr. Hubbard said problems with installing the 18-inch dishes in restricted neighborhoods hasn't emerged as an issue, possibly because the dishes can be inconspicuous.

The competition is well aware that DBS is there. And they're not standing still.

Rather than being hurt by DBS, the C-band market has actually been profiting from the growing interest in all satellite TV, dealers say. Not far from Cowboy Maloney's in Jackson, Doug McHenry at the Satellite Shop said his sales are up in spite of the DBS frenzy across town. In Baltimore, Mr. Frazier said some customer stopped by his showroom to ask about DBS but decided to buy a big dish after hearing about their 350-channel capacity, superior reception and the low monthly cost of programming.

Meanwhile, makers of the big dishes are taking no chances. Uniden, the industry leader, recently cut the price on its basic $7\frac{1}{2}$-foot dish by $300. Meanwhile, another producer called Unimesh has released a 5-foot mesh C-band dish that sells for $1,499, further narrowing the price and size gaps.

And the cable industry has taken to the skies too. Six of the largest operators banded together to launch a satellite TV service called Primestar, which announced its

Baltimore rollout [in August 1994]. The 65-channel service, which expects to upgrade to 150 channels in 1996, minimizes the upfront costs by renting its proprietary 3- and 4-foot dishes to consumers. So far, the venture claims 70,000 subscribers nationwide.

Compete with All Comers

But that doesn't mean cable companies have given up on the ground game. Most of the biggest players in cable are committing vast sums to upgrade their networks to compete with all comers—in telephone service as well as video.

Even the cable industry's detractors have to respect the fact that cable TV penetrates more than half the households in America. And in spite of the industry's image, there are many well-run cable companies with a loyal customer base. Even middling performers have inertia on their side.

Still, those cable monopolies that have spent years mistreating and overcharging their customers may get their comeuppance. "Certain systems may be dead," said Larry J. Yokell, president of Convergence Industry

The Specs on Satellite Services

Direct broadcast satellite

Technical: High-powered (120 watts) signal transmits digital audio and video programming to an 18-inch dish from two GM Hughes satellites.

Channels: 65–75 [September 1994], 150 expected in October [1994]. Further expansion depends on technology.

Program providers: DirecTV, USSB.

Upfront costs: $699 for one-TV dish, $899 for two-TV dish. Prices expected to drop after RCA exclusive expires after millionth dish is sold.

Monthly charges: $21.95 for DirecTV basic package of 30+ cable channels plus 30 music channels. USSB, which controls programs from HBO, Cinemax, Showtime, MTV, Nickelodeon and others, offers packages from $7.95 to $34.95.

Other costs: Optional installation cost of $200. Basic cable service or antenna required to receive local broadcast stations.

Advantages: Relatively inconspicuous small dish, audio and visual signal generally superior to cable. Signal quality expected to improve further when more advanced video standard is adopted. Dish is portable.

Drawbacks: Dish barred by some housing association covenants, southwest exposure required, vulnerable to signal loss or degradation during rainstorms, slight risk of catastrophic satellite failure, doesn't receive local broadcast channels, providers don't compete.

Prospects: Early response exceeds expectations. Aggressively targeting dissatisfied cable customers.

Primestar

Technical: Medium-powered (48-watt) signal transmits digital audio and video programming to a 36-inch dish from a single satellite.

Channels: 65 [September 1994], 75 expected by year-end [1994] and 150 in 1996. Further expansion depends on technology.

Program provider: Primestar.

Upfront costs: $195 for dish installation, $75 for additional outlet.

Monthly charges: $34.95 basic package includes dish rental and popular cable channels; 6 music channels; 10 pay-per-view movie channels, 14 regional sports channels. Variety of optional packages. $55.95 package includes all premium options. Additional $4.50 for network programming (only in weak-reception areas).

Other costs: $18.95 a month for optional separate programming to second outlet. $20 for TV Japan option. Basic cable

Associates in Boulder, Colo., and a veteran of the cable industry.

Telecommunications industry analysts say the advent of DBS will set off a chain reaction in the industry.

Cable companies will have to cut their rates to match DBS, especially on the premium services. DirecTV and USSB will have to respond to maintain their differential. Telephone companies with video ambitions will have to come in with lower rates than they anticipated. And everybody's going to be seeking a technological edge over the other guy.

Price Fall Predicted

Hardware prices will also fall as the volume of sales rise. Ed Creamer, an RCA distributor whose territory includes Pennsylvania and Virginia, said that after the first million DBS dishes are sold, consumers can expect the first of several major price cuts as programmers subsidize dish sales to gain subscribers.

"I wouldn't be surprised if in the next 3–5 years [by 1999] we see this product marketed for free, like a cellular phone," said Mr. Creamer, branch manager of Consumer Satellite Systems

service or antenna required to receive local broadcasts.

Advantages: Low upfront costs; 3- and 4-foot dishes less conspicuous than C-band; audio and visual signal generally superior to cable; company bears burden of maintenance, risk of technological change.

Drawbacks: High monthly cost; dish still barred by some housing association covenants, southwest exposure required, vulnerable to signal loss or degradation during heavy rainstorms, slight risk of catastrophic satellite failure, doesn't receive local broadcast channels, single provider.

Prospects: Service 70,000 customers. Ownership by cable companies limits aggressive marketing in cabled areas.

C-band
Technical: $7\frac{1}{2}$-foot dish to pick up low-powered (20-watt) signals from 20 satellites.

Channels: Estimated 350, ranging from popular programming to niche players such as Ostrich and Emu Channel. Some signals free, others require unscrambler. Picks up some unscrambled network feeds.

Programming providers: Many.

Upfront costs: $2,500–$4,200 for $7\frac{1}{2}$-foot automatically adjustable dish, depending on options. $1,500–$2,000 for 5-foot and 6-foot dishes with manual controls, lesser reception.

Monthly charges: Packages to pick up scrambled signals start at $9.95 in a competitive market. Rates for premium channels about 50 percent to 60 percent below cable.

Other costs: Basic cable or antenna required to receive local broadcast stations.

Advantages: Superior channel selection and signal; widest access to sporting events, including all NFL games; best resistance to rainstorms; low monthly costs, choice of providers.

Drawbacks: High upfront cost; dish barred by many housing association covenants; aesthetic objections even where allowed; southwestern exposure required; doesn't receive local broadcast channels.

Prospects: Loyal base of 2 million or more residential subscribers. Strong recent sales. "Stealth" devices to conceal dishes opening new markets. Equipment prices dropping.

in Arbutus. "The C-band hardware's going to go the same route."

But you won't have to become a satellite customer to benefit, said Mr. Grant, the University of Texas professor, who has seen the effect of DBS on the Austin market.

"The biggest group of people benefiting from DBS are those that didn't subscribe but get lower rates because DBS is competitive with the local cable companies. In other words, everybody wins except the cable companies."

"Cable Gets Big Competitor in Little Satellite Dish," by Michael Dresser, *Baltimore Sun,* September 4, 1994. Reprinted by permission of The Baltimore Sun. Dow//Quest Story ID: 0000358421DC.

Is Federal Funding Necessary for PBS to Survive?

Because public broadcasting depends on federal taxpayers as the largest single source of funding, a noisy congressional battle erupted in 1995 when the Republican majority in Congress proposed cuts in federal funding for PBS. This article by Nina J. Easton and Judith Michaelson of the *Los Angeles Times* describes how PBS is funded and why the debate is so important to the future of public broadcasting.

Consider:

1. If PBS is such a small part of the federal budget, as Easton and Michaelson explain, why is the issue of PBS funding such an important debate in Washington?

2. Explain the major arguments for cuts in federal funding of PBS and the major arguments against the cuts.

3. What does House Speaker Newt Gingrich mean when he calls PBS "a sandbox for the rich"? Do you agree? Disagree? Explain.

4. What is the alternative to federal funding for PBS? Do you believe that the alternative funding plan for "privatization" proposed by some members of Congress would maintain access to PBS programming in the United States? Why? Why not?

PBS: Behind the Sound and the Fury

Why should taxpayers support a 'sandbox for the rich'? critics ask;

Who would want to kill Barney? backers cry; Politics and rhetoric

obscure fight over federal funds for public broadcasting

Nina J. Easton and Judith Michaelson
Times researcher Caleb Gessesse contributed to this story.

At .0003% of the federal budget, public broadcasting doesn't even rate a mention in the fat document's index. But to Newt Gingrich, the $285-million appropriation is a vivid example of how an out-of-touch liberal Establishment has captured control of the nation's purse strings.

So, at a recent [1995] news conference, the House Speaker stepped up to the plate, just as he's done routinely since launching his campaign to halt taxpayer subsidies for what he calls "this little sandbox for the rich."

"The only group lobbying (for public broadcasting)," Gingrich declared, "are a small group of elitists who want to tax all the American people so they get to spend the money."

Across town at the National Press Club, Lamb Chop's sidekick was helping Public Broadcasting Service President Ervin Duggan plead his case. If Gingrich wants to play the political game of "us vs. them," who better for the PBS crowd to trot out as the face of "them" than doe-eyed puppeteer Shari Lewis, the ebullient redhead who is entertaining a second generation of children on public TV?

Over a cup of coffee before Duggan's speech, Lewis branded charges of elitism as "dumb" — 60% of the households who watch PBS make less than $40,000. The argument that government should not be involved in culture, she said, is "barbaric" — Canada and England spend more than $30 per person on public broadcasting each year, compared with America's $1. And the system does not waste taxpayer dollars, she said, noting that her wardrobe designer on "Lamb Chop's Play Along!" buys the cast's shoes at Ross Dress for Less.

Welcome to Washington's culture wars, Act I, Scene I: the fate of public broadcasting. Nobody pretends that federal funding of the Corporation for Public Broadcasting is more than a nick in the federal budget. But the tug of war over its future makes for grand political theater, rich in the symbolism of the times. Lawmakers and interest groups on both ends of the ideological spectrum see much political capital to be gained by drawing attention to it.

So far, public broadcasting's prospects appear grim. Executives at the Corporation for Public Broadcasting [CPB], the federally funded agency that doles out taxpayer money to local stations — 14% of the system's total budget — are girding for deep cuts from the Republican-controlled Congress; more pessimistic scenarios point to a gradual elimination of federal funds altogether. And some legislators are talking of schemes to privatize the system by selling off all or some of it to investors.

How that would ultimately affect the 110 million people who watch public television and the 18 million who listen to public radio each week is anybody's guess: The system is a complex pastiche of nearly 1,000 locally controlled stations in varying states of health. But it's likely that rural areas would lose stations, while everyone else would find slimmer pickings in their program guides.

That doesn't bother conservatives, who extol the range of options in broadcast and cable that the free market has spawned and see nothing wrong with public TV competing in that market.

With an explosion of media outlets, "the original justification for taxpayer funding of public broadcasting due to 'market failure' no longer holds water," says Sen. Larry Pressler (R–S.D.), who plans to introduce legislation to privatize the system.

In a symbolic nod to free-market media, Gingrich overlooked PBS icons Barney and Big Bird to bring Fox-TV's "Mighty Morphin Power Rangers" to Congress on its opening day [in January 1995]. Banned from many preschools because of the real-life karate kicks they inspire, the Rangers epitomize to public-broadcast allies the crass commercialism spawned by profit-seeking producers. The Rangers were uppermost on Lewis' mind when she said: "You cannot trust the market to take care of our kids."

But to many Republicans, Barney and Big Bird are the ones who have something to answer for: These critics argue that a handful of producers are getting rich off lunch buckets bearing pictures of plump purple dinosaurs and goofy yellow birds while PBS goes begging to Congress for money.

Rep. Dana Rohrabacher (R–Huntington Beach) insists that he and his colleagues don't want to kill Barney and Big Bird, "We just want to transform them from government bureaucrats to free-market entrepreneurs."

The attack on public broadcasting comes from three fronts: fiscal conservatives who want to prove that in these tight times all nonessentials must go; free-market devotees who see CPB as the next grand experiment in privatization, with harder-headed business decisions and investors filling in for government subsidies; and ideological conservatives who complain of a liberal bias in public programming.

Democratic lawmakers see in Gingrich's "elitism" comments a calculated political strategy: When budget-cutters come under attack for trimming programs for the poor, they can point to CPB as an example of a program for the "rich" that was axed.

Lost in this war of words are the seemingly mundane details of how stations will struggle to survive in a world without federal money. Southern California's KCET-TV Channel 28, which is getting a grant of $2.4 million from CPB this year, says it very likely would have to eliminate "Life & Times," its signature local public-affairs series.

Ruth Seymour, general manager of KCRW-FM, says the Santa Monica station would take a $600,000 hit that would necessitate "a reassessment of everything we do — everything."

Classical-music station KUSC-FM says it might drop Garrison Keillor's popular "Prairie Home Companion." Jazz-outlet KLON-FM would consider a shorter broadcast day. At KPBS-TV and KPBS-FM in San Diego, program manager Pat Finn says she would have to consider scrapping local documentaries, the promotion department, the program magazine and perhaps the radio news department. And an estimated 2 million Spanish speakers around the country who listen to the programming produced at KSJV-FM in Fresno would probably lose a major source of news and public affairs.

"This is not rich people's radio," says Hugo Morales, executive director of Radio Bilingue, which operates KSJV and four other Spanish-language stations from Modesto to El Centro. Without its $917,000 from CPB — which is 53% of its annual budget — "we'll just be spinning more records."

PBS President Duggan calls the elimination of federal funds "assisted suicide" and likens the 14% subsidy to "money that a farmer spends on his seed. If you destroy the seed, the rest of the planting can't be done."

CPB Chairman Henry Cauthen says that one-third of the system's TV stations would go under without the subsidy. And radio might have it worse. "I'm already bareboned," complains Judy Jankowski, general manager of KLON-FM at Cal State Long Beach. "I'm sitting here with a diaper on. I can't take any more off."

But it's difficult to accurately predict what would happen if Congress zeroed-out support, because the mix of funding at each station varies dramatically.

"Public TV is not a network," explains CPB's chief executive officer, Richard Carlson. "Each station is member-owned. It's like a rickety house with a strong foundation, a house held up with mop handles." Ditto for public radio.

CPB, an umbrella agency whose overhead and executive salaries are set by Congress, directs more than 90% of its federal appropriation to 351 television and 629 radio stations. The stations raise another $1.5 billion from other sources, including corporations, individuals, foundations, universities and — with the exception of a few states, such as California — legislatures.

Rural stations, with fewer community resources on which to draw, inevitably would be hit the hardest. Indeed, their plight could provide a nub of compromise. Gingrich told reporters [in January 1995] that he was interested in a proposal by Rep. John Porter (R–Ill.) to end help for financially secure stations, mainly in big-city markets, while continuing funding for the small-market outlets.

But it's those big-city stations — such as

KCET, Boston's WGBH and New York's WNET — that help produce the major national programs that define public television.

Without federal dollars, public broadcast officials insist that funding for new programming would dry up. While CPB does not produce or own shows, it does provide grants to local stations and independent producers who put together programs, typically relying on tax dollars as seed money to attract other investors.

"Puzzle Place," a daily series that premiered on PBS [in January 1995] in an effort to promote racial harmony and self-esteem among preschoolers, would not exist without federal funding because it was CPB that commissioned the project, said William Kobin, president of KCET, which is producing the series with Lancit Media.

"Without that ($4.5-million CPB) grant, we wouldn't have been able to go to Southern California Edison for (another) $3.5 million," Kobin says. "Though federal money is only 14% of all the money in public television, it is absolutely critical to enabling us to leverage four to five times more money."

Republican lawmakers fearful of angering constituents who enjoy public broadcasting insist that the most popular shows will survive without federal support — if the stations stop giving away the store by failing to take a cut of the millions earned on licensed merchandise by producers of "Barney and Friends" and other popular shows. Critics also point to the video earnings of producers such as Bill Moyers and Ken Burns, only a fraction of which flows back to public broadcasting coffers.

But CPB officials argue that their agency cannot demand a share of those revenues greater than its original investment. "Our claim is only on CPB's share of the show, which is typically a very small part of the overall production budget," says CPB spokesman Michael J. Schoenfeld. "The people who produce these programs take the risk."

Moyers' shows typically are fully funded by outside sources, officials say, and PBS merely pays a fee to broadcast them. The creators of "Barney and Friends," they add, made the initial investment in the show and had an underground hit on their hands before they brought it to PBS.

Even so, CPB officials are eager to show they are not naive. They are renegotiating the "Barney" contract, obligating the dinosaur's creators to fully reimburse PBS for its outlays on the show. And [in January 1995], the CPB board declared its intention to claim in future agreements "an appropriate share of ancillary income."

That's not enough to satisfy critics, who say that airing shows like "Barney and Friends" amounts to indirect advertising, so public broadcasting should share in the profits. These critics also note that, despite its name, PBS already airs commercials in the form of "enhanced underwriting" credits extolling the virtues of major contributors in spots that run before and after a program.

Still, the numbers that many of these critics throw out in suggesting that ancillary income could fill a $285-million federal funding gap are wildly exaggerated. Pressler continually refers to the $1 billion a year that "Barney" grosses and $800 million brought in by "Sesame Street." In fact, independent industry analysts say that "Barney" merchandise grossed about $500 million in 1993 — but most of that was eaten up by cuts toy manufacturers, department stores and the like. "Barney's" producers pocketed an estimated $84 million, according to *Forbes* magazine.

"Barney" is, in industry parlance, a fad, and that fad is fading fast. One Wall Street analyst estimated that gross revenues fell to about $200 million [in 1994], with only about $20 million going to the producers.

"Sesame Street" products — known as "evergreen" for their lasting popularity — have grossed as much as $750 million in a year. CPB officials say the nonprofit Children's Television Workshop plows the $20 million it earns from those licenses back into the show, which does not receive direct federal funds (although critics have highlighted a $600,000 salary made by the CTW executive who used to be in charge of those licenses).

Even when revenues from licensing Lamb Chop dolls and the like are factored in, Shari Lewis says, her Canadian partners have not turned a profit on her four-year-old series.

Station managers say it is unrealistic to expect them to squeeze more contributions out of corporations, whose funding for public TV is on the wane, or viewers, who would rather change channels than watch more fundraising drives that insiders cynically label "beg-a-thons."

"To me it is ill-informed at best, disingenuous at worst, to say you support Big Bird and public TV but let someone else pay," says Raymond K. K. Ho, president of Maryland Public Television. "Who's the someone else?"

It's difficult to gauge actual voter support for funding public broadcasting. A CNN/USA Today poll [in January 1995] showed a majority of those surveyed support continued funding. But when *Los Angeles Times* pollsters at about the same time asked whether they'd support cuts in public broadcasting "in order to reduce the federal deficit," a bipartisan 63% answered yes.

Even before Congress has decided the fate of the system, Pressler is busily shopping it to private buyers. He's drawn some interest from the Eastern phone company, Bell Atlantic, and from Colorado-based Jones InterCable.

CPB doesn't own any broadcast licenses or programming, so it's unlikely that this agency will be a candidate for a takeover. But Bell Atlantic spokesman Eric Rabe says that his company sees potential profits in becoming a business partner in public TV programming. Ken Burns' "Baseball" series, for example, could find a broader audience — and bring in more revenues — if a company such as his of-

fered episodes on pay-per-view, Rabe says.

Under a different regulatory arrangement — which could emerge with the advent of high-definition TV — public TV stations also might provide an outside buyer such as Bell Atlantic with a lucrative entree into major media markets where there are no more frequencies left, industry officials say.

Public broadcast officials, meanwhile, reject calls for privatizing their system. "Will the American people be happy with the transmogrification of nonprofit, non-commercial educational television into just another TV channel," asks Duggan, "driven by ratings, the lowest denominator of public taste and appetites of advertisers?"

Prompted by editorials on their local stations, the public broadcasting audience has inundated Capitol Hill with calls and letters. Despite this display of support, the writing is on the wall. An appropriations bill cutting already-allocated dollars to CPB and a wide variety of federal programs is expected to go to the House floor for a vote [in February 1995]. And in the Senate, even some of public broadcasting's Republican supporters are saying CPB will have to face cuts, just like other programs.

Rep. David Dreier (R–San Dimas), a close ally of Gingrich, is a longtime fan of public broadcasting. He listens to "Morning Edition" and "All Things Considered" on the radio. He makes public pitches during fundraising drives. Right now, however, he is focused on balancing the federal budget.

Federal subsidies for his favorite shows "are a wonderful luxury if there's a massive government surplus," Dreier says. "But we have some tough decisions that have to be made about our priorities."

"PBS: Behind the Sound and the Fury," by Nina J. Easton and Judith Michaelson, *Los Angeles Times* (Washington Edition), January 31,1995. Copyright 1995, *Los Angeles Times*. Reprinted with permission.

CHAPTER 9
The Movie Industry

First New Studio Since United Artists

In 1994, three of Hollywood's biggest powerbrokers formed a new independent studio. This was the first time since 1919 that a new studio was created to challenge the established system. Steven Spielberg, David Geffen, and Jeffrey Katzenberg announced their plans on October 11, 1994, even before they had named the company they had formed, which they subsequently named Dreamworks SKG.* The following article from *The New York Times,* written the day after the announcement was made, describes some of the possible ramifications the creation of the new studio may have for the movie business.

Consider:

1. Why is the formation of this new studio such an important event?

2. How much money did it take to start the studio? What does this tell you about the economics of the movie industry?

3. What advantages do these three partners have over the current studio owners? disadvantages?

3 Hollywood Giants Team Up to Create Major Movie Studio

Katzenberg to Join with Spielberg and Geffen

Bernard Weinraub

In a seismic shift within Hollywood's traditional studio system, Steven Spielberg, David Geffen and Jeffrey Katzenberg announced plans [in October 1994] for a new motion picture, animation, television and entertainment company whose creation could involve reclaiming ownership of Universal Pictures from the Japanese.

The union of three of the most powerful brokers in Hollywood to own and run their own studio marks the biggest merger of talent since Charlie Chaplin, Mary Pickford, Douglas Fairbanks and D. W. Griffith founded the United Artists movie empire in 1919. It

also underscores the financial and creative turmoil rocking Hollywood studios, including Sony Pictures, which also has Japanese owners that have lavished hundreds of millions of dollars on salaries, buildings, buyouts and, in many cases, failed movies.

"This has got to be a 'dream team,'" said Mr. Katzenberg, who angrily quit his job as chairman of Walt Disney Studios in August [1994] after failing to gain a promotion at Disney. "Certainly it's my dream."

Mr. Katzenberg was flanked at a packed news conference at the Peninsula Hotel in Beverly Hills by his two close friends, Mr.

Spielberg, the most successful director in movie history, whose net worth is more than $600 million, and Mr. Geffen, a billionaire record impresario, investor and producer.

Mr. Katzenberg went out of his way to speak warmly of his former boss, Michael D. Eisner, despite their ferocious public feud in [September 1994]. But the new studio could have a direct and long-term negative impact on Disney, notably in animation.

One possible development that could shape the structure of the new studio is that the company for which Mr. Spielberg currently produces movies, MCA Inc., and its Universal Pictures unit, may be repurchased from the Matsushita Electrical Industrial Company of Japan. Matsushita bought MCA for $6.1 billion in 1990, but MCA's top executives have bridled under the foreign ownership.

Industry executives said . . . that Lew R. Wasserman, chairman of MCA Inc., and his second in command, Sidney J. Sheinberg, are scheduled to meet in Hawaii . . . with top Matsushita executives to discuss the future of their relationship—including a possible buy-back of MCA. If Matsushita were willing to sell, industry executives said, the new company being created by Mr. Spielberg, Mr. Geffen and Mr. Katzenberg might be combined with MCA.†

MCA executives declined to comment. . . . Even if the MCA deal does not materialize, Messrs. Spielberg, Geffen and Katzenberg would seem to have the financial wherewithal to create a powerful new film and entertainment company. The three men, who said they expected the first of their studio's movies to go into production [in 1995], joked about their wealth throughout the news conference.

Although they declined to discuss the initial costs of the venture publicly, the three are believed to be combining more than $100 million of their own funds as a start-up. During the next five years, one of them said afterward, the necessary capital would probably reach $1 billion to $2 billion. But Mr. Katzenberg contended that raising financing would

not be a problem, given the track record and reputations of the partners.

"We start off self-financed," Mr. Katzenberg said, sipping a Diet Coke out of a bottle. "We're very confident. Already the phones have been going off the hook." The new studio, he said, appeared to have "unlimited financial resources" from Wall Street and the business community.

Privately, one of the partners said that once filmmaking began the company would use investors and partnerships to reduce the financial risks.

"I want to start something great, even investing in it myself," Mr. Spielberg said. "Over the years I've had almost a religious fervor in not investing my own money in show business. Not in my wildest imagination would I have guessed that this trio would have come together. Now I can't think of a better place than to invest in our own future."

Within Hollywood, the Spielberg-Geffen-Katzenberg venture sparked extraordinary interest largely because it is unusual to have a film maker like Mr. Spielberg running a studio. In recent years, with Wall Street's increasing involvement in Hollywood and the purchase of studios by conglomerates, the executive ranks have turned hierarchal and decisions have been made by committee.

The new studio is, in many ways, a return to the past, when film makers like Mr. Spielberg, and big executives like Mr. Katzenberg and Mr. Geffen, controlled decision-making and were not beholden to corporate empires.

"I want to find ways to insure film makers, both established and new, that they have a new home, that they are free to explore and share successfully in every success," Mr. Spielberg said. "When we all sat down we didn't talk about infrastructure and senior positions and management. We began talking about movie ideas and music ideas and television. It instantly became a very fertile arrangement."

The three partners did not publicly discuss the possible purchase of MCA from

Matsushita, although industry executives said the three were well aware of the significance of the impending trip to Hawaii by Mr. Wasserman, who has been head of MCA for 48 years, and Mr. Sheinberg, his president for the last 22 years.

People familiar with the MCA executives' plans said the Japanese owners would be approached about a buyback. Should Matsushita refuse, these people said, Mr. Wasserman and Mr. Sheinberg would probably quit the company.

Such a step could prove especially damaging to the Japanese owners since Mr. Spielberg also plans to stop producing films for MCA's Universal Pictures once he has fulfilled his current commitment to the studio.

"Jurassic Park," produced for Universal by Mr. Spielberg's Amblin Entertainment Company, is one of the biggest money-makers in movie history, grossing more than $900 million worldwide.

Executives involved in the looming negotiations with Matsushita said that any attempt by Mr. Wasserman and Mr. Sheinberg to buy back the studio would be joined by the Geffen-Spielberg-Katzenberg team, who would most likely have a large ownership stake. Mr. Sheinberg declined to discuss the possible negotiations with Matsushita.

Should the MCA deal fall apart, the three will begin their own studio, which is still unnamed, and start producing movies by next year. How the films will be distributed remains vague. "We intend to explore all possibilities," Mr. Geffen said.

Both Mr. Katzenberg and Mr. Spielberg made it clear that they were intent on rapidly building a strong animation unit at the new studio. Accordingly, Mr. Katzenberg will seek to enlist the help of animators and executives at Walt Disney Studios who are close to him, once their contracts expire.

The depletion of Disney's animation ranks, coupled with the loss of executives and producers loyal to Mr. Katzenberg, would

have the effect of undermining Disney. But Mr. Katzenberg, Mr. Spielberg and Mr. Geffen insisted that across-the-board competition with other studios would only improve the quality of movies throughout the industry.

Under the arrangement Mr. Spielberg will fold his company, Amblin, which is currently at Universal, into the new studio. Mr. Geffen's movie production unit will also be merged with the new company. The three men will be equal financial partners, but their specific management duties have not been defined, although Mr. Katzenberg will most certainly run the operations of the studio, Mr. Geffen will oversee the financial side and Mr. Spielberg will immerse himself in script decisions as well as directing. Mr. Spielberg made it clear . . . that he would not be tied solely to the new studio and would accept offers to direct from other studios as well.

Mr. Katzenberg said the studio would focus on five primary businesses: films, animation, television production, records and an ambitious interactive media business.

Mr. Spielberg said with passion: "Hollywood studios were at the zenith when they were driven by point of view and personalities. Together with Jeffrey and David, I want to create a place driven by ideas and the people who have them. I regard Jeffrey and David as pioneers. I'd like to be one, too."

Mr. Katzenberg and his partners insisted that their commitment to the new studio would endure and perhaps even last a lifetime.

"We're looking at this as a lifetime commitment for the three of us and we're young enough so that this gets measured in decades, not months," said Mr. Katzenberg, the youngest partner at 43. Mr. Spielberg is 46 and Mr. Geffen is 50.

"There's opportunity for us here to have a revolution," said Mr. Katzenberg, who ran Disney Studios for more than a decade.

Mr. Spielberg said nothing was quite fixed yet, but the studio would take shape quickly. "What did Forrest Gump say: 'Life is like a box of chocolates?' " he asked.

Mr. Geffen added: "That's the catch phrase of '94, and I think that's true. You never know what you're going to get."

"3 Hollywood Giants Team Up to Create Major Movie Studio," by Bernard Weinraub, *The New York Times,* October 13, 1994, p. A-10. © 1994 by The New York Times Company. Reprinted by permission.

*Note: SKG stands for Spielberg, Katzenberg, and Geffen.

†Note: In 1995, MCA was purchased by the Canadian company Seagram, and not by Dreamworks SKG.

Overcoming Stereotypes

The movies *Dances With Wolves* and *Thunderheart* represented an important departure from many of the movies about Native Americans that preceded them. Director Kevin Costner, for example, introduced several elements to the movie that were new — casting Native Americans to play Indian roles and using the Lakota language in about 30 percent of the film, for example. This article, written by John Coward from the University of Tulsa, discusses how and why movie portrayals of Native Americans are changing.

Consider:

1. How did the portrayal of Native Americans in *Dances With Wolves* differ from previous movie portrayals?

2. According to Coward, what are the four major strategies that Hollywood used to change the authenticity of these portrayals?

3. How does the portrayal of Native Americans in *Thunderheart* differ from the portrayal of Native Americans in *Dances With Wolves*, according to Coward? Why is this difference important?

Reconstructing the Hollywood Indian

John Coward
University of Tulsa

Even before *Dances With Wolves* won the Academy Award for Best Picture of 1990, the movie industry was being praised for its newly enlightened image of the American Indian. "Hollywood's War On Indians Draws to a Close," *The New York Times* proclaimed.[1] In *Dances,* the Sioux warriors — usually portrayed as bloodthirsty savages — were fully rounded characters, as capable of love as of treachery. Director Kevin Costner cast actual native people to play Indian roles, used the Lakota language in about 30 percent

of the film, and revealed the human side of the Sioux so long overlooked in previous Westerns.

After decades of formula Indians, the popular and critical response to *Dances With Wolves* signaled Hollywood's belated discovery of "realistic" Indians, characters who were portrayed more accurately and humanely than in the past. Indeed, Costner's epic was the most visible film in an entertainment industry trend that included *Powwow Highway, Black Robe, Thunderheart, The*

Last of the Mohicans and *Geronimo: An American Legend.* But this newly reworked "good Indian" was the creation of the same Hollywood system that produced the original "bad Indian," a fact that inspires more questions than confidence. Is the new Hollywood Indian substantially different from the old? If so, how and why?

This essay examines the entertainment industry's reconstruction of the Native American image in several recent films. Specifically, this [article] examines the idea and meaning of the Hollywood Indian by analyzing the films themselves, the industry practices that created them and the popular response to these films.

Race, Representation, and Movies

In *Racial Formation in the United States,* Omi and Winant argue for a new understanding of race and its role in American life. Specifically, they propose a theory of racial formation that emphasizes the ways in which race and racial ideas are arbitrary as well as artificial, constructed not from the realities of biological difference but out of existing social and political inequalities.[2] This [article] builds on such ideas by considering movies as important sites for the production of racial meanings, identities and differences. Moreover, these meanings, identities and differences are produced within an economic and cultural system that has its own peculiar and distorting practices.

Film and television, Omi has noted, have been "notorious in disseminating images of racial minorities which establish for audiences what these groups look like, how they behave, and, in essence 'who they are.' "[3] For Native Americans, Hollywood's fractured imagery has been especially harmful because it has been so popular and so closely tied to American myths of progress and Manifest Destiny.

The misrepresentation of Indians in American culture began well before the in-

vention of the motion picture. Friar and Friar connect early movie Indians to a series of earlier popular forms, including the captivity narratives of the colonial era, the novels of James Fenimore Cooper, nineteenth century Western dramas, dime novels and penny dreadfuls, and wild west shows. Given the popularity of such fictional Indians, they write, it is little wonder that many early moviemakers began to use — or, more accurately, misuse — Indians in their stories. The formula was so popular that moviemakers repeated it *ad infinitum,* producing hundreds of Indian films in the years before World War I. "No other race or culture depicted on film has been made to assume such a permanent fictional identity," Friar and Friar write.[4]

The bad Indian proved useful to early moviemakers for several reasons. First, Indian stories had been popular for decades, and film, as a medium of sight and sound, capitalized on this popularity by revealing Indians as exotic action characters. Moreover, silent westerns needed evil, easily identifiable villains, and the bad Indian stereotype was perfect for this role. Finally, native life was easy for filmmakers to expropriate: a few feathers, some rustic-style clothing, a few

Kevin Costner on the set directing *Dances With Wolves.*
Artwork © TIG Productions, Inc.

painted horses and — presto! — "authentic" evil Indians.

If the bad Indian was the most common villain in early Hollywood, it was not the only one. Indeed, some early moviemakers quickly developed a competing "good Indian" character, idealized most often as the Noble Savage. From Rousseau, Cooper and other sources, moviemakers began developing good Indians as the natural and virtuous children of the forest, unsullied by civilization. Hollywood used this theme as early as 1908, when *Pocahontas* first appeared on the screen.

Despite the rise of the Noble Savage stereotype, the evil Indian remained more popular in early Hollywood. Friar and Friar explain this in economic terms: "Whereas the noble red man attracted many, it was the savage Indian who made money for the studios."[5]

The Reconstructed Hollywood Indian

Hollywood's interest in Native Americans has waxed and waned over the years. The most recent rise in interest followed the rebirth of the western in novels, television mini-series and movies. These productions gave Hollywood still another chance to portray native people and their cultures "realistically" and "authentically," although these terms were not well defined.

Hollywood responded with four primary strategies: (1) casting natives to play native roles, (2) greater attention to historical accuracy in costume, location and language, (3) more complex and empathetic native characters whose actions and motives are explained, and (4) a new prominence for native roles and stories. With varying degrees of success, Hollywood used such strategies to construct a more sensitive and accurate Indian image.

Racially Appropriate Casting

The list of white actors who have played Indian roles is long if not always distinguished: Don Ameche, Ann Bancroft, Yul Brynner, Tony Curtis, Buddy Hackett, Boris Karloff, Bela Lugosi, Rita Moreno, Jack Palance, Anthony Quinn, Donna Reed, William Shatner, John Wayne, Loretta Young and others.[6] Given this history, the casting of natives to play native roles would seem a simple solution to a long-standing problem. Yet casting has remained a controversial issue, primarily because native actors are not box office stars.

Nevertheless, Hollywood has made progress. *Dances With Wolves* featured native actors in several major roles and Graham Greene, a Canadian-born Oneida Indian, was nominated for an Academy Award for Best Supporting Actor. The success of Greene and other native actors has helped increase the number of Indian actors working in Hollywood.

But the casting issue is not always so straightforward, as Robert Redford discovered when he sought a native actor for *The Dark Wind*. Redford and producer Patrick Markey spent more than a year looking for a native to play the Navajo detective who is the mystery's main character. Markey told *The New York Times,* "We've considered 2,500 people for that role and have on tape 300 candidates. All of us were committed to finding a Native American to play that role." The role eventually went to Lou Diamond Phillips, a Texan who won critical acclaim in *La Bamba*. The decision to cast Phillips, who says he is part Cherokee, was criticized in the Native American community. Markey defended the decision. "He's a very good actor, can open a movie and he's someone whom the American public will buy tickets to see," he said. "He's also very concerned with Native American issues."[7]

Markey's logic demonstrates how Hollywood practices have ideological consequences. Phillips is not Navajo, but he claims to be part Cherokee. Despite a host of differences between these cultures, Phillips' "Indianness" was sufficient to qualify him for the part. Also, Phillips' sympathy to Indian issues was used to justify his casting. Most importantly, Markey acknowledged Phillips' box office appeal, a consideration of overriding importance in Hollywood.

Bonnie Paradise, executive director of the American Indian Registry, has criticized this continuing emphasis on stars: "We get a lot of important roles, but rarely the major roles because Hollywood still wants to go with names."[8] In the end, the use of Indian actors alone is no guarantee that native roles will be any more accurate or representative than in the past.

Historical Accuracy

If the devil is in the details, as the saying goes, then recent movies have tried to rid themselves of the demon of historical inaccuracy. Most prominently, *Dances With Wolves'* producers went to great lengths to ensure correct historical detail in wardrobe, props and location. "The filmmaker's job today is to make it real, whether it's about Native Americans or Eskimos or blacks," said Jim Wilson, *Dances'* co-producer.[9] Costume designer Elsa Zamparelli did her part for reality, collecting 625 bearskins for costumes. *Entertainment Weekly* was so taken with the movie's commitment to accuracy that it ran a full page feature on Cathy Smith, described as "a 19th-century Plains Indian expert," and artifact consultant Larry Belitz, the man who created about 400 buffalo-hair robes and other props. Belitz assured the magazine: "This was as authentic as Hollywood could get."[10]

The contemporary Indian story *Thunderheart* also made a claim to accuracy of place and tone. Screenwriter John Fusco drew on his experiences living in the Pine Ridge Reservation to make his story more realistic. Moreover, Fusco was described as "a lifelong student of American Indian religions and philosophy and . . . a Sioux honorary adoptee."[11] Presumably, these factors give him the insight to write a more accurate screenplay.

Finally, the increased use of native languages would seem to be an easy way of adding realistic detail to Indian films. For decades, ersatz Indians spoke broken English or gibberish and directors avoided subtitles for fear of alienating the audience. In the case of *Dances With Wolves,* however, the extensive use of Lakota with English subtitles probably helped the movie because it increased the film's perceived authenticity.

Historically accurate details in costume, location and language — what art historians call "surface realism" — may be signs of increased respect for native traditions in Hollywood; certainly they are taken that way in the popular media. Yet accuracy in details is no guarantee of "realism" or "authenticity" concerning Native Americans in film; these terms are, after all, complicated and themselves embedded in ideology.

Accuracy of detail, then, is perhaps best seen as a necessary but insufficient part of the effort to construct a more representative native image. Without accurate details, such an image is problematic; with accurate details, it is at least possible. By this measure, *Dances With Wolves* and *Thunderheart* can be seen as improvements to Hollywood's checkered past.

Beyond the Stereotype

If the native image in film has been narrowly two-dimensional, recent moviemakers deliberately attempted to enlarge the range of native characters. *Dances,* for example, developed a range of positive Sioux characters, expanding the Noble Savage cliché. Such roles gave the producers a chance to reconstruct the Sioux image, revealing them as normal human beings with a variety of qualities, a characterization remarkable only because it has been applied so infrequently to the Sioux.

Other recent films have tried to remake the evil Indian. Despite its emphasis on action and overtly romantic storyline, the 1992 version of *The Last of the Mohicans* attempted to humanize the savage. Wes Studi, a Cherokee who played the vengeful Magua in *Mohicans,* noticed the improvement. "We always got the idea before that these bad Indians were being bad because 'that's the way they are,'" Studi said. "But in this movie we acknowledge that there is something human involved in their actions."[12] The explanation of Indian motives was also evident in *Thunderheart,* where the portrayal of native corruption could be understood as an ordinary human failing, not a failing unique to Indians.

The trend toward sympathetic Indian characters has not gone unchallenged, however. Cultural conservatives have complained that the new Hollywood Indian is yet another return to the romanticism of the Noble Savage. The problem, wrote Paul Valentine of the *Washington Post,* is that *Dances With Wolves* and other movies have recreated the good Indian not to serve historical accuracy but as a way of purging five hundred years of white guilt.[13]

Such comments point to the problematic and political nature of "truth," "accuracy" and "authenticity" in the popular portrayal of Native Americans. Nevertheless, both Hollywood and its critics seem to agree that Native Americans deserve recognition as full human characters capable of a variety of human emotions and actions. On this score, *Dances With Wolves, The Last of the Mohicans, Black Robe,* and *Thunderheart* have advanced, if only slightly, the humanity of the Hollywood Indian.

The Marginalized Indian

The western has been a popular genre for so long that new movies can be compared and contrasted to the standard conventions of the form. Berkhofer, for example, has noted that the fictional frontier is a place where civilization meets savagery and, in accordance with American ideals, "savagery must recede before the vanguard of White society. . . ."[14] In this classic formula, the Indians might be either good or bad, but they remain outside of civilized society. Most importantly for the

Indian, Berkhofer notes, the classic western marginalizes native people: "No matter how important the Indian might be to the Western plot and genre, he usually served in the end as the backdrop rather than the center of attention. . . ."[15]

With some notable variations, *Dances With Wolves* repeats the classic formula. Lt. John Dunbar (Kevin Costner) asks to be posted in the West, a place of vast expanses on the edge of white civilization. This is, of course, a thoroughly romantic impulse. Moreover, Berkhofer points out that the classic western hero frequently represents a blend of savagery and civilization, a characteristic which soon turns up in Dunbar. The movie makes this clear when Dunbar is posted to the abandoned Fort Sedgewick and immediately begins to clean and repair the site. Yet the longer he stays there, the more "savage" he becomes and the more respect he has for his Sioux neighbors.

It is significant too that *Dances With Wolves* is a historical depiction of Indian life, repeating yet another critical part of the classic western. In *Dances* and most other Hollywood movies, Indians are imagined as people of a more majestic time. It is clear that Costner and writer Blake intended to celebrate native life in the movie, but *Dances* itself is unashamedly nostalgic. Wrote Blake, "I love the west as it once was, teeming with buffalo and wolves. And I love the reverent, free people from whom I have learned so much."[16]

Such motives, however, do not alter the fact that the film perpetuated the idea of the Indian as an artifact. The film's emphasis on the romantic past, its conventional story line, and Costner's preeminent position as star ensures that, in ideological terms, the natives in *Dances With Wolves* remain secondary characters, a colorful backdrop for the story of Lt. John Dunbar.

The 1991 Canadian-Australian movie *Black Robe* also treated Indians as historical characters. In contrast to *Dances,* however, *Black Robe* provided an unromanticized view of the past. Directed by Bruce Beresford, the Australian director best known for *Driving Miss Daisy, Black Robe* tells the story of French Jesuits among the Algonquin in Quebec in 1634. The movie focuses on the Indians' profound indifference to Christianity and the contrast between a dedicated priest's ambitions and forces of the Canadian wilderness, a contrast that shakes the faith of the weary priest.

By concentrating on such subtle matters, Beresford provides some insight into a seventeenth century native consciousness, no small feat by Hollywood standards. It is notable, however, that the film was not a box office hit, probably because it offered none of the classic romance expected in an Indian story: no sweeping vistas, no buffalo stampedes, no spiritual Epiphanies. Instead, the movie portrayed fallible human beings trudging through a bleak Canadian snowscape on a quest of dubious merit. The themes of the big Hollywood western were missing from this non-traditional Indian story. The result was a deeper, and more wide-ranging native image that — for just those reasons — few people cared to see.

One of the few recent movies that dared to treat contemporary Indians was *Thunderheart,* an action-drama set on a Sioux reservation. Screenwriter John Fusco and director Michael Apted made a point of showing both the good and the bad sides of reservation life. On a more positive theme, Fusco showed native spirituality, using humor to keep the spirituality from being excessively mystical. Finally, *Thunderheart* offered both positive and negative native characters and provided them with individual motives as a way of getting Indian individuals, not mere Indian types, on the screen.

In small ways, *Thunderheart* attempted to challenge the traditional Hollywood Indian. Unlike *Dances With Wolves* and *Black Robe, Thunderheart* told a story of living native people, [faults] and all. Yet *Thunderheart,* in contrast to *Black Robe,* made significant con-

cessions to Hollywood conventions. The lead character, an FBI agent who is one-eighth Indian, was portrayed by Val Kilmer, an actor with star appeal but without native ties. Like the producers of *The Dark Wind,* Fusco rationalized this casting decision, noting that Kilmer's presence would "result in more exposure for this film. That's what Native Americans working on this project want."[17] Indeed, the film achieved modest box office success.

Perhaps the most successful recent effort to tell a contemporary native story was *Powwow Highway.* Released in 1989 with a little known cast, the movie put an off-beat native twist on the conventional Hollywood "road" movie. Moreover, the movie used humor to reveal its native characters as ordinary human beings, a refreshing change from the cardboard Indians of Hollywood's past. Despite the movie's obvious charms, *Powwow Highway* was not widely seen, a fact that does not bode well for the future of native perspectives in Hollywood.

A Question of Power

Movies about Indians, like all Hollywood productions, are designed to make money. This fact helps explain the stability of the Hollywood Indian: filmmakers have been reluctant to make fundamental changes to formulas that have demonstrated box office success. As *Dances With Wolves* has shown, the public is still enamored of the American West and the Noble Savage. Less romantic Indian stories, such as *Black Robe,* remain largely unseen. Thus the new Hollywood Indian, like the old, has been restrained by Hollywood's desire to tell stories more romantic than true.

Nevertheless, renewed public interest in Native Americans in the last decade has helped improve the old Indian stereotype. Filmmakers have made good-faith efforts to avoid the excesses of the past and offer more thoughtful treatments of Indians and their cultures. That being said, these advances have not addressed the fundamental racial ideology that underlies Hollywood's movie-making process.

Indian stories continue to present Native Americans from a white point of view, as if that were the only possible way to represent them. The new Hollywood Indian, then, is not substantially different from the old. Native actors, historical accuracy and sympathetic characters are not the same as the power to promote stars, control stories and produce movies from a native point of view. Ultimately, the Hollywood Indian will change only when Native Americans attain such power, a power only recently realized by African-American directors such as Spike Lee and Mario Van Peebles. In the mid-nineties, no Native American actor or director had achieved this status.

End Notes

1. *The New York Times*, October 7, 1990, H1.

2. M. Omi and H. Winant, *Racial Formation in the United States.* New York: Routledge & Kegan Paul, 1986.

3. M. Omi, "In Living Color: Race and American Culture." In I. Angus and S. Jhally (Eds.), *Cultural Politics in Contemporary America.* New York: Routledge, 1986, 115.

4. R. E. Friar and N. A. Friar, *The Only Good Indian . . . The Hollywood Gospel.* New York: Drama Book Specialists, 1972, 2.

5. Friar and Friar, *The Only Good Indian,* 104.

6. Friar and Friar, *The Only Good Indian,* 281–83.

7. *The New York Times,* October 7, 1990, H18.

8. *The New York Times,* October 7, 1990, H18.

9. *The New York Times,* October 7, 1990, H15.

10. "How 'Dances' Got Real," *Entertainment Weekly,* March 8, 1991, 22.

11. *The New York Times,* October 7, 1990, H19.

12. *Tulsa World,* September 20, 1992, H1.

13. *Fort Worth Star-Telegram,* April 28, 1991, B7.

14. R. F. Berkhofer, Jr., *The White Man's Indian.* New York: Vintage, 1979, 97.

15. Berkhofer, *The White Man's Indian,* 98.

16. K. Costner, M. Blake and J. Wilson, *Dances With Wolves: The Illustrated Story of the Epic Film.* New York: Newmarket Press, 1990, xvi.

17. *The New York Times,* October 7, 1990, H19.

"Reconstructing the Hollywood Indian," by John Coward, adapted from "Reconstructing the Hollywood Indian," a paper presented at the 1994 Annual Convention of the American Journalism Historians Association. Reprinted by permission of the author.

Negatives in the Movie Business

As the movie business searches for a new audience for each motion picture, the temptation grows to avoid controversial storylines, according to *Los Angeles Times* Hollywood reporter Jack Mathews. He calls the new Hollywood moguls "nattering nabobs of negativity" for their tendency to reject most of the projects they review. The process seems to work against new ideas and "nonbankable" stars, says Mathews.

Consider:

1. According to Mathews, why is the successful production executive "not the one who can 'smell' a hit," but "the one who is quickest at thinking of reasons why to turn projects down"?

2. List ten "no-nos," according to Mathews. Why are these ideas risky?

3. Do you agree with filmmaker Henry Jaglom, who says "the conventional wisdom is just that, conventional, and it lasts until it's broken by the public"? Why? Why not?

Rules of the Game

Jack Mathews

Any fool can make a rule,
And every fool will mind it.
　　　　Henry David Thoreau, in 1860, before the
　　　　first Hollywood production executive was born.

No dust, no snow, no foreigners. No unsympathetic protagonists. No sports, no politics, no cripples. An interracial love story? Not on your life. Westerns? Not now, not this year. No saints, no sinners, no old people, no kids, no gay romance. Jazz is out, coming-of-age has come and gone, the future's been done to death, and period costs too much. If people want to see costume dramas, they can turn on TV and see the hell Roseanne Barr puts a size 18 through.

Look, let's make this easy. No historical dramas, no musicals, no futuristic adventures, no mysteries, no war stories. We're not looking for fantasies, cinema verité, political satire, family sagas, farm life, or anything with Pacific Rim, Central American or

Eastern European settings. And do yourself a favor: Forget you ever heard the words *glasnost,* AIDS, Greenpeace or apartheid.

Thanks for thinking of us and come back when you've got something new, something different or something for Eddie Murphy.

Speaking of nattering nabobs of negativity, Hollywood's new breed of production executives sure know when to say no — whenever someone pitches an idea that comes unattached to a bankable star. Saying no is easy, expected and inexpensive. Saying yes always costs money and often costs jobs.

"There is a tendency for everyone to have excuses why not to do something," says Hollywood agent J. J. Harris, "Once you commit to doing it, you're {risking} money and your future."

The really successful production executive is not the one who can "smell" a hit, as each sucessful one will claim, but the one who is quickest at thinking of reasons why to turn projects down.

"There are executives who have long lists of no-no's, rules that they expect people to follow," says writer-director Phil Alden Robinson, whose *Field of Dreams* — like Ron Shelton's *Bull Durham* and numerous other movies — violated Hollywood's ironclad "no baseball" rule. "Most of them are custommade rules, conceived on the spot. 'We don't do stories about left-handed barbers.' That sort of thing. I've asked them, 'Do you have a list of these rules so I can take them home and study them?' I still haven't seen a list."

What are the accepted rules in Hollywood? What is it you cannot do in a script, besides having a herd of camels race through Central Park, which would — as screenwriter William Goldman pointed out in *Adventures in the Screen Trade* — be too expensive? If everyone knows what cannot be done, why don't they publish the list? Think of the nice library companion it would make for all those books on the selling of screenplays that are written by people who never have sold one for people who never will.

In talking to more than two dozen Hollywood insiders, these things became clear: While everyone says there are rules, no two people named the same ones, and for every rule mentioned, you can think of at least one movie that broke it.

Some rules are broken for obvious reasons. There's a rule, a good one, that movie stars not play against type, but as J. J. Harris said, if Tom Cruise wants to do slapstick next, he can do it, even if everyone signing on for the project knows the joke's on them. Tough guys don't sing? Sylvester Stallone and Clint Eastwood did, both badly, in *Rhinestone* and *Honkeytonk Man,* respectively.

Eastwood was so important to Warner Bros. that when he cast black actress Vonetta McGee as his love interest in the 1975 *The Eiger Sanction,* no one batted an eye.

"No, nobody even mentioned it," Eastwood said, when asked if there were raised eyebrows when he announced his selection of McGee. "I just said, 'She's right for the part,' and they said, 'Fine.'"

Sure, make *his* day. But how many lesser beings do you suppose were thrown off studio lots for suggesting such eccentric casting? When it comes to certain stars, there are no rules, not even the vaunted "Thou shalt not throw bad money after good," which is what Warner did with *Bird,* Eastwood's righteous, self-indulgent ode to jazz great Charlie Parker. Jazz? Drug addiction? Miscegenation? Bite your tongue.

It's hard to say no to Arnold Schwarzenegger these days, too. For 10 years people had been trying to get financing for *Total Recall,* a science-fiction story conceived by the same writing team that gave us *Alien.* The story is set 100 years in the future, it takes its hero from Earth to Mars and requires so many special effects that it was deemed by every major studio as financially impractical. But when Schwarzenegger told Carolco Pictures that he wanted to do it, Carolco bought the rights for him. The film, which [was released in summer 1990], cost an estimated $60 million.

The one rule that seems safe for the moment [1990] is the feature film ban on AIDS stories. Safe sex jokes are OK. What's more festive than a condom? (Answer: Two glow-in-the-dark condoms stretched to capacity in what appears to be a laser sword fight, in Blake Edwards' colossally tasteless *Skin Deep*.) So write in all the safe sex jokes you want, but don't mention the disease that promoted the practice.

Eventually, some daring producer will do a commercially successful film about AIDS and, after a flurry of failed imitations, that success will be dismissed as the exception that proved the rule, and the subject will again be verboten.*

There are simply so many rules that every film has to break some.

Danny DeVito's *The War of the Roses* broke at least two major rules: You cannot have unsympathetic protagonists, and you cannot kill off your heroes.

Spike Lee's *Do the Right Thing* broke several rules: You cannot have a mainstream film about black issues. You cannot have a sympathetic character (Lee's Mookie) do major harm (Mookie starts the eventual riot). And a major studio cannot give an inexperienced, noncommercial director final cut (Lee got it from Universal Pictures).

Oliver Stone's *Born on the Fourth of July* violated somebody's rule against having a disabled hero and would have violated the rule against Vietnam movies if Stone hadn't already successfully broken that rule with *Platoon*.

Platoon producer Arnold Kopelson has broken more rules than a Central American dictator, most recently with *Triumph of the Spirit*, a film set almost entirely in a Nazi concentration camp. "I had been trying to get *Triumph* off the ground for seven years," Kopelson says. "I took it to all the major studios, and they said, 'You can't make a film about the Holocaust today and have it be

a major motion picture. People are sick of it, and you're wasting your time.'" When *Triumph of the Spirit* was released in December, its biggest problem wasn't the Holocaust, but the fact that the film was competing against two others with Holocaust backdrops (Paul Mazursky's *Enemies, a Love Story* and Costa-Gavras' *Music Box*) that came out at the same time.

Kopelson has broken some rules on the other end of the taste spectrum, too. When he was shopping the script for *Porky's,* he says executives were relatively appalled at its raunchy treatment of high-school sexual fixations. The rule they quoted: Don't go too far with kids and sex. . . .

Kopelson finally found a taker at 20th Century Fox, and *Porky's* went on to spawn two sequels and a seemingly endless string of crotch-digging imitations, which brings up a different rule: "The only absolute rule in this business," says J. J. Harris, "is that if you make a hit movie, you get to make another movie immediately."

Porky's director Bob Clark not only got to do *Porky's II,* but also extracted a studio commitment for his own high-risk project, a Jean Shepherd short story that he had been wanting to adapt for years. Clark's *A Christmas Story* proved to be as enchanting as *Porky's* was foul, and gave Clark a moment of euphoria before he fell on his face with *Rhinestone* (where he violated the director's rule not to make a film with stars who direct themselves).

Producer David Weisman had a different problem from Kopelson's when he began looking for financing for an adaptation of Manuel Puig's novel *Kiss of the Spider Woman*. The story was about the relationship between two inmates of a South American prison cell, one a radical political dissident, the other a transvestite who passes time narrating his own Hollywood fantasy.

"When I sent the script around, the reaction was universal," Weisman says. "They would congratulate me for this amazing script . . . then say it's not the type of project they were getting involved with. They would all say it's a marketing nightmare — a movie about a fag and a Commie in a jail cell together? What could be worse? I never encountered any classical homophobic reaction to the film, but one studio executive asked, 'We're not going to see him giving a blow job, are we?' He wasn't joking. He was seriously concerned about that."

Kiss of the Spider Woman was made independently for $3 million and distributed by Island Pictures. It grossed nearly $14 million, sold 131,000 videocassettes and won an Oscar for William Hurt, whose performance as the prison queen broke a major actor's rule (don't play a gay; people will believe you are one).

Still, in marketing *Spider Woman,* Island played by the rules. "The conventional wisdom is that the mass-market American public is put off by gay-theme films," says Cary Brokaw, who headed Island then and is now in charge of Avenue Pictures. "Our ad showed the Spider Woman {Sonia Braga} emerging from the jungle with a dark web behind her. We promised an exotic experience. That was the only way we could get people to come see the movie."

There wasn't anything Brokaw could do to camouflage the theme of Gus Van Sant's *Drugstore Cowboy,* which Avenue released [in 1989] to both critical raves and waves of protest. The film, about a quartet of '60s junkies who stay stoned on the drugs they steal from pharmacies and hospitals, was compared to two classic rule breakers — *Bonnie and Clyde* (no criminal protagonists) and *Days of Wine and Roses* (no addicted heroes) — and added a violation of its own. Its nonjudgmental tone flew in the face of the nation's noisy antidrug war.

"There was a lot of smirking around town when we initiated it," Brokaw says. "What is Avenue doing making this film that is a drug movie but not didactic in its condemnation of drugs? Our feeling was that to really understand the problem of drugs, you have to understand their appeal."

Van Sant told one interviewer that studios have no problem with drug movies, it's just that research shows that drug movies won't make money. "So they go out and make these films like *Bright Lights, Big City* and *Less Than Zero,* and they take all the drugs out so you can't figure out what's really going on," Van Sant said. "And they don't make money because they're bad movies. So they wreck the films and then they don't make money {because they're about drugs}."

Research, the Zen of Hollywood's '80s, has inspired all sorts of impromptu legislation. Ron Leavitt, who created TV's raunchy *Married . . . With Children* with partner Michael Moye, said that after they showed the pilot to Fox Television executives, Fox ordered some audience testing on the episode and invited them back to hear the results.

"{This guy} made this hour-long presentation with graphs, these fucking fat booklets and other kinds of graphs. . . . Finally, when he summed it up, he said, 'What I'm trying to say, guys, is if you made these people more obviously love each other, if you made them more caring . . . I think you might have a hit series.' And I said, 'You, sir, are the reason television sucks.' "

Leavitt says that after going through the dog-and-pony show, Fox decided to ignore the research and go with the original concept of *Married . . . With Children.* "Fox was a brand-new network," Leavitt says. "Their philosophy at the time was, We have to give people something they can't get on the big three."

The paradox among film and TV executives is that it takes something bold and different to draw attention to itself, but in a game where only one in four films makes money (the success ratio is even lower in TV), who wants to step up to the plate? Who wants to break the rules? The dilemma was always thus.

"I think it's the same as it's always been. The unanswerable question is, What makes a dollar?" says Stanley Kramer, who began challenging convention and breaking rules in the late '40s. "Half the time, the financial people have been right, and half the time, they've been wrong."

Kramer ticks off evidence to support both sides. Despite almost universally sanguine reviews for his 1960 *Inherit the Wind* (which broke the rule that you don't take sides in the debate between creationists and evolutionists), the movie bombed at the box office. On the other hand, he says, three weeks before production started on the eventual hit *Guess Who's Coming to Dinner* (which violated the rule against interracial romance), Columbia wanted to pull out.

"I'd like to say that I was bright enough to feel from the beginning it would be a smash, but I didn't know that," Kramer says. "I was just trying to make as good a movie as I could."

Kramer began breaking the rules as a young producer right out of the army. Fight films don't make money, he was told when he shopped the script for *The Champion* around. But with box-office heavyweight Kirk Douglas starring, the film got made in 1949 and United Artists had a hit. Nearly 30 years later, the same studio reluctantly agreed to break the "no boxing" rule again, and made the first of several fortunes on Rocky Balboa.

When Kramer proposed *Home of the Brave*, a way-ahead-of-its-time story about racial prejudice during World War II, he says UA execs told him, " 'We'll never book it in the South.' It was booked all over the South. . . . There are people who claim they know what will do well at the box office. That's ridiculous, because no one does."

Fifteen years after Kramer crossed the color line, director Larry Peerce stepped across again with *One Potato, Two Potato*, a film based on several true cases. In *One Potato*, a white man sues for custody of his daughter when he discovers that his ex-wife has married a black man. A judge agrees that the interracial environment is unhealthy and takes the girl away from her mother.

"We made the film totally independently," Peerce says. "A lot of studios saw it and seemed to like it, but said they couldn't release it in light of the color line. They were afraid they couldn't get theaters, so they walked away."

The film's theme played much better in Europe, and when Barbara Barrie won the best actress award at the 1964 Cannes Film Festival, the heat was on. *One Potato, Two Potato* was picked up for U.S. art-house distribution by independent Cinema V and grossed a then-hefty $2 million.

Peerce has worked mostly within the system since, although he got a tiger by the tail when he went against the establishment and directed *Wired*, the surreal biography of John Belushi. There were two major rules broken there: No movies about entertainment personalities, and, no movies that make powerful enemies in Hollywood.

"The big, tough guy says, 'Don't do what I tell you not to do,' that's what it was all about," Peerce says, alluding to attempts allegedly made by Creative Artists Agency to keep the film from being made and then distributed. "It was a hideous experience."

The word that emerges most often when you talk to Hollywood insiders about the rules of the game is *fear*. People in power are afraid to exercise their power, except to give the safety-first *no*. "It's a terrorist state where everybody's well-dressed, drives a nice car and is afraid," says actress-writer Karen Klein. "The suck of the business is to get a good racket that makes you a lot of money, protect your turf and don't be controversial."

"It's just the limited minds of people scared for their jobs," adds maverick filmmaker Henry Jaglom. "In the 20 years I've been in this town, I've heard {that} every single idea is impossible, wrong, the public will not pay attention to it. The conventional wisdom is just that, conventional, and it lasts until it's broken by the public."

Jaglom was one of several young editors (the list included Jack Nicholson) who edited Dennis Hopper's 1969 break-out rule-breaker *Easy Rider.* The film was made for about $400,000 and grossed more than $50 million for Columbia and caused a lot of studio people to throw out their rule books.

"When he showed it to the studio, it broke every single rule of that time, of what a major studio could or would release. There were language violations, drugs, attitude and that ending. . . . I mean, you couldn't end a movie with the heroes being killed. As soon as it became a hit, they started doing bad imitations of it."

Screenwriter Michael Eddy has adopted the rule of not arguing with executives because you don't change their minds.

"The basic rule is, if they don't want to do something, they won't do it. You can give them every sensible argument in the world, and nobody's going to change their minds, period."

Case in point: Eddy says he recently came up with a plot line for a sequel to a major studio movie that involved a serial killer. "One of the producers stopped me and said, 'No, this doesn't work.' I said, 'Why?' He said, 'We don't do maniacs here.' They tried to sell me on the idea that murderers are not interesting because they're crazy and you never know why they do what they're doing.

Finally, one of them said, 'Why don't you spend an afternoon in the library, go to the crime section . . . and see what kind of stuff you come up with.' I did, and I came back and said, 'Well, 95 percent of the books are on murders.' This same producer says, 'I told you so,' as if that validated his opinion that murderers were not interesting."

So, what is the secret of success?

"I don't think anybody knows," says Eddy. "I always had a theory that if you took all these script submissions and spread them out on a desk and sent in a chimpanzee with a banana, and you made every movie that the chimp touched with the banana and skipped the others, his track record would be as good as any of the studios."

It's an interesting notion, but nobody will try it. Ever since the failure of Fox's *Project X,* the 1987 film about lab monkeys who rebel against their working conditions, chimpanzees have been persona non grata in Hollywood. It's a rule.

"Rules of the Game," by Jack Mathews, *American Film,* Vol. XV, No. 6, March 1990, pp. 32–59. Used with permission of Jack Mathews.

*Note: After this article was written, Tom Hanks successfully appeared in the movie *Philadelphia,* about a lawyer stricken with the AIDS virus.

Imagining Filmmaking's Future

Digital technology is transforming the movie industry just as fast as it is affecting other media industries. In this article from *American Film* magazine, Randall Tierney speculates about how digitizing will affect filmmakers in the next century.

Consider:

1. How will the use of "image digits" change the way filmmakers work?

2. Describe how a global digital film network would work. What are its advantages for filmmakers?

3. What did Ansel Adams mean when he said, "The negative is the score but the print is the performance"? How will that apply to digital filmmaking?

Filmmaking 2000: The Digital Filmmakers

Randall Tierney

Two figures are hunched over a glowing box. They could be playing Super Mario Brothers—but they're too old for that and far too serious. On a monitor, images pop on and off as the louder of the two calls out orders to the other, who responds at the controls. The one in charge is a film director, though there is no celluloid in sight. The one at the controls, well, they're still trying to come up with a title for him. This is filmmaking 2000—when the director will be as familiar with the click of a computer mouse as he is with the slap of the clapboard—and the operative word is *digital.*

Simply put, digital film technology allows a movie to be fed into a computer and atomized into image digits. Each frame of film can then be manipulated on the screen like electronic clay, recolored, resized, replicated or eliminated. When the movie has been revised, the new pictures are converted back into film and a new negative is run out of the computer like paper from a printer. Such creative capability in the post-production phase of filmmaking could have a profound impact on the way movies are made.

At present, there are only a handful of visual-effects houses across the country doing digital film work on their own systems, mostly to create otherworldly images: Boss Film Studios (*Ghost*), R/Greenberg Associates (*Predator 2*), Metro Light Studios (*Total Recall*) and Industrial Light and Magic (*Willow, The Abyss*). As the technology advances, more filmmakers are turning to digital for their work, and not just for special effects.

Industrial Light and Magic, based in San Rafael, California, used digital techniques in *Die Hard 2* to pull off a scene that would have been a logistical and budgetary nightmare to shoot on location. A painted background of the airport tarmac was photographed in four different sizes, the images fed into a computer and manipulated to simulate a pull-back shot. Actors and moving vehicles, shot separately, were digitally blended in and color-corrected in the process. The result is seamlessly realistic.

What's changing most quickly in the digital domain is the role of the cinematographer. Says Ed Jones, director of post-production at ILM: "Cinematographers are used to how film reacts, but how do you combine the painterly skills of a cinematographer with those of a computer person?"

The answer to that question may be just around the corner. In the fall of 1992, Kodak's High Resolution Electronic Intermediate System [was] unveiled. C. Bradley Hunt, director of advanced technology products for Kodak's motion picture and television products division, sees the Intermediate System as the first step toward a global digital film network, in which a movie could be pieced together over phone lines. "Say you need a moon in the background," offers Hunt, "you could call up a [stock house] and order a moon, then they download to you and you composite it in."

There is one major technological leap on the way to realizing Hunt's scenario: data storage. Some effects, like ILM's pseudopod creature in *The Abyss,* can be created without using overwhelming amounts of data, simply because the image is transparent and in motion. Opaque, still figures require more memory to create. And storing an entire film with today's technology is almost beyond comprehension. The amount of storage needed for one frame of 35mm film: about 40 megabytes, the capacity of the average personal computer.

"The big problem that no one has thought of yet is archiving," says Jones. "We calculated one film to be $7^1/_2$ terabytes — terabytes being millions. A lot of research is being done, but when you get into image files, not just data files, it's a whole different ball game." Right now, Jones and other special-effects wizards are employing digital technology mostly as "another arrow in our quiver." . . .

Says cinematographer Allen Daviau (*Avalon*), "Digital is going to be part of the cinematographer's repertoire. If you've recorded something and you want it properly interpreted, you have to be there in the digital domain. It's analogous to what Ansel Adams said with regard to dark-room printing: The negative is the score but the print is the performance."

The possibilities with digital are mind-boggling. Eventually, production schedules could be cut in half. Preservation would be a cinch: A film could be touched up on the computer with a digital pen, then stored for eternity. And if anthropologists wanted to screen a movie in a thousand years, they could create a print as fresh as the original. One clear danger in the brave new world of digital is the movie hacker. With films accessible through phone lines, any kid with a 21st century PC could crack, say, the *Casablanca* file. Forget about colorization — he could change the ending.

"Filmmaking 2000: The Digital Filmmakers," by Randall Tierney, *American Film,* Vol. XVI, No. 4, April 1991, p. 51. Used with permission of Randall Tierney.P

PART III
Support Industries

CHAPTER 10
Advertising

Re-imagining Advertising

The transformation of television programming and delivery systems is shaking up the advertising community, according to Jay Mathews in this article from the *Washington Post.* It is possible, says Mathews, that television in the future won't carry advertising. This, of course, could dramatically change the advertising business.

Consider:

1. Why did one advertising executive say, "We can't be sure ad-supported TV programming will have a future"? Do you agree? Disagree? Explain.

2. How is the mass audience for television changing? Why is it changing?

3. How could these changes affect the advertising business? What changes would the advertising business have to make to respond?

Are the Ads Infinitum? Madison Avenue Fears the Day May Come When Television Won't Carry Commercials

Jay Mathews

Television without advertising? The embattled American channel clicker might consider that an amusing, even an enchanting concept.

But in certain concrete canyons of Manhattan where advertisers dwell, and where this notion has begun to take hold, it is not the least bit funny.

And now the head of Procter & Gamble Co., a man as important to U.S. advertising as turnips are to a pig, has said out loud what many only agonized over in private: Someday there may be no commercials on the tube.

"From where we stand today," Edwin L. Artzt told the annual conference of the American Association of Advertising Agencies in May [1994], "we can't be sure ad-supported TV programming will have a future in the world being created."

He might as well have lectured his neighborhood nursery school on the nonexistence of Santa Claus, or told Congress it could no longer use the public mails.

In the weeks since Artzt, chairman and chief executive of Procter & Gamble, made his chilling declaration, the advertising industry's journals, newsletters, bulletin boards and meetings have been full of talk of how likely this revolution in American viewing habits is, and what it means for an industry considered essential for the survival of thousands of businesses.

They see the possibility that popular tastes and the advertising that feeds off them will break into so many little pieces that the mass messages that have defined American life in this century no longer will have an audience.

"Mass television advertising as we know it may become almost obsolete," said Eric Hatch, a senior vice president at the Bethesda-based Earle Palmer Brown Associates Inc. advertising agency. "We are developing media that may be much more personalized, and there will be more choices of what forms it will take."

But don't write off the American television advertising industry just yet. It would never have accumulated its bulging $35 billion in annual sales without a keen survival instinct.

For years it has noticed the cable markets expanding, pay-per-view events prospering and wondered if it was in trouble. Now, as technology and communications channels expand exponentially, agencies realize that consumers may be seeking their entertainment, and some very specialized advertising, from their computer bulletin boards, their hobby-oriented cable channels, their interactive TV channels and a hundred other new communication byways that have little to do with mass network television.

So what is American advertising without its TV?

One image forming in some advertising executive nightmares is of television without seams, one program flowing into the next without promotions for antacids. For this privilege the viewer would pay a fee, or choose to resign from program-watching altogether to play the video game channel for a monthly subscription.

To combat this, executives argue, advertising agencies may have to pool their resources with advertisers to produce their own programs, with the corporate logo placed at proper moments to remind the viewer, without offending him or her, who was paying the bills.

Sound familiar? This is the way television was born in the late 1940s, with advertisers such as Texaco Inc. funding and producing programs such as Milton Berle's "The Texaco Star Theatre."

"You have to be a partner with your clients," said Melanie Morgan, vice president and corporate broadcast director at Earle Palmer Brown. "You need to understand the nuances of the market."

Such expensive projects as producing their own shows would, in the minds of some, make it impossible for small and middle-sized agencies to survive. The responsibility for setting American tastes, which often falls to advertising by design or default, would gravitate into the hands of the few giant marketing-advertising-publicizing conglomerates that make New York, Los Angeles and London their home.

Taking the Long View

Change, however, doesn't always happen as quickly or with as much electronic pyrotechnics as you find in your local computer magazines. Many television network executives think they have years of profitable advertising ahead of them.

"Nobody wants to be an ostrich in this business," said Jon Nesvig, president of sales for Fox Broadcasting Co., "but I think there is going to still be a real significant place for free mass media in the future. No matter how targeted your advertising message, you still have to figure out a way to reach potential new users."

Some agency executives argue that inbred American skepticism and conservatism will save them from commercial-free TV, as the fickle gods of taste and convenience protected the nation from previous fads such as 3-D movies and purple hair.

They say American consumers will be reluctant to alter cherished daily routines to shop by computer. Instead, they will insist on taking their regular drive to the mall to buy whatever they last saw advertised on "Oprah."

Television executives say there is a limit to how big a monthly check Americans will write to get TV movies and specials without advertising.

Robert Iger, president of the ABC Television Network Group, sums it up: If advertisers are no longer welcome on television, he asks, who is going to pay for all of his prime-time programming?

Preparing for Change

Fueling the flame of fear in their hearts, though, are people like Barry Diller, chairman of the TV-shopping network QVC.

Procter & Gamble's Artzt said he prepared his speech to the advertisers after meeting with several of the profit-conscious prophets of the new media age, including Diller, Tele-Communications Inc. Chairman John C. Malone and Viacom Inc. Chairman Sumner M. Redstone. Each meeting appeared to leave him more convinced that conventional approaches to advertising have to change.

Diller told him the Home Shopping Network could sell 20,000 pairs of earrings in five minutes.

"That's terrific for a company that sells impulse items," Artzt said. "But Procter & Gamble, in a given year, has to sell 400 million boxes of Tide."

Even a product as tightly woven into consumer consciousness as Tide requires regular reinforcement, or the cerebral synapses that record brand names will soak up the generic version instead. Procter & Gamble wants at least 90 percent of its target audiences to see a commercial for its brands six or seven times a month.

"The only way you can achieve that kind of impact is with broad-reach television," Artzt said, "which is why we spend almost 90 percent of our $3 billion advertising budget on TV, and why we simply must preserve

our ability to use television as our principal advertising medium."

Rather than terrorizing, the new view of the future excites some agencies.

Agencies such as Young & Rubicam Inc. have established new departments to explore the implications of interactive television — a common name for the future combination of television, telephone and computer services. They think the new machines offer ways to increase agency revenue and corporate profits even beyond today's levels.

"Traditional television is skewed in the audience it reaches," said Mike Samet, executive vice president for media and new technologies at Young & Rubicam. Consumers who watch television infrequently or not at all may be drawn in by new computer services that also include advertising. Samet said the new technologies "will open up new markets to advertising we did not know were there before."

Some executives remain skeptical of that happening in the near future, although they caution that in their business, trying to predict what will happen more than two years hence is grounds for a competency hearing.

"There are some experiments going on," said Jeb Brown, chief executive of Earle Palmer Brown, "but I believe that we are a long way from interactive TV on a wide basis."

In the interim, several advertisers point to opportunities that have materialized for special messages inserted in media outlets that did not exist a decade ago.

Rich Hollander, a former television correspondent who is president of the Baltimore-based Millbrook Communications production company, has been offering advertisers spots on local news reports wedged into the CNN Headline News channel. He has begun to do the same on the Home Shopping Network.

"I liken it to a political campaign," said Hollander, who wrote a book a decade ago about the possible impact of interactive television on politics. "You are building a series of constituencies."

For Artzt and the network executives close to him, the salvation of mass advertising may come from the stubborn frugality of American consumers even in times of affluence. Mass merchandisers have been complaining recently about how cheap their recession-weary customers have become, but now agencies see dollar signs in the national urge to hoard every nickel.

"Maybe our involvement means that a pay-per-view movie can be pulled down for half the price—or even free—if it includes commercials," Artzt said. "Or maybe it means that the ten-dollar monthly fee for a game channel can be reduced to two or three dollars if we can integrate advertising."

As advertisers have done for a generation, Artzt and others are fortified by the knowledge —buttressed by studies—that although Americans complain about commercials, they usually watch them, and might miss them if they were gone.

"We're limited only by our creativity here," he said, "and our ability to prove that it's in everyone's interest to involve advertising in these new media."

Role Reversal in Auto Ads

Women are buying more cars than ever before, and this article from *Advertising Age* describes how advertisers are changing their pitch to respond. "Long gone are the scenes of women draped over the hoods of cars," says reporter Raymond Serafin.

Consider:

1. How does the new image of women portrayed in auto advertising differ from the old image?

2. Why is the shift in advertising approaches important to advertisers?

3. What are the elements in society that have caused advertisers to change their focus, according to Serafin? Explain.

I Am Woman, Hear Me Roar . . . in My Car

Greater Purchasing Power Brings Role Reversal to Auto Ads

Raymond Serafin

In a new [1994] Pontiac Bonneville commercial, a woman daydreams about a romantic ride with an attractive male, wending along a coastal highway that brings them to an elegant restaurant. She's driving.

It's just one example of how auto marketers are putting women in the driver's seat more than ever in 1995 model year advertising. Long gone are the scenes of women draped over the hoods of cars, a onetime staple of car advertising that played to male fantasies. Nor are women confined to being the chauffeurs for groups of suburban kids.

Consider some other examples:

- A spot for the 1995 Pontiac Grand Am from D'Arcy Masius Benton & Bowles, Bloomfield Hills, Mich., depicts a savvy young woman who brings her brother to a dealer's lot. His role is to help her pick out the color of her new car.

- An introductory commercial for the Volkswagen Passat from Berlin Cameron Doyle, New York, shows a young male executive assigned to pick up the company's president. The president turns out to be an older woman who commandeers the car for a cross-country joyride.

- In a spot from Lowe & Partners/SMS, a woman driving a Mercedes-Benz E420 speeds up to beat an approaching 18-wheeler. "I am engine, Hear me roar," says the voice-over, evoking the 1970s Helen Reddy song "I Am Woman."

- Four of five introductory spots by McCann/SAS, Troy, Mich., for the GMC Jimmy sport-utility vehicle feature women, including one with a suit-clad executive who doesn't have to sacrifice her dignity getting in because of the vehicle's low step-in height.

- The most lavishly produced auto commercial for 1995 depicts a woman at a cocktail party who notices a small-scale car weaving around the wavy lines of an abstract painting. The woman suddenly appears inside the artwork, steering the Aurora luxury sedan through a world of bold, colorful curves. Leo Burnett USA, Chicago, created the spot for General Motors Corp.'s Oldsmobile.

"Women react positively to seeing themselves portrayed as competent and knowledgeable consumers," said Lynn Myers, general director-brand management and marketing, GM's Pontiac division.

At the same time, research by Pontiac and DMB&B into the new advertising indicates men accept it. "Men felt the role reversal was kind of intriguing," Ms. Myers said. "Younger men said it was relevant to their experiences, while older men recognized that times have changed."

Increasing economic clout is one factor driving newfound respect for women in auto ads. Women are making or influencing more purchase decisions, even in luxury cars and upscale sport-utility vehicles, the fastest-growing auto segment.

From 1987 to 1994, women rose from being 18.2% of the principal light-duty truck drivers to 24.6%, according to J.D. Power & Associates, an Agoura Hills, Calif.-based

market researcher. That helped drive a surge in the popularity of minivans and sport-utility vehicles.

While women make up 45.7% of the principal car drivers (down slightly from 46.2% in 1987), they represent more than 50% of the principal drivers in the basic small, lower-middle, and small sporty segments, said Tom Healey, Power's advertising and media services director.

Women now comprise 29% of luxury car principal drivers, but many more aspire to those brands. Mr. Healey said that's why a marketer like Jaguar Cars has targeted executive women for its late-model used Jaguar leasing program.

"Women are potentially a very big area of growth in the luxury car segment," said Andy Goldberg, general manager-integrated marketing communications for Mercedes-Benz of North America. "If we want to expand our franchise, we need to address them."

Cadillac earlier this year tested a marketing effort in Minneapolis aimed at women, and is putting a national program into place, said Peter Levin, advertising director for the GM division.

The Cadillac effort will include promotions with women-oriented magazines like *Elle, Harper's Bazaar* and *Town & Country,* as well as new advertising from DMB&B that features Cadillac women employees. One spot shows Veronica Issacs, roadside service supervisor, discussing Cadillac's 24-hour roadside assistance benefit.

Another reason for change in the still male-dominated auto industry is that women are making headway in marketing jobs. "We bring a different perspective to a marketing program," said Ms. Myers.

Ford division is featuring women drivers in TV spots created by J. Walter Thompson USA, Detroit, for two small sporty cars: the Probe and Mustang convertible.

Media and promotional tactics are slowly evolving, too.

For example, Mercedes-Benz, tradition-ally strong in sports programming, is putting more emphasis on prime-time programming. GM's Chevrolet is sponsoring the America3 all-female sailing team that will compete for the America's Cup in 1995, and is planning spring tie-ins to attract women buyers to the new Tahoe, a full-size sport-utility vehicle.

Pontiac has increased its use of magazines that have predominantly women readers.

"We're seeing the industry treat women as bonafide consumers who are interested in what a car is all about, not just the color," Ms. Myers said.

"I Am Woman, Hear Me Roar . . . in My Car," by Raymond Serafin, *Advertising Age,* November 7, 1994, p. 1. Reprinted with permission of the November 7, 1994 issue of *Advertising Age.* © 1994 Crain Communications, Inc.

Changing the Icons' Image

Aunt Jemima and Betty Crocker are perhaps the most recognizable icons representing American food products. This article, written by Marilyn Kern-Foxworth and Susanna Hornig Priest of Texas A&M, discusses the recognizability of these icons and how the companies have altered the images over time to reflect changes in the marketplace for the products.

Consider:

1. Why were the icons originally created? Which icon was based on a real person?

2. What are the objections to the stereotyped image of Aunt Jemima voiced by African-Americans? How did the company respond?

3. Which of the icons is most recognizable, according to the study? What does this reflect about the companies' success in marketing the changes in the icons' images?

Aunt Jemima and Betty Crocker: Two American Icons Rising to the Top

Marilyn Kern-Foxworth and Susanna Hornig Priest
Texas A&M University

Aunt Jemima and Betty Crocker are two images that have graced our kitchens and occupied our cupboards for decades. Their similarities are quite remarkable. Both are female. Both have been trademarks for baking mixes for decades. Both have withstood the social changes of the time to become the leading trademarks in their product lines. Both have undergone tremendous physical changes to keep pace with their demanding consumers.

The major difference between the two trademarks, beyond their contrasting ethnicity, is that Aunt Jemima was initially a living trademark and Betty Crocker was a composite. As trademarks, they have been invited into American kitchens for breakfast, lunch and dinner more often than friends and relatives. No wonder, since "Americans are exposed to more messages in the form of trademarks than they are exposed to any other kinds of messages."[1]

Aunt Jemima

The Aunt Jemima trademark had its beginnings in Missouri. Chris L. Rutt, a newspaperman and Charles G. Underwood, a

A history of images

Here's how Aunt Jemima has changed over the years:

1890
The caricature of a black mammy was taken from posters used to advertise a blackface minstrel act, whose cakewalk-styled song, "Old Aunt Jemima," was the hit of the day.

1902
The image was part of national campaign to increase the brand's visibility. The company went bankrupt a year later.

1905
The reorganized company added color to the caricature.

1943
Edith Wilson, a Chicago blues singer, was featured in radio and TV ads. She also appeared in movies. She was used until 1966.

1968
Her face slimmed down and her red bandanna was replaced by a headband.

1989
In her latest change, Aunt Jemima lost her headband to a perm, and pearl earrings and a lace collar were added.

mill owner, purchased the Pearl Milling Company in 1888. After the purchase they began a relentless search for a product that all America would eat.[2] After much debate they decided to make pancakes, and within a year they produced the first pancake mix.[3]

After the first ready-mix was perfected in 1889, an immediate search began for a symbol that would make the product recognizable by all American housewives.

While visiting a vaudeville house in St. Joseph, Missouri, one evening in the autumn of 1889, Rutt noticed a team of black-face minstrel comedians known as Baker and Farrell. The high point of the act was a jazzy, rhythmic New Orleans-style cakewalk performed to a tune called "Aunt Jemima."[4] The song was originally called "Old Aunt Jemima" and was one of the most popular songs of the day. The team wore aprons and red bandannas reminiscent of the traditional southern cook.[5]

Rutt knew that the song and costume projected the image for which he had been searching. He decided to mimic it, using not only the name but the likeness of the southern "mammy" emblazoned on the lithographed posters advertising the act of Baker and Farrell, thus beginning a new era in advertising. This would be the first time a living person would be used to personify a company's trademark.[6]

When Rutt and Underwood could not raise [enough money] to effectively promote and market the product, they sold their interests to the R. T. Davis Mill and Manufacturing Company of St. Joseph, Missouri, after registering the trademark in 1890. Davis was a master of promotion, and one of his first great ideas was to find a real person to portray Aunt Jemima. An article in *The Poster,* a trade magazine for outdoor advertisers that was published around the turn of the century, reported that Aunt Jemima and the Armour meat chef ["The Ham What Am"] were the two symbols most trusted by the American housewife.[7]

The Aunt Jemima Mills Company used this information to proliferate the visibility of Aunt Jemima and subsequently published a pamphlet proclaiming, "Aunt Jemima, the Most Famous Colored Woman in the World."[8] By 1910 the trademark was known in all 48 states.[9] One of the reasons for the trademark's popularity was the women who took on the persona of Aunt Jemima. The first was a former slave from Kentucky named Nancy Green. Several other Aunt Jemimas served as ambassadors for the product from state to state.

The promotional strategies used by the owners of the trademark have continued to give it a first-place status for nearly a century. As premiums for using the Aunt Jemima products, the company has distributed four million salt and pepper shakers; 200,000 plastic dolls; 150,000 cookie jars; and more than one million plastic syrup pitchers, all of which are highly sought after by collectors. None, however, received such acclaim as the Aunt Jemima rag doll, coveted by little girls throughout America. The company boasts that "literally every city child owned one." The phenomenon can be equated to the Cabbage Patch doll rage several years ago [1980s].[10]

[In 1926] the Aunt Jemima Mills Company of St. Joseph, Missouri, assigned trademark rights to the Quaker Oats Company.[11]

The first major change for the trademark occurred during the 1950s; the second major change came in 1968. In the 1960s, during the pinnacle of the Civil Rights Movement, the Quaker Oats Company stopped using live models as trademarks and resorted to using composites like those of Betty Crocker. Ron Bottrell, spokesperson at Quaker Oats, says the strategy changed for the trademark because America's values had changed. "Although Aunt Jemima was much loved by all Americans," he says, "there was a feeling that the design was denigrating to blacks in general."[12]

As a result, the officials at Quaker Oats took Aunt Jemima through a complete metamorphosis. To make her image more appealing to blacks, she lost over 100 pounds, became 40 years younger, got a new headdress and moved from the Higbee Plantation to New Orleans. In essence, when black consumers charged that Aunt Jemima perpetuated stereotypical portrayals, she was transformed from a caricature of a black mammy to a savvy Creole cooking instructor.[13] Today [in 1994] the Aunt Jemima product line represents $225 million of Quaker Oats' $5.3 billion in annual sales.[14]

To prepare for the 1990s, the Quaker Oats Company put the Aunt Jemima trademark through a complete metamorphosis in April, 1989, 100 years after the concept began. All that remained of the stereotypical Jemima was her effervescent smile. The headband was traded in for soft, gray streaked hair, and to give her a more contemporary look she now wears pearl earrings and a lace collar. By the end of the summer, 1989, the new Aunt Jemima image adorned all of the 40 Aunt Jemima products. Ironically, writers who critiqued the new image summarized the change by stating that she now looked like a "black Betty Crocker."[15]

In an unprecedented move, in 1994 Quaker Oats named Gladys Knight as the spokesperson for Aunt Jemima Lite maple syrup. Critics charged that this move was done to lure back disgruntled African-American consumers. Ken Smikle, publisher of Target Market News, asserts that, "For some consumers, there's no amount of makeover that would sufficiently offset the stereotypes associated with the name and the picture."[16]

Betty Crocker

"She's an all-American girl with blue eyes. She's a good cook, a good administrator, a good mother, civic minded, she's good at everything."[17] And she is known to the world as Betty Crocker.

In 1921 a Gold Medal Flour advertisement offered consumers a pincushion resembling a flour sack if they correctly completed a jigsaw puzzle of a milling scene. The response was overwhelming. Sam Gale, head of Washburn Crosby's, forerunner of General Mills, Inc. advertising department oversaw the personal signing of all the letters, and decided that they should be signed by a fictional person. He decided to use the name of a woman to reply to the requests. Gale recalls that her last name came from William G. Crocker, a popular treasurer and director of the company. It also was the name of the first flour mill in Minneapolis, Washburn Crosby's hometown, the home city of the forerunner of General Mills and of the food giant today.[18] The name Betty was very popular during the time. It exuded warmth and was also a familiar and friendly nickname. Thus the name Betty Crocker was selected. A company employee, Florence Lindeberg, provided the first signature in 1921. Other employees provided baking tips, suggestions, and hints from the Washburn Crosby test kitchens.[19]

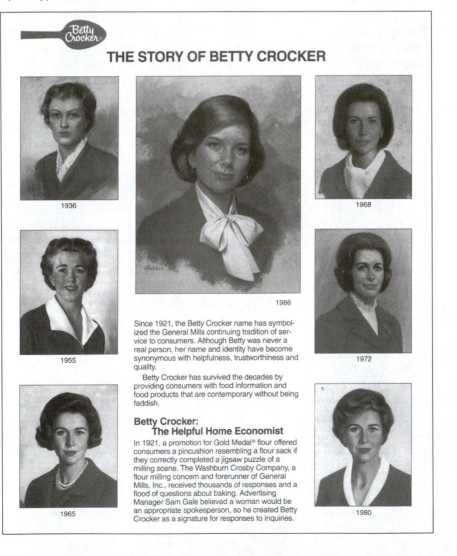

THE STORY OF BETTY CROCKER

1936

1968

1986

1955

1972

Since 1921, the Betty Crocker name has symbolized the General Mills continuing tradition of service to consumers. Although Betty was never a real person, her name and identity have become synonymous with helpfulness, trustworthiness and quality.

Betty Crocker has survived the decades by providing consumers with food information and food products that are contemporary without being faddish.

**Betty Crocker:
The Helpful Home Economist**

In 1921, a promotion for Gold Medal® flour offered consumers a pincushion resembling a flour sack if they correctly completed a jigsaw puzzle of a milling scene. The Washburn Crosby Company, a flour milling concern and forerunner of General Mills, Inc., received thousands of responses and a flood of questions about baking. Advertising Manager Sam Gale believed a woman would be an appropriate spokesperson, so he created Betty Crocker as a signature for responses to inquiries.

1965

1980

Advertisers learned early that listeners became very attached to radio luminaries who were "guests" in their homes. And in 1925 advertisers capitalized on this radio audience to bring Betty Crocker to life. A 1925 experiment with the "Betty Crocker Cooking School of the Air" in Buffalo attracted letters by the tens of thousands, according to General Mills historian James Gray. The school became the first daytime radio food service program. Blanche Ingersoll became the voice of Betty Crocker in 1924.

The show, which offered students an opportunity to graduate, continued for 24 years. By its closure over one million listeners had "graduated." By 1925 a total of 13 different Betty Crockers spoke over the radio networks in various parts of the country, offering friendly advice and providing words of confidence. The promotion became so popular that the fictitious "Betty" was writing replies to over 4000 letters a day.[20]

General Mills was very effective in creating an image for Betty Crocker and by 1940, nine out of 10 American homemakers knew her name.[21] According to *Fortune* magazine in April 1945, she also was the second best-known woman in America, following First Lady Eleanor Roosevelt.[22] The fact that company executives had been quite astute regarding her appearance also had helped the image gain momentum. American consumers were given a face to place with the voice in 1936 when, on her 15th birthday, Betty Crocker received a face. Washburn commissioned a portrait from artist Neysa McMein. Using the features of several Home Service Department members, McMein created a composite that remained in use for almost 20 years. The first portrait offered a sensible and capable appearance free of frivolity and glamour.[23] Artists have altered [Betty Crocker's] looks in promotional material from time to time to reflect the changes in American dress and lifestyle.

To keep pace with sociological transformations occurring in society, General Mills later sought to target their products to a younger-aged woman. In 1955, the company invited six artists, including Norman Rockwell, to paint a new Betty Crocker composite. A survey of 1600 women selected illustrator Hilda Taylor's concept of Betty Crocker as the best.

In 1965 and 1968, artist Joe Bowler updated Betty, making her younger and more sophisticated. In 1972, Minneapolis illustrator Jerome Ryan painted a new Betty Crocker composite. Ryan admitted that his concept of Betty Crocker was that she should not be too beautiful. She would wear a red David Crystal suit and Monet pin, both produced by subsidiaries of General Mills. The company made every effort to make the model look as real as possible and the composite was "photographically painted, so those people who knew nothing about art would think it was a real person." The 1980s composite incorporated the features of the 1965 face with softened, more casual hairstyle and clothing. Changes were made in her appearance in 1955, 1965, 1968, 1972, 1980 and 1986.[24]

The last change occurred after General Mills discovered that 40 percent of grocery shoppers are now men as compared to less than 30 percent a decade ago; that 34 percent of all men today over the age of 21 bake as compared to 22 percent a decade ago; and that 20 percent of all meals are prepared by teenagers as compared to 14 percent in 1975.[25]

The new Betty Crocker is therefore younger with a more casual hairstyle. Her smile is friendly, approachable and confident. To increase the publicity surrounding the new Betty Crocker image, General Mills' public relations staff developed seven story angles for the media and arranged interviews between the media and the portrait artist. The publicity resulting from their efforts totalled 1.3 billion impressions.[26] One author wrote of the latest change:

When Betty Crocker (now aged 52 and holding up quite well, thank you) changed her hairstyle, shed several years, and came out looking less homemakerish and more careerish, the international fashion press covered the occasion with all the attention lavished on the latest Paris *haut ton.*[27]

The Betty Crocker name appears in 10 different product categories on over 130 products, including a five-item line of ice cream novelties that was introduced in 1987. In 1986 General Mills spent $17.1 million advertising its Betty Crocker baking mixes.[28] In 1987 General Mills debuted 22 new products under the Betty Crocker trademark and allocated $35 million to an advertising campaign.[29] Additionally, in 1989, General Mills introduced the "Dear Betty Crocker" consumer cooking advice column in hundreds of newspapers.[30]

The undaunting fascination with the trademark is evidenced by the fact that there were more than 70,000 visitors to the Betty Crocker Kitchens each year before they were closed to the public in 1986. As further testimony to her influence, according to a 1989 Donnelley Marketing study conducted of 2500 households, more people would buy a product endorsed by Betty Crocker than would buy a product endorsed by Ann Landers, Bill Cosby, James Garner, or Oprah Winfrey.[31]

In 1990, the international ImagePower Survey by Landor Associates polled 10,000 consumers about more than 6,000 brands measuring not only awareness, but also whether consumers liked them. Again Betty Crocker scored high, ranking 16th on the list of Most Powerful Brands in the United States.[32]

This popularity has been spurred not only by the products that she adorns, but also by the cookbooks issued under her name. *Betty Crocker Cook Book* was introduced in 1950. It has remained one of the more popular cookbooks, and more than 27 million copies have been sold. A new Betty Crocker Cook-

book was introduced October 1, 1991, 70 years after Betty Crocker was introduced.[33]

The Trademark's Influence on Popular Culture

The purpose of this study was to provide information on how the two trademarks have been infused into American popular culture. . . . [Q]uestionnaires were administered approximately one year to the day following the introduction of the latest change for Aunt Jemima and three years to the day of the latest change for Betty Crocker.

There are over 10,000 trademarks introduced into the market each year. [Ninety] percent of the companies introducing these trademarks do not last and the trademarks therefore only last for one year. Many consumers are oblivious to . . . trademarks and cannot recall the trademark nor the companies they represent. Betty Crocker and Aunt Jemima, fortunately, are trademarks that are recognizable and popular. . . .[We] were interested in finding out the characteristics that make these two trademarks so well liked by the general public. [We] also were interested in determining which of the two is more popular and if one trademark were more popular or recognizable than the other and if so why. [We] also were interested in determining whether or not the amount of money used to let consumers know about the introduction of a new trademark made a difference in the ability of consumers to identify that trademark and sponsoring company. This was of particular interest, . . . since General Mills had spent thousands of dollars to introduce the last Betty Crocker and Quaker Oats had spent a mere $500 to introduce the 1989 version of Aunt Jemima. In fact, officials at Quaker Oats sent press releases to the media and did nothing else to alert the public of Aunt Jemima's change. The officials were fearful that focusing too much attention on the trademark would arouse too much attention within the African-American community. [We] also [wanted to] find out how many of the respondents would recognize the new Aunt Jemima one year after the new trademark was introduced.

Method

To conduct the analysis, students at a large southern university were surveyed in three different journalism classes to determine their impressions of both trademarks. Along with the 20-item questionnaire, students were given three photocopies of each trademark depicting various makeovers at strategic times in the characters' existence. The pictures of Aunt Jemima showed her appearance for the years 1936, 1968 and 1989, and the years chosen for Betty Crocker were 1936, 1965 and 1986.

Students were asked to rank each character on her attractiveness, intelligence and warmth. In addition, the respondents were asked to estimate the trademark's income level and profession. [We] also were interested in determining if the students knew what product the trademark represented, and . . . asked [the students] to identify the category in which the trademark would be found.

To increase the validity of the answers, no two students sitting beside each other had copies of the same trademark; therefore each student was provided with alternate pictures of Betty Crocker and Aunt Jemima for alternate years.

Results

Betty Crocker's newest image is more recognizable than her older two, but was only identified correctly by name, and as a food company representative, by 23% of the respondents in each case. The new Betty is seen coming from a somewhat higher socio-economic group and was classified as a professional or managerial worker by 95% of the respondents. However, the perceived socioeconomic class of the earlier Bettys was also relatively high (at $40–45,000 estimated household income), and the . . . occupational classification of respondents was also professional or managerial. The . . . results [also] suggest the second Betty presents a slightly less authoritarian and more motherly image than the first, but the [students' impression of the] third Betty . . . resembl[es] that of the first.

The early Aunt Jemima image was correctly identified by name by all respondents; 80% identified the second image used. Both images were generally classified as "food company representative" (by 85% and 84% of the respondents, respectively). The more contemporary Aunt Jemima image was correctly identified by only 42% of the respondents, and classified as a food company representative by only 63%. The new Aunt Jemima is markedly less recognizable than the older ones, but still substantially more recognizable than any of the Betty Crocker images.

The new Aunt Jemima also has a sharply different socioeconomic image, classified as professional or managerial by 68% of the respondents. Earlier images were classified as household worker by 78% (earliest photo) and 64% (second photo) of respondents. She has almost caught up to Betty Crocker on income, with the mean income category assigned by respondents falling in the $40–45,000 range. . . . [T]he new Aunt Jemima is seen as nearly as attractive as, and not much different in intelligence and authoritarianism from, the newest Betty Crocker. She remains very motherly, unlike Betty, whose newest image is even less motherly than the old.

Some of the differences between the two images are, of course, a function of generalized expectations about blacks and whites rather than a specific trademark characteristic. That even the new Aunt Jemima is seen as somewhat less attractive, authoritative, and intelligent than the newest Betty Crocker must be ascribed in part to this factor. But the new Aunt Jemima definitely presents a more positive image — as an attractive, intelligent professional, middle-class woman — than the old. And although there has been some sacrifice of recognizability from a marketing perspective, the latest Aunt Jemima is still seen as a very motherly figure.

Discussion

Trademarks have been a formidable force in business since the first trademarks appeared on early Chinese porcelain, on pottery jars from ancient Greece and Rome, and on goods from India dating back to about 1300 B.C. Since that time [trademarks] have filtered in and out of our lives on a regular basis. A synopsis of the impact of trademarks upon our lives is skillfully presented in the following:

> Trademarks evolved as accurate barometers of our constantly changing attitudes, styles, tastes and customs. They are the commercial icons, the cultural motifs, the social relics we've left strewn in our wake on our stroll through history. Some we've left behind as unsightly litter; some we've carefully stored away as museum treasures or oddities; but many, however, we keep polishing, updating, and carrying along as part of the baggage, with all the new marks that constantly sprout in our path as we move along.[34]

The "mammy" image, projected and perpetuated by Aunt Jemima, has enthralled Americans for over a century, becoming one of the most common depictions of black women in American history. The portrayal has become so much a part of American culture that it has been seen as representative of black American womanhood from slavery to the present.

Quaker Oats quickly hastened to modify the image during the 1960s when black citizens looked around and decided that Aunt Jemima did not and could never define black womanhood. It became customary within the black community that whenever another black wanted to ridicule a black female, they would call her "Aunt Jemima." Thus the concept throughout most of its existence has had a negative connotation. The phrase remained a part of popular culture in the early part of the 20th Century when the pancake mix had become very well known. Black children would gather to play a school-yard game called "playing the dozens" by saying "Ain't ya mama on the pancake box."

Betty Crocker emerged as a wholesome symbol to which all homemakers could relate over 70 years ago. Throughout the years her image has changed and the message that she conveys has been modified to align with societal trends. One of the facts that the survey suggests is that although many people are familiar with the trademark name Betty Crocker, they are not as apt to know what she looks like, evidenced by the fact that several respondents indicated that she was Margaret Thatcher, Geraldine Farraro, or Jackie Onassis. On the other hand, most people not only are familiar with the brand name, Aunt Jemima, they are also just as likely to know what Aunt Jemima looks like. Reasons for the disparity might include:

1. Aunt Jemima is the only black female trademark used to personify a company's trademark.

2. There are other white females who personify company trademarks.

3. The Aunt Jemima trademark has existed for 32 years longer than Betty Crocker.

4. The Aunt Jemima trademark has exemplified the characteristic of warmth more

than the Betty Crocker trademark and people see her as being more comforting.

They both are female, both served as trademarks for food products, and both have been loved and adored by many, although for different reasons. Both symbols have graced our kitchens for decades and continue to make indelible impressions upon American culture. They have achieved myth-like qualities and in doing so have become American icons. Additionally, Aunt Jemima's recognizability and her uniqueness as a symbol of black womanhood underscore the social significance of her image for both blacks and whites.

The questions that can only be answered by time are: Will the two symbols maintain their status in society as they evolve to keep pace with the trends occurring within society? Will Aunt Jemima lose white consumers who became comfortable with her "mammy" type image? And will Betty Crocker lose customers with her sexy new image — an image that was initially supposed to be more that of a homemaker?

The strategies used by the promoters of Aunt Jemima and Betty Crocker have made them icons and have allowed their companies to do something that 9,000 companies fail to accomplish every year — maintain their existence.

Endnotes

1. Todd F. Simon and Lauren Oliver Strach, "'Branding' Consumers: The Role of Communication and Consumer Research in Trademark Law Analysis." Paper presented to the Advertising Division of the Association for Education in Journalism and Mass Communication, Minneapolis, Minnesota, August 1990.

2. Hal Morgan, *Symbols of America.* (New York: Viking Penguin, Inc., 1986).

3. Hannah Campbell, *Why Did They Name It . . . ?* (New York: Fleet Publishing Corporation, 1964).

4. Jackie Young, *Black Collectibles: Mammy and Her Friends.* (West Chester, PA: Schiffer Publishing Ltd., 1988).

5. Marilyn Kern-Foxworth, "Plantation Kitchen to American Icon: Aunt Jemima," *Public Relations Review,* 16: 43–55 (1990).

6. Arthur F. Marquette, *Brands, Trademarks and Goodwill: The Story of the Quaker Oats Company.* (New York: McGraw-Hill Company, 1967).

7. Stanley Sacharow, *Symbols of Trade: Your Favorite Trademarks and the Companies They Represent* (New York: Art Direction Book Company, 1982), p. 62.

8. Marquette.

9. Marilyn Kern-Foxworth, "Aunt Jemima Is 100, But Looking Good," *Media History Digest* 9: 54–58 (1989).

10. Marilyn Kern-Foxworth, "Aunt Jemima," *Insite,* June 1988, p. 18.

11. Marilyn Kern-Foxworth, *Aunt Jemima, Uncle Ben, and Rastus: Blacks in Advertising Yesterday, Today, and Tomorrow,* Westport, Conn.: Greenwood Press, 1994.

12. Marilyn Kern-Foxworth, "Aunt Jemima," *Insite,* June 1988, p. 20.

13. Ibid.

14. "Aunt Jemima Trademark to Be Updated," press release issued by Quaker Oats Company, April 27, 1989, Chicago, Illinois, p. 2.

15. Julie Liesse Erickson, "Aunt Jemima Makeover," *Advertising Age,* May 1, 1989, p. 8. "Aunt Jemima Gets New Hairdo, Keeps Same Smile," *Bryan-College Station Eagle,* April 28, 1989, p. 9; "Aunt Jemima Grays," *The Houston Post,* April 28, 1989, p. A2; "Quaker Oats Is Shedding New Light on Aunt Jemima," *The Wall Street Journal,* April 28, 1989, p. A4; "You've Come A Long Way, Jemima," *Emerge,* January 1990,

p. 31; "Aunt Jemima Updated," *Houston Chronicle,* April 30, 1989, p. 2A; "Aunt Jemima Trademark to Get 1990s Makeover," *Jet,* May 15, 1989.

16. Ono, Yumiko. "Aunt Jemima Brand Hires Gladys Knight," *The Wall Street Journal,* September 16, 1994, B5 and Horovitz, Bruce. "Knight Defends Role in Aunt Jemima Syrup Ads," *USA Today,* September 30, 1994, 3B.

17. Courtland L. Bovee and William F. Arens, *Contemporary Advertising* (Homewood, Il.: Richard P. Irwin, 1982).

18. *The Story of Betty Crocker,* General Mills, Inc., July 1992, p. 2.

19. Sacharow.

20. Bovee, p. 448.

21. Carol Nelson, *How to Market to Women* (Detroit: Invisible Inc., 1994).

22. *The Story of Betty Crocker,* p. 2.

23. Ibid.

24. Dennis L. Wilcox, Phillip H. Ault, and Warren K. Agee, *Public Relations Strategies and Tactics.* (New York: Harper & Row, Publishers, 1989).

25. Cathleen Toomey, "Betty Crocker: New and Improved," *Public Relations Journal,* p. 15.

26. Ibid.

27. Dan Cody, "Icons of Commerce," *SKY,* March 1988, p. 33.

28. Julie Liesse Erickson, "General Mills Plans New-Product Blitz," *Advertising Age,* December 14, 1987, pp. 1 and 92.

29. Ibid.

30. *The Story of Betty Crocker,* p. 4.

31. Nelson, p. 133.

32. *The Story of Betty Crocker,* p. 4.

33. Arlene Vigoda, "Betty's 40-Year Recipe for Success," *USA Today,* September 19, 1991.

34. Cody, p. 3.

"Aunt Jemima and Betty Crocker: Two American Icons Rising to the Top," by Marilyn Kern-Foxworth and Susanna Hornig Priest, adapted from a paper presented at the 1994 Annual Convention of the Popular Culture Association. Used by permission of the authors.

Candidate Commercials

Public criticism of political advertising erupted repeatedly during the 1994 political campaigns. In this article from the New York Times News Service, Melinda Henneberger discusses the use of negative political advertising in several important races. She also asserts that radio advertising was much more negative than TV advertising.

Consider:

1. Why is radio "an even more effective vehicle for negative messages than TV," according to Democratic political consultant Philip Friedman? Do you agree? Explain.

2. Discuss three tactics used in political ads on radio.

3. Why is radio used more often than TV as an "attack medium"?

As Political Ads Slither into Negativity, the Real Venom Is Not on TV

Melinda Henneberger

Dennis Vacco's television commercials describe his Democratic opponent for attorney general, Karen Burstein, merely as "ultra-liberal." But on the radio, his ads go further, dubbing her "the most liberal person ever to run for statewide office in New York."

Also running for office [in 1994], according to their opponents' radio spots, are "New Jersey's No. 1 biggest spender in Congress," "the highest spender in the entire U.S. Senate," and "a member of the worst Congress in history."

In what political consultants are calling the nastiest campaign season in memory, the unkindest cuts are being made out of sight. Television ads are getting increasingly negative, they say, but radio has become the weapon of choice.

"Many people believe radio is an even more effective vehicle for negative messages than TV," said Philip Friedman, a Democratic political consultant. "And in a year when negative ads seem to be doing better than ever, radio is more important than ever."

Polls have convinced many political operatives that negative messages are the way to go, especially in the close races that are so numerous this year.

"Polls show there's nothing good about politicians that people will believe, and nothing bad they won't believe," Friedman said. "The big question in most campaigns [in 1994] is whose negative campaign is better. If it's negative, it works. If it's positive, save it for your tombstone."

Radio is considered a hot medium for potshots because political operatives are convinced that mean words go down easier without unpleasant accompanying images. And radio ads are also more anonymous — that is, less likely to be linked in the listener's mind to the candidates who paid for them, and less likely to be scrutinized by the media.

"It's more amorphous, not as visible," said Hank Morris, a New York Democratic media consultant currently working for Ms. Burstein. "Radio is more insidious, so you can have a harsher message." And newspaper reporters generally don't tape radio ads, print transcripts, or analyze their content.

A New Jersey political consultant, who spoke on condition of anonymity, said: "Clearly, radio is used as more of an attack medium. With a visual, people don't take to that. Whereas with radio, you're in your car, maybe by yourself, and it's a voice speaking that you'll listen to."

Actually, it isn't only the negative claims that tend to be more extravagant on radio than on the small screen; positive messages, too, seem to get ratcheted up when the speaker is out of view.

Television commercials for Sen. Daniel Patrick Moynihan simply tout his work on welfare reform and deficit reduction, for example. But only his radio spots, on those same topics, end with the tag line: "Protecting New York as no one else ever has, ever will. New York's Moynihan."

Because of Federal Communications Commission rules that guarantee equal time for all candidates, radio stations limit the number of political advertisements they sell to any one campaign. So it is the impact, and not the number of radio commercials that has dramatically increased this year, with more incumbents using negative advertising as they struggle to hold on to their jobs.

In New York's 5th District in eastern Queens and Long Island's North Shore, an ad for Rep. Gary L. Ackerman shows Steven McDonald, a New York City police officer paralyzed when he was shot in the spine in 1986, endorsing the incumbent, who supported the crime bill.

But on the radio, the approach is more dramatic. Of Ackerman's Republican challenger, Grant Lally, an announcer says: "Lally? His way will make the criminals who have taken over our streets happy. Make the criminals miserable. Vote for Ackerman."

Lally, meanwhile, is airing radio spots that say: "Gary Ackerman is a member of the worst Congress in history" and "Gary Ackerman. He's so liberal, he's dangerous."

Another incumbent, Democratic Rep. Nita Lowey, running for re-election in New York's 18th District in Westchester County, the Bronx and Queens, appears in two very positive television ads describing her work on welfare reform and breast cancer research. But in a series of radio spots, two characters named Joe and Harry take the gloves off in her stead.

As they wait for their morning train, Harry calls the Republican challenger, Andrew C. Hartzell Jr., "just too extreme." Joe calls him "just another politician on the attack." These unusually talky commuters also say that Hartzell, a lawyer, is "big buddies with lots of special-interest types" and "says he wants to be a national politician. Mr. Big Shot."

"This guy has had some really questionable clients, like one of the 15 worst toxic polluters in the country," the ad continues. "They even operated in Queens and Westchester," Joe says on another morning, when he is particularly agitated after spending several days at home reading the papers while nursing a cold.

Hartzell answers, via another radio ad, that he has never represented anyone in an environmental case. (In an interview, Hartzell said he has done other work for the Phelps Dodge Corp., the Arizona copper company referred to by the opposition, but he disputed the numbers cited by Ms. Lowey's camp as evidence of the company's poor environmental record.)

His own ad accuses Ms. Lowey of lying about endorsements by half a dozen different police groups. (She was endorsed by an umbrella organization representing these departments, but not by each individual organization.) And it says: "She voted to use your tax dollars to pay for her political campaigns." A spokesman for Ms. Lowey, Rob Lewis, said Hartzell was misrepresenting her support for campaign finance reform.

Amid all the wrangling over who's telling the truth, one radio spot that has sparked particular protest in an opposing camp is one for Rep. Carolyn Maloney, who is running against New York City Councilman Charles Millard in the 14th District on the East Side of Manhattan, and in parts of Brooklyn and Queens.

In the ad, a stand-in for Forrest Gump's mother explains the political facts of life to her slow but successful son.

"As you go through life, Forrest, there are a lot of things that look better than they really are," the woman says. "This Charles Millard, for example. He's pretty good looking, but he hasn't been on the council three years, and already he's running for Congress. It would be one thing if he'd actually done something, but he hasn't gotten a single bill passed while he's been there."

Lisa Linden, a spokesman for Millard, said she was outraged by what she said was the sexist nature of the ad. "Could you imagine if the Millard campaign had released this spot against her, or commented on her looks in any way?"

Jonathan Houston, a media consultant for Ms. Maloney, said Ms. Linden had made

Millard's appearance fair game by referring to his "star quality" in a neighborhood newspaper. And he said in essence, that Millard started it, with an ad saying Ms. Maloney had raised taxes 52 times.

"He went negative last Saturday, so Forrest Gump started running on Tuesday as a result," Houston said.

Inevitably in the ad, Mrs. Gump goes on to say: "Yep, politics is like a box of chocolates, Forrest. You never know what you're going to get."

Houston said: "Humorous negative ads are, it seems to me, a lot more powerful than an announcer reading a script."

Because radio ads are cheaper (costing from $50 for a middle-of-the-night minute on an obscure station to $1,000 on a major outlet during peak commuting hours), they generally run longer, for 60 seconds, and they allow candidates to localize their message, tailoring it for the demographics of the area and even the radio station. And they allow more time and more leeway for levity as well as malice.

In a spot endorsing Gov. Mario Cuomo, a familiar voice says: "This is Ed Koch, the voice of reason." Cuomo, whose three-term record Koch extols, can do even better in the next four years, he says. "He can be better than the last 12. I could have been better, too.

"He doesn't have my sweet disposition," Koch adds. "Who does?"

Even the ubiquitous "you can call me Al" commercials from Cuomo's camp, which portray Republican challenger George Pataki as a puppet of Sen. Alfonse D'Amato, is a bit more over the top than the television version, if only because it seems harder to set up: "The next time George Pataki's in your neighborhood," it says, as Paul Simon breaks once again into song, "don't be surprised when he says, 'Betty, when you call me, you can call me Al.'"

As on television, many candidates advertising on the radio creatively try to turn around perceived negatives. Third-party gubernatorial candidate B. Thomas Golisano asks New Yorkers not to waste their vote on either of the other guys.

Pataki suggests that Cuomo is unaware of New York's problems. "He needs to go home, to live as we do, to understand the fear we have for our loved ones."

And a spot for Cuomo says that Pataki raised taxes as mayor of Peekskill. "George Pataki," the ad says in closing. "Politics as usual." [Note: Pataki won the 1994 governor's race.]

"As Political Ads Slither into Negativity, the Real Venom Is Not on TV," by Melinda Henneberger, New York Times News Service, October 29, 1994. © 1994 by The New York Times Company. Reprinted by permission.

Shifting Trends

Ethnic marketing emerged in the 1990s as a new strategy for U.S. advertising agencies. In this article from *Advertising Age,* Christy Fisher describes the opportunities and difficulties in trying to reach the Asian-American market, which is more diverse than many other ethnic markets.

Consider:

1. According to Fisher, why have many companies avoided the Asian-American market in the past?

2. What is the main reason that companies may change their attitude and begin advertising campaigns targeted at Asian-Americans, according to Fisher?

3. How do advertisers' attitudes toward this emerging market reflect the changing characteristics of the U.S. media marketplace?

Marketers Straddle Asia-America Curtain

Christy Fisher

The Asian-American market is the fastest-growing and most affluent demographic segment of the U.S. population.

Long-distance telephone companies, financial services and upscale liquor brands have long been involved in the market and know its payoff. But most major U.S. package-goods marketers, automakers, retailers and fast-food chains have yet to target Asian-Americans, although they do market specifically to African-Americans and Hispanics.

That could be changing, as such big players as Sears, Roebuck & Co. begin targeting the segment.

There are many reasons why marketers have stayed out of the Asian-American market, the numerous languages and cultural traditions being the biggest barriers.

Fifty-six percent of the 4.1 million Asian-Americans five years and older do not speak English fluently, and 35% of those are "linguistically isolated," meaning they live in homes where no one over age 14 speaks English.

But the population growth and increasing buying power of Asian-Americans could convince more big companies to target these households. . . . According to figures generated within the market, Asian-Americans earn a total of about $100 billion a year.

"National advertisers are slow to see the market," concedes David Chen, managing partner at Muse Cordero Chen, a Los Angeles agency specializing in ethnic markets.

The agency handled an advertising test directed at Asian-Americans for General Foods USA's Kool-Aid brand, and in 1991-'92 created targeted ads to Asian-Americans and African-Americans for the California Department of Health's anti-smoking campaign.

"Most advertising aimed at Asian-Americans is local," says Mr. Chen.

Procter & Gamble Co. is typical of the attitude of mainstream, national marketers.

"At this point, we are not specifically targeting Asian-Americans as an audience, [and] that may or may not change," says a Procter & Gamble spokesman.

But many Asian-American agency executives think the segment is where the Hispanic market was in the early 1980s — poised for explosive growth.

There were 7.3 million Asian-Americans in 1990, 3% of the total U.S. population. The group is expected to number 12 million by 2000, a 64% increase over '90, according to the U.S. Census Bureau.

Already, Asian-Americans are a significant force in metropolitan areas such as Los Angeles, San Francisco, New York, Honolulu, San Diego and Chicago.

More major marketers will begin targeting Asian-Americans after they see high-profile targeted efforts by such national names as Sears, executives say. Sears plans to allocate $1 million of its 1995 media budget to efforts targeting Asian-Americans.

"We are talking to a lot of potential clients right now," says Jennie Tong, CEO of Lee Liu & Tong, New York, an agency billing $22 million with offices in the U.S. and Canada.

The agency grew 47% in billings [in 1993] with such clients as Bell Canada, Citibank, MCI Communications and New York Life.

"Soft drinks, fast-food, airlines are all looking at the market seriously," says Ms. Tong.

"A lot of companies . . . are standing at the precipice and have not jumped yet," says Karen Karp, strategic services director at Amko Advertising, New York, an Asian-American specialist that claims $30 million in billings and "double-digit growth" from clients such as AT&T Corp., Bank of America, Kia Motors America, Korean Air Lines and Prudential Insurance Co. of America.

The long-distance telephone companies — AT&T, MCI and Sprint — already know the value of the market, which is 66% foreign born.

Together, the three long-distance companies spend more than $20 million annually on TV, radio, print and direct mail in Chinese, Filipino, Japanese, Korean and other Asian languages.

Sprint estimates the total payoff to be $750 million to $1 billion in long-distance calling.

Asian-Americans "are big spenders, averaging between $50 and $150 a month, with the biggest callers being those who have been in the U.S. the least amount of time," says Jim Dodd, assistant VP-marketing for Sprint Consumer Services Group International.

Intertrend Advertising, Torrance, Calif., is Sprint's agency for Asian-American marketing.

Upscale liquor marketers such as House of Seagram and Remy Martin Amerique also know the value of this market, which skews younger and has a higher household income and education than the overall U.S. population.

The average income for an Asian-American family is $41,583, 18% higher than the national average, according to the census bureau.

As of 1990, 38% of Asian-American adults 25 and older had a bachelor's degree or higher, compared with 20% for the U.S. population.

Seagram often hosts special upscale

events to introduce new products to the Asian-American market. It also does local print and outdoor advertising (via AdLand Advertising, San Francisco).

"The Asian consumer is an important spirits consumer for scotch and particularly for cognac," says Arthur Shapiro, Seagram exec VP-marketing. "They are particularly inclined to premium products. Our efforts have paid off in brand recognition, brand loyalty and sales."

These premium demographics, as well as Asian-Americans' propensity to save and invest, also make this group an attractive market for financial services and insurance companies.

"Look at Manhattan Chinatown," says Joseph Lam, president of L3 Advertising, New York, a $6 million shop with clients such as Chemical Bank, Remy Martin and the U.K.'s British American Tobacco. "There are over 30 banks there with more than $3 billion in deposits."

Asian-Americans tend to buy top-of-the-line, high-ticket items, but they don't necessarily shop on Rodeo Drive. This represents a significant untapped opportunity for marketers, says Eleanor Yu, president-CEO of AdLand.

"Asians are very cost-conscious," she says. "They will not buy the cheapest item, but the best item for the cheapest price."

But as rosy as this market segment sounds, the drawbacks are significant and are causing some marketers to proceed slowly — and others not at all.

Language is probably the most troublesome aspect. According to the census bureau, the U.S. Asian population comprises Chinese (24%), Filipino (20%), Japanese (12%), Asian Indian (12%), Korean (12%), Vietnamese (9%) and 11% others.

This diversity also is reflected in the segment's splintered media offerings, such as newspapers with large but unaudited circulations like *The Korea Times* and *The World Journal,* which appeals to Mandarin speaking

Chinese-Americans or those from Taiwan; *Sing Tao Daily,* aimed at Cantonese speaking Chinese-Americans and those from Hong Kong; and *The China Press,* aimed at those who want news about mainland Chinese-Americans.

TV consists mainly of local UHF and cable channels in big-city markets and satellite networks such as North America TV and Asian America TV, which require hardware investments from consumers.

Several cities have channels of competitive prime-time programming, but little is available in off-hours.

Radio's AsiaOne Network claims to be the first national Asian-language radio network in the U.S., featuring ethnic programming in seven Asian dialects and languages.

Direct-mail advertising is efficient, says Ms. Yu of AdLand, yielding response rates of 10% to 15%, significantly better than the general-market average of 1% to 3%.

"Asian-Americans don't often get much direct mail in their own language, so they pay attention to it," agrees Amko's Ms. Karp.

Event marketing, such as corporate tie-ins or promotions to Asian New Year events, also are popular. These local events help companies establish the concept of friendship before business, which is important in the Asian market, says Ms. Yu.

The splintered languages and media have left Dayton Hudson Corp.'s Mervyn's, a specialty department store chain based in Hayward, Calif., pondering how to proceed strategically after successfully testing advertising directed at Asian-Americans in California in 1992 and 1993, via L3's San Francisco office.

The retailer's test program adapted voiceover to some of its commercials that had Asian cast members, and also included print ads aimed at various Asian-American segments.

Mervyn's wants to keep up its targeted approach, but budget limitations could hinder such plans.

"The Asian-American market tends to be

challenging because of language and casting appropriateness," says Kathy Blackburn, Mervyn's public affairs director.

"With the number of different languages represented in the Asian market, we're trying to find the right strategy and the right approach to advertising," she says.

Marketers' inability to recognize the various Asian languages makes them uncomfortable. Horror stories abound about Asian-language characters being printed upside down, embarrassing errors in translations or other cultural missteps.

For example, the number four should not be used in ads because it is the symbol of death, while the numeral eight is popular because it symbolizes prosperity, Ms. Yu says.

Red, gold and green are considered positive colors, while white, black and blue are not. The dragon is a positive symbol in Chinese culture, but a negative one in the general market.

Asian-American agencies are hopeful that new media developments, such as the Asian Broadcasting Network, might help interest national advertisers in the market.

In September [1994], ABN began rollout of the Filipino Channel, the first of nine 24-hour specialty ethnic cable and satellite channels aimed at various Asian-American groups in North America.

The rest of the channels, including two that will be pay-per-view, will be launched in mid-1995. They can be received by buying a satellite dish, receiver box and one-year subscription for $699, or through local cable operators for $13 a month where available.

Advertising eventually will be accepted once a subscription base is built up. "The more vehicles we have the better," says Ms. Yu.

"Marketers Straddle Asia-America Curtain," by Christy Fisher, *Advertising Age,* November 7, 1994, p. S-2. Reprinted with permission from the November 7, 1994 issue of *Advertising Age.* © Crain Communications, Inc.

CHAPTER 11
Public Relations

Understanding Public Relations

In this excerpt from Doug Newsom, Alan Scott, and Judy Van Slyke Turk's introductory public relations text *This Is PR,* the authors describe the different types of work public relations people do.

Consider:

1. To whom is the public relations professional responsible, according to the authors?

2. Describe briefly each of the functions of public relations.

3. How does public affairs work differ from other types of public relations?

4. How does promotion differ from publicity?

PR — What Is It?

Doug Newsom, Alan Scott, and Judy VanSlyke Turk

In my opinion, the best prevention and the most effective form of communication is behavior itself!
  Stephen A. Greyser, professor of business administration, Harvard Business School

PR Fundamentals
Maintain the integrity and credibility of yourself and your client.

Practice or adopt policies that are in the public as well as private interest.

Don't do or say or write anything you wouldn't want to see on the front page of the New York Times.
  Kerryn King, late senior consultant, Hill & Knowlton, New York

The woman sitting in front of the computer had just completed a newsletter design for a client. While that was printing, she began to proof another client's ad for a national magazine, and the logo in that ad reminded her that she needed to call a graphics artist who was supposed to show her several different logo designs for a client whose company had changed its name.

  For that client, too, she needed to review the next day's shooting schedule with the photographer. The company now needed all new brochures, media kits, and presentation folders, as well as such items as business cards and stationery. Even the sign on the building needed to be replaced with the new design. All of the organization's materials, from corporate biographies to product descriptions, had to be changed. That would involve so much rewriting that she decided to enlist the aid of a publicity writer she worked with occasionally, so her staff writer wouldn't be overloaded.

For the client undergoing reorganization, she had also agreed to do a communications audit—interviews and surveys with employees, customers and suppliers to help the restructured entity clarify its image. She had explained to the new management that mergers and restructuring tend to obscure an organization's image. Although such confusion eventually dissipates without any special planning, valuable opportunities can be lost if the organization's various publics are not actively helped to understand the changes. The woman needed to get in touch with the research organization she used to handle telephone interviews. She would have to structure the questionnaire, pretest it and then train the callers in how to use it in conducting interviews.

After completing the audit, she would be responsible for making a formal presentation of her findings and recommendations to the company's board of directors. She made a note to be sure to get the new display element for her laptop computer as soon as possible, so she would have plenty of time to practice using it while she spoke.

As the woman continued working, the fax machine began printing a message. She glanced at the cover sheet and saw that it was from an agency in Singapore she frequently worked with. A client of the agency was coming to the United States on business and would need some assistance. The fax identified the dates and places involved and spelled out the help the agency thought the client would need from her. The printout ended with a request for a return message confirming general arrangements. The woman liked working with the Singapore group because they reacted enthusiastically to her ideas and encouraged her to contribute to their broad overall plans. She laughed to herself remembering a sketch one of them had faxed to her with an accompanying note saying, "color it American." In return, she counted on their cultural help with her Pacific Rim business.

Similarly, she counted on help with the European marketplace from a former college roommate who was a German national and had returned home to work with a big public relations firm before going into business for herself. She also had a contact in Mexico City, which she had developed through several international public relations professional meetings, and she was just beginning to work with a new colleague in Canada. Although her own firm was small, her activities on behalf of clients often spanned the globe. When she came to work in the morning, she often found that the fax had been busy overnight, transmitting inquiries or requesting information from professional associates around the world.

This woman is a practitioner of public relations—a field that has emerged in recent years as a global phenomenon. The consistency of the practice, despite differences in the social, economic and political climates in various parts of the world, can be traced to the growing body of knowledge about and the general acceptance of what public relations is. The creator of the profession's international code of ethics, Lucien Matrat, offers these thoughts:

> Public relations, in the sense that we use the term, forms part of the strategy of management. Its function is twofold: to respond to the expectations of those whose behaviour, judgements and opinions can influence the operation and development of an enterprise, and in turn to motivate them. . . .
>
> Establishing public relations policies means, first and foremost, harmonizing the interests of an enterprise with the interests of those on whom its growth depends.
>
> The next step is putting these policies into practice. *This means developing a communications policy which can establish and maintain a relationship of mutual confidence with a firm's multiple publics.* [Emphasis ours.]

What Is Public Relations?

The public relations practitioner serves as an intermediary between the organization that he or she represents and all of that organization's publics. Consequently, the PR practitioner has responsibilities both to the institution and to its various publics. He or she distributes information that enables the institution's publics to understand its policies.

Public relations involves research into all audiences: receiving information from them, advising management of their attitudes and responses, helping to set policies that demonstrate responsible attention to them and constantly evaluating the effectiveness of all PR programs. This inclusive role embraces all activities connected with ascertaining and influencing the opinions of a group of people. But just as important, public relations involves responsibility and responsiveness in policy and information to the best interests of the organization and its publics.

The complexity of PR's role prompted the Public Relations Society of America (PRSA) to define fourteen activities generally associated with public relations: (1) publicity, (2) communication, (3) public affairs, (4) issues management, (5) government relations, (6) financial public relations, (7) community relations, (8) industry relations, (9) minority relations, (10) advertising, (11) press agentry, (12) promotion, (13) media relations, (14) propaganda. PRSA's definitions of these activities are listed in the Glossary.

Another organization produced a consensus definition of PR much earlier than PRSA did. The First World Assembly of Public Relations Associations, held in Mexico City in August 1978, defined the practice of public relations as "the art and social science of analyzing trends, predicting their consequences, counseling organizational leaders, and implementing planning programs of action which will serve both the organization and the public interest."

As a practical matter, good public relations involves confronting a problem openly and honestly and then solving it. In the long run, the best PR is disclosure of an active social conscience.

Ten Basic Principles of Public Relations

We can describe the function and role of public relations practice by stating ten basic principles:

1. Public relations deals with reality, not false fronts. Conscientiously planned programs that put the public interest in the forefront are the basis of sound public relations policy. (*Translation:* PR deals with facts, not fiction.)

2. Public relations is a service-oriented profession in which public interest, not personal reward, should be the primary consideration. (PR is a public, not personal, service.)

3. Since the public relations practitioner must go to the public to seek support for programs and policies, public interest is the central criterion by which he or she should select these programs and policies. (PR practitioners must have the guts to say no to a client or to refuse a deceptive program.)

4. Because the public relations practitioner reaches many publics through mass media, which are the public channels of communication, the integrity of these channels must be preserved. (PR practitioners should never lie to the news media, either outright or by implication.)

5. Because PR practitioners are in the middle between an organization and its publics, they must be effective communicators — conveying information back and forth until understanding is reached. (The PR practitioner probably was the original ombudsman/woman.)

6. To expedite two-way communication and to be responsible communicators, public relations practitioners must use scientific public opinion research extensively. (PR cannot afford to be a guessing game.)

7. To understand what their publics are saying and to reach them effectively, public relations practitioners must employ the social sciences—psychology, sociology, social psychology, public opinion, communications study and semantics. (Intuition is not enough.)

8. Because a lot of people do PR research, the PR person must adapt the work of other, related disciplines, including learning theory and other psychology theories, sociology, political science, economics and history. (The PR field requires multidisciplinary applications.)

9. Public relations practitioners are obligated to explain problems to the public before these problems become crises. (PR practitioners should alert and advise, so people won't be taken by surprise.)

10. A public relations practitioner should be measured by only one standard: ethical performance. (A PR practitioner is only as good as the reputation he or she deserves.)

PR and Related Activities

Public relations may include all of the following activities, but it is never confined to any one of them: press agentry, promotion, public affairs, publicity, and advertising. PR activities also coexist with marketing and with merchandising, which are not synonymous terms. Since many people confuse public relations with one or more of these activities, let's distinguish among them explicitly.

Press Agentry

Because PR's origins are associated with press agentry, many people think that press agentry and public relations are the same. But press agentry involves planning activities or staging events—sometimes just stunts—that will *attract attention* to a person, institution, idea or product. There is certainly nothing wrong with attracting crowds and giving people something to see or talk about, provided that no deception is involved. Today's press agents are polished pros who steer clear of fraud and puffery, unless it is done strictly in fun and is clearly recognizable as such.

Although a press agent's principal aim is to attract attention, rather than to educate or promote understanding, some press agents manage to do both. For example, one summer the Dallas Symphony Orchestra put on a series of free outdoor concerts with a program of light classical music to stimulate interest in its season ticket sales drive. The events attracted a warm response from music lovers and probably helped people see the symphony as a "fun-giving" rather than as solemn and formal. Press agentry can thus be an effective element in a larger public relations effort.

Promotion

A hazy line separates yesterday's press agentry from today's promotion. Although promotion incorporates special events that could be called press agentry, it goes beyond that into *opinion making.* Promotion attempts to garner support and endorsement for a person, product, institution or idea. Promotional campaigns depend for their effectiveness on the efficient use of various PR tools; and in many cases more is not better. . . . Examples of promotion are the various fund-raising drives conducted by churches, charities, health groups and conservation interests. Among the most successful promoters in the country are the American Red Cross, American Cancer Society and United Way. Promotion, fund raising and all the attendant drum beating constitute one variety of PR activities that may be incorporated into an overall public relations program. What makes promotion activities worthwhile is the merit of the cause.

The legitimacy of the cause is also important from a purely pragmatic viewpoint: It won't receive media coverage if it isn't legitimate news and if it can't maintain public support.

Public Affairs

Many public relations people use the term *public affairs* to describe their work, but this is misleading. Public affairs is actually a highly specialized kind of public relations that involves *community relations* and *governmental relations* — that is, dealing with officials within the community and working with legislative groups and various pressure groups such as consumers. It is a critical part of a public relations program, but it is not the whole program. For example, eighteen months before the Dallas/Fort Worth Airport was to open, two PR firms were hired — one to handle public affairs, and the other to handle media relations. There were good reasons for having two firms. Public affairs were complex, not only because the airport was paid for by cities in two different counties, but also because the airport was located astride two counties and within the municipal boundaries of four suburban cities. The media relations were complex, too, since they involved arranging special events, advertising and publicity connected with the opening; producing informational materials about the airport; and conducting media relations that were international in scope.

In agencies of the federal government, including the military, the term *public affairs* is commonly used to designate a broader responsibility than *public information,* which consists merely of publicity — handing out information. Thus a public information officer is a publicist, whereas a public affairs person in government often has policy-making responsibilities. Because a rather short-sighted law precludes government use of people identified as public relations person nel (see Why the U.S. Goverment uses the term "Public Affairs" box below), military public affairs officers often have responsibility for all facets of internal and external public relations.

The unfortunate effects of this law could be countered at the very highest level of government, since the President of the United States appoints the country's most visible PR person, the presidential press secretary. It might make sense to rename the job "public relations counselor" and then employ an accredited public relations practitioner in that

Why the U.S. Government Uses the Term "Public Affairs"

An October 22, 1913, Act of Congress often is interpreted as precluding governmental use of public relations talent. The prohibitive words were attached to the last paragraph of an Interstate Commerce Commission statute: "Appropriated funds may not be used to pay a publicity expert unless specifically appropriated for that purpose."

The amendment to the bill was introduced by Representative Frederick H. Gillett and thus is referred to in public relations literature as the Gillett Amendment. Most public relations activity of that period was publicity, and the intent of the amendment was to identify and control publicity. Legislators were concerned that the government would become involved in propaganda directed at U.S. citizens. Most responsible PR practitioners would like to see this amendment repealed, since government currently carries out PR functions anyway, but masks them. As a result, taxpayers cannot get any information about how much money is spent for PR.

post. That person could name a publicity chief for news announcements. A public affairs department could then be set up to work with Congress, and a public affairs officer in the State Department could be appointed to handle relationships with other nations.

Publicity

A college student's first awareness of public relations activity is often through some personal experience with publicity. A note comes from home, "Congratulations on making the dean's list. Love, Aunt Susie." A clipping is attached. How did that get into the hometown newspaper? Mother? No. The university's news bureau sent the paper a story with the student's name in it.

Because publicity is used to call attention to the special events or the activities surrounding a promotion, there is confusion about this term. *Public relations* is often used as a synonym for *publicity,* but the two activities are not the same. Publicity is strictly a communications function, whereas PR involves a management function as well. Essentially, publicity means *placing information in a news medium,* either in a mass medium such as television or newspapers or in a specialized medium such as corporate, association, trade or industry magazines, newsletters or even brochures (such as quarterly corporate reports).

Publicists are writers. Use of the term *public relations* by institutions to describe publicity jobs is unfortunate. Publicists perform a vital function—disseminating information—but they generally do not help set policy. Only PR counselors, usually at the executive level, are in a position to effect substantive management changes.

Publicity isn't always good news. In a crisis, for example, it's often important for the organization to tell its story before the news media develop it on their own. In these situations, the publicist is an inside reporter for internal and external media.

Publicity is *not* public relations. It is a tool used by public relations practitioners.

Some writers do choose careers as information writers, but they are *publicists,* not public relations practitioners.

Advertising

Public relations differs from both advertising and propaganda. Matrat explains why:

> The strategy of advertising is to create desire, to motivate demand for a product.
>
> The strategy of propaganda is to generate conditioned reflexes which will replace reasoned actions. *Public relations is the strategy of confidence, which alone gives credibility to a message.* [Emphasis ours.]

Designing ads, preparing their written messages and buying time or space for their exposure are the tasks of advertising. Although advertising should complement a total PR program, it is a separate function. A public relations person who has no expertise in advertising should arrange to hire an agency to work under his or her supervision.

Advertising is needed for special events and for successful promotion. Although it is a major part of marketing, it has its own needs for research and testing. Advertising in the form of paid-for time or space is a PR tool often used to complement publicity, promotions and press agentry. . . .

Marketing

As in advertising, research and testing play a vital role in marketing, but the kind of testing used in advertising may be only a part of market research. Marketing specialists want to know two things: Is there a need or desire for a product or service? If so, among which audiences and in what form is it most likely to be well received? Marketing is directed toward consumers, although it also interacts with other publics such as the sales force, dealers, retailers and the advertising department. Market research is invaluable to the PR practitioner because it provides information about consumers—an important PR public.

All marketing activities have public relations implications, and occasionally they have a direct impact. For example, a marketing campaign launched to promote a new type of double-edged razor blade turned into a public relations problem when samples of the product (enclosed in an envelope with promotional literature) were inserted into newspapers, provoking complaints that, for instance, a dog cut its mouth and children got to the blades before their parents. On another occasion some recipients of a strongly lemon scented dishwashing powder that had been sent to households as a sample mixed it with water and drank it, mistaking it for instant lemonade mix. Most often, however, marketing is an asset to public relations.

In the 1980s the term *marketing/public relations* became popular as a way to describe public relations activities involved in marketing, but it caused further muddling of the component terms. In reality, the activities involved are not PR, but they do include promotion (usually sales promotion), press agentry (special events, special appearances) and publicity.

The 1985 definition of *marketing* adopted by the American Marketing Association (AMA) shows the relationship: "Marketing is the process of planning and executing the conception (product), pricing, promotion and distribution (place) of ideas, goods and services to create exchanges that satisfy individual and organizational

THE LITTLE WOMAN

DON TORIN
9-29

© King Features Syndicate, Inc., 1975. World rights reserved.

"So you're in public relations. Is that where you get me to like something I wouldn't like at all if you didn't do what you do to make me like it?"

objectives." The AMA includes in that definition the activities (ideas and services) of nonprofit organizations as well as products sold for profit.

Merchandising

In contrast to marketing, merchandising is concerned with the *packaging* of a product, an idea or perhaps even a president. Its research asks what subtle emotions play a part in acceptance of the product, what shape of package is easiest to handle, what color is likely to attract more attention or what kind of display will make people react. The answers are important to salespeople and dealers and provide a valuable supplement to the marketing and advertising research in a campaign. Merchandising experts are strong in graphics, color, tactile responses and emotional reactions to physical imagery. Their work is a frequent and vital part of the public relations milieu. However, it is not in itself public relations.

The PR Practitioner

The practice of public relations is traditionally viewed as falling into one of three forms: the PR staff person working in-house for an organization; the PR firm or agency person working with and representing clients; or the independent PR practitioner, who often is a counselor. These three types of practitioners are often seen as personally taking on either the role of technician (that is, someone who performs the mechanics of the job as suggested by the client or management), or the role of manager (that is, an active participant in planning and decision making).

One determinant of which role a practitioner ultimately plays may be the environment in which the person tries to practice. This may also be a factor in the maturity or type of public relations being practiced. Four models of PR practice have been developed: press agentry/publicity; public information; two-way asymmetric (often found in marketing communications); and two-way symmetric (generally recognized as the most desirable and effective model).

The value of public relations lies in its power to serve a two-way link and negotiator between an organization and its publics, to build understanding and resolve conflicts. In this role, public relations can strengthen management's sense of social responsibility. But although offering counsel in the area of social responsibility is one of the jobs of public relations, such counsel is not always well received. In any case, the most valuable service PR people provide to an organization is as problem finders, solvers and preventers, and as interpreters of communications between the organization and its publics.

The common public perception of PR is unflattering, and fallout from popular misunderstandings can be experienced even by college students on their own campuses. Overcoming these misunderstandings in order to educate people about what public relations practice can and should be is one of the biggest challenges facing practitioners.

"PR—What Is It?" by Doug Newsom, Alan Scott, and Judy Van Slyke Turk, from *This Is PR*, 5th ed., Belmont, Calif.: Wadsworth Publishing Company/ITP, 1993, pp. 2–9. Used with permission of Wadsworth Publishing Company/ITP.

Overseas PR

After a 1994 visit to Great Britain, public relations consultants Ray Josephs and Juanita Josephs observed several ways in which public relations in the United Kingdom differs from public relations in the United States. Following are their conclusions, which first appeared in an article in the *Public Relations Journal.*

Consider:

1. List three ways in which public relations in the United Kingdom and public relations in the United States differ.

2. How are public relations in the two countries similar?

3. What important trends in British media industries will affect U.K. public relations, according to the authors?

Public Relations, the U.K. Way

Ray Josephs and Juanita Josephs

Princess Di, Fergie, and the rest of the royal clan may have had their public relations problems over the years, but it's not for lack of available counsel. The country that brought you fish and chips and lukewarm beer also happens to have the second-largest public relations industry in the world. While public relations in the United Kingdom is different from that of the United States in several key respects — most notably, in solicitation of new business and the degree of knowledge among clients and higher-ups about what public relations can do — boundaries between the United States and its neighbors "across the pond" are gradually blurring.

These are just a few of the conclusions we reached during a recent two-month visit [in 1994] to Great Britain. We interviewed top executives with the 10 largest U.K. public relations firms and many smaller firms, every U.S. public relations firm with a major presence there, and a smattering of associations, boutique agencies, academic sources and others.

Here's what we found.

More than 48,000 people are employed in public relations in Britain, according to a study by the Institute of Public Relations, an association headquartered in London. In contrast, there are 155,000 people in the United States employed in public relations, according to U.S. Bureau of Labor Statistics.

By most estimates, about 70% of the British public relations industry is concentrated in London. Firms in Wales and Scotland account for 20%, with the remaining 10% located primarily in the Midlands, particularly the cities of Manchester and Birmingham. These ratios may soon be changing, however. As the British government privatizes utilities and other companies, many local public relations firms are rushing in to capitalize on opportunities for new business. These "provincial players" are certain to be a growing force, according to a number of industry insiders.

Economic Climate

As in the United States, British public relations practitioners are clawing their way out of a recession in which budgets and staff were slashed. The British recession began earlier than the most recent U.S. recession and, unfortunately, is taking longer to reverse. Still, the country's public relations industry is faring better than its counterparts in advertising. While U.K. ad agency revenues stayed flat throughout 1992 and 1993, public relations firms grew about 5% to 15% each year. Small- to medium-sized firms were the biggest gainers, reported Stephen Farish, editor of *PR Week,* a tabloid newspaper covering the public relations industry. Some specialty firms, such as those in health care and environmental public relations, saw robust growth. Other firms, such as those specializing in mergers and acquisitions and financial public relations, did not do as well because of limited activity in those fields.

"While the economy improved in 1993, growth is still weak, with more clients offering assignments, not annual retainers," said Roger Haywood, chairman of Kestrel Communications Ltd. in London. This trend is echoed elsewhere throughout the global economy, he said, as companies attempt to keep a lid on fixed costs, starting and stopping projects as needed.

Other industry leaders held a more cynical view. "Clients think [contracting on a per-project basis] gives them better control and keeps us more on our toes," said John de Upbaugh, deputy chief executive of Dewe Rogerson's European office in London.

As for 1994 business prospects, Colin Thompson, director of the Public Relations Consultants Association in London, forecast that business volume will increase about 10%.

U.S./U.K. Ties

"There has been so much interaction in ownership, affiliation, movement of personnel and exchange of information that differences in public relations practice and performance between the world's two major English-speaking countries are gradually narrowing," said David Wright, chief executive of Citigate Communications Group Ltd. in London.

There are several factors driving this trend. British ownership and/or partnership with U.S. firms is on the rise. For example, Shandwick, the largest agency in the United Kingdom and the second-largest in the United States [in 1994], derives over half its volume and profit from U.S. business. Omnicom, headquartered in New York City, purchased a controlling interest [in 1993] in Countrywide Communications, the sixth-largest firm in the United Kingdom. And, Citigate Communications and Dewe Rogerson have recently opened offices in New York. Such moves serve to blur the boundaries between the U.S. and U.K. public relations industries.

Still, British practitioners, firms, and clients retain certain idiosyncrasies. Among them:

• Many sources said that U.S. clients generally have a better understanding of the value of public relations and use it more effectively than clients in the United Kingdom. Many British clients still feel that public relations people are "too aggressive in projecting what an individual or corporation is, wants to be, or would like to be perceived as," said Colin Trusler, managing director for Shandwick's U.K. office in London. This devotion to understatement is likely to change soon, however, as increased immigration to Britain and the European Community makes the public relations industry's work force more diverse, he added.

- U.S. firms do a better job of merchandising placements and other client activities. "Some in the United Kingdom don't do this sort of thing or consider it 'boosting' that's in poor taste," said Nicholas Deluca, an American who is corporate affairs manager with The Grayling Group, a British firm headquartered in London.

- British firms are likely to have simpler, less elaborate offices than their U.S. counterparts, said Prince Yuri Galatzine, a longtime veteran of the relations industry and formerly with the International Public Relations Company in London. One exception is firms whose clients are mostly large corporations or financial institutions. It's important for these firms to be perceived as substantial, established organizations, he said.

- British firms use more advertising to publicize their services and capabilities. One tabloid newspaper that carries such advertising is *PR Week*.

- U.K. clients often have unrealistic expectations of what public relations can do, said Alan Ogden, deputy chairman of Hill & Knowlton in London. "We and other responsible firms make it a point to clarify objectives, how we propose to reach them and, finally, how results will be evaluated in terms of client benefits," he said.

- The largest firms in England tend to offer full communications capabilities in-house or with the help of a concentrated group of suppliers, observed Alison Canning, managing director of Cohn & Wolfe in London. U.S. firms, on the other hand, are much more likely to parcel out pieces of a project to specialists, she said.

Getting New Business

Few firms do cold solicitation calls. However, one firm, Countrywide, has reported profitable results doing this, especially for its wholly-owned network outside London.

First-time prospective public relations users frequently consult agency lists — categorized by size and specialization — carried in *PR Week* and in the *Hollis Directory of British and European Firms*. Such prospects often send out bidding invitations, which are frequently declined by larger firms but eagerly pursued by many medium- and smaller-sized firms.

Several referral services also act as intermediaries between firms and clients. PR Register, a London referral service, charges agencies $1,500 to be included in its listings. The Public Relations Consultants Association also runs its own referral service.

Growth Areas

For many London firms, visibility within the European Economic Community's Brussels headquarters, as well as individual countries, has become an important business generator. Competition for this lucrative market is keen. Heads of British firms claim that they are best positioned to service continental Europe because of London's strong global communications capabilities.

"While there are few truly global clients, London is the perfect platform for coordinating pan-European work," said Alan Capper, chairman, Rowland Worldwide, London/New York. That accounts for the "public affairs boom" in the U.K., Capper added.

Alasdair Sutherland, joint managing director, Manning, Selvage & Lee, London, reported that 40% of MSL's U.K. billings were international, mostly to U.S. companies. He added that 60% of the firm's work in Brussels is billed to U.S. or other non-Belgian multi-nationals.

Changes in media, especially television in the United Kingdom, are another opportunity for more public relations placements, added Rowland's Capper. The protection of reputation—through issues management and crisis prevention—is another growth area, he said.

Health care public relations, especially for pharmaceutical firms in Switzerland, the United States and Great Britain, is another growth area. Several sources agreed that health care was the only specialty immune to recession.

Fees and Salaries

Service costs to clients in the United Kingdom are somewhat lower than in the United States. Not all British firms bill hourly rates, but those who do said their rates were less than U.S. firms for the same level of executive time. Consequently, U.S. firms in London have had to charge lower rates to British clients to remain competitive, said Michael McAvoy, chairman of London-based GCI Europe.

Although the cost of living and tax rates in the United Kingdom are as high as in the United States, salaries and bonuses are lower, said Ian Metherell, chairman of Proclaim Network Ltd. in London. Account directors of major public relations firms may command £24,000 to £30,000 [sterling pounds] but upper-level compensation generally reaches only £55,000, although many executives receive company cars. [Other benefits include pensions, medical insurance, and profit-related bonuses.]

Over the next few years, it's unlikely that the British public relations industry will grow as spectacularly as it did in the 1980s, when firms sold shares on the London Stock Exchange and blossomed into international prominence. Nonetheless, given the U.K.

industry's size, diversity, sophistication and dynamism, U.S. practitioners would do well to watch and learn from their counterparts across the Atlantic.

British Public Relations Associations

There are two major U.K. professional societies.

The Public Relations Consultants Association was founded in 1969 to encourage and promote the advancement of companies and firms engaged in public relations consulting. Its principal objectives are to raise and maintain professional standards, and to provide opportunities for various publics to confer with public relations consultants as a body and ascertain their collective views. The organization also acts as a spokesperson for consultancy practices and helps educate clients.

Other activities include publishing an annual directory in which member firms list their clients, and participation in an International Committee of Public Relations Consultants, a 14-country association of trade groups. A professional practices committee within the international association oversees standards and arbitrates complaints.

For further information, contact: Colin Thompson, director, Public Relations Consultants Association, Willow House, Willow Place, Victoria, London SW1P 1JH. Telephone 071-233-6026; Fax 071-828-4797.

The Institute of Public Relations is dedicated to providing a professional standard for public relations practice, enhancing the ability and status of members as professional practitioners, providing opportunities to meet and exchange views, and offering a wide range of services for professional and personal benefit.

This group's concentration is on education and training. It also sponsors "Sword of Excellence" awards, similar to PRSA's Silver Anvil program.

For further information, contact: Pamela Taylor, president, Institute of Public Relations, The Old Trading House, 15 Northburgh Street, London, EC1 VOPR. Telephone 071-253-5151; Fax 071-490-0588.

British Media Trends

The two major national dailies in the United Kingdom — *The Times* and *The Daily Telegraph,* and the tabloids, the *Daily Express* and the *Daily Mirror* — are thriving. Their business pages are often major targets for public relations practitioners. The up-market Sunday newspapers, including *The Sunday Times, The Observer,* and *The Independent* on Sunday, run separate from the dailies and have important circulations. Their abundance of sections provides vital feature placement potential.

The *Financial Times,* with editions in the United Kingdom, United States and Europe, has the strongest business coverage but is putting more emphasis on many lifestyle topics. Knowledgeable writers and editors bring considerable weight to their coverage and often speak at FT-sponsored symposia which present platforms for news-making companies.

The *Economist,* with more readers in the United States than in the United Kingdom, is another high-level target. Coverage focuses on broad issues rather than companies.

There are numerous local newspapers, but they tend to concentrate on operations within their own circulation areas. Local non-English dailies and continental imports abound. *USA Today* and *The Wall Street Journal* are also readily available.

As in the United States, there are many trade publications in virtually every field, as well as a full range of consumer periodicals.

Televisions and radio are gaining in importance. In addition to the official British Broadcasting Corp., new independent broadcasters offer a range of programs on financial, health, beauty, fashion and sports topics. These programs are fast becoming key publicity targets. Morning talk shows, the equivalent of our "Good Morning America," are a relative newcomer in Britain. Video news releases are not welcome, as stations prefer to cover local events.

Radio is starting to become more important to many practitioners. Independent stations are offering a broader programming range than was previously available, upping placement potential.

The BBC, which sells yearly licenses to viewers and listeners who want to receive its television and radio broadcasts, is now undertaking a much-publicized full review of its mission for the decade ahead. According to Pamela Taylor, BBC's director of corporate relations, "change is inevitable."

For listings of British media, consult *Bacon's International Media Directory,* published by Bacon's Information, Inc., in Chicago; *International Media Guide,* published by IMG, Inc. in Nashua, NH; or *Ulrich's International Periodical Directory,* published by R. R. Bowker in New Providence, NJ. — R.J.

On-line PR

PR Newswire celebrated its 40th birthday in 1994. In this article chronicling the history of PR Newswire and its plans for the future, Charles Marsh of the University of Kansas outlines the value of this service for public relations practitioners.

Consider:

1. **Why is public relations important to the media, according to Marsh?**

2. **How is PR Newswire different from other sources of public relations information for the media?**

3. **How is PR Newswire changing to adapt to new systems of delivery?**

Influencing History's First Draft: PR Newswire and the News Media

Charles Marsh
University of Kansas

On March 9, 1954, *The New York Times* announced quietly the birth of the world's first news-release wire service: "The wire service, PR News Association, Inc., will service a long list of civic, charitable and commercial clients by teletypewriter to the New York daily newspapers."

[In 1994], more than 40 years later, PR Newswire—born as PR News Association—is the world's largest news-release distribution service, transmitting company information to thousands of newsrooms not only in the United States but also in Canada, Colombia, Cameroon, Croatia, Kazakhstan, Kyrgyzstan—the list includes more than 130 nations and territories.

Serious students of mass media should now whisper two magic words that put the screws to any bit of new knowledge: *So what?*

Recent studies of the news media show the following:

- *The Wall Street Journal* gets up to 45 percent of its news story ideas from news releases.

- A plurality of journalists say they rely on news releases for five to 10 stories a week.

- Journalists prefer electronically delivered news releases to phone pitches ("Have I got a story for you!"), personal visits or traditional mail (also known as "snail mail").

223

If today's news media provide the first draft of history, then news releases supply much of the raw material, the proto-history. And for more than 40 years, no one in the world has given more journalists more news releases, in the form they prefer, than PR Newswire.

Computers and Satellites

How does PR Newswire (PRN) work? Say you're director of public relations for Funeste Inc., a leading manufacturer of glow-in-the-dark pillowcases. Next month you're launching several new fabric patterns, and that's a light you're unwilling to hide under a bushel, so to speak. If you're a PRN member — which, for $100 a year, you can be — you type up a news release, fax or modem it to any one of . . . 20 regional U.S. bureaus, pick a distribution menu from more than 60 distribution lists, pay a transmission fee, and hope that you've produced a story worthy of media attention.

US1, the largest PRN NewsLine, or distribution menu, reaches more than 2,000 newspapers, wire services, magazines, television stations and ratio stations throughout the United States. Four hundred words on US1 cost $450. Each additional 100 words cost $110.

The fees, you may have noted, can escalate — but so can the cost of stamps, per, envelopes, copying machines, fax machines, phone bills, electricity and staff time if you're a do-it-yourselfer.

Meanwhile, PR Newswire has formatted your release into standard layout, converted it into an electronic signal, bounced it off a satellite and into newsroom computer systems — all at no cost to the recipient. If you prefer, PRN will fax your release to the media on one or more of its hundreds of fax NewsLines, or it will use a fax-distribution list that you've prepared. If you're hopelessly low-tech, PRN will even mail the release for you.

Other Services

Besides transmitting your news release to the news media you've chosen, PR Newswire, at no additional charge, will transmit it to more than 25,000 investment companies throughout the world via its Investors Research Wire. Also, at no additional charge, PRN will send your news release to leading trade magazines in your field. For example, news of your new glow-in-the-dark fabric patterns could reach such publications as *Discount Store News* and *Home Textiles Today*.

"I would like first and foremost to be known as a service company," says Ian Capps, PR Newswire's president and chief executive officer. "Secondly, I'd like us to be known as a company that is expert in handling information for other people. But service comes first."

That service includes more than the transmission of news releases. PR Newswire can also transmit photographs — black and white or color, with captions — of your new glow-in-the-dark pillowcases to more than 300 newspapers, including *The New York Times* and *USA Today*. And, for one year, PRN will electronically store the photo in a database available to journalists throughout the world.

Data storage, in fact, has become an important secondary business for PR Newswire. PRN can store news releases as well as other company information in personalized fax-on-demand databases, allowing reporters, investors, employees and others to quickly acquire company documents. News releases, annual reports, earnings statements, personnel biographies, maps and diagrams, statements in times of crisis — all can be stored, retrieved by the public and printed out at any fax machine, at no charge to the recipient. Unlike the best PR representative, a fax-on-demand database never sleeps, it can talk to more than one reporter at once and it always says just what you want it to say.

With reporters constantly complaining about the daily blizzard of news releases, is it possible that fax-on-demand will replace standard news-release delivery? Will PR Newswire and similar companies one day be only complacent databases, patiently awaiting contacts from reporters?

Highly unlikely, says Capps. "Part of the value of our service," he explains, "is that we're active. One of the problems of databases, including fax on demand, is that they're passive. The job we do for our customers will always require, at some point, that we proactively transmit the news release so that there's no way recipients can miss the fact that it exists."

Just in case recipients were dozing, however, PR Newswire places members' news releases on the Internet, as well as in dozens of other national and international databases, including Nexis, Dow Jones News/Retrieval, Dialog and PressLink. That not only gives reporters a second chance; it also means that anyone with a computer and a modem can retrieve the full text of company news releases, thus circumventing the news media, which traditionally edit such releases to reduce length and bombast.

Such leveraging of news releases just might keep PRN members loyal in the face of growing in-house possibilities. For example, any of the large telecommunications companies could assist Funeste Inc. in setting up a "fax tree" that could simultaneously transmit your pillowcase release to dozens of newsrooms. As director of public relations, you could launch it from your computer screen without ever printing it. So why join PR Newswire?

Besides free database storage and free transmission to investment companies and trade magazines, there's good old-fashioned service, says Capps.

"In our faxing, for example, there's the guarantee that your release goes out," he says. "There's the report back on who received it and who didn't — and if they didn't, why they didn't. There are our retry methods."

Or suppose you want to send your release to Moscow, he asks. Will your in-house fax tree translate it into Russian? Newswire will.

"We are not simply a commodity," he says. "We are a service."

One service that PR Newswire doesn't offer, however, is distribution of video news releases. "That's a dog-eat-dog business," Capps says. "Right now, we just don't have any interest in becoming a 'me too' and joining the dog fight. That really wouldn't make sense because the practitioners who are in it right now are very good at their business."

Libel, Obscenity and Saying No

Among the hundreds of thousands of documents PR Newswire annually processes, it occasionally finds something it chooses not to transmit.

"We say no to a news release that is not from a bona fide source," says Capps. "We say no to a news release that is out-and-out advertising. We say no to news releases that don't clear our own fact-checkers. And of course we're very careful with libelous or obscene material. We have the absolute right to refuse to carry traffic. Now how often does that happen? Very, very rarely."

PR Newswire's History

PR Newswire had no direct competition when it began more than 40 years ago. In 1954, Herbert Muschel, one of the founders of *TV Guide,* launched the company with little more than himself and teletypewriter links to the New York dailies. By 1963, PRN had expanded to two bureaus, with a staff of six, and was moving about 26 news releases a day. On Oct. 19, 1987, the day the stock market crashed, PRN's New York bureau alone transmitted 175 news releases, up from the bureau's daily average of 100.

PR Newswire's chief competitor, Business Wire, began in San Francisco in 1961. Today [in 1994], like PRN, that company has electronic links to thousands of newsrooms and investment companies throughout the world.

"Business Wire is a strong competitor, a very good company," says Capps. "I like to think of good, intense competition as being to the benefit of the customer, because it means we do our job better in order to stay ahead."

PR Newswire's seventh employee, David Steinberg, was a prize-winning business reporter for *The New York Herald Tribune.* In 1963, during a newspaper strike, Steinberg was working for *The New York Report,* a temporary strike-born newspaper, when he asked Muschel to install a PRN printer to speed the makeshift newsgathering process. After the strike, Steinberg left the *Herald Tribune* for PRN. Thirteen years later, in 1976, Steinberg became PRN's chief executive officer, a position he held until 1992, when he was succeeded by Capps.

In 1971, Muschel sold PRN to Western Union, and it became a wholly owned subsidiary of that company. In 1982, United Newspapers, a British publishing conglomerate and PRN's current owner, purchased the PR Newswire for almost $10 million.

Today [1994], PR Newswire has almost 200 employees, 20 bureaus in the United States and affiliates around the world. It transmits more than 100,000 news releases a year for more than 17,000 members. Its fax operations transmit more than 2 million pages a year.

PR Newswire's Future

The complementary needs of PRN members and the news media, says Ian Capps, will drive PR Newswire's future.

"The key to the next generation of editorial management systems," he says, "is going to be managing a complete document as an image — as opposed to, at the moment, managing photographs, graphics and text in different environments and bringing them together through electronic cutting and pasting.

"In the future, what's going to happen is that the total image — text, photographs, graphics, letterhead, a handwritten signature — will be transmitted as one multimedia package, capable of being manipulated by the recipient. Each part of the package will be manipulable."

Company-information transmission will be a thriving new frontier, he says, offering multimedia presentations and interactivity. "Everybody will have an opportunity for great and very effective expansion," he says. "PR Newswire just intends to get more of it than anyone else."

"Influencing History's First Draft: PR Newswire and the News Media," by Charles Marsh. Expanded from a Research in Progress presentation, "Influencing History's First Draft: PR Newswire and the News Media," at the 1994 Annual Convention of the American Journalism Historians Association. Written expressly for this text.

Getting Attention

This article, written by Howard Kurtz of the *Washington Post,* presents an example of the use of publicity in attracting attention for a story. (For a definition of publicity, see Perspective 11-1, "PR—What Is It?"). To get press coverage about the high percentage of saturated fat in theater popcorn, the Center for Science in the Public Interest "carefully stage-managed the news," according to Kurtz.

Consider:

1. List three approaches that the Center for Science in the Public Interest used to get attention for their story.

2. In your opinion, which elements of the story were so appealing to the media?

3. Was the story a legitimate news story? Which principles of public relations does this case study demonstrate about the relationship between public relations and the news media?

The Great Exploding Popcorn Exposé

Howard Kurtz

It was, says Art Silverman, "a grand slam" that got his group on CBS, NBC, ABC and CNN—and ricocheted onto the front pages of *USA Today,* the *Los Angeles Times* and the *Washington Post*'s Style section.

But the Great Popcorn Exposé of 1994 didn't just happen. Silverman, communications director for the Center for Science in the Public Interest, carefully stage-managed the news that movie theater popcorn is drenched in saturated fat.

The story had obvious appeal, but Silverman further whetted appetites for the April 25 [1994] news conference in Washington by faxing the popcorn study to a dozen reporters under a strict embargo. He leaked the findings to two news organizations, set the table with colorful visuals and helped the center's officials serve up tantalizing sound bites.

The story "just took off and seemed to reach critical mass," Silverman says. In fact, Executive Director Michael Jacobson was rousted from bed at 11:30 one night by a Johannesburg radio station looking to talk about popcorn—and this was two days before the South African election.

The publicity proved so overwhelming that the major theater chains have either announced plans to abandon the use of artery-clogging coconut oil or are offering air-popped popcorn.

Every activist in town understands that he needs something — a gimmick, a celebrity, a demonstration — to break through the media static. It is that imperative that once led six members of Congress to take sledgehammers to a Toshiba radio to protest Japanese imports, and an environmental group to trot out actress Meryl Streep for some congressional testimony on pesticides.

Randall Robinson's 26-day fast to protest U.S. policy toward Haitian refugees may have been an act of conscience, but it was also a magnet for media coverage. In *The Post* alone, Robinson's fast was covered by columnists William Raspberry, Richard Cohen and Donna Britt and in a lengthy Style section piece.

"The trick is to take what's legitimately important and package it in a way that will have appeal for editors and producers," Silverman says. "Popcorn has that appeal. Saturated fat has zero appeal. It's dry, it's academic, who cares?"

Recalling that the newsweeklies ignored the group's previous studies on Chinese and Italian food because they were announced midweek — making them old news by the following Monday — Silverman cut a deal with *Newsweek* to break the popcorn story that Monday morning.

"I jumped out of my seat when he told me about the research," says *Newsweek* reporter Laura Shapiro. "It was just such a completely unexpected source of outrage.

My greatest pleasure in life is to sneak into the movies and sit in the back and eat popcorn."

Silverman also arranged a Bryant Gumbel interview on that morning's "Today" show, but it got bumped by Richard Nixon's death.

At the Hyatt Regency news conference, Jacobson declared that a medium box of buttered popcorn contains as much saturated fat as a bacon-and-eggs breakfast, a Big Mac and large fries for lunch and a steak dinner combined — and all that greasy food was laid out for the TV cameras. The center also laid out 15 hot dogs, which provide the fat equivalent of one large tub.

Television devoured the story; center officials appeared on "CBS This Morning," "Entertainment Tonight" and "Crossfire." Leno and Letterman weighed in. And headline writers had a field day: "Popcorn Gets an 'R' Rating" (*New York Daily News*); "Movie Popcorn 'The Godzilla' of Snacks" (*USA Today*); "Lights, Action, Cholesterol!" (*Newsday*); "Theater Popcorn Has Fatal Attraction" (*Baltimore Sun*).

Silverman, who has taught media strategy classes, says the press gobbled it up because popcorn is "ubiquitous" and "affects the lifestyle of people in the media."

And what kind of stories has he had the least success peddling? "Anything substantive without a hook."

"The Great Exploding Popcorn Exposé," by Howard Kurtz, *Washington Post,* May 12, 1994, Dow//Quest Story ID: 000010315WP. © 1994 *The Washington Post.* Reprinted with permission.

PART IV

Issues and Effects

CHAPTER 12

Ownership Issues
Press Performance Issues

The Big Four Newspapers

In the United States, the four newspapers with the largest and most influential audiences are *The New York Times, The Washington Post, The Wall Street Journal,* and the *Los Angeles Times.* This article, written by Michael Krantz of *Mediaweek,* analyzes the role that each of these influential newspapers is likely to play in the future media marketplace.

Consider:

1. How is each of these media institutions adapting to the changing media marketplace?

2. Will these newspapers, according to Krantz, be able to "maintain their opinion-shaping mandate"? Why? Why not? Explain.

3. Newspapers in the United States have been called the media's agenda-setters because they have traditionally initiated and focused attention on the issues that their editors consider to be important to the country, and the other media (especially broadcast) often follow newspapers' lead. Do you believe this function of newspapers as agenda-setters is likely to continue into the 21st century? Explain.

Newspapers: Still Setting America's Agenda

Four major daily newspapers continue to determine what is news in 1994. But what about tomorrow? Will they remain the arbiters of the important? The New York Times, The Washington Post, The Wall Street Journal *and the* Los Angeles Times *come to terms with their post-print age.*

Michael Krantz

For the newspaper industry, the past decade has brought both the best and worst of times. From 1979 to 1985, if you were the publisher of one of America's greatest papers, all the arrows pointed up. The overheated economy was boosting your profits along with everybody else's. Classified was strong. Circulation was strong. Retailing was strong. Real estate was strong. Hell, everything was strong.

But at the same time, some disturbing trends were under way. Cable television was reaching critical mass and beginning a steady foray into local advertising. Local TV stations were winning retail business and free-standing advertising inserts were slipping over to direct mail. The spread of electronic culture—everything from video games to MTV News—meant fewer young people were acquiring the daily paper habit. Readers'

232

average age crept steadily upward, foretelling demographic catastrophe.

Then came the Crash of '87. The next six years were a shocking comedown, even for the notoriously cyclical newspaper industry. Classifieds collapsed. Retail collapsed. Real estate collapsed. Hell, everything collapsed.

Except, that is, the papers themselves. Two years into the great multimedia boom, amid myriad predictions of print's imminent demise, America's four great opinion-making newspapers—these being, almost inarguably, *The New York Times, The Wall Street Journal, The Washington Post,* and the *Los Angeles Times*—still set the national agenda on a daily basis, as they and their forebears have done throughout the century. When the executive editor of *The New York Times* steps aside and a new one is crowned, as happened two weeks ago [in April 1994], it's a public event on a par with the crowning of a head of state. And when news happens—an air strike in Bosnia, riots in Rwanda, a revelation in Little Rock—senators and Ordinary Joes alike might get the story from CNN, but they rely on the *Times,* the *Post,* the *Journal* and the *Times* to explain what it means.

What's more, there are good arguments favoring the great papers' continued preeminence in the [21st] century. For one thing, the more information we have access to, the more we'll need perceptive editors to sift it into presentable form—and who's more perceptive than, say, the editors at *The New York Times*?

But [in 1994], after the highs of the '80s boom and the lows of the '90s recession, the great papers stand at a crossroads. In the past few years all four have undergone change at the publisher and editor levels, and as much as a newspaper is influenced by institutional identity, individuals do put their own stamps on the present—sometimes out of necessity. As new media further obviate the great papers' original news dissemination role, will they be able to maintain their opinion-shaping

mandate? In changing with the times, will they change too much, thus losing the strengths that made them great?

I: The State of the Church

Everybody loves *The Wall Street Journal.* The business community that composes its prime, 1.8 million-strong audience relies on the newspaper's incomparable Wall Street coverage. Washington, D.C., enthralled on both sides of the aisle by Robert Bartley's infamous editorial page and its scathing, right-wing-in-exile pyrotechnics, scours the paper more than any other save their own beloved *Post* (90 percent of the press and senior federal officials read the *Post,* 62 percent the *Journal,* 45 percent the *Times* and 4 percent the *Los Angeles Times*). Even the liberal media intelligentsia is unanimous in its praise for both church and state in the *Journal,* though they cite the entertainment value of the editorial page and the quality journalism of the rest of the paper.

Like the *Post* and the *Times* (if not just yet the *L.A. Times,* thanks to the lingering recession in Southern California), the *Journal* has a healthy and wealthy parent in Dow Jones Co. Dow Jones' far-flung media enterprises, say analysts, including a healthy sampling of futuristic electronic information delivery projects, ensure a strong bottom line for the foreseeable future. "They have a very specific niche," says one analyst, "and they're doing quite well." The newspaper itself, under the leadership of publisher Warren Phillips (then, as of three years ago [1991], Peter Kann) and managing editor Norm Pearlstine, rose to financial dominance along with Wall Street in the 1980s. Circulation and ad lineage skyrocketed, and, in turn, the newspaper beefed up its product, becoming a player in political and international news reporting and even adding a well-received arts page. Pearlstine, a glamorous figure cut from Ben Bradlee's swashbuckling cloth, cruised into (and, apparently, out of) the newsroom like a rock star. With former page one editor James B. Stewart, his front page turned the scandal- and merger-ridden, boom-and-bust '80s into the stuff of journalistic legend. In the space of a generation, the *Journal* transformed itself, as the *Post* had a decade before, from a snoozy tip sheet for financial types into the hot paper for young journalists to work at.

Yet, like everyone else in the Gray Nineties . . . *The Wall Street Journal* faces an uneasy transition into a quieter era of what some are calling diminished expectations. The '80s are gone, and so are Phillips, Pearlstine, Stewart, Bryan Burrough and many other luminaries of the *Journal*'s golden age. Opinions differ as to how the change of managing editorship actually occurred. "He got pushed out," says one industry insider. "Peter Kann just f—ed him," says another. "It came out of the blue. Norm was blindsided." *Journal* management, however, claims Pearlstine (who declined to be interviewed) resigned on his own. Paul Steiger, now the managing editor of the *Journal,* also dismisses such talk, saying it is "simply not true."

What isn't in dispute is that, Pete Townshend's warning notwithstanding, the new boss, Steiger, is not the same as the old boss. "It's a safer, more boring paper," says a former reporter at the *Journal.* "It's more conservative. Norm was more creative than Steiger; he was an '80s editor." Today, says the reporter, "the paper is returning to its roots, which is covering business and finance in a thorough way. The quality is still high, but what it doesn't have is that knock-your-socks-off appeal."

For others, their new leader's relative conservatism is not necessarily a negative trait. "The first thing you notice about Steiger," says *Journal* copy editor Ron Chen, "is that he's a very hands-on person. You feel like you're working for someone who's in charge. Norm was very good at burnishing his own image. The pair [Pearlstine and Kann] fit the go-go '80s: Norm peeling a banana with his toes, Peter's parties in Hong Kong. But when you actually work with them, you decide a lot of this is just stories."

Pearlstine, says Chen, "probably gave up control of the newsroom two or three years before he got pushed out. He was shopping himself. It was clear that the guy was not going to end his days at some stuffy newsroom. He was using it as a launching pad for his future."

Speaking of which, that's just what one discovers the *Journal* is doing right now. Some readers and media commentators may bemoan the paper's newer, drier feel — but that says as much about the paper's prime territory as it does about the paper. In fact, the *Journal*'s strategy in the '90s appears to be to play to its strength — a specific, and very profitable, journalistic niche — while expanding its presence in some canny arenas such as overseas development and new media proliferation.

Internationally, *Journal* editions now include steady Asian and European five-dayers and this summer's [1994] *Wall Street Journal Americas,* a two-page Spanish language insert produced in New York for addition to eight Latin American dailies with a combined circulation of more than 1 million. The Asian and European editions still are small, but, notes Steiger, the European edition is close to overtaking *The Financial Times* on the continent.

Steiger also is quite bullish on new media, which, alone among the publishers and editors interviewed for this story, he seems to consider integral to his paper's future. New media, he says, will play "a huge role. The question is timing. How fast can we get into the marketplace with approaches that are smart and that will attract a large following?" The answer, apparently, is: Quickly. "By this time [in 1995]," Steiger says, "we are going to be doing a full-fledged interactive edition of *The Wall Street Journal.*" If that means being able to talk back to Bob Bartley and the sharks on the editorial page, Dow Jones looks like a good investment.

II. The Pacific Century?

When Shelby Coffey arrived at the *Los Angeles Times* from *The Washington Post* to succeed executive editor Bill Thomas early in 1989, he expected to preside over the *Times'* continuing emergence as a newspaper of national, even international, stature.

Instead the '80s ended, and Coffey watched the roof cave in. "We're downsizing, but we're also expanding," says *L.A. Times* spokeswoman Laura Morgan four years later. "I think a lot of people have trouble understanding that." Well, that's understandable. The *L.A. Times* has always been rife with contradictions: a local paper with international aspirations; a nationally-known paper with, at least according to its critics, a provincial perspective. Boasting the largest editorial department of any American newspaper, a West Coast monopoly on serious international news coverage and a front-row seat at the arrival of the Pacific Rim nations on the world's economic stage, the *Times* would appear primed to flourish.

So why doesn't anybody like it? "There's a general sense of stasis, of being under siege and behind the eight ball," says the paper's media critic, David Shaw. Margo McGee (a pseudonym), who writes the "Our Times" column about the *Times* for L.A.'s *Buzz,* is blunter. "Don't you think the *L.A. Times* is a pretty big dropoff?" she asked, told of the four newspapers covered in this report. "It's rather embarrassing and a shame that it's so inferior." In information-saturated Washington, D.C., writers and government workers report seeing, and reading, the *Post,* the *Journal* and *The New York Times* almost religiously. The streamlined, five-day *L.A. Times* edition, by contrast, has precious little visibility in the nation's capital.

Though the paper is acknowledged to produce strong international coverage — perhaps largely due to its size and wealth — complaints about the *Times'* content are persistent and manifold. They include: iffy editorial judgment; insufficiently edited, long-winded articles; the lack of what one editor calls "an identifiable personality"; and an East Coast-focused inferiority complex and scant attention to the paper's own hometown. In many ways, say its critics, the *Times* has not yet risen above local paper status: "The *Seattle Post-Intelligencer,*" McGee writes, "with a lot more money."

The paper's biggest problem may be that it tried to rise too far too fast. "Clearly, over the years, the changes were much for the better," says contributing editor Bob Scheer, a 17-year *Times* veteran. "We went from being a poor regional paper to being a national paper." But after decades of slow, steady growth under the Chandler family (whose family still controls the company's class-B voting stock but, since the retirement of Otis Chandler in 1980, no longer involves itself with the newspaper's affairs), the *Times,* under the leadership of publisher David Laventhol, expanded rapidly in the '80s. A longtime Times Mirror executive once thought to be CEO Robert Erburu's chosen successor, Laventhol travelled west in 1989 hoping to make the *Times* a national paper. Under his leadership, the *Times* launched editions to the south in San Diego and to the east toward Phoenix. But the company has since abandoned the San Diego experiment, and the *Times* is still locked in a fierce battle in L.A.'s suburbs with the archrival *Orange County Register* and the *Los Angeles Daily News.* Three employee buyout offers [between 1991 and 1994], while whittling the huge staff to a more Wall Street-friendly size, have cost the paper more marquee writers than it expected. "You can't tell a writer, 'I'll give you two years pay and medical benefits,' and expect him not to take it," says Scheer, who took it. "If I hadn't, it would have looked like I had nothing better to do."

Where that's left the paper is in a bind — trying to get better while getting smaller, in what remains one of the toughest economies in the country. "Their marketplace is still in turmoil," says one financial analyst who is edgy about Times Mirror. "That company is going to go through some changes."

The men on the spot are the new publisher, longtime Times Mirror executive Richard Schlosberg, and editor Coffey. "I feel a little sorry for Shelby," says Shaw. "He came on in '89 to edit what was then the richest paper in the country. His selection suggested an appetite for change. Then, boom, almost before he's in his seat, the recession hits, and all his great ideas died aborning."

"Obviously, the last three years have not been great," Coffey says . "We've been able to make some advancements, but we've had to make some retrenchments." But help may be on the way. After three years of recessionary freefall that saw the paper's ad lineage drop 12 percent (the bread-and-butter classifieds dropped a startling 46 percent), Southern California's economy appears finally to have turned. Under Coffey, the paper has embarked on what seems a sound recession-weathering strategy: eliminating costs that were lower priority, adding new features and improving coverage of its prime territory. "We've tried to work section by section," says Coffey. "We're building on an extraordinary foundation Otis Chandler laid in creating the modern Times; our aim is to be the finest paper in the land. Over time."

The best news yet may be at the publisher level. Laventhol, who is suffering from Parkinson's disease, abruptly resigned late last year [1993]; the early returns on his successor, Richard Schlosberg, have been quite positive. "I've heard from editors here who've been unhappy that this is the best thing to happen in the past 10 years," says one source close to the Times. Even Margo McGee agrees. "With Schlosberg, people's spirits have lifted," she reports. "He wrote a thank-you note to the staff for its earthquake coverage," she adds by way of example. "People were very happy and stunned."

In the end, the Los Angeles Times seems to mirror the region it covers: huge and rich but, deep down, perhaps a bit shallow, compared to its East Coast brethren. Aggressively expansionist in the '80s, now shellshocked by the recessionary, disaster-prone '90s.

Still, there's no real competition out there; as long as the Southern California economy manages to right itself, under Schlosberg and Coffey, the Times should manage to muddle through as well. Either the biggest local paper in America, or the most parochial big paper. Take your pick. After all, L.A. is a company town.

III: After Kay and Ben

No newspaper in America has the degree of influence in its home city that The Washington Post enjoys in Washington, D.C.; the paper's 60 percent circulation penetration assures it of a preeminent agenda-setting role in the nation's capital. The paper's coverage of Watergate in the 1970s, under legendary editor Ben Bradlee, changed journalism forever, and remains the standard by which investigative reporting is judged. "The Post," says former staffer Chuck Conconi, now a writer for The Washingtonian, "is the major institution that touches everyone." And the larger Washington Post Co.— with a wide range of newspaper, magazine, cable TV, broadcast TV stations and telephone services holdings as well as an aggressive profile in the growing new media arena— remains an enormously profitable company that weathered the recent recession better than many of its competitors.

But, like the L.A. Times, today the Post finds itself in a difficult period of transition. [In 1991] the paper lost its two charismatic leaders: Owner Katharine Graham turned the reins over to her son Donald, and Ben Bradlee retired, replaced by the quiet, staid lifer Leonard Downie and, under him, the preternaturally ambitious managing editor Robert Kaiser. The changes came as a shock to the Post's staff. Perhaps no other newspaper in the country was so closely associated in the public mind — not to mention its own — with a specific editor and publisher. Bradlee's staff of journalistic rock stars — names such as Larry Stern, Haines Johnson and William Grieder — are now largely gone, and those that remain feel the *Post*'s peak years might be behind it. "While the *Times* was brightening itself up," says Conconi, "the *Post* was stumbling. [In 1992], during the campaign, *The New York Times* beat the hell out of the *Post,* day after day. The Style section has been flat. The business section isn't very good. People say even the *Times* has a better sports section."

There is a widespread notion that the Rev. Sung Myung Moon-owned *Washington Times* has beaten the *Post* on metro coverage. Strengthening the local news report had been one of Don Graham's primary ambitions in choosing Downie, a 15-year veteran of the *Post*'s Metro section, as his next editor, especially since Metro under Bradlee had been considered either a training ground or a graveyard. The *Post* has launched expensive regional editions in order to reach local customers in Washington's widespread wealthy suburbs, but so far, Graham's ambition hasn't been realized on the paper's home turf. "D.C. is a black town," says one analyst, "but you wouldn't know it from reading the *Post*."

For some, the problems start at the top. "Those guys are wrong for *The Washington Post*," says one longtime staffer of Downie and Kaiser. "They're nit-picking. They're not good for morale. Bradlee was always cruising and schmoozing; he carried with him this aura. Downie can't do that at all. Kaiser is so acerbic and in many ways, mean-spirited and self-righteous. And everyone who knows him knows he won't sit still being No. 2 to Downie."

Both Graham and Downie are sanguine about the paper's current challenges. "We consider ourselves local, national and international," says Downie. "We have to serve all those audiences at the same time. First and foremost, we have to be a strong local paper,

but when your local base happens to be Washington, D.C., then first and foremost you are also a national and international paper.

"We didn't drift away from local news coverage," Downie continues. "While the majority of D.C. is black, in the region we serve, black people number only about 10 percent. We've had to learn a lot about how to cover minority communities. However, it remains more of our emphasis than ever." For his part, Don Graham seems content to leave *The Washington Post* in Downie's hands. "Publishers of papers like this really only do one important thing," says a self-effacing Graham. "If all I'm going to be remembered for is picking Len Downie as editor of the *Post,* well, that's fine with me."

IV: Fit to Print

A visitor to the office of *New York Times* publisher Arthur Ochs Sulzberger, Jr., must first pass through Pulitzer Row, a long, daunting hallway hung with portraits of esteemed Timesmen (Timepersons now) who, over the years, have brought glory to the newspaper. David Halbertstam in Vietnam. Walter Kerr on theater. Brooks Atkinson in Russia. Sidney Schanberg in Cambodia. Cyrus Sulzberger in Yugoslavia. Anna Quindlen for her column.

The paper's circulation and ad lineage have recovered from the brutal Northeast recession; the national edition continues to gain subscribers. With its recent billion-dollar purchase of *The Boston Globe* and the electronic news deal with America Online, the New York Times Company would seem poised for continued growth and prosperity.

Just so long as people keep reading the damn paper. But increasingly, industry insiders wonder whether that will be the case. The *Times'* long-held reputation for unparalleled journalistic excellence precedes any examination of Planet Earth's "paper of record," rendering both startling and sad [1994's] pervasive complaints that the paper has gone soft, that in adapting to a mutating and highly competitive media landscape the *Times* has lost the impassive, imperial objectivity that made it irreplaceable in the first place.

The changes began in mid-1970s under executive editor A. M. Rosenthal. They continued in the late '80s, when Rosenthal was succeeded by Max Frankel, who instituted a breezier, "softer" journalistic style to complement the *Times'* hard news reportage. Along with bulletins from Congressional hearings and reports from war-torn nations, the front page now also featured articles on rising hemlines and single women's falling romantic expectations. Says one former *Times* staffer, echoing the thoughts of many peers: "It's hard to write an article about building bird cages out of popsicle sticks and not sound trivial." As longtime Timesman John Corry once said, the paper's front page is no longer about what happened yesterday. Now it's about what might happen tomorrow, or what should happen tomorrow. That's a big difference.

Frankel also enthusiastically promoted the voices of what one *Times* source calls his "young, fun, hip" reporters. Literary stylists such as Anna Quindlen, Frank Rich, Michael Kelly, Maureen Dowd and Alex Wichtel began replacing venerable old guarders who found themselves marginalized and finally ousted under the Frankel regime: names like Sydney Schanberg, E. J. Dionne, Bill Kovach, Hedrick Smith and David Shipley, many of whose faces decorate Pulitzer Row. "This whole 'Look at me, ma, no hands' journalism thing," says the former staffer, "has reached the point where it's in the obscene category. The Frank Rich piece (a memoir that ran recently on the cover of *The New York Times Sunday Magazine*) is a species that never would have gotten into the magazine 10 years ago."

"Max really just wasn't up to the job," says one writer at the *Times* who witnessed the transition from Rosenthal to Frankel. "We all knew the good gray lady was too boring to make it into the 21st Century intact. But unfortunately, Max's model was *USA Today*. I think it's pretty obvious that the *Times* is in a lot of trouble . . . bringing in Roberts is a clear acknowledgement of that."

That last is a reference to Eugene Roberts, the *Philadelphia Inquirer* editor (and former Timesman) who, upon Frankel's recent early resignation and Joseph Lelyveld's ascension to executive editor, was named the *Times'* new managing editor—the first time such an appointment has been made from outside the newspaper's own ranks. There are two schools of thought on the 62-year-old Roberts' appointment. The optimists say he's an outstanding short-term caretaker while such rising young stars as Gerald Boyd, Howell Raines and Anna Quindlen* jockey for position. The pessimists view Roberts' appointment as a clear indication that Sulzberger and Lelyveld have accepted the view that their paper needs to recover the hard-news excellence that once was its uncontested bailiwick.

For the record, *Times* editors defend Frankel's editorial changes and the era of what one wag calls the Maureen Dowd School of Journalism. "You can say politics is what happens in a legislature or a parliament," says editorial page editor Mitchell Levitas. "But what if you went out into a neighborhood to find out what people thought of that legislation? By journalistic conventions, one's a hard story and one's a soft story. But which tells you more? Soft is not necessarily a dirty word."

And at the end of Pulitzer Row, one finds a calm, cheerful and confident publisher named Arthur Ochs Sulzberger, Jr., leaning forward in his chair, sipping coffee from a thermal mug and peppering his conversation with words like "s—" and "cool," the scion of the Sulzberger publishing dynasty blithely defends the editorial changes over which he, Abe Rosenthal and Max Frankel have presided. News has changed, Sulzberger says, since "the time when news was a bill or a war or a treaty. . . . News started to be viewed as more than that: medical advances, why women buy dresses, how people eat and sleep and watch TV." That saw the paper win three Pulitzer Prizes.

And what about new media? Could they upsurp the daily paper's news-reporting role?

"You mean like radio?" he says with a wry smile. "I think the use of the term *information superhighway* is a sign of sloppy and shallow thinking. It's easy to say that, and everybody nods sagely. But people who use it haven't taken the beginnings of the next step: what is it? . . . I want to provide the content that I'm proud of."

That may not include the *Times'* most revolutionary journalistic experiment, the heartbreaking hip Style section shepherded by former *Seven Days* wunderkind Adam Moss, which is termed by one former *Times* writer "an utter disappointment" to the paper. Asked whether the Style section will survive, Sulzberger sighs and says. "I wish I knew the answer to that," before adding, "In one form or another, certainly."

So the flagship of U.S. journalism sails forward into an uncertain future, aware of the enormity of change it's making, yet serene in its belief that the path it chooses will ultimately be judged correct — as it happened in the past. "When you look around at the newspapers in this country," says Levitas, "you want to cry. Local papers don't come within a dog's life of what a good newspaper should do — what you find in the *Times.*"

"Newspapers: Still Setting America's Agenda," by Michael Krantz, *Mediaweek,* April 25, 1994. Dow//Quest Story ID: 0000400508ZF. © 1994 *Adweek,* L.P. Used with permission from *Adweek's Mediaweek.*

*Note: Anna Quindlen resigned from the *Times* late in 1994.

Networks Take Biggest Broadcast Share

U.S. television network programming reaches almost everyone in the United States every day. This makes the networks very attractive to advertisers, and the majority of viewers in the television audience seem reluctant to abandon network television for cable programming, according to Paul Farhi of *The Washington Post*.

Consider:

1. **What makes the tug of network programming so strong, according to Farhi?**

2. **Why does Farhi say that "even when the new age of communications does arrive, the broadcast networks are likely to remain the only free, mass-market medium"? Why is this "free media" role important?**

3. **Which factors could change the future strength of the television networks, according to Farhi?**

Advertisers, Suitors Zoom in on TV Networks

Paul Farhi

Only two years ago [in 1992], in the midst of a recession that ravaged the television industry's revenues and self-confidence, ABC President Robert Iger made a gloomy prediction. Warily noting the 500-channel world to come, Iger offered that the future would hold "fewer networks."

Then again, TV executives are often wrong.

Rather than imploding, network television—the dominant source of news and entertainment in American households for decades—is in the midst of a revival.

Advertisers recently lavished a record $4.6 billion on the four major networks (ABC, CBS, NBC and Fox) to buy time on the [1994] fall shows. For the full year, analysts are projecting nearly $12 billion in sales, also a record.

The TV networks business has become so attractive that major media companies are racing each other to start one of their own—or buy an existing one. The list of would-be suitors pitching buyouts and joint ventures at broadcasting's Big Three seems to lengthen by the day: Barry Diller's QVC Inc., Walt Disney Co., Time Warner Inc., Ted Turner, Tele-Communications Inc., ITT Corp.

Meanwhile, Time Warner and Viacom Inc.'s Paramount studio both are poised to launch their own mini-broadcast networks . . .*

---

*Note: Time Warner and Viacom did launch fifth and sixth networks in 1995.

All of which underscores a point that wasn't obvious until recently: The networks, once thought of as an endangered species, are resurgent.

"A year ago, people were talking about the death of broadcasting," said Reed E. Hundt, chairman of the Federal Communications Commission. "If broadcasting died, it went to heaven."

The networks have benefited from a combination of better management, slowing competition and a revival of spending by advertisers. At bottom, however, they always have had a powerful advantage: No other medium can reach virtually every household every night of the week.

Much of the industry's current good fortune is because of an improving economy, which has driven up the demand for network advertising and hence what the networks charge advertisers. Prices for commercial time are at record levels on many shows. A 30-second ad on ABC's "Roseanne," for example, [in 1994] costs more than $300,000, according to one network official.

What's more, the recession taught the three leaders how to control their costs, particularly program budgets. A key reason for the proliferation of primetime "reality" programs and news "magazines" such as ABC's "Primetime Live," is that such shows are cheaper to produce than dramas and sitcoms.

All of this is occurring as the fierce competition for viewers' attention is cooling off.

Cable TV, home video and independent TV broadcasters took millions of viewers away from the networks during the 1980s and early 1990s. But with fewer homes left to wire and the VCR nearly ubiquitous, viewing habits have stabilized.

"The networks have actually done a pretty good job of giving viewers the news and entertainment they want," despite inroads from rivals, said Betsy Frank, senior vice president of the Saatchi & Saatchi advertising agency.

Since the early 1980s, she said, the number of channels available in the average household has tripled, while the share of audience watching the broadcast networks has slipped to about 62 percent from 90 percent. "Yes, there's been a decline [for the networks], but if you didn't know better you'd think it would be much worse," Frank said.

While a growing economy and maturing competition could be short-term pluses, the longer term is starting to look better for the networks, too.

"The truth of the matter is that plain old television is going to be around for quite a while," said Viacom Chairman Sumner Redstone, whose company owns MTV, Paramount, the Blockbuster video-store chain and, soon, a fifth broadcast network.

Why, with the coming of the information highway, does "plain old television" appear to have staying power? The answer is a mix of technology, economics and politics.

For one thing, the supposed threat to broadcasting posed by the information highway is years away. Despite all the media attention, most households won't be able to receive interactive services or hundreds of TV channels until well after the turn of the century, according to a majority of industry executives recently surveyed by the Arthur Andersen accounting firm.

And even when the new age of communications does arrive, the broadcast networks are likely to remain the only free, mass-market medium. It's not clear that the same claim can be made of any of the communications technologies under development.

The networks' ability to reach 98 percent of the U.S. population via hundreds of affiliated local stations is the biggest source of their power, said Jack Valenti, who heads the Motion Picture Association, Hollywood's leading lobbying group. "Any entity that can throw out a net and cover the entire nation . . . is going to have the most efficient, cost-effective way to reach the public," he said.

This scale, which is difficult for others to duplicate because of the limited number of local TV stations, gives the networks the ability to attract the kind of advertising support that enables them to underwrite more original, high-quality programs than anyone else.

A half-hour sitcom such as "Seinfeld" or "Murphy Brown" costs about $750,000 an episode to produce, an executive of a major studio said. One-hour dramas such as "Law & Order" cost about $1 million a show, while special-effects-laden serials such as "Lois & Clark" can approach $1.4 million. The budget for a two-hour made-for-TV movie averages about $3.4 million, and sports rights such as the National Football League's recent $1.6 billion contract with Fox are costlier still.

No other media can spend as much as the networks on programming because no other media reaches so many people. While a top-rated cable program might be tuned in by 2.5 million homes, a primetime program drawing the same rating on ABC or CBS would be quickly canceled.

Even now, the most consistently popular program on cable [in 1994] is an old network show, CBS's "Murder, She Wrote," in re-runs carried on the USA Network. Its rating doesn't come close to the least-watched program on the broadcast networks.

In short, the networks' dominant position has an almost self-perpetuating quality: With big-budget original programming, they attract the largest audiences, which in turn attracts the largest share of advertising money, which in turn finances the networks' ability to buy more original programming.

But the economics of network television aren't foolproof. A bidding war for a hot sports package, such as NFL or Olympic rights, or escalating demands by popular actors and producers can make some programming unprofitable. It can, in fact, make an entire network unprofitable, which is what happened to top-rated CBS [in 1992], primarily because of its costly Major League Baseball contract.

The most consistently profitable part of ABC, NBC and CBS is not their network operations but the local TV stations these companies own in a handful of major markets, such as New York and Los Angeles.

Network TV Time Sales (in Millions)						
	THREE NETWORKS					
	ABC	CBS	NBC	Total	Fox	Total
1990	$3,234	$3,177	$3,721	$10,132	NA	$10,132
1991	3,198	2,920	3,338	9,456	NA	9,456
1992	3,036	3,361	3,576	9,973	NA	9,973
1993	3,272	3,375	3,184	9,381	1,062	10,893
1994*	1,880	2,239	2,016	6,135	690	6,825

* = Jan.–July

Source: CMR/Media Watch

"People watch programs, not networks," said John Malone, chief executive of Tele-Communications Inc., the world's largest cable TV company. "Competition for unique programming," said Malone, threatens the networks' long-term profitability. "It's not a good news–good news situation."

And lately, the networks are grappling with another problem: how to maintain their national lineups of affiliated local stations.

Rupert Murdoch's Fox network set off a scramble within the TV industry in May [1994] when Fox paid $500 million to a group-station owner to switch all of its 11 stations' network affiliations to Fox. CBS, NBC and ABC responded by raiding each other's affiliates.

Once this game of musical chairs stops, independently owned stations in Baltimore, St. Louis, Cleveland and 10 other cities will have changed their network loyalties.

The affiliate switches frighten the networks because they go to the core of what they are: distribution chains comprised of affiliated stations, one in each market, that carry programming selected by executives in New York.

"We're being very aggressive in [preventing affiliate defections] because access to distribution is a very scarce commodity," said Neil Braun, president of the NBC network.

To prevent defections, NBC, CBS, ABC and Fox will pay their affiliates about $250 million [in 1994] for agreeing to air network shows — roughly double what they paid in "compensation fees" [in 1993].

But even as they giveth, the networks also are about to get.

Thanks to a series of court and regulatory decisions, CBS, ABC and NBC soon will be freed from legal restrictions that have prevented them from participating in the lucrative market for re-runs.

For the past 24 years, the financial interest and syndication rules have kept the networks and Hollywood studios at arm's length. For example, a company could own a network or a TV production operation but not both. Fox,

as a fledgling fourth network, was given an exemption from that rule by the FCC.

By forcing the networks to rent their shows from independent producers, the rules effectively kept the networks from dominating both the distribution and production of television programs.

With the rules set to expire by November 1995, the networks will be able to produce all of their first-run programs in-house, instead of paying the studios for them. Further, the networks will be able to resell these shows to cable networks, satellite, independent and foreign broadcasters, as well as proposed video systems owned by telephone companies.

This new freedom isn't without risk — many network shows are flops, after all — and no one expects the networks to produce all of their shows themselves, at least at first. But the networks clearly see new revenue opportunities in syndication as well as the ability to gain greater control over their costs.

"To have a place in the future of the television business, you can't think of yourself as just a network," NBC's Braun said. "You have to think of yourself as a network, a syndicator, a cable company, an international programmer, and you have to know how all those pieces fit together."

Hollywood's response: If you can't beat the networks, join them — or buy them.

It's no accident that Time Warner and Disney lately have been the two most active companies discussing the purchase of a network. This is because Disney and Time Warner, through its Warner Bros. Studio, are the leading producers of network fare. Disney, for example, produces TV's most popular program, ABC's "Home Improvement."

Rather than see their biggest customers slip away as the networks ramp up their own productions, the studios want to ensure a place for their programs by owning the network.

Time Warner and another studio, Paramount, have a fallback position, too. Both are starting broadcast networks of their own, in conjunction with the owners of independent TV station groups.

Time Warner's WB network [went] on the air Jan. 11 [1995] with two hours of new sitcoms every Wednesday night. The United/Paramount network [was] launched on Jan. 16 [1995] with two nights of programs a week, including "Star Trek: Voyager," another spinoff from Paramount's venerable "Star Trek" franchise.

"There's no longer any issue about whether the networks will be around," said Frank Biondi, chief executive of Viacom, Paramount's parent. "The question is, how profitable will they be, and whether the answer will be 'more than today.'"

"Advertisers, Suitors Zoom in on TV Networks," by Paul Farhi, *Washington Post,* October 31, 1994. Dow//Quest Story ID: 0000121235WP. © 1994 *The Washington Post.* Used with permission.

Covering High-Profile Cases

The O. J. Simpson case offered the platform for critics and supporters of television news programming to analyze the impact that media attention to a specific story can have on society. In this article, O. J. Simpson's lawyer, Robert L. Shapiro, discloses how he uses the media to garner attention for his clients.

Consider:

1. Do you agree with Shapiro that "the lawyer's role as spokesperson (for his or her client) may be equally important to the outcome of a case as the skills of an advocate in the courtroom"? Explain.

2. Why does Shapiro feel that "no comment" is "the least appropriate and least productive response"? Do you agree? Explain.

3. List four of Shapiro's recommendations for dealing with the news media. What does this tell you about the relationship between the news media and central figures during high-profile media events? Explain.

Secrets of a Celebrity Lawyer
How O. J.'s Chief Strategist Works the Press

Robert L. Shapiro

As trial lawyers, our skills are honed in the courtroom. We practice our craft and improve to the point where our skills allow us to handle those important cases that the media deem newsworthy. When we are retained for those high-profile cases, we are instantly thrust into the role of a public relations person—a role for which the majority of us have no education, experience, or training. Our job switches from advocate to manager and commentator. To further compound the difficulties, when the media call, they come in droves. The lawyer's role as spokesperson may be equally important to the outcome of a case as the skills of an advocate in the courtroom.

The importance and power of the media cannot be overemphasized. The reporting of an arrest always exceeds the reporting of the acquittal. The first impression the public gets is usually the one that is most important. Unfortunately, in criminal cases, this generally is the biased report issued by the investigating law enforcement agency and, subsequently the prosecuting agency.

Immediately upon the arrest of a well-known person — a public figure, entertainer, athlete, or businessperson — the story is framed in a way to give the prosecutor's version of the case the greatest weight. If the case is big enough, the head of the prosecuting agency will personally appear and announce a vigorous prosecution highlighting the strongest pieces of evidence showing guilt. This often takes place before a suspect has retained counsel, and any response to the media at that time is generally limited to statements from the suspect himself or from close family members.

The lawyer who is finally retained will be bombarded with inquiries from the press to comment on the allegations that have been levied by the police and prosecution. While the lawyer is busy becoming familiar with the facts of the case, beginning interviews with the client, starting the investigation, and arranging to have bail set or lowered so the client can be released, the attorney is now also obliged to be a spokesperson for the client.

Although California ethical rules do not place restrictions on an attorney's statements before trial, the majority of states do. Therefore, lawyers in states with restriction on free speech may be compelled to a simple "no comment" approach.

Otherwise, "no comment" is the least appropriate and least productive response. Coming at the end of a lengthy story, it adds absolutely nothing and leaves the public with a negative impression. At the same time, a cliché response that "these are trumped-up charges, politically motivated," accomplishes little good. An obvious exception would be if there are serious racial overtones or direct political implications.

The initial statement must be carefully crafted. It is never a good idea to lie to the press. To simply make up facts in the hope that they will later prove correct is too big a risk. Remember that everything you say will be recorded on videotape, audiotape, and in voluminous handwritten notes. Questions will appear and reappear throughout the case based on your initial response.

My personal preference is to prepare an open-ended response stating that we have recently been retained, that many of the facts will be in dispute, that we are conducting our own intensive investigation with the best experts in the field reconstructing the crime scene, and that we will not be able to make any specific comments until all the facts are in. This is also an appropriate time to let the public know that your client has support from his family and friends, that you are currently working with the family to arrange for bail or that you will be appearing in court to have bail set, and that you are optimistic about the ultimate outcome of the case.

If you release the story to the wire services, you can expect a barrage of calls from newspapers, radio, and television stations. In addition, free-lance writers will begin to prepare articles for magazines, and, finally, the tabloids will try to get the inside scoop on the case.

Initial relationships with legitimate members of the press are very important. The working press has a job to do. Many times a lawyer will feel it is an intrusion to be constantly beset by seemingly meaningless questions that take up a tremendous amount of time which could be better spent on trial preparation. Relationships can and should be cultivated with all legitimate members of the press. It is important for the lawyer to act as a conduit so that the real workings of the legal system can be known. My experience is that most reporters couldn't tell you the difference between a preliminary hearing and a pretrial conference. They know little or nothing of how bail is posted and what the legal requirements are. By answering these simple questions, a lawyer not only can develop a relationship with the press, but can also educate the public on the true workings of our justice system.

The initial headlines of the arrest often make the sacred presumption of innocence a myth. In reality, we have the presumption of guilt. This is why dealing with the media is so important. To make inroads into the mind-set that "if the press reported it, it must be true" is the lawyer's most challenging task.

Dealing with the members of the press with whom you have a pre-existing relationship presents no particular problems. However, the majority of the time you'll be dealing with new and different people. Be responsive to their inquiries. The wire services depend on immediate updates. Therefore, all calls should be returned as quickly as possible. The wire-service reporters are generally interested in basic factual material and do not do in-depth interviews. They will want factual background material regarding dates of court appearances, assignment of judges, specific questions regarding the charges and the potential consequences. They also, however, provide immediate distribution of anything you have to say worldwide.

Wire-service reporters can also provide a valuable source of information to you. Many times they are aware of factual material yet to be released, but which is important to lawyers.

Care should be taken to release the same statements to all wire-service reporters within the same time framework. Many reporters who work out of the courthouse share adjoining offices. It is a good idea to constantly keep in touch with wire-service reporters and let them know any updates that are important. By opening lines of communication, you will develop an invaluable sense of trust.

Newspaper reporters require a different approach. They have more time to investigate their stories, have later deadlines, and generally will stay with a case until its conclusion. These reporters, therefore, have tremendous power, and their stories can easily affect the outcome of the case. Newspaper reporters will try to present a balanced story. However, they are sometimes hampered in this endeavor by lack of communication with the defense lawyers.

The police department and prosecuting agency have longstanding relationships with most members of the press. High-profile cases provide an excellent opportunity for top-ranking police officials and prosecutors to use the press to their advantage. The defense lawyer who has never dealt with the press, or has no pre-existing relationship with a particular reporter, is at a severe disadvantage. In order to overcome this, the lawyer must cultivate a line of communication with the reporter so the client's point of view can be expressed in the most favorable way.

Just as you would do in trial, anticipate the questions a reporter will pose. Think out your answers carefully. My personal preference is to initially talk to a reporter off the record and get an idea what questions the reporter is interested in and where the story is going. After I get a general feel for the reporter's interests, I then respond to the questions that are appropriate. If there are questions that cannot be answered, or should not be answered, I simply tell the reporter that I cannot respond at this time. Remember, everything you tell a reporter, whether it's on or off the record, will be remembered even though it's not printed.

Use great care in choosing your words for the record and for attribution. Keep your statements simple and concise. Reporters generally will not use more than two or three sentences as a quote. If you do not feel comfortable, you may want to write out statements in advance and see how they appear to you. After a statement is given to a reporter on the record, do not hesitate to ask the reporter to read it back. This will insure that the reporter got the statement correctly and also give you a chance to change any words or thoughts.

As in any relationship between professionals, give-and-take can be mutually beneficial.

This is not to say that reporters will take your point of view out of favoritism. I have never seen that occur. However, by the nature of the questions a reporter will ask, you can get an idea as to what people have been telling the reporter.

Perhaps the most difficult problem in dealing with the press is dealing with the tabloids. Sensational headlines which often have little or nothing to do with the story that follows can have a severe impact on a high-profile criminal defendant. My experience is that cooperating with tabloid reporters only gives them a legitimate source of information which can be misquoted or taken out of context and does little good for your client. The practices of ethical journalism are not followed.

My personal approach is not to cooperate with tabloid reporters. In response to questions raised in those publications, I generally point out that most stories are bought and paid for and, therefore, the sources have a financial stake in the story being printed. Thus, their credibility is undermined.

However, tabloids cannot be ignored and can potentially influence the outcome of a high-profile case. I have had occasions when individuals have attempted to extort me and threaten the sale of stories to the tabloids if financial demands were not met. My practice is to report such communications immediately to the police and district attorney.

I initially tried to cooperate with television tabloid shows. I had reporters and producers try to persuade me that they would present balanced versions for broadcast. However, my experience was that they are geared totally towards sensationalism. With television's editing ability, and the instant effect of reading out-of-context statements from police reports, I am now reluctant to cooperate with many of the TV tabloid shows.

It should be noted that some of the producers are so hungry for celebrity coverage that they will give you complete creative control over your client's presentation on a segment. Although such offers have been made, I have felt that it is best for my clients and their families to generally stay away from the media and have declined what appears to be a generous offer. My thinking is, again, that editing and follow-up stories can only be detrimental.

Another aspect of dealing with the press begins after the case is under way and they are reporting the day-to-day coverage of a case in progress. Here, I make a distinction between members of the press. I always try to notify legitimate working press — ahead of court appearances — as to what is to be anticipated and what procedures will be used. Further, if the case is going to be advanced or continued, I notify the media so that they can adjust their schedules and avoid coming to court when nothing will take place. Such consideration helps to develop a relationship of trust which will be greatly appreciated.

After a day in court, a lawyer in a high-profile case will be inundated by the media. The first people I talk to are legitimate members of the print media. I gather the newspaper, wire-service, and legitimate magazine representatives together. These are the people who are going to have to write the most in-depth stories and are facing tremendous pressure from deadlines, especially for evening edition newspapers.

The end of a court day is a time when most of us are exhausted and must go on to prepare for the following day. Take time and be patient with the reporters. Many of the questions they ask may seem simple and sometimes irrelevant. But bear with them. They have a job to do, and your cooperation with them is always appreciated.

Do not assume that courtroom reporters understand court procedures. Take your time to explain motions that are filed, the theories behind them, and the reason for the motion. If a story appeared that you liked, compliment the reporter on his or her objectivity. Maintain a list of all reporters covering your case. Get not only their office phone numbers, but their home numbers as well. I have yet to meet a reporter who did not want to be called when something was happening on a story.

Reporters are always looking for a scoop. However, to maintain good relationships with all members of the press, it is important that all material be released simultaneously. For example, if a probation-sentence recommendation is going to be filed at the end of a case, have simultaneous deliveries to all of the media. But make sure that the court and prosecuting attorney have the recommendation before it is released to the media.

Dealing with television presents additional problems. Not only is the content critical, but how it's said, where it's said, and your appearance are equally important. The television media, either consciously or unconsciously, create an atmosphere of chaos. Immediately upon arriving at the courthouse, you are surrounded by television crews. Reporters press their microphones at your jugular. You would think the most important event in the world was the arrival of your client and you at the courthouse. We have all seen people coming to court and trying to rush through the press with their heads down or covering them with newspapers or coats. Nothing looks worse. There is no way to avoid having your client's picture on television. Therefore, do everything you can to have yourself and your client appear in the most favorable light.

I always instruct my clients upon arrival at the courthouse to get out in a normal manner, to walk next to me in a slow and deliberate way, to have a look of confidence and acknowledge with a nod those who are familiar and supportive. Although the reporters will be shouting questions from all directions, answer no questions at this time. I simply tell the press a statement will be given at the end of the court day.

If your client is in custody, take special care to make sure that he or she appears neat, well-groomed, and in civilian clothes, even for perfunctory appearances. Television producers are notorious for editing in pictures of your client in the most unflattering light. Their preference is for pictures taken immediately upon arrest or transportation to court after your client has been up all night, unkempt and in jail clothes. They will continue to edit in this picture months after the fact. When this has happened, I have called station news directors and producers, and told them my concerns. If they told me they had no current pictures, I immediately sent them one. Almost all were sensitive to my request and stopped running the negative photographs.

In the California state court system, all judges now allow microphones and cameras in the courtroom. You must therefore be constantly aware that every movement you make and every word you say will be recorded.

At the end of a court session, the television crews will form a semicircle, effectively blocking any exit from the courtroom. The attorney will be backed up against the courtroom doors with television lights glaring in his eyes and microphones thrust in his face.

To avoid this, I tell the reporters in advance that I will be making a statement at the end of the day, and I direct them to an area outside the courthouse. I prefer a lawn with trees or some other attractive background. As I stated before, I talk to the print media first. This allows me time to compose my thoughts and outline in my mind the statement I will give.

The most important lead story on an hour newscast allots only 15 or 20 seconds for a statement from an interview. These sound bites must be concise and easily understood. In order to insure what you say is aired on the news, limit your statements. The less choice you give the news director or reporter, the greater chance you have of airing the precise words you want aired.

If you feel it is appropriate to answer questions, remember that only the answers are aired — never the questions. Pick and choose the questions you want to answer. You do not have to be concerned with whether the answer precisely addresses the question, since only the answer will be aired.

By taking time to compose your thoughts before you come outside, you will have a chance to relax. I always have my client, if not in custody, or family members close to me, but do not allow them to answer any questions. Do not lower your head and look at the microphone. This will cause your eyes to close and give you a dazed appearance. The best way to see how people come off well on television is to watch professionals. A good rule is to try to look over the cameras. This will cause you to keep your chin up. John Wayne, when asked about his success, was fond of telling young actors, "Speak low and speak slow." Trial lawyers, who are used to quick cadence and firing fast questions on cross-examination, must rethink their delivery for television. Look neat and well-groomed. Rather than be intimidated by cameras, think of them as a friendly audience to whom you are trying to tell a very short and important story.

In dealing with all members of the press, avoid clichés. Referring to a case as a tragedy or to a client as being framed does not convey a thoughtful message. To describe an unfortunate death situation, I use the term "a horrible human event." Come up with phrases that you believe in and are comfortable saying. Repeat them continuously, and they will be repeated by the media. After awhile, the repetition almost becomes a fact. That is your ultimate goal.

In one murder case, I was faced with a situation where I wanted to leave our options open for trial, but also to attempt to resolve the case on a favorable basis. Rather than try to explain the difference between first-degree murder and second-degree murder and voluntary manslaughter and involuntary manslaughter, I use the phrase "accidental manslaughter." This was a perfect phrase for television, although it has no legal significance. The idea

that I wanted to convey came across loud and clear. It was a death that was unintentional, that may have legal consequences, but was nothing more than an accident.

Be concerned with time constraints on all legitimate members of the press. The television media begin their news coverage at 5 P.M. If you are leaving the courtroom at 4:30 P.M. and conducting a news conference at 4:45 P.M. that gives very little time for preparation. Thus, reporters will conduct a live-from-the-courthouse segment and then edit in the comments you have just made. These brief press conferences are of tremendous importance. Try to watch the first news of the day if at all possible, or have someone record it for you. The news is repeated throughout the evening. I have often called reporters to point out mistakes in their initial newscast, and an hour later saw a different and more accurate version. Your input will be respected.

Reporters in high-profile cases will continuously ask you to come on live news segments or for private interviews. My policy is the same as with the written media: I want everybody to have equal access and not create any animosity through favoritism. Therefore, I kindly thank reporters for such inquiries and tell them that I must decline for the above stated reasons.

There is no question that media coverage can and does affect the ultimate outcome of widely publicized cases. Just as it is important to cultivate relationships with judges and prosecutors, it is equally important to establish and maintain such relationships with the press. When bail was set for Christian Brando, more than fifty journalists were camped outside the county jail awaiting pictures and comments upon his release. I knew the legal requirements in posting a property bond would delay Christian's release for several weeks. I therefore contacted all members of the press covering the story and informed them there was no need to camp out, and I would notify them when his release would take place.

At first, most reporters remained on the scene. As the days went by, their ranks dwindled. Finally the local television crews and a few tabloids were the only ones left maintaining all-night vigils. I personally contacted the local crews and again told them that I would tell them exactly when Christian's bail was posted and coordinate a release through the sheriff's department. The sheriff's department was extremely happy to cooperate because the reporters were causing a security problem at the jail. Even though Christian's bail was posted late in the day on a Tuesday, and he could have been released any time that night, I fulfilled my promise and coordinated with the sheriff's department a release at 11 A.M. This allowed the press enough time to gather and allowed the sheriff's department to set up proper security for the safety of the reporters and for us.

Creating and cultivating such relationships pays great dividends. Remember: the press, including reporters, photographers, cameramen, and backup crews, all have a job to do. Making their job easier can only serve you and your client's best interests.

"Secrets of a Celebrity Lawyer: How O. J.'s Chief Strategist Works the Press," by Robert Shapiro, *Columbia Journalism Review,* September/October 1994, pp. 25–29. Used with permission from *The Champion.*

PERSPECTIVE 12-4: PRESS PERFORMANCE ISSUES

The New Press Criticism

Criticism of the press as the "nabobs of negativity" harks back to the days when former Vice President Spiro Agnew used that phrase to describe journalists during Richard Nixon's presidency. This article, which appeared on the opinion page of *The New York Times,* revives the argument that the press spends too much time focusing on what is wrong with society and not enough time focusing on possible solutions for the problems.

Consider:

1. Do you agree with press critics who say, according to William Glaberson, that journalists "often deliver a self-canceling message: every-thing—from a celebrity murder case to the health care debate and on to journalism itself—is a game about nothing more than winning or losing"? Explain.

2. Why does Kathleen Hall Jamieson believe that journalists "are now creating the coverage that is going to lead to their own destruction"? Explain.

3. Do you believe that the answer to these press critics is for journalists to de-emphasize coverage that focuses on conflict and to emphasize more positive news stories? Explain.

News as the Enemy of Hope

William Glaberson

Criticism of the press is in vogue again. That may be due in part to what might be called the O.J. effect, the odd reality that the same public that consumes tabloidism also loses respect for the medium that conveys it.

But the anti-press mood may be more fully explained by what amounts to a new critique of journalism today that is being embraced by critics from the left and the right, from academia and from some in the working press itself.

Journalists, these critics argue, are so wedded to cynicism that they often deliver a self-canceling message: everything—from a celebrity murder case to the health care debate and on to journalism itself—is a game about nothing more than winning or losing.

"We're now at a point of believing it's all a scam, everyone is looking out for his own narrow interest and the job of the reporter is to reveal the scam," said Thomas E. Mann, director of government studies at the Brookings Institution.

This notion that cynicism has replaced a necessary skepticism as the core of American journalism may be supplanting the more traditional criticism that coverage is warped by ideological (usually liberal) bias. Many critics now worry about a potentially neutral bias that shapes news coverage by declaring that all public figures, indeed all people in the news, are suspect. In this version of journalism, all politicians are manipulative, all business people are venal and all proposals have ulterior motives.

This journalism may be undermining its own credibility.

"Journalists are now creating the coverage that is going to lead to their own destruction," said Kathleen Hall Jamieson, dean of the Annenberg School for Communication at the University of Pennsylvania. "If you cover the world cynically and assume that everybody is Machiavellian and motivated by their own self-interest, you invite your readers and viewers to reject journalism as a mode of communication because it must be cynical, too."

The criticism has been expressed in a remarkably consistent collection of recently published scholarly work and popular criticism and buttressed by several new statistical reports. Thomas E. Patterson, a professor of political science at Syracuse University, published an analysis that argued that "the press nearly always magnifies the bad and underplays the good" in coverage of the White House.

Others, like Ms. Jamieson, have compiled statistics that demonstrate how frequently the press transforms serious issues into personality contests. At the same time, Ken Auletta of *The New Yorker* and other journalists argue that many of their colleagues have changed the rules of the game to benefit themselves.

Several national polls show widespread distrust of television and newspapers. One released [in September 1994] by the Times Mirror Center for the People and the Press found that 71 percent of Americans think the press "gets in the way of society solving its problems."

Reporters establish their independence, critics like Mr. Patterson say, by casting doubt on everything. In the absence of a new Watergate and in a post-Vietnam War generation distrustful of authority, the critics say, journalists substitute snideness for skepticism. Subtleties, such as the possibility that political leaders sometimes have altruistic motives as well as selfish ones, occasionally get lost.

Under the guise of analysis, the critique continues, journalists have begun to supply judgments. Talking-head television gives reporters a shot at money and fame — and the more outrageous their opinions, the greater the potential reward. The implication is that these clever people have the answers that are missed by dimwitted or excessively political public figures.

Some of the new studies suggest that such coverage amplifies public frustration because it oversimplifies problems and fails to incorporate the often complex reasons behind policymakers' positions.

In response, news professionals are experimenting with coverage that tries to reflect the greater complexity of public issues. Many of the journalists say these experiments in what they call "public journalism" are needed because their readers and viewers have turned their frustration against the messenger itself.

Lately, there has been a flurry of suggestions in publications like *TV Guide, The New Yorker* and *The Washington Post* that the large fees earned for speeches by celebrities like ABC's Sam Donaldson and Cokie Roberts compromise their independence and display a double standard. Although ABC has recently changed its rules to limit speeches, the controversy became shorthand for the idea that the inside-the-beltway pundits have become so powerful they need as much watching as the people they are supposed to be watching.

Critics of convoluted Whitewater coverage have been making the press squirm with the assertion that Watergate-hungry journalists have lost perspective. But the more troubling debate among some news professionals is whether the casting of suspicion has merely become a journalistic habit.

The Health Game

"In the post-Watergate, post-everythinggate culture, no reporter wishes to appear insufficiently prosecutorial," Gene Lyons, a columnist for *The Arkansas Democrat-Gazette,* argues in an article in *Harper's* [in October 1994]. Mr. Lyons accuses *The New York Times* of distorting innocent events to create a Whitewater scandal.

Even the failure of health-care reform has brought the assertion from health-policy analysts, elected officials and even some news professionals that news organizations, ever fascinated with political gamesmanship, may have so confused the public that journalists should shoulder some of the blame for the impasse.

A study by Ms. Jamieson and a colleague, Joseph N. Cappella, found that some of the country's most influential news organizations dedicated 54 percent of their health-care coverage to the strategic aspects of the debate, such as which politician was "winning" and which was "losing." Only 35 percent of news accounts were primarily issue oriented or factual.

Even the coverage on issues increased public cynicism about the political process, the researchers found, by assuming that Americans were already knowledgeable instead of supplying basic information.

One of the more interesting findings comes from the Center for Media and Public Affairs, which tracks positive and negative references from reporters and their sources on network news broadcasts.

During the Bush Administration, the Washington-based center often reported negative press treatment of President Bush. But because it receives much of its financing from conservative foundations, its research was often dismissed as partisan.

The center's latest research, however, indicates statistically what many press critics have observed anecdotally: the putatively liberal press has been much harder on Mr. Clinton, supposedly one of its own, than it was on Mr. Bush. During the first 18 months of Mr. Clinton's term, network news references to him were 62 percent negative as against 51 percent negative during the same period for Mr. Bush.

The analysis evokes a chicken-or-egg argument: do journalists shape their reports to fit their preconceptions or do negative reports arise from negative events? And in a world of political spinmasters and corporate message makers, perhaps cynicism itself has become a subject journalists need to cover. How, for example, are they to describe the role of professional media manipulators like Lee Atwater, the late Republican National Chairman, or David Gergen, an image-maker for President Ronald Reagan and now for Mr. Clinton?

The answer from some journalists is they simply have to continue doing what they have been doing: providing information and leaving to others the task of assessing its impact. Criticism of endeavors like investigations into Whitewater, some journalists say, suggest a naive belief that without the press the news would somehow be better.

Richard C. Wald, ABC's senior vice president for news, said in an interview that much of the current complaining is based on nostalgia for imagined better days. There are cycles of press popularity, he said, and the current lows must be viewed in that context. "There is a societal skepticism that erodes the influence of all institutions," including the press, Mr. Wald said.

But what may be most significant about the criticism of the press is that it has a growing number of adherents among journalists. Some reporters and editors talk about de-emphasizing coverage that focuses on conflict. Others say they are rethinking old aversions to positive news stories.

And it is becoming common to hear journalists wonder whether it is time to review how they do their jobs. "Journalists owe it to the public and to themselves to ask whether there's a problem that goes beyond the general cynicism about all institutions," wrote Gerald F. Seib, the political editor of *The Wall Street Journal,* in a recent [1994] column. "There probably is."

In an interview, Geneva Overholser, the editor of *The Des Moines Register,* said her readers often suggest that the negativity and cynicism of news coverage leaves them uncertain of whether they are getting a real picture of the world.

"The public is right to question whether newspapers are acting in the public interest," Ms. Overholser said. "I think what readers are asking is, 'Are you really giving us a reflection of what is happening or are you just discouraging us?' We're so good at reporting all the negatives and all the in-fighting that we give people a sense it is all hopeless."

Hearing About Harassment

The 1991 confirmation hearings for Clarence Thomas' appointment to the U.S. Supreme Court attracted the public's attention not only to the hearings but also to the way the press covered the event. In this analysis, William Boot examines the criticism.

Consider:

1. List the major criticism of the press coverage of the hearings. Then, beside each criticism, explain whether you agree or disagree. Did Boot overlook any points of criticism? If so, what are they?

2. What does Boot mean by the "Perry Mason Factor"? the "Shovel Factor"? Do you agree with Boot's criticism? Why? Why not?

3. Which important stories did the press overlook, according to Boot? And how would you suggest that members of the press improve their future coverage of important public issues, based on their experience with this event?

The Clarence Thomas Hearings

Why Everyone—Left, Right, and Center—Found the Press Guilty as Charged

William Boot

It is an old newsroom axiom that if reporting on a particular event draws protests from both right and left, the journalists on the story have probably done a balanced job. But what if the coverage prompts rebukes not only from the left and right, but from the center as well? What if it arouses the ire of countless generally apolitical people, black and white, female and male? What if it even provokes certain news organizations to attack each other's coverage? If all those factors apply, we can only be talking about the Clarence Thomas–Anita Hill sexual harassment dispute, which polarized the country [in 1991] and made for the most bizarre national news story to come our way in years.

Now that Thomas has been confirmed to the Supreme Court, it is time to take stock of the various objections to news coverage that this controversy provoked. First, an assessment of complaints from the right. Many conservatives were convinced that reporters were out to block Thomas by exploiting a news leak. Closely held Senate Judiciary

Committee information had been disclosed to *Newsday*'s Timothy Phelps and NPR's Nina Totenberg. Their stories about Hill's allegations jolted the country on Sunday, October 6 [1991]. Coming just two days before the Senate was scheduled to vote on Thomas, the leaks seemed to many to be politically motivated, timed to derail his nomination. The leaks prompted the Senate to delay Thomas' confirmation vote for one week, so the committee — under attack for not having taken Hill's allegation seriously — could probe the charges. For the first time Thomas' nomination seemed to be in real jeopardy.

Conservatives began denouncing the leaks with fierce indignation, demanding a formal investigation . . . and offering to pay a bounty of more then $30,000 to anyone who could identify the leaker. This reaction was, of course, part of a long tradition of selective outrage over leaks (a leak is monstrous if it hurts politically but not nearly so heinous if it helps, and Republicans themselves leak like crazy when it suits them). But what was the substance of their case against this particular leak? For one thing, they argued that reporting it was unethical, because it would damage Hill, who wanted to keep her allegations confidential. "This is going to be one of the saddest chapters in American journalism," Senator Alan Simpson predicted during an October 7 [1991] ABC *Nightline* confrontation with Totenberg. Casting himself as a protector of women, he said that disclosing Hill's name was like disclosing the name of a rape victim: "You've blown the cover of a person on a sexual harassment charge . . . you will have destroyed this woman." Of course, it was Simpson and his allies who immediately set about trying to destroy her. Judiciary Committee Republicans accused her of concocting her story and of committing perjury and eventually branded her mentally unstable.

There is no question that journalists trespassed on Hill's privacy in exploiting the leak. Senate staffers had approached her, having heard that she had been harassed, and Hill had provided details on condition that they not be made public. But then someone leaked her affidavit to reporters, who leaped on the story. Thus, against her will, Hill was placed in the spotlight. On balance, this intrusion seems justified, considering that most of the senators preparing to vote on Thomas were not even aware of the allegations against him, and should have been. (Judiciary Committee members say they kept their knowledge of Hill's allegations under wraps to protect the privacy of the nominee and his accuser.)

Thomas' defenders also suggested that reporters who exploited the leak were, in effect, assassinating the federal judge's character on behalf of the Democrats. This argument confuses two issues — the motivation for the leak and the question of whether the allegations were true. The leakers may well have been Democrats out to get Thomas because he is a conservative (I'd be surprised to learn they were anything else). Even so, it is still possible that Thomas was guilty of sexual harassment. This surely was a serious matter that had to be explored by the media. Since the Judiciary Committee had opted not to explore it, reporting the leak was necessary to force the Senate into action. Reporters' responsibility is to try to get to the bottom of things, not cover them up, even if some news subjects suffer as a result. (It does seem that the possible motivations of leakers should be addressed in a story like this. What both the Phelps and Totenberg pieces lacked was a section that, without giving away the leakers' identities, could have suggested what might have prompted this disclosure at the time it occurred — i.e., only after Thomas' foes had exhausted their other anti-Thomas ammunition.)

Another, more considered, objection to the leak reporting comes from Brent Baker of the conservative Media Research Center. Baker argues that Phelps and Totenberg reported their leaks too hastily, recklessly jeopardizing Thomas' reputation before they had done enough reporting to justify their stories.

He noted in an interview that Hill's allegation was far different from a claim that nominee X was guilty of something that definitely could be proven, such as stock fraud. Hill's allegation was an instance of her-word-against-his (as is generally the case in sexual harassment cases); there were no witnesses and real corroboration was impossible. Baker contends that, given those limitations and the inevitable damage to Thomas' reputation that disclosure would cause, Phelps and Totenberg should have held their stories until they had established, among other things, that there had been some *pattern* of misbehavior, with other women claiming he had been guilty of sexual misconduct with them. (*Charlotte Observer* editor Angela Wright eventually contacted the Judiciary Committee to allege that Thomas had put sexual pressure on her when she worked for him at the EEOC.)

Baker makes a strong case, but he does not give sufficient weight to the high-pressure situation in which Phelps and Totenberg found themselves. The Senate vote was just a couple of days away that Sunday, and if the story had not gotten out immediately there might never have been a Senate investigation. Given the time constraints, the two reports were not irresponsible. They cited "corroboration" from a friend of Hill's, who said Hill had complained of being sexually harassed at the time of the alleged conduct in the early '80s. The Totenberg piece carried Thomas' denial of the allegations. Phelps, unfortunately, could not reach him for comment, but he did include quotes from employee Phyllis Berry-Myers, who had worked for Thomas and who said it was inconceivable that he could be guilty of harassment.

Leaks aside, conservative groups like Baker's complain of a pervasive liberal bias in coverage. Even *The Wall Street Journal* editorial board got into the act, accusing *The Washington Post* and *The New York Times* of taking a "politically correct" pro-Hill approach to the issue (October 17 [1991] lead editorial). Conservative critics are able to cite some specific instances of slanted reporting (see Smolowe and Gibbs below), but overall it does not appear that liberal bias was much of a factor during the Hill-Thomas hearings. On the contrary: a report by the Center for Media and Public Affairs in Washington concluded that Thomas got much better press than Hill during the hearings. This study of some 220 network news broadcasts and newspaper articles found that, after the hearings began, nearly four out of five individuals quoted in news accounts backed Thomas. (Just prior to the hearings, a majority had been critical of him.) As to Hill, "more than three out of four [sources] expressed doubt or outright hos-tility towards her allegations." These data hardly suggest pervasive liberal bias. Instead, they suggest that pro-Thomas forces dominated the debate during the hearings on Hill's allegations of sexual harassment and that the media rather passively reflected this, just as they reflected the domination of pro-Hill advocates in the days prior to those hearings.

As to specifics of bias, consider these excerpts from the October 21 [1991] edition of *Time,* cited in the conservative newsletter *Media Watch. Time* associate editor Jill Smolowe wrote: "Given the detail and consistency of her testimony, it was almost inconceivable that Hill, rather than describing her own experiences, was fabricating the portrait of a sexual-harassment victim. . . ." In fact, it is not "almost inconceivable" that she was fabricating — the polls indicated that millions of Americans found the idea quite conceivable. In the same edition, senior editor Nancy Gibbs declared:

> Harriet Tubman and Sojourner Truth were slaves by birth, freedom fighters by temperament. Rosa Parks was a tired seamstress who shoved history forward by refusing to give up her seat on the bus. . . . The latest to claim her place in line is Anita Hill, a private, professional woman unwilling to relinquish her dignity without a fight.

In fact, Hill is another Rosa Parks only if one assumes she is telling the truth.

Elsewhere, of course, one could find pro-Thomas biases. *The New Republic's* Fred Barnes asserted without evidence on the October 12 [1991] *McLaughlin Group* broadcast that Hill was spinning "a monstrous lie," and Morton Kondracke, also of *TNR*, bolstered the theory, saying Hill might be compared to Tawana Brawley. John McLaughlin (himself no stranger to sex harassment allegations) compared Hill to Janet Cooke.*

For some less ideologically driven critics, a major complaint centered on sensationalism of this story. Political scientists Norman Ornstein, a barometer of centrist conventional wisdom, said in an interview that television coverage revealed warped news priorities at NBC, CBS, and ABC. They ran hours of Hill-Thomas testimony, whereas they had not provided live coverage of his pre-Hill confirmation hearings, at which big issues like abortion were on the table. This showed that ratings drove their news decisions and that personal scandal wins out every time over drier but equally important issues.

This is true, up to a point. Commercial networks do pander shamelessly. But as Ornstein acknowledged in a second interview, Hill-Thomas was, by almost any measure, a bigger story and deserved more coverage than the first round of Thomas hearings (where the nominee spent hours ducking the abortion issue and revealing as little about himself as possible). Once Hill's allegations became public, much more drama was to be had: there was a substantive issue (sexual harassment), and there were multiple conflicts (one man vs. one woman, men vs. women, black men vs. black women, women vs. Congress, Congress vs. the White House). And, of course, there was sex. Judiciary Commit-

tee chairman Joseph Biden described the high megatonnage of the story: "I know of no system of government where, when you add the kerosene of sex, the heated flame of race, and the incendiary nature of television lights, you are not going to have an explosion" (quoted on an *ABC Town Meeting,* October 16 [1991]).

Other objectors offered a kind of prude's critique, complaining that it was a travesty to bring all that graphic talk about Thomas' alleged references to sex with animals, and porn star Long Dong Silver, and pubic hairs on Coke cans into our living rooms, where children and old ladies could be watching. According to an ABC News poll released after the hearings, news media were rated lower for their Hill-Thomas performance than were the Democrats, the Republicans, Congress, or George Bush. One has to assume that the low rating was due in part to the graphic subject matter.

Of course, even those who voiced disgust kept watching. They could not do without the details. The story could not be told adequately without them. In fact, some TV journalists issued warnings to parents that simultaneously served as advertisements for the juicy material to come. Dan Rather, at the start of the Saturday October 12 [1991] hearings, said earnestly: "Now we want to *strongly* caution parents . . . there may once again be *extremely graphic testimony* that you may not want your children to watch. You may want to think about that." A few moments later, correspondent Bob Schieffer voiced awe at a case so unprecedented that it had forced the anchor of CBS News to say such a thing:

SCHIEFFER (intense, portentous delivery): Let me just go back to the words you used at the start of this broadcast. We want to warn parents that what they may hear might be offensive to their children. Have you *ever* begun a broadcast of a Senate hearing with those kind of words?

RATHER: Never.

*Cooke, a reporter for the *Washington Post,* won a Pulitzer Prize in 1981. After she won the prize and was questioned by her editors about her sources, she admitted the story was a "fabrication" and resigned. — Ed.

SCHIEFFER: It seems to me that this illustrates and underlines just how *very different* this is. . . .

Come now, wasn't this laying it on a bit thick?

Enough of the prudes — on to the feminists, who had quite different objections. One was that the news media, especially TV, were manipulated by the Republicans and used as tools to demolish Hill. Judith Lichtman of the Women's Legal Defense Fund argues, for example, that, during the hearings, journalists failed to draw the attention of viewers to Republican strategies and to the fumbling of committee Democrats. She contends that the networks and newspapers should have brought in experts to challenge questionable claims like the allegation that Hill had committed perjury, the insinuation that Hill might be "delusional," and Thomas' striking claim that he was the victim of "a high-tech lynching for uppity blacks." Instead, Lichtman says, most reporters were mere conduits: "The media portrayed what was presented to them — they therefore were manipulated. . . . We were let down by the media."

Lichtman is correct that reporters had seemingly little impact on public perceptions during the hearings. She is a bit off the mark as to why. Networks and newspapers actually did make some effort to provide the sort of commentary she says was lacking (as well as counter-opinion from conservatives). But, for reasons we'll get to shortly, this news analysis does not appear to have mattered much.

Here are some examples of the critical commentary. NBC's Robert Bazell, on the October 13 [,1991] *Nightly News,* interviewed New York psychiatrist Robert Spitzer, who voiced extreme skepticism about the assertion that Hill was living in a fantasy world. Black commentator Bob Herbert on NBC's *Sunday Today* (October 13) sharply questioned Thomas' claim to be a victim of racism. In a series of live network interviews, sexual harassment experts like University of Michigan law professor Catharine MacKinnon disputed a Republican claim that no genuine harassment victim would have followed Thomas to a new job, as Hill did in 1983. (Hill went with Thomas from the Department of Education to the Equal Employment Opportunity Commission.) Reporters also tried to give audiences an idea of Republican strategy and Democratic timidity. "One had the impression that . . . Orrin Hatch sort of played the part of Mike Tyson," Dan Rather told CBS viewers October 11. "Before Senator Biden could sort of get off his stool, Hatch was at him, all over him, and decked him." ABC's Tim O'Brien (*World News Sunday,* October 13) reported that Biden had acquiesced to Republicans, giving Thomas the big p.r. boost of live prime-time exposure.

As the opinion polls suggest, however, the impact of all this critical reporting was marginal. Why? The main reason, I suspect, is that this was a riveting live television event. Millions were watching and drawing their own conclusions. They did not need reporters to provide a news filter, so viewers may have listened even less closely than usual to commentary and analysis.

Live TV was only part of the press' "control" problem. In some cases, we lost control over some of our own debilitating impulses, which helped to undermine whatever small influence critical commentary might otherwise have had. For instance, there was the "Babble Factor": much of the intelligent news analysis (liberal, moderate, and conservative) was simply drowned out by the compulsive babbling and hyperbole that this event seemed to arouse in journalists. On October 11, Peter Jennings said of the Judiciary Committee, which has its share of dim bulbs: "One of the things we of course might remind people as they watch these proceedings . . . is that these senators are all profoundly intelligent men on this committee. In many cases they're all lawyers." Over on CBS, Dan Rather was groping for simple solutions. "If the FBI can't determine who's lying between the two, let's have some homicide detective out from Phoenix or New York City to spend a few days on this," he blurted on October 12. NBC's Brokaw said on October 11 that it would be bad if the hearings were to last several days because "it's in the national interest to have this all done as quickly and efficiently and completely as possible." As if doing it quickly were compatible with doing it efficiently and completely! (In order to meet the tight Senate-imposed timetable, the committee decided not to call any expert witnesses at all—making a thorough investigation virtually impossible.)

Then, for a few minutes on October 15, just before the Senate vote on Thomas, NBC seemed to lose complete control of its critical faculties. The network jumped from Capitol Hill coverage to Pinpoint, Georgia, where Thomas' mother could be seen live, rocking back and forth and praying in a neighbor's kitchen ("They're trying to keep him from helping us, Lord, but I ask you, Jesus, to please give it to him!" etc.). The sequence was captioned "NBC News Exclusive." The network seemed to be boasting, but why was difficult to fathom.

Another way in which journalists got sidetracked might be called the "Perry Mason Factor." Refusing to heed warnings from calmer heads, like ABC correspondent Hal Bruno, an astonishing number of journalists accepted a Republican comparison between the hearings and a trial. Republicans (and some Democrats, including the feckless Biden, at times) advanced the trial metaphor, emphasizing that Thomas must be judged by the standard of innocent until proven guilty, even though other nominees have been rejected on grounds of reasonable doubt and no candidate has a *right* to a seat on the Supreme Court. Reporters took the bait and reinforced a presumption-of-innocence message. "A political trial [is] effectively what we have ing on here today. . . . There is a kind of trial aspect to all of this after all," said Brokaw during the coverage of the October 11 hearings. "We have four institutions and people

on trial . . . in a nonlegal proceeding," said Bryant Gumbel on the same broadcast. "I guess in a sense it is a trial in a way [and] we're seeing the defense lay out its strategy here," said Bob Schieffer over on CBS on October 12; "It is a trial in a way," agreed his boss, Dan Rather. And so on. By the eve of the confirmation vote, over half the public agreed that Thomas should get the benefit of the doubt, according to a CBS-*New York Times* poll. Senate Republican leader Bob Dole said polls like that were what assured Thomas' confirmation.

Finally, there was the "Shovel Factor." Reporters (including me) failed to dig hard enough on their own during the Senate's consideration of Thomas. Why weren't the sexual harassment allegations against Thomas disclosed earlier? After all, Phelps of *Newsday* says reporters were hearing about the allegations as long ago as [July 1991]. Why wasn't more done to investigate Thomas' alleged taste for pornography, an allegation that became very pertinent in sizing up Hill's veracity? Why didn't reporters explain why Angela Wright, who complained that Thomas had sexually pressured her, was never called as a witness?

Before Hill's accusations became public, why wasn't more done to explore allegations that Thomas had breached conflict of interest standards? In one case, he ruled in favor of Ralston Purina, rather than recusing himself, even though his mentor and patron, Senator John Danforth, had a big interest in the company. In another case, Thomas was accused of delaying release of one of his controversial appeals court decisions, possibly to bolster his confirmation prospects. (Thomas denies any delay.) I was able to find fewer then ten stories devoted to the Ralston Purina issue and only a few focusing on the delayed ruling controversy. Meanwhile, as the left-leaning Fairness and Accuracy in Reporting group points out, news organizations ran dozens of articles about Thomas' climb from rags to riches—the Horatio Alger theme that the administration played up to divert attention from the nominee's meager judicial experience. Reporters had, once again, bought the Republican sales pitch.

Pro-Thomas salesmen continued to pitch successfully even after the nominee was confirmed, with Justice Thomas actively participating (which is highly unusual conduct in that Supreme Court members have traditionally been media-shy). Thomas cooperated in the ultimate puff piece, a seven-page, November 11 [,1991] *People* magazine cover article, "How We Survived," told in the first person by his wife, Virginia. In it, she asserts that Hill "was probably in love with my husband" and that her charges "were politically motivated." She makes a point of describing the importance of home prayer sessions to the family. In a photograph illustrating the article, the two pose on a sofa, reading a Bible together. . . . [And] if new derogatory stories about the judge are broken in the months ahead, I would not be too surprised if we hear even more about the Thomas family's devotional habits — stopping short, one can only hope, of another urgent TV prayer bulletin from Pinpoint, Georgia.

"The Clarence Thomas Hearings," by William Boot, *Columbia Journalism Review,* Vol. XXX, No. 5, January/February 1992 ©, pp. 25–29. Used with permission of *Columbia Journalism Review* and Christopher Hanson.

U.S. Press and Foreign Policy

The Gulf War in 1991 focused much attention on the way the U.S. press covers international conflict. William A. Dorman, author of *The U.S. Press and Iran,* maintains that the most productive role for the media to play should come before war starts. The media, Dorman says, can become a better warning system for the public about potential crisis spots.

Consider:

1. Do you agree with Dorman that "the institutions of civil society are simply no match for the forces of nationalism and jingoism unleashed by modern warfare"? Explain.

2. What reasons does Dorman give for the press' reluctance to criticize U.S. foreign policy decisions in the early stages of conflict? Do you agree? Explain.

3. Do you agree with Dorman that media institutions, often controlled by corporate interests, are "more likely than ever to identify with . . . the power structure"? Explain.

The Media's Civil Voice

William A. Dorman
California State University, Sacramento

The [1991] war in the Gulf focused more sustained attention on the role of the press in international conflict than at any time since the Vietnam War. The subject crept into public debate briefly at the time of the U.S. invasions of Grenada and Panama, but not nearly to the degree that characterized the 1991 confrontation with Iraq. Yet for all the dismay expressed in debates, conferences, studies, panel discussions, articles, and academic papers about the U.S. news media's performance during hostilities,

this emphasis on how the press behaves during wartime may be misplaced.

The historical record is clear: The period of concern about press performance should come before a war starts because once a war does begin, good journalism is too late. Mainstream journalism in any society at any time tends to defer to the state's perspective during a shooting war, particularly during the early stages. The U.S. press in the Gulf (or Vietnam, Grenada, or Panama, for that matter) was no exception, underscoring the truth of Christopher Lasch's observation that war always represents a "monstrous intrusion of the public in the private." In other words, the institutions of civil society are simply no match for the forces of nationalism and jingoism unleashed by modern warfare.

The assumption that at least open societies are somehow exempt from this dictum should have been put to rest with World War I — and if not then, by the examples of the French press during Algeria and the British press during the Falklands War. Such deference during open hostilities is as natural a feature of the political world as rain or earthquakes are of the physical, and although lamentable, should be no more surprising.

In the case of the Gulf, then — for all of the more recent concern about military censorship, security reviews, the pool arrangement, careerist-cum-compliant correspondents, and television's war-as-miniseries approach, the journalistic period of real significance began with Iraq's invasion of Kuwait in early August 1990 and lasted until the first air mission was flown against Baghdad. It was during this earlier phase that the lasting boundaries of public thought and discourse about U.S. policy were formed and a range of acceptable policy alternatives was established. Most important, it was during this early period that the foundation was laid in public opinion for the escalation that would follow.

Yet there is ample evidence that during this critical early period, long before tight military controls hamstrung reporters at the front or even before there was a front to cover, the mainstream press failed to raise pointed questions about the Bush administration's interpretations, labels, and policy prescriptions.

The largest shortcoming in this regard was the failure to examine U.S. policy toward Iraq under the Reagan and Bush administrations for the decade before August 2, 1990. Details of the whole sordid story — of how

the Bush administration, right up until the invasion of Kuwait, had vigorously pushed for a broad range of economic, military, and agricultural assistance to Saddam Hussein despite his horrific human rights record and evidence that he was intent on building weapons of mass destruction — would, of course, eventually surface in the U.S. news media. However, the journalistic drum would not begin to beat until fully one year and a half after the war had ended, long after many in the United States, locked in a seemingly endless recession and confronted by a whole new set of international crises, had ceased to care.

It was not as if the press did not know these things in the late summer of 1990. On the eleventh day of the crisis, *The New York Times* published a particularly strong front-page analysis by Michael Wines, the tone of which was clearly set in the lead: "For 10 years, as Iraq developed a vast army, chemical weapons, nuclear ambitions and a long record of brutality, the Reagan and Bush Administrations quietly courted President Saddam Hussein as a counterweight to Iran's revolutionary fervor. Now, critics say, Washington is paying the price for that policy." According to Wines, Iraq had achieved its power "with American acquiescence and sometimes its help," and he went on to detail the forms of assistance provided to Iraq by official Washington. Had the *Times* and other news media, particularly television, pursued this line of inquiry in a systematic fashion, the warp and woof of public discourse might have been markedly different.

Why should the absence of relevant historical context matter so much in the Gulf crisis? For one thing, from the very beginning the Bush administration explained U.S. behavior in moral terms rather than geopolitical ones. To the degree that the president and his advisers succeeded in portraying the crisis as a morality play, they made it exceptionally difficult for opponents of the Bush policy to be taken seriously until it was far too late to stop the momentum toward war. Even more significantly, however, the results of a University of Massachusetts survey of public attitudes and knowledge in February 1991 revealed this central fact: Those who knew the most about the history of the region and about Iraq's relationship with the United States and Kuwait were the least likely to support the use of military force to get Iraq out of Kuwait.

But instead of historical content (a Nexis study of the prewar period yielded only a handful of stories that examined the history of the U.S.–Iraq relation), what most journalists focused on was Bush's efforts at building a coalition, the mechanics of deploying U.S. troops to the region, home-front human interest stories, possible military scenarios, and the likening of Saddam Hussein to Adolf Hitler. Indeed, the greatest success of the Bush administration during the early period was to convince the U.S. population that a Third World country with the gross national product of Kentucky was as dangerous to world peace as Hitler's Germany.

What alternative frames might the press have adopted instead of "Saddam as Hitler" and the invasion of Kuwait as the worst crisis since World War II? Elihu Katz has suggested the "feuding neighbors" frame, which is the way the media encouraged the U.S. public to view Iraq's eight-year war with Iran, which also involved an invasion and far more casualties. And, of course, as suggested here, the press might have adopted a frame of "this is what you get when you encourage someone like Saddam—but let's not compound the problem."

To be certain, there was a period of time before the Gulf War began when something approaching at least a nominal debate over the administration's assumptions and policies did occur in the press and public. This period was touched off by the November 8, 1990, announcement by President Bush that 150,000 additional ground, sea, and air forces would be sent to the Gulf area to provide, in

his words, an "adequate offensive military option." It was at this juncture that many important opinion elites began to speak out publicly, voicing concern about a clear change in U.S. policy. The dissenting voices ranged from former chairs of the Joint Chiefs of Staff and national security advisers to retired foreign services officers and diplomats, not to mention key congressional leaders. The expanded concern was reflected in news coverage and commentary.

What is interesting about this period from the standpoint of a student of the news media and the foreign policy process are the forces that brought it about. According to the tenets of democratic theory and the Libertarian model of the press, the information media are assumed to be the institutional means for stimulating critical thought about the state. By extension, then, the press is expected to open national debate about dubious policy. Moreover, there has been considerable popular opinion following the Vietnam War to the effect that whatever else it may be, the press is critical of the state in the realm of foreign policy, perhaps too critical.

Yet there is a body of evidence that suggests that the press since World War II has not performed the function assumed for it in the free marketplace of ideas theory. To the contrary, the news media throughout the Cold War have rarely initiated critical discourse about foreign policy matters and instead merely reflect the doubts and debate of opinion elites after they have defected from a policy consensus. In other words, when it comes to opening debate, the press waits for permission.

The pattern was repeated in the confrontation with Iraq: Sustained challenges to the administration's chosen course did not begin to appear in news columns until after influential opinion leaders raised them. When people say they remember a vigorous debate about the president's Gulf policy, invariably it is this period of nominal debate that they have in mind. Pressed for examples, they will cite coverage of the Senate Armed Services Committee hearings and the debate in both houses over a resolution approving the use of force should Iraq ignore the UN's January 15 deadline. Energetic as these debates may have been, and however comprehensive the news coverage they generated, discourse opened up very late. The Armed Services Committee hearings did not begin until November 27, 1990, or almost four months after the confrontation with Iraq began. The congressional debate about the force resolution did not begin until January 10, 1991, or only five days before the UN deadline, and the final vote came only three days before.

In sum, public debate came far too late to serve as an effective counterweight to the momentum for war built up during a time when the executive branch was the dominant force in public discourse and — if Bob Woodward's *The Commanders* can be believed — long after the Bush administration had already decided on the course of war.

Perhaps the most important question of this discussion has to do with why the press behaved as it did during the early phase, before harsh military restrictions were placed on the news process. There are a number of reasons, some more significant than others.

There was the possibility, for instance, that journalists got caught up in the same feeling of euphoria that swept official Washington in the days following the invasion of Kuwait, as the capital's sense of self appeared to be restored by the Gulf crisis. As the world's attention after 1989 had shifted to the astonishing transformation of Eastern Europe, it was apparent that the movers and shakers of Washington were feeling ignored if not unwanted. The confrontation with Iraq restored their ever-present need to feel self-important. As a writer for *Newsweek* magazine observed, to understand the nation's capital fully it helps to keep in mind that official Washington is essentially a city of former student-body presidents.

A second possibility, as one veteran correspondent observed on a different occasion, is "Too many reporters pamper their sources, relish their proximity to power, or simply fall unwittingly onto a 'team.'" By "team" he means that reporters either begin to identify with the national security apparatus and the military or they find it too difficult to swim against the current.

Another foreign affairs reporter of long standing argues: "If the correspondent takes up new things he [sic] has discovered, which challenge stereotypes or the conventional wisdom, or contradict what the newspaper's people in Washington are being told by officials, he is likely to be advised that what he is writing is 'counterintuitive' or simply can't really be so." In other words, the field correspondent is likely to be told to "get back on the team."

All of this said, the main thing that undermines contemporary journalism of foreign affairs is the national security state and a journalism of deference. Journalism of deference is the willingness of the press in most situations most of the time to defer to Washington's perspective on the world scene and policy agenda. News workers have tended to internalize or psychologize the assumptions of the national security state. As a result, the news media throughout the Cold War have more often than not tended to validate rather than challenge a whole string of arguably disastrous policy assumptions by official Washington. The Gulf War is only the most recent example.

The media's deference on national security matters can be traced to the sense in the United States of continuing crises since World War II, which has created a particularly powerful worldview. Journalists in the mainstream media are as likely as anyone else to hold widely shared assumptions about the world, consisting, among other things, of the notion that the Soviets were an implacable enemy with whom the United States was engaged in a life-and-death struggle. Moreover, it is hardly reasonable to assume that journalists alone were immune to the reality that nuclear weapons represented an unprecedented threat to the homeland and to the species. Finally, there is no evidence to suggest that the journalistic system has rejected the idea that Western liberal democracy was morally superior to all other forms of political life and, accordingly, that Third World peoples are merely pawns in a great power struggle. These elements of belief are so deeply rooted that one might even term them personality factors.

The concept of deference as it applies to the individual editor or correspondent is hardly the same thing as abject submission. Nor does it suggest that journalists deliberately bow to doctrine or that they consciously color their reporting according to individual ideological bias. Rather, what is at work is a nonpartisan, collective bias that what is good for the United States is good for the world—in a word, ideology. Understand that widely shared bias or ideology appears to be no bias at all, and no journalistic system has been devised yet to eliminate it. As a journalist who covered the Middle East for *The New York Times* during the 1950s once remarked to me about the subtle effects of Cold War ideology on his work, "Is a fish aware of water?"

But perhaps even more significant than the orientation of the individual is the reality that the institutions of the mass media, like so many other segments of society ranging from the academy and science to commerce and industry, have been transformed by the Cold War and its implicit requirement that civil society subordinate its usual interests in the name of national security. For a variety of complex reasons, the professional practices associated with defense journalism favor the official policy agenda, official sources, and therefore the official perspective. Coupled with this is the reality that the media have, since World War II, moved from the periphery of the economy to its very core and therefore are now more likely than ever to identify with other elements of the power structure.

In sum, the problems of journalism in the post–Cold War period are deeply structural, rooted as they are in some 45 years of nuclear anxiety, competition for global power with the Soviet Union, flawed professional practice, and the economic transformation of the media themselves. The result is that most journalists most of the time do not need to be told how to portray something, what procedures to follow, what sources to quote, and so on. The system's givens are internalized; performance is therefore reflexive, not usually considered or deliberate.

For those who had hoped that an end to the superpower confrontation would also mean an end to the journalism of deference, the Gulf provided little for which to cheer. The press did not perform much differently during the first major post–Cold War crisis than it has for the past forty years. The U.S. press has yet to regain its civil voice, which Robert Karl Manoff has described as one with "proud recourse to moral authority, dependence on unmediated expression, respect for individual opinion and independent judgment."

A modest first step to restoring journalistic autonomy might be for the press to work toward anticipating major policy debates and crises in the world rather than waiting for the White House to set the agenda. Saddam Hussein did not undergo a sudden personality change on August 2, 1990. The press should have been investigating U.S. support for this man long before he decided to invade Kuwait. Without such warning, preventive policy will always give way to coercive policy and the devastation of war.

If the press is ever to move in this direction, the journalistic system must also begin to develop sources outside the golden circle of Washington policymakers, bureaucrats, and the defense intellectuals. Journalists must widen their definition of quotable authorities to include those who dispute Washington's goals and not just its tactics.

These are only first small steps toward re-capturing the civil voice that U.S. journalism might take in order to fulfill the promise dem-ocratic theory holds for it. Unfortunately, the mainstream press seems disinclined to admit that there is even a problem, let alone a need to correct it. In the final analysis, it may be that the U.S. press has been too long under the sway of the national security state to abandon the habits of mind that kept it from developing the Gulf story when it might have made a difference in public discourse.

"The Media's Civil Voice," by William A. Dor-man, *Peace Review,* 1993, pp. 11–17. Used with permission of Lynne Rienner Publishers.

CHAPTER 13

Media Effects

Whose Fault Is It?

Media scholars today generally agree that the media have different effects on different types of people with differing results (called *selective perception*). That is, the media affect what we do, but it's difficult to predict who, when, and how we will be affected.

In Perspective 13-1, Robert MacNeil (former co-anchor of public television's MacNeil/Lehrer NewsHour) challenges the usefulness of television. He says that two of the dangers of television are that it distracts us from other activities and that it trivializes events. In Perspective 13-2, ABC commentator Jeff Greenfield says that we overestimate the effects the media have on our lives.

Consider:

1. What does MacNeil mean when (quoting a Quebec newspaper) he says that television's approach is *"mitraillant de bribes*—machine-gunning with scraps"?

2. Do you agree with MacNeil that "this society is being force-fed with trivial fare with only dimly perceived effects on our habits of minds, our language, our tolerance for effort, and our appetite for complexity"? Why? Why not?

3. Which effects does Greenfield concede to television? Which effects does Greenfield say are debatable? Do you agree? Why? Why not?

4. Do you agree with Greenfield that "television . . . has shown precious little power over the most fundamental values of Americans"? Why? Why not?

5. Which of these arguments is most persuasive? Why?

Is Television Shortening Our Attention Span?

Robert MacNeil

I don't know much about the business of education, but I do know something about my own business, television, and I have a prejudice that I believe is relevant to the concerns of educators.

It is difficult to escape the influence of television. If you fit the statistical averages, by the age of twenty you have been exposed to something like twenty thousand hours of television. You can add ten thousand hours for each decade you have lived after the age of twenty. The only activities Americans spend more time doing than watching television are working and sleeping.

Calculate for a moment what could have been done with even a part of those hours. Five thousand hours, I am told, are what a typical college undergraduate spends working on a bachelor's degree.

In ten thousand hours you could have learned enough to become one of the world's leading astronomers. You could have learned several languages thoroughly, not just to the level required to pass a college course, but fluently. If it appealed to you, you could have read Homer in the original Greek or Dostoyevsky in Russian. If that didn't appeal to you, you could have invested that amount of time and now be at the forefront of anything — nuclear physics, aerospace engineering — or you could have decided to walk right around the world and write a book about it.

The trouble with being born in the television age is that it discourages concentration. It encourages serial, kaleidoscopic exposure; its variety becomes a narcotic, not a stimulus; you consume not what *you* choose and when, but when *they* choose and *what*.

In our grandparents' eyes, such a prodigious waste of our God-given time would have been sinful because that time was not used constructively — for self-improvement, for building moral character, for shaping our own destinies. Our grandparents would have regarded it as sloth, as escapism, as perpetually sucking on visual candies. Yet, our grandparents would probably have found television just as difficult to resist as we do.

Almost anything interesting and rewarding in life requires some constructive, consistently applied effort. The dullest, the least gifted of us, can achieve things that seem miraculous to those who never concentrate on anything. But television encourages us to *apply* no effort. It sells us instant gratification. It diverts us *only* to divert us, to make the time

pass without pain. It is the *soma* of Aldous Huxley's *Brave new World*.

Television forces us to follow its lead. It forces us to live as though we were on a perpetual guided tour: thirty minutes at the museum, thirty at the cathedral, thirty for a drink, then back on the bus to the next attraction; only on television, typically, the spans allotted are on the order of minutes or seconds, and the chosen delights are more often car crashes and people killing each other. In short, a lot of television usurps one of the most precious of all human gifts, the ability to focus your attention yourself, something that only human beings can do.

Television has adopted a particular device to do this, to capture your attention and hold it, because holding attention is the prime motive of most television programming. The economics of commercial television require programmers to assemble the largest possible audience for every moment (because that enhances its role as a profitable advertising vehicle). Those programmers live in constant fear of losing anyone's attention — the dull or the bright, the lazy or the energetic. The safest technique to guarantee that mass attention is to keep everything brief, not to strain the attention of anyone but instead to provide constant stimulation through variety, novelty, action, and movement. You are required, in much popular television fare, to pay attention to *no* concept, no situation, no scene, no character, and no problem for more than a few seconds at a time. In brief, television operates on the short attention span.

It is the easiest way out. But it has come to be regarded as a given, as inherent in the medium itself, as an imperative — as though General Sarnoff, or one of the other august pioneers of video, had bequeathed to us, from wherever he now rests, tablets of stone, commanding that nothing in television shall ever require more than a few moments' concentration.

I see that ethos now pervading this nation and its culture. I think the short attention span has become a model in all areas of communication, where the communicators want to be modish, up to date. I think it has become fashionable to think that, like fast food, fast ideas are the way to get to a fast, impatient public reared on television. And I think education is not exempt.

In the case of news, this practice was described a few years ago by a Quebec newspaper as *"Mitraillant de bribes,"* machine-gunning with scraps. The description is very apt.

I believe, although my view is not widely shared, that this format is inefficient communication in terms of its ability to encourage absorption, retention, and understanding of complexity. I believe it is inefficient because it punishes the attentive and the interested by impaling them on the supposed standard of the *in*attentive and the *un*interested.

I question how much of television's nightly news effort is really absorbable and understandable. I think the technique fights coherence. I think it tends to make things ultimately boring and dismissable (unless they are accompanied by horrifying pictures), because almost anything is boring and dismissable if you know almost nothing about it.

If I may pause for a commercial, the "MacNeil/Lehrer Report" was founded on the conviction that the attention span of thirty seconds or a minute, which formed the basis of most television journalism, was an artificial formula imposed on the nation by the industry. To claim that it was the only way large numbers of people could be held by news about the real world was false and also insulting to large numbers of intelligent Americans.

We are now [twelve] years along in an experiment to prove the contrary. And we are having some impact. [In] September [1986] we expanded the program from thirty minutes to an hour, the "MacNeil/Lehrer News-Hour."

I believe that catering to the short attention span is not only inefficient communication, but it is also decivilizing. Part of the process of civilizing a young person, surely, lies in trying to lengthen his attention span, one of the basic tools of human intelligence.

A child may or may not have original sin, but he is born with original inattention. He is *naturally* inattentive, like a puppy, except to his basic biological needs.

Rearing a child consists in part in gradually trying to get his attention for longer periods, to cause him finally to direct it himself and to keep it directed until he finishes something. The older or more mature a child is, the longer he can be made to pay attention.

But what so much of television does is precisely the opposite. It panders to a child's natural tendency to be scatterbrained and inattentive, to watch this for two minutes and play with that for two minutes. It is giving up the struggle. It starts from the assumption that he will be bored. It is like conceding that a child likes sugar, therefore you should give him only cereals with lots of sugar in them, or he may not eat and will hate you and grow up to write mean novels — assuming he *can* write — about what wretched parents you were.

I do not think education is immune to the virus. And the responsibility of education is enormous. Educators should consider the casual assumptions television tends to cultivate that bite-sized is best, that complexity must be avoided, that nuances are dispensable, that qualifications impede the simple message, that visual stimulation is a substitute for thought, and that verbal precision is an anachronism.

There is a crisis of literacy in this country and a tendency to excuse it by throwing up our hands and saying, "Well you can't fight the impact of the visual culture. Perhaps we can only join it." But we do not have to resign ourselves to the brilliant aphorism of Marshall McLuhan that the medium is the message. It *is,* but it is not a sufficient message. It may be old-fashioned, but I was taught to believe the Kantian idea that thought is words arranged in grammatically precise ways.

The message of the television medium fights that notion in several ways. One is obvious and perhaps trivial: it ingrains popular verbal habits, like the grammatical shortcuts of Madison Avenue. More seriously, it steals time from and becomes a substitute for deriving pleasure, experience, or knowledge through words. More subtly, even for sophisticated people, it encourages a surrender to the visual depiction of experience, necessarily abbreviated by time constraints, necessarily simplified, and often trivialized.

If American society is to maintain some pretence of being a mass literate culture, then far from reversing the appalling statistics of functional illiteracy, I think the struggle is to prevent them from growing worse. As you know, it is estimated that twenty-five million Americans cannot read or write at all. An additional thirty-five million are functionally illiterate and cannot read or write well enough to answer a want ad or understand the instructions on a medicine bottle. That adds up to sixty million people — nearly one-third of the population. And, since close to one million young Americans drop out of school each year, it is probable that the country is producing at least that many *new* illiterates, or semi-literates, every year.

They land in a society where rudimentary survival increasingly depends on some ability to function in a world of forms and schedules and credit agreements and instructions. They enter a society that already faces the growing problem of finding something productive for most of its citizens to do. It is already a society with a cruelly large number of people who are in some sense redundant, whose share of the American dream is pitifully small.

Literacy may not be a human right, but the highly literate Founding Fathers might not have found it unreasonable or unattainable. We are not only *not* attaining literacy as a nation, statistically speaking, but also falling farther and farther short of attaining it. And, while I would not be so simplistic as to

suggest that television is the cause, I believe it contributes and is an influence: for the dull it is a substitute; for the bright it is a diversion.

The educators of this country, especially in the public schools, have had enough burdens thrust on them by society. But I frankly see no other force than educators in the society that can act as a counterweight to the intellectual mush of television. Of course, the home environment is primary, and millions of parents try very conscientiously. But television is now an essential part of every home. The Fifth Column is there, often in many rooms. It is virtually a utility. The school is the only part of a young person's regular environment where television isn't — or where television wasn't, until recently.

To the extent that schools and universities feel the only way they can reach young people's minds is by importing the values of television, I feel they risk exacerbating the problem. I don't mean there should not be television sets in schools or that television may not be, in a limited sense, a useful tool. Obviously, not all television programs are worthless, and teachers may be able to encourage more critical, more selective viewing — I believe it is called "television literacy" — and may be able to use television to whet the appetite for other disciplines. And there are fine programs designed specifically for instruction. That's not what I'm talking about.

I am talking about the tendency I notice to surrender to the ethos that television subtly purveys: the idea that things are gotten easily, with little effort; that information can be absorbed passively: that by watching pictures children are absorbing as much information as they might through print. That is what I mean by pandering to the easy virtues of television, of letting young people believe that ideas are conveyed by tasty bits; that intellectual effort need not be applied; that you can get it (as they say) quickly and painlessly.

A few years ago I said to my small son, then age nine, "Would you like me to read

Treasure Island?" He said, "Naw, I know it. I saw it on television." I felt very defeated, since that book happens to be one I love. Later, on a boat, I got him in a captive environment with others who wanted to hear it. I read it and he liked it. But I think of his first response as the equivalent in my generation of saying, "Naw, I read it in Classic Comics." Are we content to let a generation grow up without knowing *Treasure Island* in its complete form? If not, there is only one way and that is by gentle forcing. That is what education used to be all about, and some of the forcing was not too gentle.

Why is that important? On one level, to get the sound of English prose, its rhythms and its rich vocabulary stirring pleasurably in their brains. Because it will echo there all their lives. The other is to stimulate their imagination. I know Walt Disney was a genius. But I personally deplore the way he has made so many classics so visually lit-eral, substituting his (often cloyingly sweet) imagination for that of the child. And television is Walt Disney and his lesser imitators wholesale.

In politics, in sports, in entertainment, in news, if television doesn't like something the way it is, it is assumed that the wide public won't, so American institutions rush to change themselves so that television will like them. Television viability becomes *the* viability. My own code phrase for that pervasive influence on the culture is the short attention span.

Everything about this nation becomes more complicated, not less. The structure of the society, its forms of family organization, its economy, its place in the world have become more complex. Yet its dominating communications instrument, its principal form of national linkage, is an instrument that sells simplicity and tidiness — neat resolutions of human problems that usually have *no* neat resolutions. It is all symbolized in my mind by the hugely successful art form that television has made central to the culture, the thirty-second commercial: the tiny drama of the earnest housewife who finds happiness in choosing the right toothpaste. That . . . has also become the dominant form of political communication, transforming the choice of elected leaders into a slick exchange of packaged insults and half-truths, with the battle weighed heavily in favor of the candidate with the most money and the cleverest ad agency.

Whenever in human history has so much humanity collectively surrendered so much of its leisure to one toy, one mass diversion? Whenever before have all classes and kinds of men, virtually an entire nation, surrendered themselves wholesale, making their minds, their psyches, their bodies prisoners of a medium for selling?

Some years ago Judge Charles Black wrote: ". . . forced feeding on trivial fare is not itself a trivial matter. . . ." Well, I think this society is being force-fed with trivial fare with only dimly perceived effects on our habits of minds, our language, our tolerance for effort, and our appetite for complexity. If I am wrong, it will have done no harm to look at it skeptically and critically, to consider how we should be resisting it. And I hope you will share my skepticism.

"Is Television Shortening Our Attention Span?" by Robert MacNeil, *National Forum,* Vol. LXVIII, No. 4, Fall 1987, pp. 21–23. Used with permission of *National Forum.*

Don't Blame TV

Jeff Greenfield

One of the enduring pieces of folk wisdom was uttered by the 19th-century humorist Artemus Ward, who warned the readers: "It ain't what you don't know that hurts you; it's what you know that just ain't so."

There's good advice in that warning to some of television's most vociferous critics, who are certain that every significant change in American social and political life can be traced, more or less directly, to the pervasive influence of TV.

It has been blamed for the decline of scores on scholastic achievement tests, for the rise in crime, for the decline in voter turnout, for the growth of premarital and extramarital sex, for the supposed collapse of family life and the increase in the divorce rate.

This is an understandable attitude. For one thing, television is the most visible, ubiquitous device to have entered our lives in the last 40 years. It is a medium in almost every American home, it is on in the average household some seven hours a day, and it is accessible by every kind of citizen from the most desperate of the poor to the wealthiest and most powerful among us.

If so pervasive a medium has come into our society in the last four decades and if our society has changed in drastic ways in that same time, why not assume that TV is the reason why American life looks so different?

Well, as any philosopher can tell you, one good reason for skepticism is that you can't make assumptions about causes. They even have an impressive Latin phrase for that fallacy: *post hoc, ergo propter hoc.* For instance, if I do a rain dance at 5 P.M. and it rains at 6 P.M., did my dance bring down the rains? Probably not. But it's that kind of thinking, in my view, that characterizes much of the argument about how television influences our values.

It's perfectly clear, of course, that TV *does* influence some kinds of behavior. For example, back in 1954, *Disneyland* launched a series of episodes on the life of Davy Crockett, the legendary Tennessee frontiersman. A song based on that series swept the hit parade, and by that summer every kid in America was wearing a coonskin cap.

The same phenomenon has happened whenever a character on a prime-time television show suddenly strikes a chord in the country. Countless women tried to capture the Farrah Fawcett look [in the 1970s] when *Charlie's Angels* first took flight. Schoolyards from Maine to California picked up — instantly, it seemed — on such catch phrases as "Up your nose with a rubber hose!" (*Welcome Back, Kotter*), "Kiss my Grits!" (*Alice*) and "Nanu-nanu!" (*Mork & Mindy*). Today [1986], every singles bar in the land is packed with young men in expensive white sports jackets and T-shirts, trying to emulate the macho looks of *Miami Vice's* Don Johnson.

These fads clearly show television's ability to influence matters that do not matter very much. Yet, when we turn to genuinely important things, television's impact becomes a lot less clear.

Take, for example, the decline in academic excellence, measured by the steady decline in Scholastic Aptitude Test scores from 1964 to 1982. It seemed perfectly logical to assume that a younger generation spending hours in front of the TV set every day with Fred Flintstone and Batman must have been suffering from brain atrophy. Yet, as writer David Owen noted in a . . . book on educational testing, other equally impassioned explanations for the drop in scores included nuclear fallout, junk food, cigarette smoking by pregnant women, cold weather, declining church attendance, the draft, the assassination of President Kennedy and fluoridated water.

More significant, SAT scores stopped declining in 1982: they have been rising since then. Is TV use declining in the typical American home? On the contrary, it is increasing. If we really believed that our societal values are determined by news media, we might conclude that the birth of MTV in 1981 somehow caused the test scores to rise.

Or consider the frequently heard charge that the increase in TV violence is somehow responsible for the surge in crime. In fact, the crime rate nationally has been dropping for three straight years [1983–1986]. It would be ludicrous to "credit" television for this: explanations are more likely to be found in the shift of population away from a "youth bulge" (where more crimes are committed) and improved tracking of career criminals in big cities.

But why, then, ignore the demographic factors that saw in America an enormous jump in teenagers and young adults in the 1960s and 1970s? Why *assume* that television, with its inevitable "crime-does-not-pay" morality, somehow turned our young into hoodlums?

The same kind of problem bedevils those who argue that TV has triggered a wave of sexually permissible behavior. In the first place, television was the most sexually conservative of all media through the first quarter-century of its existence. While *Playboy* began making a clean breast of things in the mid-1950s, when book censorship was all but abolished in the *Lady Chatterly's Lover* decision of 1958, when movies began showing it all in the 1960s, television remained an oasis—or desert—of twin beds, flannel nightgowns and squeaky-clean dialogue and characters.

In fact, as late as 1970, CBS refused to let Mary Tyler Moore's Mary Richards character be a divorcée. The audience, they argued, would never accept it. Instead, she was presented as the survivor of a broken relationship.

Why, then, do we see so many broken families and divorces on television today? Because the networks are trying to denigrate the value of the nuclear family? Hardly. As *The Cosby Show* and its imitators show, network TV is only too happy to offer a benign view of loving husbands, wives, and children.

The explanation, instead, lies in what was happening to the very fabric of American life. In 1950, at the dawn of television, the divorce rate was 2.6 per 1000 Americans. By 1983, it had jumped to five per thousand; nearly half of all marriages were ending in divorce. The reasons range from the increasing mobility of the population to the undermining of settled patterns of work, family and neighborhood.

What's important to notice, however, is that it was not television that made divorce more acceptable in American society: it was changes in American society that made divorce more acceptable on television. (Which is why, in her new sitcom, Mary Tyler Moore can finally play a divorced woman.) In the mid 1980s, divorce has simply lost the power to shock.

The same argument, I think, undermines most of the fear that television has caused our young to become sexually precocious. From my increasingly dimming memory of youthful lust, I have my doubts about whether young lovers really need the impetus of *Dallas* or *The Young and the Restless* to start thinking about sex. The more serious answer, however, is that the spread of readily available birth control was a lot more persuasive a force in encouraging premarital sex than the words and images on TV.

We can measure this relative impotence of television in a different way. All through the 1950s and early 1960s, the images of women on TV were what feminists would call "negative"; they were portrayed as half-woman, half-child, incapable of holding a job or balancing a checkbook or even running a social evening. (How many times did Lucy burn the roast?) Yet the generation of women who grew up on television was the first to reject forcefully the wife-and-homemaker limitations that such images ought to have encouraged. These were the women who marched into law schools, medical schools and the halls of Congress.

The same was true of the images of black Americans, as TV borrowed the movie stereotypes of shiftless handymen and relentlessly cheerful maids. We didn't begin to see TV blacks as the equal of whites until Bill Cosby showed up in *I Spy* in 1966. Did the generation weaned on such fare turn out to be indifferent to the cause of black freedom in America? Hardly. This was the generation that organized and supported the civil-rights sit-ins and freedom rides in the South. Somehow, the reality of second-class citizenship was far more powerful than the imagery of dozens of television shows.

I have no argument with the idea that television contains many messages that need close attention: I hold no brief for shows that pander to the appetite for violence or smarmy sexuality or stereotyping. My point is that these evils ought to be fought on grounds of taste and common decency. We ought not to try and prove more than the facts will bear. Television, powerful as it is, has shown precious little power over the most fundamental values of Americans. Given most of what's on TV, that's probably a good thing. But it also suggests that the cries of alarm may be misplaced.

Creating Fear

According to many media critics, crime news receives too much media coverage, especially on television. The result, claim the critics, is that media attention focuses on crime at the expense of other issues, such as health care or education. This article, from the *St. Louis Post-Dispatch*, examines how newspeople view the issue of crime news in St. Louis. This discussion reflects the important issues in the national debate about the role of the news media in the coverage of crime.

Consider:

1. Do you agree with former news director Ian McBryde who says that "Crime news gets a disproportionate amount of a newsroom's time, sources and attention, to the exclusion of news that truly affects everyone"? Explain.

2. According to news director Steve Hammel, what are the primary differences between crime coverage on TV and crime coverage in newspapers? Do you agree? Explain.

3. Should television news directors tone down the sensationalism in TV news crime coverage? If so, how can they accomplish this? If not, why not? Explain.

Prime Time Crime: TV Coverage Heavy

Harry Levins

At 10 P.M., computer-generated graphics roll across your television screen to pulsing music. They give way to the anchor's face and the inevitable opening words: "Good evening."

But usually, it isn't a good evening. It's another evening of crime.

If you were watching KMOV (Channel 4) on July 14, [1994,], the first story on your screen detailed the arrest of a child-molesting suspect in Tower Grove Park.

If you pushed your remote channel-changer to KSDK (Channel 5), you saw a reporter broadcasting live from outside the hospital treating a pipe-bomb victim.

Click to KTVI (Channel 2): You're back in Tower Grove Park with the child-molester case. . .

Click to Channel 5: A serial rapist terrorizes the Shaw neighborhood area. . .

Click to Channel 4: Police in St. Charles are looking into an infant's death at a motel. . .

Click to Channel 2: The Shaw rapist again, which gives way to the discovery of a car used in the serial murders of homosexuals. . .

And so it goes on the 10 o'clock news, at least on many evenings. In the week of July 10–16, [1994,] crime or violence accounted for 24 percent of the 14-plus minutes each station devotes to general news on the 10 P.M. news.

Channel 2 anchor Don Marsh says part of television's emphasis on crime stems from the simple fact that violent crime is up in St. Louis.

But he adds, "It probably seems as if there's more crime than there really is because of the heavy amount of coverage."

Marsh once reported to Ian MacBryde, formerly news director at Channel 2 and now an independent producer here.

MacBryde says, "Crime gets a disproportionate amount of a newsroom's time, sources and attention, to the exclusion of news that truly affects everyone—health, education, local government and so on. As a result, the public is not well-served."

Channel 2's news director Bill Berra takes tart exception to that idea. He says, "I think 267 people killed in St. Louis [in 1993] is an epidemic, an atrocity."

If crime seems to dominate the news here, we weren't alone. Consider that:

- Network crime coverage has jumped. The Washington-based Center for Media and Public Affairs reports that [in 1993], the network news shows doubled their coverage of crime—and tripled their coverage of murder—from the year before.

- In Miami, several hotels have erased that city's Fox affiliate, WSVN, from their cable systems. The reason: WSVN programs eight hours of news a day, heavily spiced with blood and gore. The hotels say WSVN is scaring their guests.

- [In] winter [1993], the Chicago Council on Urban Affairs paid for a 10-week study of local television news. The major finding: Chicago's three network affiliates give crime 60 percent of their newscasts.

"You Can't Be Sensational"

The news directors of the three stations studied here say the 24 percent figure for crime coverage in St. Louis seems accurate, and typical.

"Here, you have a more conservative market," says Tim Larson, the news director at top-ranked Channel 5.

"You can't be sensational in St. Louis," Larson says. "You have to relate your newscast to your audience. If you're very sensational, racy and crime-laden, your newscast won't be watched as much here."

At Channel 2, Berra notes that many newscasts open with a non-crime story. "It depends what's going on," he says. "If a major crime happens, it'll be right up there. If something bigger happens, maybe not."

Channel 4's news director, Steve Hammel, says: "It's not in anyone's interest to have more than a quarter of the news about crime. Crime isn't the only thing going on in our area. Going heavy on it would be a disservice."

At any rate, Hammel notes a key difference in the way the public perceives crime coverage on television and crime coverage in the newspaper: "With a newspaper, people have the choice of reading the front page or going straight to the sports section. On television, the story of the moment is the only story.

"Even if we run a crime story in the fifth spot on the newscast, at that moment, it's the most important story."

Crime Made for TV

To a large extent, crime and television are perfect suitors because of television's unique qualities. Consider that television:

- Competes with itself as a medium. No television station enjoys a monopoly like the *Post-Dispatch*'s. In the scramble for viewers, stations must offer what they think viewers want. "There's tremendous pressure to be No. 1 in the market," MacBryde says, "which means that you can't be Ed Murrow today" — that serious journalism has a limited audience.

- Needs pictures. Channel 4's Hammel repeats a maxim as old as television itself: "Television is a visual medium." Marsh, the anchor, says producers base a lot of news decisions on visuals. Crime scenes teem with visuals: flashing lights on emergency vehicles . . . wide-eyed witnesses . . . weeping relatives. . .

- Abhors abstractions. In television, few things are worse than "a talking head" — an anchor reading a story, a politician answering questions. Since the arrival of the remote-control channel changer, news directors have fretted that a talking-head story will prompt an orgy of zapping. The medium favors action; crime provides it.

- Craves immediacy. The amount of local news on television has risen sharply in the last 15 years — partly because viewers want more news, partly because news makes money. To keep each newscast fresh, stations need new news — and they can usually find something freshly violent.

- Often lacks context. "At times," says Channel 4's Hammel, "television news doesn't do a good job of putting stories in perspective. That's a fair criticism — but it applies to all stories, not just crime." It's the nature of the beast: TV demands brevity; on television news, 60 seconds is a long time.

- Rations its time. Television is stuck with a 24-hour day. That means stories must be brief, and most murders can be reported briefly: good guys, bad guys, dead guys. And back to you, Steve.

- Shuns specialties. No television station here comes close to matching the 52 local reporters at the *Post-Dispatch*. (Channel 4's Hammel and Channel 2's Berra declined to say how many reporters their news

operations had. Channel 5's Larson has 25, but he says the figure might include weather and sports people.)

As a result, a few television reporters cover specialized "beats." There are exceptions; Channel 5's Mike Owens shows up often at City Hall, for example.

By and large, TV reporters are generalists — and, as Channel 2's Marsh says, "Anybody can cover a crime. You don't have to know a community's history; you don't have to know its movers and shakers."

Hammel says it bluntly: "Crime coverage is easy coverage."

MacBryde elaborates: "You drive the truck out. You set up the camera so the police-line yellow tape is showing. It's not hard work; there's no investigation involved. You ask a few questions, and that's a wrap."

He adds: "I don't think this serves the public well. Crime coverage doesn't have much to do with what the public needs to know."

Who's Following Whom?

Says Channel 4's Hammel, "The purpose of news is to reflect, to mirror, society. If people are afraid — if they're locking their doors and windows — it's not because of television news."

In fact, people here are locking up. Sales of home burglar alarms in this area [St. Louis] are booming, even though burglaries have fallen sharply since 1980.

But if the public is overreacting, Channel 5's Larson refuses to take the blame. "Here in St. Louis, it's an unfair rap," he says. "In some other markets and on some other shows — the syndicated tabloid programs, for example — things may be different."

Channel 2's Berra says: "We have had some spectacular crimes in St. Louis — the missing girls, the I-70 serial killer. They'd be big stories in any market."

True. And when an even more sensational story comes along — the Great Flood of '93, for example — it all but washes crime from the news. Lately, television has had no monster flood, no Gulf War, no national recession. Crime fills the vacuum.

Nor does Berra think newspapers come into the issue with clean hands. "You follow us now," he says. He calls television "an easy target," made even easier by brash tabloid shows like "Hard Copy" and "A Current Affair."

Says Larson: "The lines have blurred. We get blamed for many of the sins of the tabloid shows."

In the end, says anchor Marsh, it all comes back to what viewers want. "Nothing will change television faster than people not watching," he says.

Tips for TV: No Mug Shots, Flashing Lights

What can television news do to turn down the temperature on crime coverage?

A recent study in Chicago by journalism Professor Robert M. Entman offers a few possibilities. His suggestions:

- Show suspects less frequently. Entman writes, "These are normally 'talking heads' (or, more usually, silent heads) and have little visual interest. But they identify the ethnicity of the accused and thereby could heighten racial antagonism."

- Minimize shots of "violence images," like flashing emergency lights. Entman says the images have become clichés. "They add almost no information," he writes. "But they do heighten the sense of a world unhinged."

- Downplay events of little general import, like fires and accidents. "Rather than continuing to follow the maxim, 'If it bleeds, it leads,'" Entman writes, "stations might consider offering more directly useful news reports."

- Guide audiences toward "a new recognition of the possible utility of news." Entman cites experiments in Minneapolis and elsewhere with "family-sensitive" news. He suggests viewers have a latent appetite for more information and less violent news. With careful planning, he says, television news can nudge its audience in that direction.

For this study, Entman pored over 10 weeks of tapes of local news in Chicago, beginning last Dec. 6 [1993].

His conclusion: On their local newscasts, Chicago's three network-affiliated stations devoted about three minutes of every five to crime and violence.

Sponsoring his study was the Chicago Council on Urban Affairs. It's all part of that group's larger effort against violence in the Chicago area.

At the time, Entman taught at Northwestern University. He has since moved to North Carolina State University.

[In] spring [1994], the British Broadcasting Corporation drew up its own guidelines for crime coverage. The network's Polly Toynbee summarized them this way in a British newspaper, *The Guardian:*

- Report only crimes "that raise issues of significance or new points in law."

- Avoid gruesome details; steer clear of "shots of blood on the pavement, or wounds."

- Refrain from crime re-enactments, unless they're organized by the police.

Says Toynbee, the BBC's social affairs editor: "We do not have crime reporters, only home and social affairs correspondents, who are expected to keep crime in context."

Post-Dispatch Joins the Ride on Crime News Wave

With all the to-do about crime coverage on television, what about newspapers? What is the *Post-Dispatch* like when it comes to covering crime?

The answer: More circumspect than the television stations, but perhaps less circumspect than it used to be.

In the sample week of July 11–17, [1994,] the *Post Dispatch* gave 15 percent of its "news hole"—its space for general news—to news of crime and other violence, like fires, car wrecks and so on.

That same week, the three network affiliates in St. Louis devoted 24 percent of their "news hole" on the 10 P.M. local newscast to similar news.

But one of the reporters who must sell crime news to the editors at the *Post-Dispatch* says the job seems to be getting easier.

That reporter is Bill Bryan. Like the tumbledown office furniture in the press room at city police headquarters, Bryan has been a fixture there for two decades—first with the old *Globe-Democrat* and, for the last 10 years, with the *Post-Dispatch.*

"Until the last few years," Bryan says, "the *Post-Dispatch* frowned on crime news— sort of stuck up their noses at it. Now, the *Post* is more interested in crime—if it can be featurized."

By "featurized," he means analyzed, put in context and told, whenever possible, in English that skips clichés and jargon and gets to the point.

The editors splashed one such story across the top of the front page on the last Sunday in June [,1994].

Over a four column color photo of grieving relatives praying over a murder victim being wheeled from an apartment, a bold headline read: "Killings Put Strain On City Police."

In the story, Bryan and colleague Kim Bell tried to put the rash of homicides into some kind of statistical focus—and to describe its human impact.

The story ate up 45-1/2 column inches, with 15 more column inches devoted to a map and 9-1/2 inches to a "sidebar," or related story.

Bryan's editor, assistant city editor Peter Hernon, says he thinks newspapers can give crime news a depth impossible on television.

"We can go deeper and further," he says. "We can try to get to the root causes because we have the luxury of more space and a little more time. We can put crime in perspective, and that has a big impact."

On television, he says, "they'll lead the 10 o'clock news with an ambulance every night. It's exciting. It's bells and whistles."

Not that the newspaper always does better, he hastens to add.

"We haven't tried hard enough to put crime in perspective," Hernon says. "Polls say the country is less violent than people think—but a small part of St. Louis is very violent.

"We need to say why, and we need to tell people in Creve Coeur or Ladue why they should care."

Hernon thinks his topic gets the space it deserves. "I think we have the right balance," he says.

News editors, working at night, function as the paper's gatekeepers. They decide which stories get in, and on which page, and at which length.

At the *Post-Dispatch*, the news editors answer to Carolyn Kingcade, the assistant managing editor for news. She concedes that readers might think the *Post* has played up crime news in recent years.

"Those homicide tally boxes we ran in '91 probably made it look as if we were more interested in crime news," Kingcade says.

"In recent years, we've tried to analyze the causes of crime. We've run profiles of victims. We've run profiles of suspects. So that increases the amount of space we give to crime."

Still, she says, "because homicides are so common now, a lot that once would have been played big don't even make Page 1A. Sometimes, a double homicide is held to six inches and played inside the paper."

In fact, Kingcade notes, "a lot of killings wind up as a single paragraph of agate [smaller] type in the Police-Court summary box."

"In my talks with groups," Kingcade says, "most people say they hate crime news — street killings and all the other horrible stuff. But when they calm down, they say they want to know about crime.

"They don't want it overblown — but they want to know it happened."

"Prime Time Crime: TV Coverage Heavy," by Harry Levins, *St. Louis Post-Dispatch*, August 14, 1994. Dow//Quest Story ID: 0000355407DC. Reprinted with permission of the *St. Louis Post-Dispatch*, © 1994.

Does Media Attention Distort the Issues?

Some critics charge that by overemphasizing an issue, such as AIDS, the press is manufacturing news. The result of intensely targeting one topic for press coverage is called agenda-setting—the ability of the press to influence the choice of issues under discussion at any one time. Focusing so much attention on one topic gives that topic disproportionate public attention, the critics say, at the expense of other important issues. In this article, written in 1987, journalist Ron Dorfman argues that AIDS deserves the attention it is getting.

Consider:

1. Has the issue of AIDS been the subject of a "media-fed national panic," as *New Republic* editor Charles Krauthammer charges? Why? Why not?

2. Do you agree with Dorfman that the AIDS story is "not about a disease, but about our society"? Why? Why not?

3. Marlene Cimons of the *Los Angeles Times* says "the media as a whole downplayed the AIDS story until they realized it wasn't 'just a gay man's disease.'" Do you agree with Cimons? Why? Why not?

4. Dorfman says that in one week he clipped 27 articles about AIDS. Are there other medical stories you feel deserve as much attention today? Why? Why not?

AIDS Coverage: A Mirror of Society

Ron Dorfman

In an October 5 [1987] *New Republic* piece captioned "Time to cool it," Senior Editor Charles Krauthammer argues that the American people have entirely too much information about AIDS.

Writing after community hostility and a suspicious fire drove the Ray family from Arcadia, Florida, he says: "Obsessive coverage does not create cures. It creates panic."

Krauthammer is an M.D. and is indignant that many people refuse to accept scientific assurances on how difficult it is to transmit HIV, the virus associated with AIDS.

Since a child in Arcadia "is as likely to die by earthquake as he is by sitting in [his] homeroom with young Ray, and far more likely to die in an auto accident," and since the people there "have been told a thousand times who gets AIDS and how they get it," their "selective irrationality in the face of improbability is not the product of ignorance but of a media-fed national panic."

To the extent that this is a complaint against news reports and commentary exaggerating the likelihood that AIDS will infect people in the "general" population — which is to say, people who are not homosexuals, not hemophiliacs, and not heroin addicts — it is true enough. But it is a truth unfortunately detached from journalistic and political reality.

"It is not more AIDS information that drug abusers need but treatment for their addiction," Krauthammer writes. "It is not more condom ads scientists need, but money to pursue their studies."

But research money and addiction-treatment programs are political products, not scientific discoveries.

Dr. James Curran, director of AIDS programs at the national Centers for Disease Control, observed at a recent Washington meeting on media coverage of AIDS that with this story "scientists and journalists become part of the political process." And the politics of AIDS has more to do with demography than with virology and epidemiology.

As long as the disease was perceived as a threat only to gays and drug addicts, the government was content to let it run its course, proposing no appropriations until 1984 and in fact reducing spending on drug-treatment programs.

Under the circumstances, both the research community and advocacy groups had an interest in emphasizing the small but real threat of heterosexual transmission and the ease of prevention by use of condoms, soap, and water. Journalists no doubt reflected that emphasis, and it's a bit unfair to suggest that they should have independently calibrated the scale of risk.

It's not unfair, however, to observe the very real journalistic bias toward aspects of the story that affect the heterosexual majority.

Steve Findlay, responding to a survey in *ScienceWriters,* the newsletter of the National Association of Science Writers, said of his editors at *USA Today:* "They are big on covering AIDS, but clearly in the last year [1986–1987] the editors are much more interested in heterosexuals and they don't want to hear about gays and drug users. It's a desire to shift the story in ways that may not be warranted."

Marlene Cimons of the *Los Angeles Times,* writing in *Mother Jones* magazine, makes this comparison: "Much as *The New York Times* largely ignores the hundreds of black people murdered every year in the South Bronx and Harlem, but runs prominently on page one the story of a white drama student stabbed to death on a Manhattan rooftop, the media as a whole downplayed the AIDS story until they realized it wasn't 'just a gay man's disease.'"

Both science and journalism strive to report facts, but facts are not policy, and the problem for both, as Curran noted at the CDC-sponsored meeting in Washington, is "how to tell important or inevitable stories without causing panic."

He cited as examples the reports of three health workers who became infected in freak accidents and a case of transmission of the virus through transfusion of blood that had passed screening.

"Even though we knew they would cause problems," Curran said, "we had to report these cases," and so did journalists. Not to have reported them would have led to their ultimate discovery — by political opponents of what Krauthammer thinks is "rationality" — and to the discrediting of the entire public-health education project that both science and journalism have signed on to.

By the same token, media reports of public response to the available knowledge at any given stage of the epidemic have undoubtedly fueled further hysteria. But it is pigheaded to imagine that some journalistic compact or conspiracy could have kept those events under wraps, or prevented them from occurring in the first place.

In Atlanta [in] February [1987], Laurie Garrett, science correspondent for National Public Radio, noted in a speech to a scientific conference on pediatric and heterosexual AIDS that the critical year was 1983, after the first reports of AIDS in children and in blood-transfusion recipients:

"In San Francisco, for example, gay-owned businesses were boycotted, the police donned masks and gloves before entering gay neighborhoods, firefighters refused to give artificial resuscitation to homosexuals, and people boycotted restaurants. I don't think these and other public responses . . . were created by the media or that the media went out of [their] way to exacerbate them. We simply reported these occurrences."

Also in 1983, Garrett said, funding became a major issue and "I think many of you [scientists] in this room know that you deliberately leaked horror stories about predictions for the AIDS epidemic, cases of unpaid clinical treatment, research problems that were unfunded, and so on. And the media covered those stories."

Whatever was the case in the past, AIDS has ceased to be a story that is primarily about science. The science journalists assembled for the meeting in Washington recognized that fact and wondered what good might come of their discussion.

As Ron Kotulak of the *Chicago Tribune* put it, "It's not our story any more. . . . This disease has become politicized."

B. D. Colen of *Newsday* said "the reaction story has become the tail wagging the dog."

Garrett of NPR said she feels "more and more like a cultural anthropologist, going into Vienna in A.D. 1150 and seeing how the community responds to the Plague."

The one strong recommendation that came out of the meeting, mentioned both by the CDC's Curran and several of the journalists, was the need for vetting of these non-science stories by science editors.

"There's got to be a way for you to peer-review stuff at your own papers," Curran said. "It's bad to see somebody writing stupid stuff at a paper where I know there are two or three experts."

Jim Bunn, who covers AIDS full-time for KPIX-TV in San Francisco, said that for a few years his editors "were sure to ask me to review AIDS stories" done by other reporters. Now, he said, he has to actively check to see who's doing what, "because there are other people who are at a point on the learning curve where they think they know what they're talking about."

Garrett said she knew of a reporter in California who was reprimanded for attempting to correct inaccuracies that had appeared in the paper.

But even where there is a concern for accuracy, and especially at the major media, the autonomy of divisional editors (national, metro, features, editorial, Sunday, etcetera) often precludes the left hand from knowing what the right hand is doing.

And, in the minds of many editors, there was such a thing as too much accuracy; as Cimons of the L.A. *Times* said, the media's greatest contribution to the inappropriate sense of public panic may have been the several years in which the euphemistic "exchanging bodily fluids" survived the knowledge that semen and blood, transferred in traumatic ways such as anal intercourse or hypodermic injection, are the only fluids we really need to be concerned about.

The AIDS story, like "the economy" or "civil rights," has simply disappeared as a discrete editorial entity.

I have a file of clippings on AIDS that I've been accumulating for about a year and a half and which is now about 15 inches deep. With a few exceptions — "Rock Hudson," "obits," and "condom ads," topics I wrote about early in that period — the file is undifferentiated and by now nearly useless.

The volume and variety of coverage have escalated and AIDS has ceased to be a story that goes by that name; it would have to be an editor pretty deep in the sticks who would today instruct a reporter, "Do a story on AIDS."

Instead, there are a multiplicity of AIDS-related stories. The week during which I wrote this column is probably typical. I clipped 27 stories. Not one of them had anything to do with science or medicine. Rather, the stories were about politics, religion, business and economics, lifestyle, the arts, education, and the law. Nearly half of them appeared on a single day, October 1 [,1987].

- The Pasteur Institute in Paris prepares to observe its centennial. It was at Pasteur that Dr. Luc Montagnier first identified human immunodeficiency virus (HIV), the apparent cause of AIDS. Construction is to start in 1988 on a new AIDS and virology laboratory financed by the $50 million realized from the sale at auction of the late Duchess of Windsor's jewels.

- A suburban Dallas pediatrician is forced to close his practice after the local newspaper banners his HIV-positive status, gleaned from a lawsuit.

- The *Journal of the American Medical Association* reports a Harvard study resulting in a negative cost-benefit analysis of premarital AIDS testing; with 3.8 million persons marrying each year, the tests can be expected to produce only 1,200 true HIV-positives, along with 380 false positives and 100 false negatives, at a cost of about $100 million. Three-quarters of all children born with AIDS are born to unmarried women.

- The President's Commission on AIDS is urged by members of Congress to recommend that the president get involved in public education.

- Although a lawyer who alleged that he was fired from Baker & McKenzie because he had AIDS has died, his complaint charging the firm with violation of New York's anti-discrimination law will be pursued.

- Elizabeth D. Eden dies of AIDS-related pneumonia at the age of 41. She was the

former Ernest Aron. In 1972, Mr. Aron's lover, John Wojtowicz, took a number of hostages in an attempt to rob a bank in order to finance Mr. Aron's sex-change operation. The financing eventually was obtained from Mr. Wojtowicz's share of the profits from the film *Dog Day Afternoon*. (*The New York Times* reports, tantalizingly: "Before her sex change, Ms. Eden married Mr. Wojtowicz in 1971.")

- District of Columbia officials are counting on House-Senate conferees to remove from the 1988 D.C. budget an amendment sponsored by North Carolina Senator Jesse Helms that forbids the District to spend any money until it repeals its local ordinance prohibiting insurance companies from considering HIV status in determining insurability.

- A Chicago woman saved a man's life by administering CPR when he collapsed on the street. He turned out to be an intravenous drug abuser and to have bleeding gums. Authorities, citing confidentiality requirements, refuse to give the woman information as to the man's HIV antibody status.

- Governor George Deukmejian of California says his state's new drug-testing law will not circumvent the Food and Drug Administration's authority generally, but will merely permit speedier clinical trials of AIDS drugs.

- The Illinois division of the American Civil Liberties Union criticizes, for irresponsible abdication of leadership, school boards that refuse to enroll children with AIDS knowing that the courts will order them to do so and that their timidity will encourage community panic.

- Longmeadow, Massachusetts, mourns the death of 18-year-old Todd White, who had suffered with AIDS since December 1985 and who had been an inspiration to his classmates and teachers at the local high school. Though blinded by complications of the syndrome, White was graduated in June and planned to start college.

- Federal officials kick off "AIDS Awareness and Prevention Month" by unveiling print and broadcast public-service announcements and educational materials produced by Ogilvie & Mather under a $4.6-million contract with the Centers for Disease Control. At least some of the television networks will run some of the spots, but none will run any dealing with the use of condoms, leaving decisions on those spots to local stations.

What we have here, clearly, is a story, not about a disease, but about our society.

In urging the media to do less reporting about the "terrors of AIDS," in an effort to reduce the level of hysteria, *The New Republic*'s Charles Krauthammer is, in effect, urging that we blink the collective eye that we keep on that society.

But our nightmares tell us as much about ourselves as do other dreams, and confronting them may in itself be therapeutic.

"AIDS Coverage: A Mirror of Society," by Ron Dorfman, *The Quill,* Vol. 75, No. 10, December 1987, pp. 16–18. Used with permission of Ron Dorfman.

Prejudice and the Press: The 1983 Case of Fred Korematsu

The way the news media portrayed Japanese-Americans in the United States during World War II reflected the biases and fear spreading through the country at the time. This article, written by Gerald Kato and Beverly Deepe Keever of the University of Hawaii, gives historical perspective and analysis to a contemporary example of the press' role in inflaming prejudice. Kato and Keever analyze the way six newspapers covered the 1983 court hearing in the case of Fred Korematsu, who petitioned the U.S. government to overturn his conviction for violating a U.S. Army evacuation order during World War II.

Consider:

1. What were the three central events in the Korematsu case covered by the study?

2. What are the findings of the study about coverage of the case in each of the six newspapers analyzed?

3. What evidence do Keever and Kato present to support their conclusion that "the net impact of these misrepresentations was to tilt news coverage favorably toward the government side"? Do you agree? Explain.

Re-living News of the Internment: A Study of Contemporary Japanese-American Experience

Gerald Kato and Beverly Deepe Keever[1]
University of Hawaii, Manoa

The American news media have traditionally seen themselves as a watchdog over government, scrupulously on the lookout for government abuse.

But in the 10 weeks following the Japanese attack on Pearl Harbor on December 7, 1941, the watchdog often was transformed into the proverbial lapdog. Or even worse, it became a megaphone for the virulent racist agitation that led to rounding up and expelling 100,000-plus persons of Japanese ancestry from the West Coast and sending them to desolate inland camps.

"The press amplified the unreflective emotional excitement of the hour" after Pearl Harbor and before February 19, 1942, when President Roosevelt empowered the War Department round-up, according to a congressionally mandated Commission (Commission on Wartime Relocation and Internment of Civilians [CWRIC], 1982, p. 6). This amplification role, especially by newspapers along the West Coast, was also noted by scholars (Grodzins, 1949; Chaisson, 1991), but in the remote interior of the country, the press was silent (Stromer, 1993).

Although the policy was justified on grounds of military necessity, there was not a single documented act of sabotage, espionage or fifth-column activities being committed by an American citizen or by a resident Japanese alien. No internee was ever charged with disloyalty, espionage or sabotage (CWRIC, 1982).

The War Department roundup was historic. "It was the first time that the United States government condemned a large group of people to barbed-wire inclosures [sic]" (Grodzins, 1949, p. 1). Dissenting U.S. Supreme Court Justice Murphy described the racial restriction of the roundup as "one of the most sweeping and complete deprivations of constitutional rights in the history of this nation in the absence of martial law" (Murphy, 1944, p. 235). The Commission termed it a "grave injustice" (CWRIC, 1982, p. 19).

Against this historic backdrop, this article examines the press coverage of an amazing sequel to the wartime internment decision. This sequel centered on fresh evidence presented in court that the highest wartime officials in the Justice Department and the War Department had trumped up reasons to justify interning the Japanese. This sequel played out in 1983 — just nine years after the press had exposed such widespread and high-level wrongdoing that Richard M. Nixon became the first president to resign. In short, the 1983 sequel did more than rewrite World War II history; it also sketched a 1940s pattern of government misconduct that became more relevant with the 1970s Watergate scandal that was to be followed by the 1980s Irangate scandal.

This article argues that in their coverage of the sequel of the 1983 court action, the six newspapers examined here continued to maintain somewhat in peacetime the pro-government tilt evidenced in some press coverage of World War II. This pro-government tilt in the 1983 coverage is in evidence when analyzed within the framework of the eight methods of media misrepresentation devised by political scientist Parenti (1992) in *Inventing Reality: The Politics of the News Media.*

Parenti's eight methods of media misrepresentation are: (1) omission, (2) selectivity, (3) placement, (4) labeling, (5) lies and face-value transmission, (6) false balancing, (7) auxiliary embellishments such as headlines and photographs and (8) the greying of reality by dwelling on surface details. This article seeks to test Parenti's eight methods of media representation, thus confirming or rejecting the theory of the press' watchdog role.

Beyond the scope of this limited study, however, are Parenti's extrapolations from his rejection of the press' watchdog role. He asserts that the news media:

- while posing as an objective chronicler of the events of the day, actually function more as a public relations conduit for government agencies and their leaders, the privileged and the powerful;

- slight the underprivileged and the powerless;

- are significant, exerting a persistent influence in defining the scope of respectable political discourse;

- make major distortions that are repeatable and systemic.

This [article] further argues that the press would do well to impose a critical self-appraisal upon itself by studying the criticism of reputable persons. It could then consider whether specific self-correcting actions or institutional improvements should be initiated.

Background

The 1983 news coverage analyzed here hinges on a soft-spoken former shipyard welder named Fred Korematsu, who was then 64 years old. His route to newsmaking began shortly after World War II broke out. He was picked up by police while he was walking down the street with his girlfriend in San Leandro, California. Then 22, he was charged with violating the U.S. Army's evacuation order. He was convicted, placed on probation for five years and sent off to the internment camp he was trying to avoid.

That criminal conviction set the stage for his appeal to the U.S. Supreme Court. In 1944, the Court on a 6–3 vote upheld the constitutionality of the military orders that led to evacuation and internment of the Japanese. The majority opinion, written by Justice Hugo Black (1944)—described as the court's foremost civil libertarian—insisted that Korematsu was being sent to a camp because of the real dangers of espionage and sabotage that the military had determined were posed by the Japanese on the West Coast.

The dissenting justices held that the military orders were unconstitutional, "falling into the ugly abyss of racism" (Murphy, 1994, p. 233) and forming a "legalization of racism" (Murphy, 1944, p. 242). Korematsu was born in America of parents born in Japan. Remaining near his home was a crime only if his parents were of Japanese birth. But a German alien enemy, an Italian alien enemy, even a citizen of American-born parents convicted of treason but out on parole would not have violated the military evacuation order, Justice Jackson (1944) wrote in his dissent. Of the four types, only Korematsu would have committed a crime because he is "the son of parents as to whom he had no choice, and belongs to a race from which there is no way to resign" (Jackson, 1944, p. 243). Korematsu remained a convicted criminal for four decades.

Then in 1981 a great accident of American history occurred. Professor Peter Irons discovered key government documents in a federal records warehouse in Maryland. With

luck and persistence he had tracked down four cardboard boxes covered with 30 years of dust.

In a 1990 talk at the University of Hawaii, Irons recalled:

> The first document I looked at, I almost had a heart attack. Because — remember the Watergate tape missing 18 minutes — the smoking gun that essentially destroyed Richard Nixon? At the very top of the first box was a smoking gun. You could literally smell the gunpowder. (Quoting Irons, Kato, 1992, p. 8)

That smoking-gun document showed that the War Department had lied in reporting the urgency of evacuating the Japanese from the West Coast — and that the Supreme Court had relied on false information to reach its historic decision.

That document led to a gigantic paper chase through government archives by Irons and others. They uncovered numerous documents contradicting the military's justification for the urgent evacuation. These documents included declassified memoranda, cables, reports, transcripts of telephone conversations detailing how War Department top officers altered and destroyed evidence. The War Department officers were then joined by Justice Department officials who suppressed evidence countering claims the Japanese Americans constituted threats to national security. Thus, the government's own documents revealed officials at the highest levels of the War Department and the Justice Department knowingly altered, suppressed and destroyed relevant evidence that should have been — but was not — presented to the U.S. Supreme Court when it rendered its landmark Korematsu decision in 1944.

These documents formed the basis of the 1983 sequel to Korematsu's story. They were filed as exhibits to Korematsu's petition, made January 1983, to have his World War II conviction re-examined by the courts. Copies of these exhibits, obtained from a National

Archives regional center, were also examined by the authors.

Method

The press coverage of this 1983 sequel is examined in this article. This sequel consists of these three events occurring in U.S. District Court in San Francisco in 1983:

1. Korematsu's initial court filing on January 19. The filing consisted of a petition for a *writ of error coram nobis* — or a writ to correct a fundamental injustice — and thus a plea to erase Korematsu's wartime criminal conviction and to find that the U.S. government had erred. The writ was backed up by a 2-inch stack of exhibits of the governments' own paper trail of documents exposing misconduct at the highest reaches of the Justice and War Departments.
2. The U.S. government's two-page response, made on October 4. The government agreed to setting aside Korematsu's conviction — but did not answer the allegations of government misconduct.
3. The court hearing and then the judge's oral decision on November 10. The judge set aside Korematsu's conviction and said the government's meek response was tantamount to admitting error.

The coverage of these three events in six newspapers is analyzed, based on a close scrutiny of the news texts and photographs.

In all, 19 news articles and five photographs were found covering these three court events. Analyzed were three each from the elite *New York Times* and the *Washington Post;* four each from the *Los Angeles Times* and the *San Francisco Chronicle,* each running a January 20 followup to Korematsu's filing; three from the *Honolulu Star-Bulletin* and two from the *Honolulu Advertiser.* Although the two Honolulu newspapers relied

solely on AP or UPI wire service accounts, the discretion of their editors is significant in ways noted below.

These newspapers are not representative. But they might be expected to provide heavier spot-news coverage because of their focus on important national policy or because of a significant Japanese American population in their circulation areas.

Findings

Following are the findings made by evaluating the 19 articles, using Parenti's eight methods of media misrepresentation.

1. Omission — the single most common form of media misrepresentation, Parenti says. This form of media misrepresentation shows up in our analysis.

The *Honolulu Advertiser* carried no article about Korematsu's initial filing that was backed up by the numerous exhibits detailing government misconduct. Yet, it found space to promote a book it was distributing in-house on Hurricane Iwa — and it did its promotion in a two-column article containing a spacious mail-in coupon. And, while it ignored Korematsu's petition being filed in San Francisco, the *Advertiser* found space to tuck within its national-news roundup column a four-paragraph article from Sacramento about California tax refunds possibly being paid off in IOUs. In contrast, both California papers and the *Honolulu Star-Bulletin* ran articles on Korematsu's filing.

The *New York Times* — America's newspaper of record — omitted coverage about Korematsu's filing for 11 days. It carried its first news story about the lawsuit on Jan. 31, 1983, 11 days after it was first filed, as Odo (1992) notes.

Thus, Parenti's most common method of media misrepresentation is evident in two of the six newspapers.

2. Selectivity — defined by Parenti as favoring those who have power, position and wealth.

The 19 articles seem to slight the U.S. government's misconduct evidenced in the two-inch stack of exhibits comprising most of Korematsu's initial filing. Given the choice, writers mixed information gleaned from news conferences and interviews rather than the damning documents.

The exceptions to the interview-based sourcing were the two California newspapers. The *Los Angeles Times* published the most comprehensive document-based article on January 19. Filed from Washington by staff writer Jim Mann, the article captured the highlights of reports from the FBI and the Federal Communications Commission contradicting the military claims that the Japanese were dangerously using ship-to-shore signaling by lights or radio to submarines off the West Coast.

Mann's account was the only one mentioning the top War Department officials' ordering the recall and the burning of original copies of a draft military report stating that time was not the crucial factor dictating the mass evacuation.

Even so, Mann's account omitted the riveting Exhibit K, written from the Presidio by a warrant officer. Dated June 29, 1943, it succinctly stated: "I certify that this date I witnessed the destruction by burning of the galley proofs, galley pages, drafts and memorandums of the original report of the Japanese Evacuation" (Smith, 1943/1992, p. 47).

The *San Francisco Chronicle*'s article of January 20 also focused conspicuously on Justice Department officials' ignoring a memo from FBI Director J. Edgar Hoover stating that Japanese Americans on the West Coast posed no security threat to the country.

In contrast to this stack of exhibits was the two-page government response in October. The *Washington Post* relied on this two-pager for the most prominent of its three articles. Casting the story favorably, writer Fred

Barbash (1983, p. A-5) wrote that government "took the extraordinary step" of asking the court to set aside Korematsu's conviction. Yet the article fails to indicate the government was forced to take this extraordinary step because of Korematsu's initial filing. And his article — like articles published in the five other newspapers — neglected to mention the government's failure in court to address Korematsu's charges of fabricated evidence. Yet this weak governmental response was tantamount to a confession of error, Judge Marilyn Patel later held (*Korematsu* v. *U.S.*, 1984).

Thus, outside of the California papers, the four other newspaper accounts were conspicuous in their pro-government selectivity by virtually ignoring the paper trail of court exhibits documenting the government's suppression of evidence that undermined the policy decision to evacuate the Japanese.

3. Placement — described by Parenti as burying articles in obscure places.

Only one of the 19 articles was placed on page 1. That one was the *Los Angeles Times'* article datelined Washington and published on Jan. 19 as Korematsu was about to file his court petition. This article ran in the bottom, left-hand corner — that day's least prominent Page 1 spot, given the eye-catching, top-of-the-page photographs (Garcia and Stark, 1991). The story was jumped twice on inside pages.

The other 18 articles were relegated to inside pages. The most-buried one — the *New York Times* article on Judge Marilyn Patel's overturning Korematsu's conviction and accepting his petition that the government had fabricated evidence — ran in the second section on page 7.

In all papers, articles on Judge Patel's ruling were generally buried in more obscure spots than were stories on the other two court events. News articles on the dramatic court hearing and judge's ruling of November 10 were published November 11 — Veteran's

Day. Advertisements, editorials and veterans-related articles often further obscured the inconspicuous placement of Korematsu's joyous legal victory.

The *New York Times'* 11-day-late story about Korematsu's initial filing — based on the damning documents — was run on page 14, the back page of its first section. In contrast, that day, as Odo (1992) notes, the *Times* editors placed on page 1 under a two-column headline the pre-publication leak of a book criticizing Margaret Mead for misrepresenting the Samoan culture in the 1920s.

In sum, some evidence of obscuring or slighting news coverage of government misconduct is clearly found in this analysis.

4. Labeling — words designed to convey politically loaded meaning, Parenti explains. In the 1983 coverage, one journalist, Edward Iwata (1983a, p. 2) showed sensitivity to this method of media misrepresentation. He did so in his *San Francisco Chronicle* article by placing quotation marks around *relocation* camps.

In a broader sense, however, this method of media misrepresentation is classically exemplified in Korematsu's 40-year-old legal battle. By 1983, 40 years after the War Department roundup, the euphemisms of *relocation centers* or *internment camps* had served to sanitize the language describing these historic encampments. In contrast, however, during World War II, debate over the use of the words *concentration camps* occurred in the Supreme Court opinions on Korematsu's case. Justice Black (1944, p. 223), writing for the majority, argued, "We deem it unjustifiable to call them concentration camps with all the ugly connotations that term implies." But three pages later, dissenting Justice Roberts (1944, p. 226) wrote that Korematsu represented "the case of convicting a citizen as a punishment for not submitting to imprisonment in a concentration camp." Roberts (1944, p. 230) also referred to "so-called Relocation Centers, a euphemism for concentra-

tion camps."

The justices were arguing these linguistics before the horrors of the German death camps had been exposed. Much later, in its 1982 report, the Commission on Wartime Relocation and Internment of Civilians (CWRIC, p. 27) wrote in a footnote, "There is a continuing controversy over the contention the camps were 'concentration camps' and that any other term is a euphemism." The Commission rejected using that phrase, explaining that after World War II, with full realization of the atrocities committed by the Nazis in the death camps of Europe, that phrase came to have a very different meaning.

Others disagreed (Daniels, Kitano and Taylor, 1991; Okamura, 1982). Okamura (1982) wrote the government's use of the words *evacuation* and *relocation* served as a cover for either embarrassing or horrible truths.

The words used to depict an event are crucial to one's perception and understanding of the occurrence, Okamura argues, examining the philosophy of Austrian-British philosopher Ludwig Wittgenstein. Earlier, Wittgenstein had maintained that language proceeded from reality — that the structure of the real world determined the structure of speech. "Now he had come to believe that the reverse was the case: language, as a vehicle for understanding reality, determined the way in which people saw it" (citing Hughes, Okamura, 1982, p. 105).

In sum, this analysis of 19 articles written in 1983 hint at, but leave unexplained, the historic, 40-year labeling debate within the Supreme Court and elsewhere about whether *concentration* camps was the proper term to denote the barbed-wire encirclements — complete with watchtowers and armed guards — that warehoused the Japanese for the war years.

5. Lies and Face-Value Transmission — described by Parenti as passing on without rebuttal information considered to be false.

Again, one example of this method of misrepresentation shows up in our analysis.

Exemplifying this type of face-value transmission was a UPI story published in the *New York Times* of January 31. The story included use of quotation marks around the first reference to the "leaves of absence" taken by Los Angeles city employees who were forcibly uprooted from their World War II jobs and were decades later being repaid for their lost time. This official euphemism was used in the lead paragraph but on the second reference the quotation marks were dropped. Omitting these quotation marks transformed the euphemism into a fact.

6. False Balancing — described by Parenti as the journalistic practice of supposedly tapping competing sources to get both sides of an issue. "But in the major media, 'both sides' of an issue sometimes are nothing more than two variations of what is essentially one side" (Parenti, 1992, p. 200).

A pattern of one-sideness in some of the 19 articles was noticeable. Articles about Korematsu's filing his January petition cited only documents and attorneys supporting that side. Later in October articles about the response of the government cited only its document and attorney.

In addition, Parenti argues, both sides are not necessarily all sides; important but less visible sides are often cut out of the questioning. Perhaps understandably, spot-news-of-the-day articles contained no references to any third party. But Mann's day-after article in the *Los Angeles Times* on January 20 did quote an official of the American Civil Liberties Union who had represented Korematsu during the war years. Other articles were silent about the implications of Korematsu on the civil rights of other racial or ethnic groups.[2]

7. Auxiliary Embellishments — described by Parenti as such peripheral framing devices

as photographs and headlines that can package a story so as to influence perceptions of its content.

In our analysis, some evidence of minimizing the government's wartime conduct shows up here.

Only the two California newspapers ran photographs to accompany their articles. A total of five photographs were published. Only the *Los Angeles Times* ran file photos capturing the pathos of the 1942 roundup. One of its two file photos showed a Japanese American child awaiting a train to transport her to an internment camp. The other showed elderly Japanese American men on a train. The third remaining photo in the *Times* and the two in the *Chronicle* were of Korematsu alone or else at a news conference with others.

Headlines are important, Parenti says, because they can mislead anyone who skims a page without reading the story or they can establish a mind-set that influences how one reads the text.

Exemplifying a pro-government slant was the *Washington Post*'s headline reading, "U.S. Seeks to Undo 1942 Japanese Ruling." That headline over the *Post*'s Oct. 5 article implied the U.S. government's response was "an act of executive grace," (Irons, 1989, p. 23) rather than a defensive one required by Korematsu's initiative. The four-column headline was more prominent than those over the *Post*'s other two articles on Korematsu's January filing or the judge's November ruling.

In contrast, more suggestive of U.S. government wartime misconduct was the *Los Angeles Times* headline that read on page 1 "Suppression of Internment Data Charged" and the *San Francisco Chronicle*'s six-column-long headline that read: "FBI Memo Exonerated U.S. Japanese."

8. The Greying of Reality — by scanting content and dwelling on surface details, the media are able to neutralize the truth while giving an appearance of having thoroughly treated the subject, Parenti explains. The resulting misrepresentation neutralizes the subject matter, often giving it an innocence it may not deserve or else glossing-over, toning down or muting quite shocking events.

The surface details of Korematsu's complex litigation involving 40-year-old events are likely to be difficult to squeeze into pre-determined column inches. Even so, many articles seemed to neglect explaining the magnitude of the litigation or its possible impact on other minority groups in the future.

One writer who inched toward this broader dimension was the *Chronicle*'s Iwata. He did so by quoting an assistant U.S. attorney that the threat of another internment does not "lie around like a loaded gun" (Iwata, 1983b, p. 5).

Iwata's use of this quote indicates a sensitivity to dissenting Justice Jackson's wartime warning. Jackson (1944, p. 246) wrote that by validating for all time such racial discrimination in criminal procedure, the Court creates a principle that "lies about like a loaded weapon ready for the hand of any authority that can bring forward a plausible claim of an urgent need. Every repetition imbeds that principle more deeply in our law and thinking and expands it to new purposes." This landmark loaded-weapon principle in *Korematsu* v. *United States* has not been overturned—and was not mentioned in the other 18 articles.

Conclusions

These findings made in this 19-article analysis uncovered evidence supporting in varying degrees elements of Parenti's eight methods of media misrepresentations. The net impact of these misrepresentations was to tilt news coverage favorably toward the government side by omitting or scanting details that graphically portrayed in words or

photographs the historic nature of the official misconduct and cover-up. This impact thus undercut the theory of the press' role as watchdog of the government.

Omitting, scanting or slanting coverage deprives readers of mainstream print media of empathizing with the problems and sentiments of racial minorities. And this omission may lead to an invisibility that forces the minority group to adopt attention-grabbing tactics (Johnson and Sears, 1971).

Misrepresentation by favoring those with power, wealth or position suggests conscious attempts might be made to broaden the range of sources and topics covered. Placement of articles, even on sporadic issues, may deserve more careful monitoring that may be easily facilitated by computer-assisted programs.

The problem of labeling deserves more exploration to find new devices to defuse politically loaded words. More or better use of glossaries or matrixes might be utilized, for example.

Ways to combat misrepresentations of lies or face-value transmission need to be explored. Perhaps newspapers can adopt the fact-checking and research-prone practices of magazines.

The realization needs to be fostered that two sides to a story are an increasing rarity in an increasingly complex world; reporters and editors may deserve more time and training to broaden the spectrum of viewpoints included in the news product.

Photographs, headlines and other packaging embellishments may deserve more sensitive care as research shows they are the most eye-catching elements on a page.

To reduce the greying of reality, journalists may need and deserve more resources to explore more fully the dimensions of problems and the alternative approaches to addressing them.

This article suggests that greater sensitivity was needed in 1983 in covering this landmark racial issue. This article also suggests that journalists have much to gain—or at least nothing to lose — by self-reflection on their everyday professional practices. This self-reflection may form the basis for self-correcting options that are worth considering during today's massive media restructuring and changing press-government relationships.

Even a decade after Korematsu's writ, greater sensitivity in news coverage of minorities is sometimes warranted. For example, Democratic Representative Norman Mineta (1992) questioned two dozen reporters present when former Treasury Secretary Nicholas Brady referred to Japanese as "Japs." Only one reporter thought it was newsworthy enough to write about Brady's using a term long considered derogatory.

Jerry Nakatsuka: On Being a Japanese American Reporter in Honolulu on December 7, 1941

Gerald Kato

In 1939, Lawrence "Larry" Nakatsuka became the first Japanese American hired as a reporter for the *Honolulu Star-Bulletin.* On December 7, 1941, when the imperial Japanese forces attacked Pearl Harbor, the 21-year-old Nakatsuka ran to the *Star-Bulletin* city room from his home two miles away.

Other reporters were being assigned to cover hospitals and government officials. But Nakatsuka did not get a clear assignment. Finally, he spoke up. Nakatsuka (1992) recalls that the editors

> didn't know what to do with me. They were concerned because with a Japanese face, going out into the street, I might get into trouble, might get shot at by hysterical people, individuals. Finally, someone said . . . "Send Larry to the Japanese Consulate," since that was part of my beat anyway.

So I dashed up there and I asked the consulate general, "What's going on?" very naively. But, of course, can't you see the sky has the antiaircraft smoke already? He said he doesn't know. . . .

So I said, still naively, "Let me go back to the *Star-Bulletin*" because I knew a first edition was going to be out then. So right away I dashed back to the office. I got the first edition, dashed back to the consulate general, and said: "Here is this. Look at it. War, big time." And then I said, "I would like to have your comment." And he said something to the effect that he wants the Japanese community to stay calm.

Nakatsuka was talking to the consulate general on the back steps of the consulate office when two police detectives dashed up the steps and pushed them aside. Nakatsuka continues:

> We dashed in the back and then they spotted these Japanese consulate staff stuffing papers in the back room. I was not supposed to go in but, as the eager-beaver, I went right in there. I went to see, I wanted to see what was going on. So I saw the wash basin where the staffers were tossing papers into it. I couldn't see what it was but later on found out those were codes. Naturally, they would burn it. By that time, one of the police detectives, a Japanese American whom I knew personally, said something to the effect, "Larry, get the hell out of here."

So I dashed back to the *Star-Bulletin* to write the story of what I saw.

It was a memorable day for Nakatsuka. He remained on the staff until 1951, when he was awarded the prestigious Neiman Fellowship at Harvard University. He went to work as press secretary for two Hawaii governors and served as an administrative assistant to the former U.S. Senator Hiram L. Fong.

When asked by Mineta's office, the *Washington Post* reportor said the paper published "everything we considered newsworthy." The *New York Times* reporter expressed shock that Brady had said "Jap." But "I just overlooked putting it in" (Mineta, 1992, p. A-10).

Mineta's inquiry underscores that Fred Korematsu's 40-year quest for justice may still be unfinished. It will be unfinished if the press continues to treat his story as merely a page of history rather than a lesson for the journalists of today and tomorrow.

References

Barbash, Fred (1983, October 5). U.S. Seeks to undo 1942 Japanese ruling. *Washington Post,* p. A-5.

Black, Hugo (1944). *Korematsu v. United States,* 323 *United States Reports* 214.

Chaisson, Lloyd E. (1991). An editorial analysis of 27 West Coast newspapers. *Newspaper Research Journal, 12,* 92–107.

Commission on Wartime Relocation and Internment of Civilians. *Personal Justice Denied* (1982). Washington, D.C.: U.S. Government Printing Office.

Daniels, Roger; Kitano, Harry H. L.; and Taylor, Sandra C. (Eds.) (1991). *Japanese Americans: From Relocation to Redress.* Seattle: University of Washington Press.

Garcia, Mario and Stark, Pegie. (1991). *Eyes on the News.* St. Petersburg, Florida: The Poynter Institute for Media Studies.

Grodzins, Morton (1949). *Americans Betrayed: Politics and the Japanese Evacuation.* Chicago: University of Chicago Press.

Irons, Peter (1989). *Justice Delayed: The Record of the Japanese American Internment Cases.* Middletown, Conn.: Wesleyan University Press.

Iwata, Edward (1983a, January 19). U.S. reportedly lied to justify Japanese camps. *San Francisco Chronicle,* p. 2.

Iwata, Edward (1983b, November 11). Victory against internment—40 years later. *San Francisco Chronicle,* p. 5.

Jackson, Robert (1944). *Korematsu v. United States,* 323 *United States Reports* 214.

Johnson, Paula; Sears, David (1971). "Black Invisibility, the Press, and the Los Angeles Riot." *American Journal of Sociology 76,* 698–721.

Kato, Gerald (1992). Introduction. In Beverly Keever (Ed.) *Military secrets: a case of government misconduct in the wartime internment of Japanese Americans* (pp. 5–9). Unpublished manuscript originally designed and distributed by Asian American Journalists Association, Hawaii Chapter, and now available from Beverly Keever, Department of Journalism, University of Hawaii, Honolulu, Hawaii 96822.

Korematsu v. United States, 323 *United States Reports* 214 (1944).

Korematsu v. United States, 584 *Federal Supplement* 1406 (1983).

Mineta, Norman. (1992, August 26). *Washington Post* syndicated column published in *The Honolulu Advertiser,* p. A-10.

Murphy, Frank (1944). *Korematsu v. United States,* 323 *United States Reports* 214.

Nakatsuka, Lawrence "Larry." (1992, December 2). VHS-videotaped oral history conducted by Gerald Kato and on deposit at the University of Hawaii's Department of Journalism, Honolulu, Hawaii 96822.

Odo, Franklin (1992). Following the paper trail. In Beverly Keever (Ed.) *Military secrets: a case of government misconduct in the wartime internment of Japanese Americans.* (pp. 11–12). Unpublished manuscript available from Beverly Keever, Department of Journalism, University of Hawaii, Honolulu, Hawaii 96822.

Parenti, Michael (1992). *Inventing reality: the politics of the news media.* (2nd ed.) New York: St. Martin's Press.

Roberts, Owen (1944). *Korematsu v. United States,* 323 *United States Reports* 214.

Smith, Theodore E. Memorandum dated 29 June 43 included as Exhibit K in the court filing; it is reprinted (p. 47) in Beverly Keever (ed.) (1992). *Military Secrets: A case of government misconduct in the wartime internment of Japanese Americans.* Unpublished manuscript available from Keever at address cited above.

Stromer, Walt. (1993). Why I went along: 1942 and the invisible evacuees. *Columbia Journalism Review, 31,* 15–17.

Notes

(1) The authors are grateful for the insightful comments of Professors Michael Haas and Michael Parenti and the generous assistance of Lawrence "Larry" Nakatsuka.

(2) Korematsu and other wartime decisions on the relocation of Japanese Americans provided an interesting footnote to the Supreme Court's decisions that brought legal segregation in America to an end. Among other things, Korematsu stands for the proposition that "pressing public necessity" must exist to justify racial classifications as in the exclusion of Japanese Americans from the West Coast. No such public necessity was found in the separation of races in the public schools, the court held in a series of cases starting with *Brown* v. *Board of Education* in 1954.

"Re-living News of the Internment: A Study of Contemporary Japanese-American Experience," by Gerald Kato and Beverly Deepe Keever. Article written for this text.

PERSPECTIVE 13-6

Defining Images

In 1993, "mainstream media came out of the closet with respect to covering gay and lesbian issues," according to Marguerite Moritz of the University of Colorado. The way the media fashioned these gay and lesbian images is the subject of this article.

Consider:

1. How are the media beginning to reconstruct and expand their notions of sexuality, according to Moritz?

2. What is the definition of the term *polysemy*? How does that term apply to the issue of the portrayal of gays and lesbians in the media, according to Moritz?

3. Do you agree with Moritz that "newspapers, film and television all offer many . . . examples of lesbian invisibility, even as they increase the attention they give to gay issues"? Explain.

Magazines, Media, and the Fashioning of Sexualities

Marguerite Moritz
University of Colorado

If any single year can be seen as the one in which mainstream media came out of the closet with respect to covering gay and lesbian issues it is 1993. The debate over gays in the military captured headlines in newspapers and airtime on television stations around the country. The Gay Rights March on Washington got similar attention and pretty soon even the gay press was noting the phenomenal explosion of interest by its straight counterparts.

Women's magazines, which follow trends in media as much as in fashion, were no

exception. *Mademoiselle* may have started the exodus from the closet with what *Folio: The Magazine for Magazine Management* described as a "back of the book feature on twentysomething sapphists, or 'baby dykes. . .'" *Glamour* followed with a sexuality "survey of readers' feelings about gays." *Harper's Bazaar* and *Mademoiselle* added to the textual offerings with cover photos that each "highlighted a pair of mirror images models in a subtle caress." The editors called the photos a fashion statement on the "fluid and gentle look of the nineties," not a reference to, much less an endorsement of, lesbians. (*Folio*)

General interest magazines showed no such hesitation. *New York* magazine kicked off what was to become a flurry of interest in lesbians with a cover story in May 1993 entitled "Lesbian Chic." *Newsweek* followed one month later with a cover photo of a smiling lesbian couple and a headline that asked, "What Are the Limits of Tolerance?" By August, *Vanity Fair* was out with a cover profile of singer k.d. lang, complete with a camp photo session of (butch) k.d. lovingly embracing (fem) model Cindy Crawford.

The media attention to lesbians was so striking and so unusual that it became a story itself in the gay press. *Out* offered a lengthy piece that highlighted the lesbian look created throughout that year by the competition: *Seventeen, Allure, Elle, Harpers* and *W.*

"The fundamental thinking," editor Sarah Pettit told *Folio*, "was to encompass the range of opinion on the meaning of these covers and features. Some people were happy with the coverage, some were queasy, and some were ambivalent . . . some of it was good and some was appalling." Indeed, one of the *Out* photos featured a model depositing *Newsweek*'s cover story in a trash can. The *San Francisco Bay Times* offered a similar critique, issuing a copy-cat cover called *Dykeweek* that featured a smiling heterosexual couple and a headline that asked "What Are the Limits of Tolerance?"

While the gay press bashed some of the lesbian chic coverage, *Folio* offered another interpretation, saying that perhaps "these mainstream editors are trying to fashion a compromise between reader interest in gay issues and advertiser skittishness."

I would argue that it is just this kind of compromise that media products must offer on a variety of controversial topics to maintain their currency with a diverse or mass audience.

Nowhere is this negotiation more apparent than in presentations involving sexuality and gender, two of the most highly contested issues of the last several decades. Images of working women, to take a simple example of shifts in gender stereotypes, were rare in the 1950s but are now commonplace. Similarly, media products are now beginning to reconstruct and expand their notions of sexuality. But this re-fashioning is designed to retain many aspects of the familiar, not to displace them. The result is a seemingly new look that wears very well with most of what has been on the rack for years.

In communication studies, this concept of constructing texts with more than one meaning is called *polysemy*. The idea is that in structuring multiple possibilities into a text, that text makes room for contradictions that have not been resolved in the culture. In so doing, magazines such as the ones described above offer their readership something new and interesting yet not completely threatening. They may hint at, or even highlight, gay and lesbian themes, but typically they also retreat or recuperate such ideas, returning to the endorsement of heterosexuality as either the normative space, or in some cases the only legitimate space.

Approach to the Study

Just as it is problematic to write about women and indeed about lesbians as one undifferentiated group, so too is it misleading to write about media as a monolithic enterprise in which all products are seen as having essentially the same content. We know that there is a great deal of difference in the definition of women's issues and in the framing of these topics in *Ms., US News & World Report* and *Cosmo,* for example, even though all three are mass circulation magazines produced in the U.S. Television products have important differences from print products; [and] cinema is not the same as advertising. . . .

Nonetheless, there are instances when it is useful to speak of mass media in a general way. For example, depictions of women in the 1950s in all mass media are not the same, at least not in terms of surface content, as today's media depictions. News media practices, both in print and in electronic media, are also evolving. We can see major difference in all news media products, for example, in terms of coverage of lesbians and gays, when we compare the 1960s and the 1990s. My point here is that mass communication analysis cannot ignore history and that, when writing about different time periods, it can be appropriate to generalize about media industries.

In this essay, I am attempting to examine contemporary media accounts of lesbians. I approach this study knowing that I am writing about a particular historical moment; that current professional practices are not uniform; that media content is not the same across industries; and that what I have chosen to examine is a select set of media products. I attempt to distinguish in this piece between current media practices and products and those that existed and emerged from earlier historical moments. By placing this analysis in a historical framework, I hope to illustrate the ways in which professional practices change and the ways in which they remain relatively constant over time.

To be more specific about my selection of media products, I began with a reading of three articles in major mainstream magazines, all of which appeared in 1993 and all of which featured lesbians on their covers. This seemed a logical starting point precisely because these articles appeared as historical firsts and because they in turn generated media attention as well as public debate.

In the issue following its cover story on lesbians, *Newsweek,* for example, reported having received hundreds of phone calls and letters to the editor commenting on the article. In seeking to establish how these three accounts fit into the larger media picture, my selection process is more random than systematic. I am writing about examples I have encountered in a variety of ways, sometimes as a media consumer, sometimes as a mass communication researcher, sometimes as a political activist, sometimes as a lesbian reader.

My method of analysis is qualitative and largely informed by feminist theories on film and television. One important approach, for example, is to distinguish between surface features of media products and underlying structural content. This is what feminist film theorists did when they critiqued the so-called New Women's films of the 1970s, revealing how these films structurally position women as dependent on and subservient to men, even though the surface features of these female characters showed them as seemingly autonomous individuals by virtue of being lawyers or doctors. One of my points of inquiry has been to look for ways in which lesbians are structurally positioned as deviant from the normative straight world and as subservient to the more visible gay male world.

Feminist film theorists such as Annette Kuhn have long claimed that the work of cultural products is to mask inequities in our social system and that the work of feminist critics is to make visible that which is invisible. Toward that goal, it is useful to examine what is not in the text for it can be as revealing as what is. Gaye Tuchman's notion of the symbolic annihilation of women in media is just such an approach and is easily applicable to lesbians. Marsha Houston's analysis of race and class provides another instance of looking for that which is absent and her work provides an important background to my reading of these texts.

My own earlier work on celebrities and media also proved useful here. I have argued elsewhere that in an increasingly competitive marketplace, mass media journalism has successfully developed a cult of celebrity that both creates and exploits high visibility personalities. In film theory, this is the star person analysis. By promoting celebrities, media narratives imply that celebrity lives represent or reflect the experiences of others in the group they supposedly represent. Thus Kurt Cobain becomes the fallen symbol of his twentysomething generation [in 1994] in much the same way Janis Joplin was mythologized two decades earlier.

Similarly, in 1980 when tennis star Billie Jean King was sued for financial support by her female secretary who revealed that she had been Billie Jean's live-in lover, the news media had a field day: all three networks carried the story as did *The New York Times, Time, Newsweek,* and the sports pages of papers large and small across the country. Five years later the media showed a similar appetite for the details of Rock Hudson's AIDS diagnosis.

Except for those notable cases, however, the ordinary lives and issues of gays, lesbians and bi-sexuals remained largely off-limits in the mass media throughout the 1980s. Coverage that did exist was often framed in a negative way; in addition, these stories were typically focused on white, affluent gay men. In the process of promoting celebrity, the everyday lives of ordinary group members remain obscured or completely invisible. In the case of lesbians, this becomes especially problematic because there are so few arenas within the culture in which they are given any significant voice.

Despite my earlier disclaimers, I do attempt to draw some general conclusions about media practices; it is the work of the careful reader to evaluate the accuracy and validity of those conclusions.

Evaluating Change

Given the fact that mainstream media by definition are not revolutionary in their approaches to contentious topics, how many critical readers evaluate the efforts they do make at incorporating contradiction and change? To answer that question, I would turn to some of the theoretical work that has critiqued media treatment of women in general. For example, more than two decades ago, Gaye Tuchman's groundbreaking work on women and media depictions used the term *symbolic annihilation* to describe the ways in which media operate as a gendered discourse that denies a voice to women and thus makes them invisible.

Certainly this has been the case historically with respect to lesbian representations in all mass media. Whatever their flaws, it is nonetheless true that current magazine depictions at the very least make it less possible to deny lesbian existence. Torrie Osborn, former executive director of the National Gay and Lesbian Task Force, stated the case this way: "You can't know the impact of all those *Newsweek*s having been delivered to all those homes ensconced in homophobia, where Dad had to pick it up off the coffee table and see the L-word. And for all those terrified teenagers who are gay, think of the boost."

Still, the depictions of lesbians in both general interest and fashion magazines have a similarity that should not be missed. Like many of the representations of women that are put forward in the very same magazine pages, these renderings often rely on an idealized standard of beauty. On some level, making lesbians chic permits mass culture to acknowledge contemporary political struggles and at the same time re-construct, recuperate or co-opt the very notion of lesbian by emphasizing Madison Avenue and Hollywood definitions of glamour, fashion and beauty.

The *New York* magazine piece, for example, offers the following description of the women they found at a lesbian bar in [Greenwich] Village: "a sexy, young, tawny skinned woman . . . thick, dark, curly hair flowing into her eyes . . . talking to her pretty blonde lover. . . . Over by the pool table, there's a woman in an Armani suit. (There's) a gorgeous brunette with a movie-star face . . . " Writing about depictions of women, Kathryn Cirksena and Lisa Cuklanz have shown how media create idealized representations which then establish the standards of beauty for the culture.

> Images of the ideal female body reproduced in advertising, film, television and other texts served to create a conception of the female body against which real people measured themselves and others . . . (So we can see that the body is) linguistically or symbolically constructed, and thus that people's understandings of their own and others' bodies were actually constrained and defined by linguistic and imagistic repetition of ideals and non-ideals.

It is my argument here that contemporary depictions of lesbians in mass media also function symbolically not only to deny lesbians a real voice in the culture but also to construct them in the same sexualized and sexist ways that women in general have been formulated. Thus media create lesbians whose personas and lifestyles convey an idealized and unattainable version of appearance, beauty and style. Lesbians who cannot meet this standard are marginalized or made invisible altogether.

When the emphasis is not on beauty, it is often on celebrity. The text of *New York*'s cover story on "Lesbian Chic" focuses almost entirely on celebrities who are either self-identified as lesbian or who have some lesbian connection such as playing a lesbian character in a film or publicly asserting a lesbian sensibility. Thus paragraph one is on Madonna. Paragraph two is on NOW president Patricia Ireland, Madonna (again) and actress Sandra Bernhard. Paragraph three refers to actress Sharon Stone, Bernhard (again) and Roseanne.

The fourth paragraph names k.d. lang who is pictured on the cover. Where is Martina Navratilova? Paragraph 10, after references to Dee Mosbacher, best-selling author Dorothy Allison, Clinton appointee Roberta Achtenberg and political activist Torie

Osborn. Before it's all over we also hear about author Rita Mae Brown and comics Lee Delaria and Kate Clinton.

The *Newsweek* article is remarkably similar in its focus on celebrity. The very first person named is k.d. lang. Then comes Sandra Bernhard, Roseanne, actress Morgan Fairchild, comic Suzanne Westenhoefer, then Roberta Achtenberg, Kate Clinton, Lee Delaria, Dorothy Allison, and so on. The lesbian couple appearing on the cover — presumably put there as representative of today's young lesbians — is not mentioned until the fifth *page* of the article. While these magazine stories do put the issue on the media agenda, they also suggest that all lesbians are upper middle class, well educated, fashionable, and white.

Still Locked Out

Despite lesbian chic, I think it is politically imperative to acknowledge that most lesbians and indeed most women do not fit the idealized model of femininity and fashion. And certainly lesbians are still largely invisible in most mainstream media. Critic Laura Flander, writing about coverage of the 1993 March on Washington, termed this ongoing phenomenon Lesbian Lock-Out:

> Just what do lesbians have to do to get a photo on the front page of the *Washington Post*? she asked in a report on the 1993 March on Washington. "Even when the Lesbian Avengers mobilized thousands of women — some bare-breasted, some on motorcycles — to demonstrate in front of the White House, the *Post* still went with a picture of gay men.

Of course, Lesbian Lock-Out is just another term that describes the invisibility and marginalization that have worked against numerous groups including women, racial and ethnic minorities, and the economically disadvantaged. Historically, invisibility and marginalization have been the hallmarks of media coverage, or more accurately non-coverage, of gay issues in general and lesbian issues in particular. This still exists and functions in many of the same ways it has for decades. Even positive stories about gays and lesbians, for example, often undercut lesbian visibility by focusing on white, gay men.

An *Adweek* article from July 1993 entitled "The Way Out . . . After Years of Silence Gays in Advertising Are Starting to be Heard" is a case in point. In its conceptualization this piece might be considered a breakthrough since it suggests that gay men and lesbians are coming out of the closet in an industry that has not always been hospitable. In its execution, however, it follows a familiar and sexist prototype, featuring the stories of eight gay men (all with prominent photos) and one lesbian. Perhaps that should not be surprising in an industry where women are still very much underpaid in comparison to their male counterparts and under-represented in virtually every realm except that of display where women are, of course, very much the center of attention.

Redbook offered a similar white, male focus in its piece on college life entitled "Gays on Campus." The headline sets the tone for the entire piece by using the word gay as an umbrella term to cover both gay men and lesbians, a fairly common media practice. The opening page of the article features four separate photos showing a total of six gay men and no lesbians. The next page of the piece features nine separate photos, three of lesbians, six of gay men. Similarly, the text uses gay as the encompassing term; the word lesbian doesn't even appear until the ninth paragraph and then only in a reference to the formal title of a campus event called Gay and Lesbian Awareness Week.

By subsuming the term *lesbian* under the heading of gay, journalistic practices tend to erase the specific experiences of lesbians who are impacted by the culture's pervasive sexism in ways that gay men are not. White gay men, after all, still benefit from white male privilege in some instances even though they may suffer from homophobia in others. In her essay on "Compulsory Heterosexuality and Lesbian Existence," Adrienne Rich argues that the lesbian experience is indeed profoundly different from that of the gay man.

> In defining and describing lesbian existence I would hope to move toward a dissociation of lesbian from male homosexual values and allegiances. I perceive the lesbian experience as being, like motherhood, a profoundly female experience with particular oppressions, meanings and potentialities we cannot comprehend as long as we simply bracket it with other sexually stigmatized existences. (Rich)

Just as the experience of lesbians is quite distinct from the experience of gay men, so too is there a crucial difference between white lesbians and lesbians of color, between those who are economically privileged and those who are not. These differences also are erased, however, by media practices that naturalize elite white subjects and make theirs not only the normative experience but seemingly the only experience.

Other Media

While the framing of images and stories about lesbians and gays remains the subject of considerable debate, there is no question that in the 1990s interest in these issues has accelerated in newspapers, films and television shows as well as in magazines. The *Washington Blade* has described this phenomenon in newspaper coverage as an explosion of interest, a "radical departure" from news practices of even the late 1980s, a "sea change," like being on "a different planet." Even the formerly distant *New York Times* has done an about face, increasing its coverage of gay and lesbian communities by "65% from 1990 to 1991 and the paper began using the word 'gay' instead of 'homosexual.'" (Fejes & Petrich). Because of its impact as the national paper of record, this change created "what many activists and media watchdogs assert is a 'ripple effect' on other media."

The lesbian cover stories may be part of the ripple effect, but in terms of media practices, I am arguing that they should not be viewed as a wave or a tidal wave, much less a sea change. Instead of underscoring the ways in which these accounts are different from past practices and from other media practices, I would like to focus on the ways in which they are very much the same.

Newspapers, film and television all offer many similar examples of lesbian invisibility, even as they increase the attention they give to gay issues. In an especially noteworthy example of lesbian erasure, a newspaper headline used the word gay ("TV's Good At Putting up 'Fences' on Gay Themes") for an article about an episode of "Picket Fences" in which two high school girls explore their mutual sexual interest. Not only does the headline use the word *gay*, but never in the piece itself does the word *lesbian* appear, even though lesbian sexuality is what is under consideration in the program.

Hollywood has its examples too. Two significant cases from 1992: not naming or showing the lesbian relationship in *Fried Green Tomatoes* and not having any lesbian ballplayers in *A League Of Their Own*. In 1994, when Hollywood's first AIDS film, *Philadelphia,* became a box office smash, *Time* asked if the movie industry could "still shun gay themes." Its lengthy feature article on the film indicated that the answer was at least a qualified no. Indeed, it listed four films (*The Normal Heart, Angels in America, And the Band Played On,* and *Good Days*) already in the offing. All feature gay men, thus leaving Hollywood versions of lesbians still locked in what Russo terms the celluloid closet.

Television remains similarly hesitant. There were no lesbian mothers in the "Murphy Brown" family values episode aimed at Dan Quayle, even though the point of the entire episode was to demonstrate the large variety of family models that exist. ABC continued this drive to keep lesbians invisible when it initially refused to air the same sex kiss episode of "Roseanne."

Conclusion

Clearly the place of homosexuality in the culture is one of the central debates of the decade and consequently media representations will continue to be contested terrain for some time to come. Representations of lesbians, whether in women's magazines or in other media in some cases, may advance the debate, increase visibility or at least put the issue on the table. It is also possible, however, that lesbian chic articles with their focus on fashion, beauty, celebrity status and upward mobility may have a negative impact by obscuring more serious issues that remain largely out of bounds in the media, including lesbians in the military, adoption, artificial insemination, medical benefits, health issues, spousal rights.

In addition, as lesbian columnist Deb Schwartz wrote, these cover stories remake lesbians into more sellable commodities. "The recent hetero media googlyness over lesbians isn't about documentation—showing the realities of lesbian lives—it's about creation: building a better lesbian, one palatable enough for mainstream consumption . . . In order to show off the new and improved qualities of these lovely ladies, a line is drawn between the fab lesbians of today and those cruddy old dykes of yore." (Martin).

Thus when we begin to look beneath the surface and unmask mass media constructions of lesbians, we begin to see that in some important ways they cover up rather than expose the interdependencies of sexism and homophobia, of racism and classism. In this sense, the chic lesbian shown in the slick mass market magazine is a creation that succeeds as a commodity but often fails as an explanation of who lesbians in all their diversity are and what they experience in this culture.

Endnotes

A Pinch of Chic. (1993, Nov. 15). *Folio: The Magazine for Magazine Management,* Vol. 22, No. 21, p. 29.

Bennetts, L. (1993, August). k.d. lang Cuts It Close. *Vanity Fair,* pp. 94–98, 142–146.

Cirksena, K. and Cuklanz, L. (1992) Male Is To Female As ____ Is To ____: A Guided Tour of Five Feminist Frameworks for Communication Studies. In L. Rakow (Ed.) *Women Making Meaning: New Feminist Directions in Communication* (pp. 18–44). New York: Routledge.

Corliss, R. (1994, Feb. 7). The Gay Gautlet. *Time,* pp. 62–64.

'Dykeweek.' (1993, July 1). *San Francisco Bay Times,* Vol. 14, No. 20, cover page.

Fejes, F. & Petrich, K. (1993, December). Invisibility, Homophobia and Heterosexism: Lesbians, Gays and the Media. Critical Studies in Mass Communications, pp. 396–422.

Flanders, L. (1993, June). Lesbian Lock-Out. *EXTRA!* Vol. 6, No. 4, p. 16.

Freiberg, P. (1993, April 23). Gays and the Media. *Washington Blade.*

Houston, M. (1992) The Politics of Difference: Race, Class and Women's Com-"munication. In L. Rakow (Ed.) *Women Making Meaning: New Feminist Directions in Communication* (pp. 45–59). New York: Routledge.

Kasindorf, J. (1993, May 10). Lesbian Chic: The Bold, Brave New World of Gay Women." *New York,* pp. 31–37.

Kuhn, A. (1982). *Women's Pictures: Feminism and Cinema.* London: Routledge & Kegan Paul.

Mansfield, S. (1993, May). Gays on Campus. *Redbook,* pp. 124–127, 140–142.

Martin, L. (1993, Aug. 29). Lesbians have Mixed Feelings About Being Mainstream Chic. *Boulder Daily Camera.* Sec. B. p. 4.

Moritz, M. (1992). How U.S. Media Represent Sexual Minorities. In P. Dahlgren & C. Sparks (Eds.) Journalism and Popular Culture (pp. 154–170). London: Sage.

Rich, A. (1980 Summer). Compulsory Heterosexuality and Lesbian Existence. *Signs* 5, No. 4.

Rosenberg, H. (1993, April 29). TV's Good At Putting Up 'Fences' On Gay Themes. *Boulder Daily Camera.* Sec. B, p. 5.

Russo, V. (1981). *The Celluloid Closet: Homosexuality in the Movies.* New York: Harper & Row.

Salholz, E., et. al. (1993, June 21). Lesbians Coming Out Strong: The Power and the Pride. *Newsweek,* pp. 54–60.

Sharkey, B. (1993, July 19). The Way Out . . . After Years of Silence Gays in Advertising Are Starting To Be Heard. *Adweek,* pp. 22–31.

Tuchman, G., Kaplan Daniels, A. & Benet, J. (Eds.) (1978). *Hearth and Home: Images of Women in the Mass Media.* New York: Oxford University Press.

Women in Love. (1993, April 15). *Folio: The Magazine for Magazine Management.* Vol. 22, No. 17, p. 24.

"Magazines, Media, and the Fashioning of Sexualities," by Marguerite Moritz. Article written expressly for this text.

CHAPTER 14
Legal and Regulatory Issues

Regulating Content

This article from the *Seattle Times* examines the legality of program content on local public access cable Channel 29. Cable programming has been interpreted by the courts to be protected speech, which means that the traditional methods the public uses to protest such content—contacting a member of Congress or the Federal Communications Commission—have very little effect on most program content.

Consider:

1. Why is nudity and profanity available on cable and not on the traditional over-the-air broadcast stations?

2. What is the difference between the public pressure that can be brought to change over-the-air broadcast programs and the public pressure on cable?

3. Which types of content have been ruled by the courts to be the responsibility of the cable programmer? Which have been excluded?

The Naked Truth About Public-Access Cable TV

Chuck Taylor

For some, free speech is like muscle. If you don't use it, you lose it.

One of the more sinewy examples of that credo, around here [Seattle] at least, is a public-access cable-television shown called "Political Playhouse."

Part talk show, part leftist diatribe, "Political Playhouse" explores in unusually frank and irreverent ways such issues as the abuse of power, censorship, health care, AIDS and the legalization of marijuana.

But what usually stops channel-surfers dead in their tracks when they encounter the weekly show is its broadcast of full nudity and the F word, to name two of the more famous things regarded as offensive in 20th-century America.

That makes it one of the more colorful programs on Public Access Channel 29, the cable-only station run by Tele-Communications Inc. and available to about 383,000 subscribers to the TCI, Viacom and Summit systems in King County.

Last month [June 1994], at 8 o'clock on a Saturday night, "Political Playhouse" ran a retrospective 4$\frac{1}{2}$-hour special in which nude program participants acted out a siege of the public-access studio just off Aurora Avenue North in Seattle to dramatize the danger of censorship.

In introducing the show, Philip Craft, the program's 28-year-old producer, stood naked, superimposed on an image of the Constitution, and suggested that viewers, too, could exercise freedom if they didn't like what they saw — with the TV's remote-control unit.

Surely, many viewers did switch away. Many also picked up the phone to call the cable companies and the Federal Communications Commission.

After years of government regulation of broadcasting, a largely commercial endeavor that caters to the whims of the vast center of the cultural spectrum, public-access TV might seem out of control.

But its occasionally risque content is perfectly legal. Aside from requesting that the cable company block the channel in their homes, offended viewers have little recourse in successfully challenging TV shows such as "Political Playhouse."

Public-access broadcasting has been embraced by the courts as a channel of free speech under the First Amendment of the Constitution, not subject to the usual regulations or economic forces that define prudent content.

If you are accustomed to sanitized TV, that can be troubling.

"Like Making a Newsletter"

The Internet of computers is getting all the headlines these days as the great enabler of free information. But public-access TV, which has evolved over two decades into a somewhat anarchic soapbox, combines language with the power of pictures and reaches more homes.

And as camcorders have become the Brownie cameras of the '90s, the ability to produce television is also in many of those homes.

"Making a video program today is like making a newsletter," said Scott Scowcroft,

the director of the Channel 29 Northwest Access and Production Center run by TCI Cable of Washington.

"People now are just beginning to get it as far as public access as a free speech medium," Scowcroft said. "They're just now realizing the power citizens have in a channel that is on the same platform as mass media."

Most of the programming on Channel 29 is fairly mundane, even boring, compared to "Political Playhouse."

Public-access managers here and elsewhere say that's the overwhelming nature of the medium. They say most shows are inoffensive, constructive, even inspired.

"I think it's important to look at controversial programming for what it is: a very narrow slice of what's on the community channels," said Allen Bushon, executive director of Capital Community Television in Salem, Ore. "To focus on that (which offends) is to devalue all the groups and organizations that use those channels positively."

Indeed, cooking, amateur comedy, sports, and music out of the mainstream, and non-English programming, can all be seen on Channel 29 and other public-access channels.

Such channels also are magnets for those with axes to grind and oxen to gore. Many of the programs can be regarded as politically or religiously fringe which, of course, is the whole point of public access.

Be you left-leaning, or conservative, or of the center, when you sit to watch a whole day of Channel 29, it's only a matter of time before you see something that makes you cringe or snort.

"Unlike other television," said Scowcroft, "what the audience wants isn't important. It's what the program providers want."

For once, TV is not beholden to ratings.

Producer: "Nothing Obscene"

"I don't objectify men or women," says Craft, the Seattle-bred producer of "Political

Playhouse," who also plays in rock bands. "There's nothing obscene about a naked person. Obscenity is defined by action."

Indeed, there is no action on the show that would meet his definition of obscenity. If the show's participants were clothed, not much would seem amiss. They are inert in their nakedness.

Well, OK: "Political Playhouse" has shown an anatomically explicit video demonstrating proper condom use. But it was clinical.

As for the F word, it is mostly employed as the sort of punctuation you might encounter in many conversations these days in board rooms or pool rooms around Seattle.

But nudity and profanity aren't what channel surfers are accustomed to encountering in their living rooms, and it presents a challenge to parents who believe in free speech but fear their kids might encounter Channel 29 unsupervised.

The forces that make possible this intrusion, as many regard it, are a morass of laws, regulations, changing morés and politics.

Confusing the issue for the average television viewer is the fact the government has always regulated broadcasting content, although the standards set by Congress and the FCC are a moving target.

Further, over-the-air broadcasters have been subject to stricter content regulation than cable systems, which the U.S. Supreme Court recently ruled are more akin to private publishers than their broadcast brethren that use the publicly owned, finite electromagnetic spectrum.

While cable programming in general is less scrutinized than broadcast TV and radio, public-access channels have been further shielded from meddling.

Public access has been around longer, but its widespread availability was created by an act of Congress in 1984 to "assure that cable communications provide . . . the widest possible diversity of information sources and services to the public." That act prohibited cable companies from exerting editorial control over public access,

educational and government channels, together known as PEG.

But in 1992, Congress tried to limit that carte blanche through the Cable Television Consumer Protection and Competition Act, permitting a cable operator to prohibit "indecent" programming, as defined by FCC rules, on access channels.

That provision was challenged by a coalition of free-speech advocates, and last year the U.S. Circuit Court in Washington, D.C., called it essentially an "outright ban" on certain content and declared it unconstitutional.

Wrote the court: "Congress and the FCC sought to create a regulatory scheme in order to restrict children's exposure to indecent material on cable access channels. We do not denigrate its attempt to protect children. However, part of its execution in this case runs afoul of our Constitution."

The court left the door open for less severe measures, such as time-of-day restrictions on adult material — a solution in favor these days with regard to over-the-air broadcasting.

Providers Take Responsibility

That's not to say anything goes on public access. Program providers, whose names are broadcast, take full responsibility for content, and if that content includes anything that is not so-called constitutionally protected speech, they — and not the cable system — are accountable.

For example, libelous and unredeeming obscene material (defined by a 1973 federal court decision) are not protected. State and local obscenity laws can apply. But matching any definition of obscenity with a real-life example has, over the years, proved to be problematic, and some call it an ideologically slippery slope.

"You've got to put it in the larger context — that we are kind of struggling with what, if anything, should be done" about expression that is offensive to some, whether it's television or rap CDs or shock radio, said Jeremy Lipschultz, a professor of communications at the University of Nebraska at Omaha who specializes in broadcast regulation and law.

"People feel that maybe there are some boundaries to free expression. But the minute you start to draw those boundaries for people, it becomes dangerous for free expression and free-speech rights."

For those who run the bigger public-access channels in the Northwest, the issue boils down simply to taking the First Amendment at face value, to let freedom ring.

Programs are not screened in advance, and in Seattle, Scowcroft does not "time-shift" into the late evening shows that might be unsuitable for young people, although program providers are encouraged to do so voluntarily.

Unlike independently run, nonprofit public-access channels in other places such as Portland, Seattle's Channel 29 is operated by TCI. Under new franchise agreements being negotiated with King County and Seattle, Channel 29 could evolve into an independent community entity. But for now Scowcroft finds himself straddling corporate and free-speech interests.

"Part of my job with both hats on is to keep public access out of harm's way, and part of the way we do that is we don't take sides," Scowcroft said of the channel's methodical first-come, first-served programming policies.

Said Debbie Luppold, general manager of independent Portland Cable Access: "You never have to protect the voice of the majority. It is the minority voice that someone is always trying to silence. Frequently the people who are calling to complain are more frightening to me than the people who are producing objectionable programming."

"The Naked Truth About Public-Access Cable TV," by Chuck Taylor, *Seattle Times,* July 15, 1994. Dow//Quest Story ID 0000344506DC. Reprinted with permission of the author.

Reporting on Rape

As *Baltimore Sun* reporter Lyle Denniston points out in this article, many news organizations have a policy against naming the victim in a rape case. The issue in the 1991 Florida case of William Kennedy Smith, says Denniston, was prior restraint — whether the court should be allowed to prevent a news organization from releasing information.

Consider:

1. What is the difference between *prior* restraint and prosecution of someone *after* a news organization has made the information public?

2. Describe the two precedents that Denniston says were established by the decision in the William Kennedy Smith case. Why are they important for future cases?

3. What does Denniston suggest as the judge's reason for revealing the victim's name, in Denniston's opinion?

Ruling on Rape Name Blazes New Trail

Lyle Denniston

A tabloid newspaper is off the legal hook — temporarily — in the most celebrated case of criminal prosecution for publishing the name of a rape victim. The constitutional victory in Florida for the *Globe* is, in fact, as sweeping as any the American press is likely to get in court these days.

Palm Beach County Judge Robert Parker threw out, before a trial, two criminal charges against the *Globe* for naming the woman who accused William Kennedy Smith of rape . . . [in] April [1991]. The judge did so in a decision that could add significantly to the press' First Amendment rights — provided his ruling holds up after a planned appeal by local prosecutors.

Many news organizations have policies against identifying victims of sexual assault and may have no need for the kind of protection the *Globe* received. But the American press would stand to benefit in a big way from the two lines of reasoning Parker followed in ruling for the *Globe*. Both have significant potential to insulate the press from legal restraints.

The first seems to free the press from a problem that can be traced back to English antecedents of First Amendment law. Sir William Blackstone, who is arguably the greatest jurist in English history, was the author of the notion that the press does not and should not get the full protection of the law unless government attempts to impose prepublication controls or censorship—in other words, "prior restraint." The press, under that rationale, is fully accountable for its publishing misdeeds—but only after the fact.

Blackstone's theory is responsible, in basic ways, for the deeply entrenched First Amendment principle that the government almost never can stop the presses in advance to prevent the dissemination of a story.

But that theory leaves the press fully exposed to a myriad of *post*-publication legal restraints or punishments. The most serious of these, naturally, are laws making it a crime to publish something that the government wants kept out of print or off the air. In that category are laws imposing criminal liability for identifying victims of sexual crimes.

The *Globe* was charged under just such a law. But Parker, in the most important part of his ruling, erased the difference between prior restraints and post-publication criminal punishment: "It no longer makes any difference whether the restriction comes in the form of an injunction or in the form of a penal 'subsequent punishment' under federal or state decisional law. Both forms of restraint are subject to careful review which requires the highest form of state interest to sustain their validity."

In what amounts to a rebuke of even Blackstone, Parker commented that the term "prior restraint" may have lost "much of its utility as an aid to First Amendment analysis." That is judicial daring of the highest order. If that were to become the law of the land, the press would enjoy much greater protection than it now does, not only under criminal laws, but also under the law of libel and invasion of privacy.

It is only fair to note that the U.S. Supreme Court has not embraced Parker's approach to the First Amendment, even though the Palm Beach County judge found language in prior rulings by that court to buttress his conclusion. But, as long as this breath of new freedom in Florida lasts, the press surely will enjoy inhaling it deeply.

The other core principle upon which Parker relied may be of greater practical value. He ruled that when a state uses a criminal law to enforce a public policy against the press (such as keeping rape victims' names confidential), it has the burden of proving that its policy is of "the highest order" and that it can be achieved in no other way than by punishing the press. In short, a doctrine of necessity.

In the *Globe* case, Palm Beach County prosecutors contended that the tabloid could defeat the criminal charges only if it could prove that the state's interest in rape victim confidentiality was *not* important enough to justify punishing the press. "Such an approach turns the First Amendment upside down," Parker declared. It was up to the state, he said, to prove it needed criminal statutes to protect victims of sexual assault from being publicly identified.

The judge noted that it was the practice of prosecutors in Florida to include the names of adult sexual assault victims in the papers they file to start a criminal case for assault. Other official documents used in such cases also include the names, he said.

"The privacy rights of [the woman in the Smith case] . . . are not even hers to command; her so-called rights belong to the state attorney," Parker wrote. "His unfettered discretion, whether to go public and when, his decision to prosecute or not, is virtually absolute. What a paternalistic, constitutional abode the state invites us to dwell in."

In the *Globe* case, he concluded, "the state has failed to carry its burden of sustaining its actions in taking the extreme step of criminal prosecution."

Perhaps to make his point, the judge included the Palm Beach woman's name in his opinion.

"Ruling on Rape Name Blazes New Trail," by Lyle Denniston, *Washington Journalism Review* (now *American Journalism Review*), Vol. 13, No. 10, December 1991, p. 52. Reprinted by permission of *American Journalism Review*.

Child Abuse Victims and the Press

In Perspective 14-2 on pages 314-315, Lyle Denniston described one aspect of the debate over whether the press should reveal victims' names. In this article, David Hechler, author of *The Battle and the Backlash: The Child Sexual Abuse War,* says that under no circumstances should the names of child abuse victims be made public.

Consider:

1. How are children as victims different from adults, according to Hechler, and why does this change the press' responsibility?

2. Describe the rewards and dangers of interviewing young victims, as detailed by reporter Madeleine Blais.

3. Under what conditions, according to Hechler, might the interviewing of a sexually abused victim be justified? Do you agree? disagree? Why?

The Source You Shouldn't Talk To

David Hechler

The debate over whether the media should identify rape victims continues. There should be no debate, however, about one group of sexual assault victims. We should not identify, through words or pictures, children who have been sexually exploited, and we should interview them only under carefully controlled conditions, if at all.

Why? Children cannot give informed consent to being photographed for the same reason they are incapable of giving informed consent to having sex with an adult: they cannot assess the potential consequences. Furthermore, in many cases their parents are equally ignorant of the stigma their children

may suffer if they are identified. So even *with* the parents' consent I don't think we should identify child victims or project their images, as HBO did in its powerful documentary *Child of Rage.*

Interviews may be conducted without revealing children's identities, of course. The rewards and dangers of such interviews are best illustrated by a generally excellent article in *Tropic, The Miami Herald*'s Sunday magazine. "Haunted Houses," by Madeleine Blais (March 22, 1987), explored the aftermath of a notorious Florida day-care case. The dramatic lead had Blais riding in a car with a six-year-old victim and her mother. The child resisted answering questions until her mother said, "Tell her how Frank [the molester] chased you with the knife. . . ." The child "reluctantly" provided details, then stopped talking and began "humming ferociously." Finally, Blais wrote, "the child's head lolls to the side, and her eyes are closed. She pretends to be asleep or drugged. At the same time, she lifts her skirt and starts to pull down her underpants."

Blais did not identify this child, or another whom she quoted later. The passages in which they appear are undeniably poignant and powerful. Even so, the interviews on which they were based were, in my opinion, inappropriate. There's no way to predict how a child will react to interviews of this kind or to know what further psychic damage may result from them. Investigators, therapists, and lawyers need to ask probing questions to help the child and to see that justice is done, but why must reporters? And if one reporter interviews a child, will the parents say no to the competition?

Moreover, in this instance, it could be argued, the interviews were unnecessary. Blais' article contained a wealth of information provided by victims' parents, including quotes from their children. When I questioned Blais about this matter, she told me the parents had invited her to talk to their children and had, in fact, asked most of the questions themselves. It never occurred to her *not* to interview the children partly because the parents felt strongly that this was the only way the enormity of the crime could be shown, she said.

"Every concern you raise is legitimate," she said, adding that she supports "any way we can protect children. But when they've been violated," she added, "is it a further violation *not* to pay attention to them, *not* to talk to them? I have no easy answers."

Is interviewing a sexually abused child ever justified? I, too, have no easy answers. But, at a minimum, we should not interview children reflexively. In most instances, other sources — which may include transcripts, videotapes, and adults in whom children have confided — will suffice. If there's something important that only the child can add, and the child and the guardians are amenable, perhaps an interview is appropriate. The reporter should make it clear, however, that the child is not obliged to answer — and should be sensitive enough to stop if it is apparent the child is suffering. Interviews should be conducted with a therapist, lawyer, or guardian present.

It boils down to this: child victims are uniquely vulnerable. When we respect ethical lines that may shield them from further damage, we demonstrate not passivity but sensitivity — a quality too seldom associated with journalists.

"The Source You Shouldn't Talk To," by David Hechler, *Columbia Journalism Review,* Vol. XXXI, No. 6, March/April 1992 ©, p. 48. Used with permission of *Columbia Journalism Review* and David Hechler.

The Law On-line

The availability of text and graphics from on-line services on any computer is challenging the current notion of copyright. If you retrieve the text of a copyrighted magazine article from an on-line database and share it with a friend, are you breaking the law? If you take an image of Disney's Little Mermaid from your computer and use it to create a party announcement, is that illegal? These are just examples of the complicated copyright questions being posed by the new electronic technology.

Consider:

1. Do you agree that violations of copyright on-line are "virtually unstoppable"? Explain.

2. What are the obstacles to successful legal challenges to copyright abuses on-line?

3. What are the implications for authors, composers, and other creative people of the widespread availability of copyrighted material?

Copyright Law in Sprawling Cyberspace Is Easy to Break

Junda Woo and Jared Sandberg

Entertainment companies are learning just how hard it is to protect copyrights on the sprawling information highway.

Not only is copyright law easy to break on the Internet and electronic bulletin boards, it is difficult to enforce because of an anything-goes attitude among some users and the evolving state of copyright law itself.

Walt Disney Co., which aggressively seeks to protect its copyrights on characters and films, appears to have made only a small dent in the array of unauthorized and altered Disney images appearing on-line. [In 1993], the company persuaded America Online Inc. and other commercial on-line services to either zap images of its characters or display only authorized reproductions.

But the vast Internet, a loose coalition of computer networks with no governing body, is another matter. "We haven't heard of any violations" there, a spokesman for the Burbank, Calif., company said.

Yet a little poking around on the Internet revealed troves of drawings of Disney characters as well as full-color scenes from Disney animated movies including *Aladdin* and *Beauty and the Beast*, scanned in by computer. One drawing showed Belle, the heroine of *Beauty and the Beast*, brandishing two gigantic waterguns. Others showed Disney heroines in indiscreet poses—the Little Mermaid, for instance, cheerfully disrobing on a rock. The Disney spokesman said he wasn't aware of Disney ever authorizing Internet distribution of Disney material.

"It's a replicating medium and it's a mess," said Michael Wolff, who is writing several books on Internet resources. He called the violations "essentially unstoppable," given how easily people can post material and cover their tracks. At a push of a keyboard button, anyone can copy drawings, computer games, photographs of supermodels, film stills, song snippets and newspaper articles. With another push of a button, copies can be sent to a vast audience without the original copyright owner ever getting wind of it, much less a royalty.

It's unclear how much money companies lose to such desktop piracy. Steve Metalitz, general counsel of the Information Industry Association, a Washington trade group, called the potential losses "gigantic and infinite" but impossible to calculate.

Lawyers who represent entertainment companies say one problem is that litigation, or the threat of litigation, is only effective against commercial on-line services. It is nearly impossible to keep up with offenders on the country's 60,000 computer bulletin board systems, or cast a searchlight over the 3.2 million computers connected to the Internet. "Cyberspace is so vast that there's a risk-reward ratio," says Mark F. Radcliffe, an attorney in Palo Alto, Calif., whose clients include units of Time Warner Inc.

Moreover, some companies are still unsure how to apply copyright and trademark law, which was written years before even the clunkiest home computer existed. When someone downloads a snippet of music from a network like CompuServe Inc., can the on-line service be held liable? When someone transmits a work, are they "copying" it in the legal sense of the word or merely "displaying" it? And how can U.S. companies stop copyright violations on foreign electronic bulletin boards?

And even when the law is clear, that doesn't necessarily stop computer piracy. For instance, at least two federal courts have said bulletin-board operators can be liable for online copyright infringement. Whether networks like H&R Block Co.'s CompuServe, essentially a collection of many bulletin boards, can be liable for such infringements is uncertain. But it's still common for some electronic bulletin boards to display copyrighted and trademarked goods.

"Right now there doesn't seem to be adequate protection and adequate awareness on the part of users" about copyright law, said Jane Schultz, editor of Knight-Ridder/Tribune Information Services, a joint venture of Knight-Ridder Inc., Miami, and Tribune Co., Chicago. The information service recently pulled copies of columns by humorist Dave Barry off some parts of the Internet when it heard that people were widely duplicating and distributing them. Newspapers that pay for and publish the column had complained.

Similarly, people regularly defy attempts by Paramount Communications Inc., a unit of Viacom Inc., to yank "Star Trek" items off the information highway. Paramount got Delphi Internet Service Corp., New York-based Ziff Communications Co. and other on-line providers to pull Star Trek items that fans had put there, including games, archives and screen savers. But users continue to pass screen savers, which display fun images when a computer is idle, via electronic mail. Indeed, cyberspace at times seems like a thinly veiled Trekkie convention; users can find unauthorized goodies as easily as they can eavesdrop on speculation that Spock and Captain Kirk had an erotic relationship.

New technology seems likely to allow even more violations. The motion-picture industry, for instance, frets about devices under development that would make digital copies of movies transmitted by computer. A government task force is expected to formally propose [in 1995] to ban such devices, a prohibition that would need Congress' approval.

Still, some commercial on-line services are trying to immunize themselves in the wake of a ruling that suggested they could be held strictly liable for subscribers' intellectual-property violations.

The December [1993] ruling involved an electronic bulletin board that offered digitized photographs of Playboy Enterprises Inc.'s Playmates. The bulletin board operator said he didn't know his subscribers had violated copyright law, but a Florida judge held him liable for the infringement anyway.

Jan F. Constantine, vice president and general counsel of News Corp.'s News America Publishing Inc., said the company's Delphi unit, based in Cambridge, Mass., has no way of telling whether subscribers are posting copyrighted material. Currently, the service issues only a warning that distributing such material is illegal.

But Ms. Constantine is working on a sort of electronic contract that Delphi subscribers soon will have to sign. They must promise, by answering a series of questions on their computers, not to violate libel, copyright or obscenity laws. Afterward, legal warnings occasionally will flash on-screen. Other on-line services have similar but less aggressive set-ups.

"It would raise the consciousness of a subscriber to know what the rules are," Ms. Constantine said. "Once you get onto the Internet, there's really a free-for-all — that's the whole idea of the Internet."

CHAPTER 15
Ethical Practices

How to Decide What's Right

The word *ethics* derives from the Greek word *ethos,* meaning the traditions and beliefs that guide a culture. In this excerpt from his book *The
Messenger's Motives,* Stanford University communications scholar John
Hulteng gives an overview of the history of ethical guidelines for the
press.

Consider:

1. Do you agree with the statement attributed to William Peter Hamilton
   of *The Wall Street Journal* that "a newspaper is private enterprise owing
   nothing whatever to the public, which grants it no franchise"? Why?
   Why not?

2. How do the authoritarian and libertarian theories of the press differ?

3. What is the concept behind the theory of social responsibility for the
   press, according to Hulteng?

4. Is it possible, in your opinion, to devise a set of absolute ethical principles by which all media should be governed? Why? Why not?

Searching for the Context

John Hulteng

From Plato to the present the subject of
ethics has absorbed the attention of
thoughtful persons in all cultures.
This has been the case partly because the
topic is so fundamental to our simple
survival — our ability to get along harmo-
niously with our fellows in an ever more
complex and interdependent society. But
it has also been a recurring subject for speculation and analysis partly because it is tantalizingly elusive — difficult to pin down in
definitive, concrete terms.

We all use the words "ethics" or "principles" or "standards" as everyday conversa-

tional coinage. But rarely are we confronted
with the necessity to go behind the label
terms and provide definitions for them; and
when such occasions do arise most of us are
hard put to come up with anything but the
broadest generalities ("Oh, you know what I
mean, doing the right thing . . . not breaking
the rules . . . being fair . . .").

Yet what is "right"? Whose rules, established by what authority? "Fair" in what
context?

If the answers don't come readily to
mind, you need not be disconcerted. You
have plenty of company.

Through several thousands of years, legions of philosophers have filled libraries with scrolls and books on the topic of ethics. The theories advanced in these volumes range over a wide spectrum, from religious to behavioristic. Some of these theories are vague and mystical; others are infinitely complex; still others coldly mechanical.

Most of the definitions of ethics that have emerged from these centuries of theorizing tend to be laid out first in broad and general strokes, and then painstakingly explained in voluminous, analytical detail that must be considered in totality to be comprehended. If you groped through the volumes in search of simple, one-sentence definitions, you are likely to find yourself back with the label terms.

One twentieth-century philosopher, George E. Moore, observes that "we find that many ethical philosophers are disposed to accept as an adequate definition of 'Ethics' the statement that it deals with the question of what is good or bad in human conduct."

If you turn from the philosophers to the dictionary you won't be much more precisely enlightened. There you will find that the word "ethics" can be used in a general sense to describe the body of moral principles or values governing or distinctive of a particular culture or group (as in "business ethics"). Or it may be used with respect to an individual as a term expressive of the complex of moral principles held, or rules of conduct followed, by an individual.

In all these attempts to set down the meaning of the word, there are open-ended, elastic variables, just as in our own amateur efforts at definition. What, exactly, do "good" and "bad" mean? What is suggested by "moral principles" or "values distinctive of a culture"? Unless you are prepared to undertake a short course in philosophy, however (and don't expect that from this book or this author), you will probably have to get along as best you can with definitional frames of reference that *are* broad and generalized, even though this will pose problems as we attempt to fit into these frames specific cases drawn from journalistic practice.

Narrowing the Focus

As one explorer in the field of journalistic ethics has pointed out, not many professional journalists have attempted to write about the subject, except to formulate generalized codes. John C. Merrill, author of *The Imperative of Freedom,* observes that:

> Perhaps one reason for this is that most editors, publishers, news directors and other journalists simply write the whole subject of ethics off as "relative," giving little or no importance to absolute or universal journalistic principles. A newspaper friend put it succinctly recently when he said that he looked at ethics as "just the individual journalist's way of doing things." Certainly a free journalist has the right to consider ethics in this way, but such a relativistic concept relegates ethics to a kind of "nothingness limbo" where anything any journalist does can be considered ethical.

At another point in his analysis of the philosophical underpinnings of journalistic freedom and integrity, Merrill touches on another reason why the topic of ethics has been one that journalists typically have treated in broad, vague terms rather than detailed specifics:

> When we leave the subject of basic orientation and allegiances and enter the area of journalistic ethics, we pass from the more solid ground of sociopsychological empiricism into a swampland of philosophical speculation where eerie mists of judgment hang low over a boggy terrain.

Yet Merrill does not hesitate to strike out into this mist-shrouded countryside, and neither should we. The footing may not be solid, but there is a trail of sorts, so let's follow it as best we can.

In journalism, as in society generally, ethics may be viewed either as a group influence, governing the behavior of all or most who are in this field of activity, or as a set of guidelines unique to an individual practitioner.

In the final analysis, whether an individual journalist behaves ethically depends upon the personal code by which he or she gauges rightness of conduct, that is, determines what *ought* to be done as a journalist.

These personal codes are of course beyond our ability to catalog or anatomize, varying as they do from person to person and reflecting many kinds of input, experience and orientation. What we *can* do, however, is sort through some of the institutionalized influences that may have shaped the personal codes.

Here, as in the earlier general discussion, it is possible to discern central ideas that run far back in time (though not back to Plato, since the press is a relatively recent phenomenon). But the central ideas (for example, the concept that it is the journalist's chief responsibility to report news honestly) have been modified from time to time by the various societal contexts in which the media of mass communication have developed since the invention of movable type.

William L. Rivers, Wilbur Schramm and Clifford G. Christians, in their *Responsibility in Mass Communication,* note several basic theories under which the press has functioned since the time mass communication first became possible.

The first journalists were obliged to operate within an authoritarian society. The rulers of the time were absolute, and the interests of the state — embodied in the ruler — were paramount. All institutions functioned within this context. As Rivers, Schramm and Christians put it:

The basis for communication ethics in such a system is clear. Stated negatively, there should be no publishing which, in the opinion of the authorities, would injure the state and (consequently) its citizens. More positively, all publishing should contribute to the greatness of the beneficent state, which would as a consequence enable man to grow to his fullest usefulness and happiness. Significantly, one need not decide for himself; there is always an authority to serve as umpire.

Authoritarian regimes still hold sway today in some parts of the world, and where they do the press must contend with an imposed ethical system (almost a contradiction in terms). In many nations, however, as absolutist governments were replaced by democratic forms, the authoritarian theory of the press similarly gave way to another concept, that of libertarianism.

This theory rejected the notion that the press must operate to support and benefit the state, and instead encouraged the free expression of ideas without governmental hindrance.

All voices should be free to be heard in the press and, as various viewpoints contended, the public would be able to discern the truth amid the hubbub. There would be an open marketplace of ideas; government must keep hands off, letting the various shades of truth and error contend for the attention of the community. Underlying this theory was the assumption that the public would make rational decisions if it had access to all ideas and viewpoints.

What ethical code figured in this theory? Again from Rivers, Schramm and Christians:

The ethical responsibility of the libertarian communicator might be expressed by John Locke's phrase, "enlightened self-interest." The degree of enlightenment, of course, varies widely with individuals. At one extreme might be a Pulitzer, who wrote that "nothing less than the highest ideals, the most scrupulous anxiety to do right, the most accurate knowledge of the problems it has to meet, and a sincere sense of social responsibility will save journalism." At the other extreme might be placed a statement attributed to William Peter Hamilton of the *Wall Street Journal:* "A newspaper is private enterprise owing nothing whatever to the public, which grants it no franchise. It is therefore affected with no public interest. It is emphatically the property of the owner, who is selling a manufactured product at his own risk." Between these extremes are the positions and practices of most publishers, broadcasters and filmmakers.

During the last several decades, the libertarian theory has undergone substantial modification. Some writers on the press and society believe that a new theory — that of social responsibility — now influences (or *ought* to influence) the thoughts and behavior of the men and women who work within the media of mass communication.

The social responsibility theory holds that the simple "hands-off" thesis of the libertarians is insufficient as a guideline for the media of today. The libertarian theory was based on the assumption that access to the means of publishing or disseminating information would be available freely to all, or most. Thus it would not matter whether what was published by some journals was distorted or biased, since these would be offset by others slanted in another direction. In the clash of contending viewpoints, the truth would eventually emerge for all to see.

Shrinking Channels

In the period when the libertarian theory was taking form, and particularly at the time that it was embodied in the American Constitution as part of the First Amendment, there may have been at least some plausibility to

the assumptions on which it was based. Although there never has been a time when the media were accessible to all, there were in the late eighteenth century relatively numerous channels available, in proportion to the literate population of the time. Newspapers, broadsides and pamphlets came and went on the journalistic scene; neither substantial capital nor complex technology was needed to launch a new communication venture — the proverbial "shirttail full of type" would serve.

But . . . the means of mass communication are a good deal less accessible to all than they were at the time of the Revolution. Now there are very few channels, controlled by relatively few persons. . . .

How many [Americans] have free access to any of the various channels for the dissemination of ideas and information? How many have the wherewithal to hire space or time on those channels? How many have the vast means that would be required to buy or launch their own communication channels to reach large numbers of their fellows?

[Today], in virtually all American cities where there are daily newspapers, there is only one such paper, or perhaps one ownership publishing a morning-evening combination. In only 3 percent of our cities does true head-to-head competition between different owners survive. Attempts to revive competition by starting new large-circulation papers have been ruinously costly (with losses running to many millions yearly) and have almost invariably failed. Only in small towns and suburban communities have new papers emerged on the scene and survived.

In most cities there are no more than two or three television stations. And to acquire a TV station is, if anything, even more costly than buying a daily newspaper. Radio stations are more numerous but typically are specialized, reaching only one or two segments of a community with target programming of music and news. The opportunity for the average citizen to find on radio an outlet for his or her views is limited. In time, the realization of the promise of cable systems should provide greater opportunities for public access to the channels of communication, but the full development of multi-channel, two-way cable networks may be years away.

So as a practical matter, the assumption on which the libertarian theory of the press once rested does not hold today. And that is why the concept of social responsibility has taken root.

This theory of the press contends that since the channels of communication now are so limited, those who own the channels, and those who gather and process the information that flows out through them, must accept a responsibility to society along with the freedom that they still enjoy from any kind of governmental interference.

In brief, that responsibility is to provide a truthful, balanced and comprehensive account of the news. Under the libertarian theory, it was possible to tolerate biased, distorted or one-sided presentations because there were many channels and many voices were being heard over those channels; the distortions would balance out, and reality would be discernible. But the social responsibility theory recognizes that when there is only one game left in town, it must be an honest one.

Unless those few channels that are available to us provide an accurate, complete flow of news and information, how else can we hope to get a true picture of the world around us, and acquire a basis for making the decisions expected of us in a democratic society?

So the proponents of the social responsibility theory would lay obligations on the journalists, as well as reaffirm their rights. (Among the proponents of the responsibility theory was the Hutchins Commission on Freedom of the Press which issued a landmark report in 1947 after an extensive investigation of the condition of the press at that time.) And from the obligations laid on the press flow ethical implications.

Most observers of the press tend to view these implications as positive. That is, they assume that journalists who subscribe to the theory of social responsibility will direct their efforts toward identifying and then serving the interests of society. The massive power of the media will be employed responsibly, and an accurate picture of reality will be fashioned for the public. Media excesses and abuses will be minimized.

But this is not the only way in which the social responsibility concept is perceived. Some see built into it ominous pitfalls. John C. Merrill warns in *The Imperative of Freedom*:

> This "theory" of social responsibility has a good ring to it and has an undeniable attraction for many. . . . Implicit in this trend toward "social responsibility" is the argument that some group (obviously a judicial or governmental one, ultimately) can and must define or decide what is socially responsible. Also, the implication is clear the publishers and journalists acting freely cannot determine what is socially responsible nearly as well as can some "outside" or "impartial" group. If this power elite decides the press is not responsible, not even the First Amendment will keep the publishers from losing this freedom to government, we are told.

Merrill's point cannot be ignored; it poses a real and valid concern. As far back as 1947 the Hutchins Commission report was hinting darkly at the necessity for the press to discipline itself or face the prospect that some external agency would step in — presumably some agency of government.

Yet most proponents of the concept of social responsibility contend that the press can make its own internal adjustments in time to avoid the prospect of intervention from outside. And they argue that in this period of shrinking channels of information, social responsibility is the only valid and acceptable guiding theory for the press. This appears to be the position of the majority of editors and educators, and of many working journalists as well. That does not mean, however, that there follows a simple step from the social responsibility theory to the definition of an ethical framework logically evolving from it. It is not that easy to pin down the basis for contemporary journalistic ethics.

The principles and standards that are influential in the workings of the mass media today stem from many sources and a variety of theories. The concept of social responsibility does indeed influence many of the men and women who own or work in the media of mass communication. But libertarians abound, too, as well as some crusty individualists who share the nineteenth-century philosophy that a newspaper is a private enterprise "owing nothing whatever to the public."

As a practical matter some ethical concepts — but only some of them — have roots in press theories. Others have grown up as craft attitudes, folkways of the news business. Still others seem to be almost visceral, instinctive in their origin and persistence.

One writer on the standards of journalism, J. Edward Gerald, contends that "the whole of journalism's dependability and usefulness rests in adequate conformance to the articles of faith upon which communication is based and upon rewards and punishments for behavior." And at another point in his overview, *The Social Responsibility of the Press,* Gerald asks: "What are the conventions journalists are taught to respect? What are the rules of their trade? What skills in communication entitle a journalist to the acclaim of his fellows? What errors bring loss of face?"

If we can uncover some answers to these questions we should have a starting point, at least, for the case-by-case exploration of ethical problems that plague the journalist today.

But be warned: the search for these articles of faith, the answers to Gerald's questions, won't be completely productive. The ethical scene in the field of journalism is almost as imprecise and generalized as is the case with the ethics of society as a whole. We can get a view of some wide parameters and some broad principles, but don't expect neat and comprehensive blueprints.

"Searching for the Context," by John Hulteng. Excerpted from *The Messenger's Motives: Ethical Problems of the News Media,* 2nd ed., Englewood Cliffs, N.J.: Prentice-Hall, 1985, pp. 5–13. © 1985. Reprinted by permission of Allyn & Bacon.

Paying for Space

The relationship between public relations practitioners and journalists is very complex (see Chapter 11). In this article from *The Wall Street Journal,* a professor said that a public relations organization representing a pharmaceutical company offered to pay him to write an editorial for a medical journal.

Consider:

1. What is the ethical issue involved when a professional consents to write an article for payment?

2. Ultimately, who is responsible for the ethical decision—the professional who is asked to write the article, the public relations practitioner who asks for the article, and/or the magazine editor who publishes the article? Explain.

3. Did Dr. Brennan act ethically? Explain. Did the public relations company act ethically? Explain.

Drug Company's PR Firm Made Offer to Pay for Editorial, Professor Says

Ron Winslow

A Harvard School of Public Health professor said a public relations firm representing a pharmaceutical company—believed to be Schering-Plough Corp.—offered to pay him $2,500 to write an editorial for a medical journal.

Troyen A. Brennan, professor of law and public health, and a widely published author of articles and books on medical ethics, medical malpractice and health policy, said he was surprised by the offer because he thought medical journal editors themselves selected the medical experts who write the signed editorials commenting on new medical research or controversies.

The offer to Dr. Brennan came from Edelman Public Relations Worldwide in New York. No specific journal was discussed as a candidate for publishing the editorial.

The subject of the proposed editorial was liability issues for doctors who prescribe drugs, such as antihistamines, that have a sedating side effect. Neither the Edelman officials nor Dr. Brennan would identify the drug company that was Edelman's client. It is believed, however, the client was Schering-Plough, which markets the antihistamine Claritan, which it claims is nonsedating. Schering-Plough representatives declined to comment.

Dr. Brennan's discussion of the offer in an article in [the week of September 8, 1994] *New England Journal of Medicine* highlights a new facet of a growing controversy over the influence of drug companies on the publication of medical research.

Drug companies generally finance clinical trials that show whether their products are effective, and most medical journals now require that the companies' sponsorship be acknowledged when articles about the research are published. More recently, following disclosures that some academic scientists owned stock in the companies that made the drugs they had tested, several medical journals began requiring scientists to disclose any financial interest they might have in the research they are reporting.

Medical journal editorials usually are written and signed by outside experts selected by the journals' editors.

"We solicit almost all of our editorials," said George Lundberg, editor of the *Journal of the American Medical Association.* "It's rare that one comes in on its own and it would be rare that anyone would have an opportunity to use a PR firm to get somebody to write an editorial."

Dr. Brennan said that Edelman agency offered him a professional writer to compose the editorial after a discussion with him, and that he, Dr. Brennan, would be able to change it as he saw fit. His total effort would involve only several hours' work.

"In many ways, what they wanted to do was to put together a position piece for a client and dress it up somewhat with another individual's name," Dr. Brennan said in an interview.

Dr. Brennan, who turned the offer down, also said Edelman sent him a brochure describing its efforts to respond to "bad publicity" about pharmaceutical products with "advertisements, special symposiums and management of the press." He also was sent several articles from medical journals "commissioned by the firm."

Richard J. Rothstein, president of Edelman Medical Communications, the Edelman unit that made the offer, said the firm often works with outside experts in projects for pharmaceutical industry clients and that any support provided by clients is clearly disclosed in materials the agency prepares. Mr. Rothstein also said the overture to Dr. Brennan was the first time it sought to prepare an editorial; other projects involved research reports and other types of articles.

Mr. Rothstein said Dr. Brennan's portrayal of the offer was "misleading" in its implication that corporate support wouldn't be revealed. He said the plan was to submit the editorial to a medical journal with the disclosure that it was supported by the client drug company. "If a pharmaceutical company is going to work with an outside expert, obviously, they're going to work together because they share a similar viewpoint on the issue," he said.

Dr. Brennan used the incident to call for even more detailed disclosure of financial interests by authors of medical articles, possibly including any fees paid for preparation of the article. "Of course, if I were to state that I was paid $2,500 to help a public relations firm write an editorial, my opinion might carry less weight with readers," he wrote. "That is the point."

Alan Hillman, director of the Center for Health Policy at the University of Pennsylvania's Leonard Davis Institute, said the episode reflects a shift in sales tactics as pharmaceutical companies market their products to large health-care providers. "They are searching for new ways to influence behavior of physicians and their choice of medications," Dr. Hillman said.

"Drug Company's PR Firm Made Offer to Pay for Editorial, Professor Says," by Ron Winslow, *The Wall Street Journal,* September 8, 1994. Dow//Quest Story ID: 0000301699WJ. Reprinted by permission of *The Wall Street Journal,* © 1994 Dow Jones & Company. All Rights Reserved Worldwide.

Advertisers and the Russian Press

This short article from *Adweek Eastern Edition,* written from Moscow by Genine Babakian, details a practice in Russian journalism called "hidden advertising." Competitors provide undocumented charges about their rivals to the news media, according to Babakian, and pay journalists to write stories using the undocumented charges.

Consider:

1. How are the ethical issues of the practice of "hidden advertising" similar to the issues faced by Dr. Brennan in Perspective 15-2, who was asked by a drug company to write a favorable editorial for a medical magazine? Explain.

2. What are the risks of publishing "hidden advertising" for journalists? For the news outlets? for the public?

3. How are the journalistic practices at *Rossiskaya Gazeta* different from the practices at *Izvestia,* according to Babakian?

Russian Sponsors Pay for Poison Press: Dirty Tricks of "Hidden Advertising" Are Growing Scandal in Print Media

Genine Babakian

Russia's tradition of hidden advertising—the practice of advertisers paying for predetermined "news" coverage—has now seen the introduction of the "killer presser." The purpose of the "killer presser," as the practice has been nicknamed by the Russian media, is not to buy positive editorial coverage, as was the original intention, but to poison the image of an unwanted competitor.

In a recent [1994] issue of the major Russian daily *Izvestia* an article entitled "How Much Did They Pay You?" revealed a new scandal brewing between Russian oil company, LUKoil, and two foreign companies which provided information to *Izvestia* maligning LUKoil. According to LUKoil, the article was baseless and filled with fabricated facts. "We are counting on you to verify all compromising materials for accuracy," the company said in an official statement to *Izvestia*, adding that it would launch a new media campaign to clear its name.

The fact this scandal hit one of Russia's most respected dailies indicates how widespread paid mudslinging is in the press, in spite of the media's efforts to deny it. Many publications maintain a discreet, but official, hidden advertising policy. But virtually no paper is without guilt.

One rare exception may be *Rossiskaya Gazeta,* a government-funded newspaper so determined to just say no to hidden advertising that it went public when one of its own reporters was caught taking bribes from a "client." The paper not only fired the offending journalist, but it published her name and warned potential advertisers that it would do the same to other journalists who accepted payment for stories.

"Russian Sponsors Pay for Poison Press: Dirty Tricks of 'Hidden Advertising' Are Growing Scandal in Print Media," by Genine Babakian, *Adweek Eastern Edition,* October 10, 1994. Dow//Quest Story ID: 0000433820ZF. © 1994 Adweek, L.P. Used with permission from *Adweek.*

Privacy Versus Curiosity

Photographs often tell stories better than words, and the issue of the camera's intrusion into everyday life is important in any discussion of ethics. In Perspective 15-4, ethics scholar Don Fry describes the different approaches two newspapers covering the same story in the same city used to decide which pictures to run with the story.

Consider:

1. What were the arguments at the *Journal* and at the *Tribune* for and against running photographs of Sage Volkman? Which newspaper made the right decision? Why?

2. Is it possible, as Fry suggests, that both papers made the right decision? Why? Why not?

3. Given the same situation, what would your decision be? Why?

The Shocking Pictures of Sage

Two Newspapers, Two Answers

Don Fry

On October 24, 1986, as Sage Volkman slept, a spark from a wood stove set her father's camper on fire. The flames burned the five-year-old girl over 45 percent of her body, destroyed her eyelids, nose, and left ear, fused her toes together, and melted the skin on her legs, arms, chest, and face. Later, doctors had to amputate her fingers.

Two local newspapers, the Albuquerque *Journal* and *Tribune,* faced a series of decisions on printing photographs of the scarred girl as she struggled through operations, therapy, and her return to public view. One paper eventually decided not to risk offending its readers with shocking pictures, while the other printed gruesome photographs in a special section. Why would two newspapers, edited for the same city, published in the same

building under a joint operating agreement, reach such opposite conclusions on essentially the same materials?

The *Journal*

The *Journal* initially ran three stories, illustrated only with a school photo of Sage *before* her accident. Then, six weeks after the fire, it sent reporter Steve Reynolds and photographer Gene Burton to the Shriners Burn Institute in Galveston, Texas, to report on Sage's treatment. Initially, Burton had some problems with feeling intrusive in the therapy sessions, but he began to think, "What wonderful pictures." He soon came to regard the Volkmans as "one of the strongest and most courageous families I've ever been involved with," the universal reaction among people who have met them.

For the December 25th [1986] issue, Reynolds wrote a story on the Volkmans's emotional struggles. Asked how the Volkmans felt about the paper's coverage, he told his editors that the family was "open to publicity." Indeed, counselors at the Burn Institute had told the Volkmans that Sage would face major problems with public reactions. The institute's former nursing director, James Winkler, had said, as reported in Reynolds' story, "She's going back into the street for the first time as an entirely different person. . . . Society is going to be very cruel to her and it's going to, not intentionally, stop and stare and she's going to be ostracized." He recommended preparing Sage's schoolmates for her new appearance.

Burton offered a portfolio of pictures, which his photo editor took to higher editors for consultation. Eventually they settled for a color picture of the parents with Sage wrapped up in her Jobst suit, an elasticized body covering. A mask covered her face. This picture ran on page A-1, accompanied on A-13 by a black-and-white of the family without Sage. Reporter Reynolds, who did not participate in the photo deliberations, called the color picture "the least offensive photo we had [of her], and the safest."

This decision matched the style of the *Journal,* a statewide paper with a morning circulation of 117,000 daily and 153,000 on Sunday. The *Journal* considers itself a paper of record, and favors hard-news treatments. Its editor, Jerry Crawford, a short, neat, cautious man, has won wide respect for his courageous stands against corrupt politicians. He consults often and broadly, and runs an aggressive paper. Crawford characterizes the *Journal* as "very careful with pictures," always cautious about its "responsibility to anticipate what the public can deal with."

Sage returned to Albuquerque on February 20, 1987, and the *Journal* ran a large picture

on the front page. Totally covered up by her Jobst suit and mask, Sage reaches toward her brother, who smiles back. Crawford called it "the most appealing picture we had taken . . . with the greatest impact in terms of tugging the heart." The editors had rejected all the other pictures as "much too graphic."

During this period, the *Journal* discussed the pictures in editors' meetings, and Crawford often took them upstairs to Tom Lang, publisher of the *Journal.* Lang manages the joint operating agreement between the *Journal* and the *Tribune.* He also heads the Albuquerque Publishing Company, which owns the building and prints the two papers. Lang rejected some of the pictures as "too graphic".

The photographer got complete cooperation from the Volkmans, who were willing to unbandage and disrobe Sage in the hospital. Although the family had preferred photos in Texas with Sage's mask on, after her return they began taking her out in public without it, as the Galveston counselors had advised. Reporter Reynolds told his editors that the family did not mind the coverage, indeed welcomed it.

The Shriners agreed to cover most of Sage's medical costs until her 18th birthday, estimated to run as high as $1 million. But the Volkmans faced other expenses far beyond Michael's means as a tree planter and Denise's salary as a kindergarten teacher. A whole series of fund-raising events helped built a trust fund for Sage.

Five of the stories in the *Journal* ended with a detailed notice on where to send contributions. Editor Crawford and Publisher Lang had several discussions about the family's need for publicity. Lang worried that the Volkmans were trying to make the paper into their advertising agency: "We didn't want to be their solicitor of funds." Crawford also suspected that the family wanted more explicit pictures in the paper.

By the summer of 1987, Sage improved remarkably, learning to walk again and even riding her bike with training wheels. The family wanted to prepare Sage and her classmates for her return to school.

On July 27, [1987] the *Journal* made a decision that affected the coverage of Sage in unexpected ways. Although staff members remember the sequence of events with slight variations, a picture of the key meeting emerges.

Burton shot a new series of photographs, mostly at a therapy clinic. He brought both black-and-white and color pictures to Dan Ritchey, the Metro Plus section editor, while reporter Reynolds worked on a long story about the many people who voluntarily helped Sage and her parents.

Dan Ritchey found the pictures shocking, but "very warm, as warm as you could shoot." He and the photographer spread the prints on a slant table outside the office of Frankie McCarty, the managing editor for news, and asked her opinion. McCarty looked them over and said, "They're pretty shocking, but we might be able to get by with this one," indicating one of the black-and-whites. She found the other pictures "gruesome," likely to offend readers, even outrage them. But she decided to consult the editor, Jerry Crawford.

Crawford came out and immediately rejected the color photos. He looked over the others, and said: "I see only one picture we can publish," paused, and said, "No, not even that one." Crawford pronounced all the pictures "too graphic." He took the pictures to his assistant editor, Ken Walz, for a second opinion, returned, and said, "Not even this one." Managing Editor McCarty left.

Crawford felt amazed that the staff had proposed such photos, because he had turned down "less gruesome" ones before. He "thought the family wanted the paper to run shocking photos to educate potential classmates." He worried about the paper's reputation, as he always does, and "didn't want to be considered reckless." But he stayed and debated the issue with Ritchey and Burton.

Crawford brought up a page-one photo in the *Journal* several weeks before, showing an injured cyclist lying in the street. Paramedics had slit the rider's pants to treat his wounds, and Crawford had to field calls about revealing the underpants. He said, "I could tell the news value overrode the shock value *there,* but what is the news value *here*?" Section editor Ritchey argued that the family wanted people prepared for what Sage looked like; with the start of school coming up, they needed the pictures to break the ice. Photographer Burton argued: "Here's a story about a little girl. We should publish a picture. If it's okay with the family, why not us?" Both stressed their desire to help the Volkmans. Crawford countered: "No, we've done that. . . . there's a fine line between our responsibility to our readers and helping this little girl."

The discussion ended.

Crawford did not think he had made a hard decision, "no big deal." But he sympathized with the disappointment he anticipated: "The staff was so close to it, so they felt let down. I felt sorry for Gene [Burton] and the writer because they wanted their work out." Managing Editor McCarty also worried about her staff's reaction, but she approved of the decision, although she felt that "any story about a person is better with a picture of that person."

Crawford saw his decision as simple: "we would not run *those* photographs on *that* story." But as the decision began to reverberate through the newsroom, staff members separately interpreted its implications for their own work. Burton, the photographer, thought the decision meant that "we can never publish another picture of that girl in this newspaper." He received no further assignments on the Volkmans in 1987, and generated none himself.

Ritchey, the section editor, felt upset by the decision, but he thinks he got a fair hearing. Like the photographer, he took the finding to mean that the *Journal* would run no further pictures of the girl. He thought "To have stories [on Sage], we have to have photos." Ritchey concluded: "It seemed dishonest to write stories about the child being accepted while saying the child's face is too gruesome to run in the newspaper." He assigned no further stories on Sage Volkman.

Reynolds, the reporter, learned of the debate, and thought: "If you're not going to use those pictures, you're not going to use any." As a writer, he worried that describing Sage's disfigurement would seem "exploitive and sensational." Only pictures could capture "the way she is in public." He felt disillusioned, and lost interest in the Volkman story. Apparently no one in the newsroom thought a policy on Sage had been announced, but many other staffers were upset by the implications.

The next day, July 28, [1987,] Reynolds's story appeared in a zoned section, with no pictures. In a later edition, the main section of the *Journal* picked it up and ran it with the old file photo taken before the fire. Section editor Ritchey angrily sealed the library copy of the mug shot in an envelope so it could never run again. He thought it was "insensitive to remind people how cute and beautiful she was." Despite a series of fund-raising events, the *Journal* published no further stories on Sage until December 4, [1987,] seven weeks after the *Tribune*'s special section came out.

The *Tribune*

Meanwhile, the *Tribune* had published nothing on Sage beyond a few city briefs. Vickie Lewis, a staff photographer, began shooting pictures with the Volkman family on her own time. One day in February or March [1987] (no one seems to remember), she tossed a half-dozen difficult photos onto Editor Tim Gallagher's desk and proposed a pictorial essay. Tim says he made no formal decision on what would become a major project involving controversial photographs; he just told Vickie "to take all the time you need." The casual style of this interchange tells a lot about the contrast between the two papers and their editors.

The *Tribune*, an afternoon daily owned by Scripps-Howard, has a circulation of 43,000, about one-third of the *Journal*'s, with only 15 percent overlap in readership. The *Journal*'s editor, Jerry Crawford, characterizes the rival paper as "less cautious . . . more likely to rush into print." He thinks "the *Tribune* has to gain attention. They're number two, so they try harder."

The *Tribune*'s managing editor, Jack McElroy, agrees with that assessment,

---

The following is the letter Sage's parents wrote for the October 16 Tribune:

Dear Readers:
We wanted this article written to make our daughter Sage's adjustment to her new life as easy as possible.

We would like you to be aware of her struggle from when she was first burned and almost through death's door to her return to us as a 6-year-old-girl with feelings who sees life in terms of Barbie dolls and her Brownie troop.

When you come upon Sage unexpectedly in a store or restaurant, your first reaction may be one of sadness.

But if you do run into her, we hope you will see her as we do — as a brave little girl.

Thank you.

From Sage's family: Michael, Denise and Avery Volkman.

P.S. We would like you to share these thoughts with your children.

praising the rival *Journal* as complete, thorough, methodical, and tenacious as a government watchdog. But he adds: "They're a tortoise; we're a hare."

The two papers differ markedly in their handling of photographs. In January 1987, when Pennsylvania state treasurer Bud Dwyer committed suicide at a press conference, the *Journal* ran two AP wirephotos inside on page A-3, one with Dwyer reaching into an envelope for his gun, and the other, waving the pistol. But the *Tribune* ran the two most disturbing wirephotos on page one above the fold, of Dwyer with the weapon in his mouth, and just after he pulled the trigger. Managing Editor McElroy says he "would like to take that one back," but concedes that it shows "the direction we tend to err in."

The *Tribune*'s Tim Gallagher looks nothing like his rival editor, Jerry Crawford. Tall and rumpled, he hunches his shoulders and looks at you out of the top of his eyes. He shouts comic remarks across the newsroom and laughs a lot. In January 1987, Scripps-Howard sent him to Albuquerque to revive a stagnant and boring paper, suffering disastrously from bad advice and falling circulation.

Gallagher recalls his older brother Charlie, who suffered from Down's Syndrome. Like the Volkmans, his parents braved the reactions of others, taking Charlie out with them in public. Other children mocked his brother, and Gallagher felt "a deep desire to have people understand Charlie, to explain why staring hurt my brother's feelings." Later, as a reporter, he wrote a highly regarded series on mainstreaming the handicapped. This concern stayed in the front of his mind throughout the Volkman project.

Managing Editor McElroy says the "question never arose of *not* publishing the photographs." Indeed, all the discussions seemed to concern packaging the pictures and the story in ways to make them acceptable and powerful for the reader. Mike Davis,

---

The picture (detail, right) accompanied this story by Julie Klein, which appeared in the Tribune's *special section on Sage on October 16:*

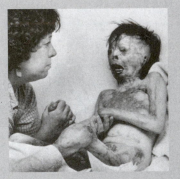

Bath time for Sage is a time-consuming ritual that begins daily at 7 p.m. For months, a typical bath took three hours. Now it's down to an hour and a half, and friends of the family sometimes schedule their evenings to help Sage with her bath.

Scabs consume the evening. They're a welcome sign that her skin is healing. But each scab must be picked with forceps. Then, the open wounds are scrubbed with anti-infection soap.

"Michael picks and I scrub," Denise said. "I'm a pretty good scrubber."

After bathing, Sage is propped up in her hospital bed in her bedroom. Her parents break pustules and cleanse them with hydrogen peroxide.

The peroxide stings more than usual. Her skin feels as if it is on fire and Sage cries about the excruciating pain.

"We don't mean to do things that make you cry," Denise said.

She reminds Sage about another burned little girl whose parents stopped giving her home therapy because she wept too much. Now that little girl can't walk.

Sage stops sobbing. Minutes later, her sullenness is followed by uncontrollable tears.

"I wish I could give my body or anything so that little girl could walk again," Sage said through her tears.

the photo editor, says the *Tribune*'s style is to ask *how* photos and text should run. The staff tends to make decisions in casual and mostly technical discussions among the players, rather than in editors' meetings. Generally, Gallagher says go and leaves them alone. Managing Editor McElroy had little direct involvement in the project, and none in the photo screening.

Through the year, the team kept adding players as Gallagher hired his new staff. Vickie Lewis, the photographer, privately recruited Julie Klein, a new reporter whose style she liked. Klein gathered materials for Sage's story on her own time, before she got the formal assignment. Eventually the team decided on a special tabloid section with no advertisements, designed to ease the reader into accepting very difficult pictures. The package included a letter from the parents printed twice, an emotional editorial, excerpts from the mother's diary, and a careful sequencing of photographs.

One night late in the process, reporter Klein sat around the kitchen table with the Volkmans and took dictation while they composed a letter to the public (see box).

Printed on page A-1 of the main paper and reprinted on page two of the special section, accompanied by an appealing photograph of Sage before her accident, the letter obviated all arguments about privacy and exploitation. Ken Walz, the *Journal*'s assistant editor, believes the letter muted potential negative reaction, because criticizing the paper would amount to criticizing the family.

The photographs and the text each follow their own logic, and seldom correspond on individual pages. The staff designed the photo sequence to ease the reader in toward the middle. On the cover, Sage's mother smiles and snuggles her. The reader sees Sage smiling and getting along with her schoolmates before coming to the harshest picture in the double truck. The *Journal*'s editor, Jerry Crawford, would later praise the *Tribune* for their "extraordinary pains to diminish the impact" on readers.

Two weeks before publication, Vickie Lewis took one final photograph that provoked the strongest reaction and the most debate, both before and after publication. This photograph will become a classic case in photo ethics debates for years to come. The double truck depicts Sage and her mother after her painful nightly bath. The naked, scarred girl sobs while her mother comforts her (above).

Tim Gallagher confesses he had "an anxiety attack" over this picture, "so graphic you couldn't help but feel her pain." But it reminded him of his parents' struggles with his disabled brother, and he knew he had to use it. He thought: "This is the private side of Sage. People have to know it." Lewis feared she had lost her objectivity as a photographer, and worried about exploitation of private grief. But the mother convinced her, and Lewis decided that "this photo tells so much from the woman's face about how she accepts her daughter." The graphics editor, Randall Roberts, held out, worried that the picture was "too strong," but he finally gave in. He then decided it "was the strongest picture, so we ran it big." But he paired it with a smaller photo of Denise cuddling Sage in her Jobst suit.

Two days before the section ran on October 16, [1987,] the values of the two organizations collided in the backshop. Persistent rumors say that two engravers, Dennis Gardner and Jeff Micono, tried to stop the pictures, even in one version taking their case directly to Tom Lang, owner of the press and a man of legendary inaccessibility. Technicians in production do not normally question editorial judgments, especially in organizations involved in a joint operating agreement. In an interview, with his production director present, Gardner insisted that he merely pointed out "excessive grain" to his supervisor.

Tom Lang gives his official explanation: the engravers called attention to a technical problem, which was then solved. That problem came to the attention of Hugh Sarrels, operations director of the Albuquerque

Publishing Company, who expressed misgivings about the pictures to Tim Gallagher, and suggested he run them by Lang.

Gallagher and Lang discussed Lang's worries about the family exploiting the newspapers, the proximity of publication to Halloween, and the very graphic double truck. Lang spoke of the balance between "offending the reader versus tugging the heart." Gallagher described the various efforts to soften the impact for the readers, concluding: "This is a story about a little kid who has more courage than any of us will ever have." Lang said, as he usually does, "It's your call."

The presses rolled, and all the players braced themselves for phone calls and cancellations. To everyone's surprise and relief, the *Tribune* got no negative reactions at all; in fact, quite the opposite. Readers deluged the newspaper with praise. Contributions poured into Sage's trust fund. The section sparked a whole new series of fund-raising events. And parents showed the pictures to their children and discussed them, as the Volksmans' letter suggested. Even Sage liked the pictures.

The *Tribune* newsroom responded joyously. George Baldwin, a columnist, called it "the best thing in my 52 years with this newspaper." On the other side of the building, the *Journal* staff reacted variously, some with surprise and fascination, some with anger, and some with dismay. Assistant editor Ken Walz thought: "I'm glad we didn't do that."

Which paper made the right choice? Both editors stand by their decisions, and neither would have done what the other did. In my opinion, both newspapers chose correctly, in that each remained true to its own identity and values. Journalism school classes and professional seminars debate photo choices like these at length and in rather high-flown ethical terms, but the two staffs made quick operational decisions, more on grounds of credibility than ethics.

But how could they come to such opposite conclusions? We can see some obvious reasons in the story above:

- The traditionally feisty P.M. chasing the traditionally gray A.M.

- a newsroom culture of risk versus a newsroom culture of restraint, and

- two editors as different as two editors could be.

This list leaves out what I consider the most important difference: the way the two papers frame questions. The *Journal* tends to talk in images of a balancing act, or of drawing lines. State editor Bruce Daniels, for example, spoke of the "fine line between arresting photos and pornography." They try to judge whether a decision would cross those fine lines or upset a balance. They ask "yes or no" questions, and they settle for "yes or no" answers. The *Tribune,* on the other hand, tends to ask process questions, not "*should* we put this in the paper?" but "*how* can we present this to the reader?"

"Yes or no" questions serve a restrained newsroom culture well, because in sticky situations, the answer usually turns out "no." But answering "no" repeatedly tends to stifle creativity and injure morale. Process questions serve a more adventurous newsroom culture well, because they get the staff deep into a project before anyone asks hard questions that might stop the project. Unfortunately, the players tend not to ask the hard questions at all, or too late. As the *Tribune*'s Jack McElroy puts it: "We're more aware today of how the ice can get thin out where we skate."

"The Shocking Pictures of Sage: Two Newspapers, Two Answers," by Don Fry, *Washington Journalism Review* (now *American Journalism Review*), Vol. 10, No. 3, April 1988, pp. 35–41. Used with permission of *Washington Journalism Review.*

The Persistence of Plagiarism

Despite policy statements and even some firings, plagiarism continues to exist in today's newsrooms, says Mike Hughes of the American Press Institute. In this article, Hughes summarizes some questions and answers posed to several editors and publishers about the subject.

Consider:

1. **Is modern technology the main reason for plagiarism? If not, what is the main cause?**

2. **Describe the hazards of plagiarism for the profession.**

3. **Which suggestions about eliminating plagiarism seem most realistic? Why?**

Deja Vu All Over Again

Mike Hughes

There is a consensus among editors that plagiarism is a cardinal sin that cannot be tolerated, but not everyone believes it's an automatic firing offense.

[In 1992], three reporters—Laura Parker of the *Washington Post* and Katie Sherrod and James Walker of the Fort Worth (Texas) *Star-Telegram*—lost their jobs for lifting material without attribution. Parker and Sherrod believe they were harshly dealt with. A part-time columnist for the San Antonio (Texas) *Light* also lost his job for plagiarism, while an editorial writer for the Fort Worth *Star-Telegram* and Fox Butterfield of the *New York Times* were suspended for one week for the same offense.

The American Press Institute posed five questions to a group of editors and publishers who have led discussions at the institute's headquarters in Reston, Va., [from 1990 to 1992].

While respondents agreed modern technology has made it easier to plagiarize material, the majority were adamant that is not the primary cause. The consensus was that a reporter intent on stealing will do just that.

They rejected the suggestion that the current practice at many major metros of not naming sources had anything to do with the recent rash of plagiarism. Most agreed the issues are separate, while one respondent—Gregory Favre, executive editor of the Sacramento

339

(Calif.) *Bee* — said that to suggest otherwise was a copout.

Others contributing to the unscientific and unofficial API survey were David Lawrence Jr., publisher of the *Miami Herald* and president of the American Society of Newspaper Editors; Thomas H. Greer, editor of the *Cleveland Plain Dealer;* Timothy M. Kelly, editor of the Lexington (Ky.) *Herald-Leader;* Tonnie Katz, managing editor of the Santa Ana (Calif.) *Orange County Register;* Cole C. Campbell, managing editor of Norfolk's *Virginian-Pilot* and *Ledger Star;* Michael Young, View editor of the Orange County edition of the *Los Angeles Times;* Joel P. Rawson, deputy executive editor of the Providence (R.I.) *Journal-Bulletin;* Michael E. Waller, vice president and editor of the Hartford (Conn.) *Courant;* Lawrence K. Beaupre, vice president and executive editor of the Gannett Suburban Newspapers in White Plains, N.Y.; and Neville Green, managing editor of the St. Petersburg (Fla.) *Times.*

The respondents were sent written questions, and they responded in writing, except for Waller, who answered by telephone.

Waller and Favre are against automatically firing a reporter found guilty of plagiarism. Both recommended an investigation of the ethical lapse in the hope the guilty party's career can be salvaged.

Favre said, "Too often we punish excessively to cleanse ourselves of shame without any regard to the circumstances that led to the ethical lapse."

There is no written policy covering the subject at several of the newspapers participating in the API survey. Some editors said they have a written policy; some have guidelines, while others are considering a written set of rules in light of recent revelations.

Lawrence said of plagiarism: "It's the damndest crime in journalism. It's just wrong, it's stupid and it's dumb."

An edited version of the respondents' answers follows.

1. Is plagiarism more prevalent today because of access to material made possible by modern technology?

BEAUPRE: Yes.

WALLER: To some degree, technology has made plagiarism that much easier because access to all kinds of information is so much greater; it's tempting and, yes, it can be a problem.

GREER: Modern technology certainly makes it easier to plagiarize. But I would hesitate to suggest that plagiarism is more prevalent today because of access. Persons who are inclined to commit such acts will do so regardless.

KELLY: I don't know whether plagiarism is more prevalent, but certainly the same material shows up more places than it used to because of electronic storage.

KATZ: I don't think so. If the implication is that computers make it easier to copy another's work, I don't agree with that either.

CAMPBELL: Modern technology makes it easier to lift blocks of copy from other published sources, so we may be seeing more repetition of background paragraphs and set definitions. But it doesn't make it easier to commit the act of intellectual theft. That requires a level of moral turpitude that is immune to technology.

FAVRE: Today's technology probably increases the risk of plagiarism because it makes an abundance of information available instantly at our touch. It allows us to be lazy. But it's what's inside a writer's head and heart that is most important, not the tools we use.

YOUNG: Although modern newspaper technology could make it easier, I don't see any proof that it's on the increase. Plagiarism is an ethical matter; those who are prone to stealing other's words don't need computers or electronic databases to prod them on.

RAWSON: I'm not sure, but it could be. A common practice when researching a story is to call up the electronic versions of other stories on the subject available in databases and on the wires. It is very easy then to define large sections of another person's story and move it into one's own. The more likely crime here may not be deliberate plagiarism as it may be sloth; attribution not made because of laziness.

GREEN: I do not know if plagiarism is more prevalent today; I certainly suspect that with electronic libraries and faxing of stories from other publications that the opportunity to plagiarize presents itself more often.

And there is one area I have not seen discussed: Graphics. In my observation, a lot of newspapers are ripping off graphics from other newspapers and publications with little acknowledgment.

2. Do you have a written policy and/or guidelines in respect of lifts from the wires, other newspapers and magazines?

WALLER: Yes, we have written guidelines; we don't want big chunks of stuff to be lifted and run virtually word for word. Our people can't do that; if they lift without attribution they run the risk of being disciplined, all the way up to dismissal which, I believe, would be a last resort. One has to learn why a reporter would do such a thing; but every case must be judged individually.

There are other forms of plagiarism I worry about; sports, for instance. Beat writers who also write a notes column should carry a tag line to indicate where they got their information — from other newspapers, magazines and by talking to other beat writers. They're passing their *notes* off as original reporting and it just isn't so.

GREER: The *Plain Dealer* subscribes to very basic guidelines: Everything written for publication which has been taken from a source other than the reporter's original and/or direct effort must be attributed to the source from which it came.

KELLY: No. However, we do credit other publications; notably, our chief competitor,

the *Courier-Journal* in Louisville, when we use their material.

KATZ: No. I don't think you need one.

CAMPBELL: In a recent edition of our in-house writing guide, we reviewed our policy following the recent, highly visible cases at other newspapers. Among the points spelled out: The golden rule of newspapering says stealing is the biggest sin, so don't borrow without giving credit.

FAVRE: Our policy is quite simple: If you use material from another source, you attribute it. Obviously, we, as all newspapers do, combine wire reports and credit same.

YOUNG: There is no written policy at the *Los Angeles Times;* editors let common sense dictate when addressing such questions. However, because of the recent publicized cases, some of the paper's top editors are considering drafting such a policy.

RAWSON: Yes. We do not use items or information from competing media without making our own check of the facts. In extraordinary circumstances, exceptions may be authorized by the ranking editor on duty. If this happens, we will give details of our efforts to reach sources and will give credit to the news outlet from which we pick up the story.

GREEN: We don't have a written plagiarism policy, but we're thinking of putting one in our new stylebook. We spend a lot of time telling staffers of the need to attribute and to acknowledge the use of wire material in staff written stories.

BEAUPRE: Yes, one specifically cautioning reporters of the need to attribute at all times.

3. Do you think the current practice at many major metros in not naming sources (especially politics) has led to an erosion in standards and indirectly to some of our current problems?

WALLER: This is a difficult one, and there is no satisfactory answer, but I don't believe the policy at some newspapers of not printing anything without attribution is necessarily correct.

We've established three criteria for use of unnamed sources: a) If there is no other way of getting the information, but the (unsourced) information helps advance the story; b) if the speaker is not launching a personal attack on an opponent; c) as long as a senior editor knows who the source is.

Things have changed in the last 25 years, and I believe, for the better. In the old days, reporters found out all kinds of stuff but never told their editors; they probably reasoned, "What's the use, it won't get in the paper." But some of that stuff should have been in the paper; at any rate editors today are alerted to what's going on.

There is no doubt our credibility is hurting by not naming sources and some readers will always remain skeptical, but I don't like the alternative.

GREER: No question about it, the practice of using unnamed sources permits reporters to take a shortcut which otherwise would be unavailable to them.

Of course, there are occasions when the use of unnamed sources is the only means of publishing information—when printing a name may cost the source his or her job, or when the source may be subjected to physical injury or worse. But these exceptions are rare and must be authorized by the highest-ranking editorial executive.

KELLY: I don't think so. But without being at any of the newspapers involved in the recent incidents, it would be specious of me to speculate.

KATZ: I think not naming sources leads to all kinds of problems. It's one of the reasons we've lost credibility with our readers. That's why at the *Orange County Register* we insist that all resources be named.

CAMPBELL: I don't think so.

FAVRE: This is a copout. I don't think the practice of not naming sources has created

any larger plagiarism problems. I don't think one has anything to do with the other.

YOUNG: No, I don't think the protection of sources in print makes plagiarism more prevalent.

Heavy competition, though, not only increases the tendency to plagiarize, but also blurs the lines a bit. Competitive papers are constantly "following" each other on stories. Is this plagiarism? Is the theft of a feature story idea plagiarism? What if the story construction is the same, but the writing is different? What if the lead is basically the same, just reworked a bit? What if the same punch line or joke is played up?

RAWSON: I think not naming sources and plagiarism are separate issues. There are times, admittedly rare, when using unnamed sources is acceptable. But if a matter of public importance will not come to light by other means, protecting sources is the right thing to do.

I'm not sure things are better or worse. Today's standards seem to me to be more strict than they were in the glory days of investigative reporting following Watergate. I think that's good.

GREEN: No, I don't see that connection.

BEAUPRE: We do not encourage use of anonymous sources, but when we have to, we have a checklist of 13 items, the most important of which are these: The unnamed source is the only source of substantive information; his or her name must be known to the managing editor; and there is a need to verify the information with another source. The assistant managing editor in charge of the newsroom makes the call.

4. What is your definition of plagiarism?

LAWRENCE: When people co-opt, purloin, borrow or otherwise; taking material from others and suggesting it's their own.

WALLER: Stealing big chunks; taking tidbits for a notes column; passing off another's work as your own. I have no problem with stealing an idea; hey, if we couldn't do that, this industry would go bust; we'd not be able to operate. After all, it's a form of flattery to copy a successful idea, or to improve on same.

GREER: The theft of an idea or previously published material for the express purpose of passing it off as original material.

KELLY: Passing another's work off as one's own, without proper credit.

KATZ: I'm happy with Webster's "To take and pass off as one's own the ideas, writings, etc. of another."

CAMPBELL: Theft of an idea or an image or a personal expression or a body of knowledge developed by someone else. You can't copyright facts, so it's hard to steal them. Literary allusions and related references are not theft and therefore not plagiarism.

GREEN: That's the nub of this problem: What is plagiarism? When we can define that, I guess we will have a written policy. Loosely, I would define it as the unattributed stealing of someone else's work.

FAVRE: Using someone else's material (words, ideas, thoughts, phrases, etc.) without acknowledging the source.

RAWSON: Using someone else's work without crediting them. This goes beyond word-for-word lifting and extends to original reporting or opinion.

BEAUPRE: Using somebody else's words as your own without attribution.

5. Plagiarism aside, what can we as an industry do to improve our public image?

LAWRENCE: Very simply, people who work for us must be clear about our standards; we need to define plagiarism; tell them (staff) what's expected of them and *insist* that the rules be observed.

I consider plagiarism the damndest crime in journalism. It's stupid. People get caught and I'm not suggesting it's wrong because you get caught. It's just wrong; it's dumb, period.

WALLER: We have an ethics beat, and I think that helps; the public knows we recognize our problems and are dealing with them. We have to impose penalties when people do wrong but, as I've said, I don't want us to be licensed, or for us all to operate under one system. We are all different, and that's how it should be. Otherwise we'd all be doing the same thing; the innovators would not be rewarded.

GREER: We must maintain the highest journalistic standards: accuracy; (be willing) to cover all sides of a question; allow everyone an opportunity to have his (or her) say; use unnamed sources in special circumstances only; stop emphasizing the negatives of a story; stop dramatizing the news.

KELLY: First and foremost, we can start by putting out newspapers that speak more to

---

Richard L. Connor, publisher of the Fort Worth (Texas) *Star-Telegram,* says he is completely perplexed by the fact that his newspaper has had to deal with three cases of plagiarism in the past year. The *Star-Telegram* has a written policy prohibiting plagiarism. "It does not offer a definition, but we assume that people know that whenever they borrow something we require attribution," he notes.

Connor rejects the growth of anonymous sources or the spread of modern technology as contributing factors. Managers at the *Star-Telegram* are mulling ways they can do more to combat plagiarism—Connor says they have rejected a firing squad—but they still do not know why it happens. "I do not think some of the people (involved) know themselves," he says.

our readers and less to journalists. This question of plagiarism — and the recent flurry of activity surrounding it — is an example of how major newspapers seize on an "issue du jour" of intense interest among themselves that may be of very little interest to their readers.

KATZ: Serve readers instead of ourselves; ban the use of unnamed sources; get reporters out of the newsroom and out of city hall and into the neighborhood.

CAMPBELL: That never varies. Be accurate, fair, honest, compassionate and clear.

FAVRE: We need to put more emphasis on training and teaching so incidents of plagiarism become non-existent. We must judge each case individually and not have a blanket policy; too often we punish excessively to cleanse ourselves of shame without any regard to the circumstances that led to the ethical lapse. You never forget it, but you can forgive.

YOUNG: I don't think there's anything official the industry needs to do. The humiliation from publicizing such cases goes pretty far, especially since journalists pride themselves on honesty and trust.

RAWSON: Quit being egomaniacal. Part of the problem is editors who must have their own story and can't stand to credit another publication. We should give our people time to do the job right, and we should tell them it's OK to use quotes from other sources as long as they are properly attributed. Take responsibility for our reporters' and editors' failures.

GREEN: There needs to be more openness about our shortcomings. When we screw up, let's tell people about it. Also, we need more internal and external critical evaluation of our performance and excesses behind the First Amendment.

BEAUPRE: Don't screw up any more than we've already done. Frankly, this recent spat of plagiarism has affected our credibility even though the issue is not one the public is connected with — we screw up and an "orgy of self-examination" follows.

"Deja Vu All Over Again," by Mike Hughes, *ASNE Bulletin,* No. 738, January/February 1992, pp. 14–18. Used with permission of ASNE and Malcolm Hughes.

PERSPECTIVE 15-6

Becoming the Victim of a News Event

In this first-person narrative, television reporter Ginger Casey describes the emotional heartaches for the victims connected to a sudden news event. Enduring the coverage of the event is sometimes as difficult as enduring the event itself.

Consider:

1. What does Casey mean when she says that, for a reporter, "the event itself becomes the backdrop; the picture is swallowed by the frame"?

2. Describe the ethical dilemmas that the reporters at such a news event must confront.

3. According to Casey, what is a reporter's ethical responsibility to the victims of a news event?

Feeding Frenzy

Ginger Casey

It was Jan. 17, 1989, when the call came in. Some guy armed to the teeth with semiautomatic weapons had gone crazy at a schoolyard in Stockton. He'd opened fire on a playground full of kids, killing five and wounding 30 before killing himself. MacNeil-Lehrer wanted someone to go in and cover the story from the second-day angle — how the town was handling the aftermath, anything new the police had come up with about this guy, why someone would kill innocent children, that kind of thing.

It was a plum assignment, really. No chasing bits and pieces of information, no holing up at the command center. It was more of a think piece, an overview.

The crew and I rode up in the van. We got the usual hospital shots at St. Joseph's, of harried emergency room workers. They were in the special mechanical overdrive that allows people to do their jobs in a crisis, but all of them were deeply shaken at the thought that someone had done this to kids . . . my God, barely-out-of-diapers kids, who learned hopscotch and horror in an afternoon.

I was able to find one of the school psychologists, but she looked as if she herself needed professional help. "Why did he have to kill himself?" she asked. "He denied us justice." She stared at her hands.

It was good stuff, but our real work wouldn't begin until the next morning. The big thing we were all waiting to hear was whether or not the school would reopen. Would any kids venture out on the playground? If they did, we wanted to be the first ones there.

345

Stockton is not a major news center. While it has its own paper and several radio stations, there are no big TV stations there, only small news bureaus serving a few Sacramento stations. News is something brought in by antenna or cable, or the occasional out-of-town crew covering some "spot" event.

So for the people who lived near the school, the scene the next morning must have been simply overwhelming. I know that when my two colleagues and I turned the corner and saw the school, we all gasped — and we've been doing this kind of work for years.

There were hundreds of journalists crowded onto the school lawn, spilling over onto the sidewalks and street. You couldn't even see them all. Up and down the street, remote vans and satellite trucks hunkered and roared like feeding elephants, trunks extended to the sky. I counted 60 cameras.

Sixty cameras. Where in God's name did they all come from?

Until just a few years ago, the media crowd at a major news story was fairly predictable. Local TV and print reporters would be there, the three network crews, possibly one or two wire service reporters. It usually meant a crowd of about 20 to 25 people, figure two or three to each camera (reporter, camera person and possibly a sound engineer). Local reporters would claim sovereignty, feeling they owned the story, all the while enviously eyeing the networks' expensive equipment and better-dressed journalists.

Times have changed. Independent news agencies and tabloid TV shows have sprung up. Satellite trucks and live gear now enable any station to have a local presence on a national story. Why wait for Dan or Peter or Tom to tell you on the network news when you can send your own anchor team or reporter to the event? Be there yourself, and show off the bells and whistles of your new technology!

The big granite slab inscribed with the school's name — it looked eerily like a giant tombstone — was littered with used Styrofoam coffee cups. One was perched inside a wreath of flowers someone had placed on the sign during the night.

Technicians and reporters called out to each other in recognition, laughing with delight to be working the same story again. "Hey Tom! How the hell are 'ya? Jesus, I haven't seen you since the Sacramento landlady!" These horrific events, when newsroom budgets are thrown to the wind and journalists are sent on expensive out-of-town trips, are reunions of a sort.

A funny thing happens when you cover a major news event. The event itself becomes the backdrop; the picture is swallowed by the frame, and the whole thing acquires an air of unreality. When you look at something through the lens of a camera, or interpret it using note pads and microphones, it doesn't seem quite as authentic — or disturbing — as when you come armed only with your senses. The hardware serves as a kind of shield of denial, a way to create structure — however illusory — out of chaos.

Making structure out of chaos — isn't that what our job is supposed to be about? Show the folks back home the gruesome details, but within the comforting, bite-sized confines of the medium. Frame the fire so it burns from edge to edge of the screen, show the bombs landing on rooftops and watch as buildings explode like smashed toys, shoot the burned-out neighborhood so it looks like Dresden, go sound up full on a wailing parent. Present the event in precise order: tight shot, medium shot, wide shot, soundbite, more pictures. For a story like Stockton, use some "symbol" shots — a single sneaker if you can find one, or an empty swing blowing in some desolate wind.

But the most important component, at least for the reporter, is the "stand-up," the moment when you are standing in front of the camera, the electronic oracle of the event. This is the time to look sage, wise, appropriately moved. They call these news packages "wraps." It's a good word for what reporters do: wrap everything up in a neat package.

I have a theory that a lot of journalists go into this profession because they need that structure. At some deep level, they are corralling their own wild stallions when they bring sense to an insane event. I joke with my friends that there are some people in this business who, if they couldn't cover a fire, would probably set one. When the news sirens start to wail, some of us go into heat.

Those sirens beckon us perilously close to the rocks. And sometimes we crash.

The school administrator stood in front of the building, obviously nervous as he faced the mob of reporters, photographers and sound technicians. "Why did you decide to open school today?" someone shouted. The man swallowed. "After discussing it with the psychologist and other administration officials, we decided it would be in the best interest of the children to try to return to our normal routine," he said. A half-dozen cameras and reporters dropped out of the crowd, and a half-dozen more dropped in. "Why is school open today?" someone shouted.

Ah, the voice on the video. So important to a boss back at the station that your voice is heard above the melee, asking the cogent question. Serious points for an ambitious reporter. Enough to drive him to ask the question even if it has been answered four times already. The principal looked around, confused. "We, uh, we discussed it with the psychologist and other administration officials and felt it would be in the best interest of the children to try to return to our normal routine." More cameras out, more cameras in. A shout came from the back. "Why did you decide to open the school today?"

Suddenly a yellow school bus pulled around the corner. The school administrator was spared. The group had found a car target, and swarmed toward it, microphone poles extended, cameras clicking, reporters and photographers jockeying for position.

"Please stand back from the bus!" the school administrator shouted. "Please stand back! Off the sidewalk please!" The crowd ignored him and surged forward as the bus pulled to the curb. Its lone passenger, a small boy with glasses, stared through a side window at the approaching mob. He was barely tall enough to see all the way over the windowsill. His eyes grew enormous.

As the crowd pushed forward and reached the door of the bus, the driver pulled away again. Quickly. The crowd began to move down the street toward the remote vans, leaving the school administrator alone on the sidewalk repeating over and over, "Please stand back! Please stand back!"

I was tapped on the shoulder. It was a woman I had worked with at a station in Los Angeles. She had been sent up to cover the story. "Christ, do you believe it?" she asked, looking over the crowd. "What a zoo. It makes me sick." We'd been talking for a few moments when suddenly she said, "Oh, God, Ginger, I just hope no one gets a kid. I'm a mother. I can't stand it." Well then, I told her, don't get one. "You know how it is," she said. "If someone gets a kid, then I have to."

She was right, of course. If someone got a kid, she would have to, as well. It's the way the game works. You don't want your competition to have any angle you don't have, and crying kids on camera were powerful images. If having your voice heard at a news conference scored points, so did interviewing a child. Your boss would tell you that you "kicked ass." Your résumé tape would look terrific.

As she walked away, I saw that several reporters had already broken from the crowd and were going door to door down the block looking for witnesses. Those with any shame at all at least had the decency to pretend to be sheepish; younger, less experienced reporters boldly knocked on doors with a sense of entitlement. I knew what they would say; I had said it myself at one time, and had even half convinced myself I believed it. "Sharing this terrible tragedy will help others"; "There are so many people concerned"; "At a time like this, it sometimes helps to talk." As if the media were some kind of cultural confessional.

Yes, I knew all the tricks. I had learned to hide my excitement when I found someone naive enough to share their pain with me. And I swallowed the shame of knowing that their tragedy would be a good career move for me.

Back in front of the school, reporters were lined up shoulder to shoulder like bowling pins for their "live shots," all of them using the front of the school as the backdrop. The coffee cups had been moved off the school marker. I hoped it was because someone had realized the disrespect; I suspected it was because the flowers were crucial to the shot. Technicians stood ready at their tripods, pools of cables snaking back along the sidewalk to the vans. The reporters were framed so no other reporters were seen doing their respective live shots. That's considered bad form: You're supposed to look as if you are the only one "live" on the scene, the solitary witness for the folks back home, spouting the inevitable opening lines: "Still more questions than answers here this morning, Dave" . . . "Officials are still trying to figure out what triggered this terrible tragedy" . . . "The one man who could explain what happened here is dead by his own hand." And the tried-and-true classic, "As the residents of this tiny town struggle to pick up the pieces of their lives . . ."

At the top of the hour, they all began, a chorus of live shots beamed home through mountaintop repeaters and satellites, ending up neatly boxed in someone's living room. Within minutes it was over, as reporters soberly signed off, promising more details as "this terrible tragedy unfolds."

It had to happen, of course. Some parents were going to bring their kids to school. They were going to try their best to carry on, to pretend that after the previous day the world still made sense. As I watched from the edge of the crowd, an Asian woman came around the corner, holding onto her child's tiny hand. Someone let out a yell.

I should preface what happened next with a short disclaimer. Most of the people who were at that school that day were, no doubt, dedicated, hard-working professionals. Most of what they were doing was proper: collecting information, digging for facts, trying to package their reports and get them back to the station in a timely manner. If the crowd had been smaller, they probably would never have done what they did. But they did.

I remember thinking how much the crowd looked like an amoeba as it began to roll toward the woman and her child. Not everyone even knew what they were heading for, only that the mass they were a part of had found something to focus on. A kind of feeding frenzy takes over at highly charged events, and reporters don't necessarily act, but react.

The woman froze and pulled her child closer to her and then turned and began to run, pulling her child with her. The crowd ran after her.

Many of the children who attended the school were Cambodian refugees, who endured God-only-knows-what to come to this country. The day before, whatever sense of safety they might have had vanished in a stream of blood and bullets. And here they were being chased by a mob, microphone poles extended like weapons, cameras trained on them, people shouting at them to stop. Some reporters even tried to interview them as they fled, yelling "Did you see it? Did you see it?"

Chances are you didn't see any of this at home. In fact, I'd say it's a safe bet that you didn't. There is a tacit agreement in this business never to pull back the curtain, never to show you the little man pulling his bells and whistles. What you see is the great and powerful Oz. When I read my script to MacNeil-Lehrer over the phone, I was told they hadn't sent me to cover the role of the media, that it was incidental to the story.

In the world of TV news, viewers see only the product of journalism, not its process. They're never told that television is a lens that both shapes and reflects. And we journalists find it easy to ignore this awkward truth, too. We never see the consequences of our presence at an event, and even more rarely do we even think about it. When we do, we have lofty philosophical discussions about whether the way we cover the news has conditioned our audience, if we have corrupted them with sensationalism. We ponder if we should force the media to "pool" coverage in these situations and limit the number of cameras.

There are good arguments on the other side, of course. We're giving people what they want. Limiting press access can lead to censorship. The First Amendment gives us a constitutional right to do our jobs.

All true. But what I learned on the playground that day is that we also have a moral and ethical responsibility that goes beyond providing objective reporting. It's the responsibility to be gentle to those in pain, and compassionate. It's the responsibility to know when we have overstepped our bounds as witnesses. And it's the responsibility, in the end, to hold the mirror up, not just to the news event, but to ourselves.

"Feeding Frenzy," by Ginger Casey, *Image,* January 19, 1992, pp. 21–26. Used with permission of Ginger Casey.

PART V
International Media

CHAPTER 16
Global Media

Technological Century

World media scholar L. John Martin, Professor Emeritus, University of Maryland, says that in the twentieth century communication has made the greatest strides since the invention of language itself. This changing communications landscape, says Martin, is causing profound changes in the media around the world.

Consider:

1. According to Martin, how have changing communications technologies transformed media ownership and financing?

2. According to Martin, what have been the effects of the communications revolution on the content and on the audience?

3. How has the relationship changed between media and their own governments and the media and foreign governments, according to Martin?

World Media at Century's End

L. John Martin, Professor Emeritus
University of Maryland

Standing on the threshold of the 21st century, this is a good time to take stock of where the world's media are heading. Unquestionably, ours has been the technological century. It also has been the century in which communication has made the greatest strides since the invention of language itself. True, the rotary press and telegraph appeared in the first third of the 19th century, and the telephone, the phonograph and the linotype machine were invented in the last quarter. But these inventions pale in the light of the deluge of communication technology that has flooded the 20th century.

At or about the turn of this century, we were introduced to wireless and motion pictures. Commercial radio broadcasting began in the 1920s, as did sound recording on tape; the talkies came around the '30s and so did the invention of the copying machine (which, however, was not too common in offices until the '60s); commercial television became vi'able at the end of the '40s and early '50s, a decade that also saw the widespread use of the videotape; the '60s brought forth color television and the communications satellite; the '70s introduced the videocassette recorder (VCR) and the personal computer;

in the '80s, fax machines and desktop publishing, the mobile phone and the beeper revolutionized communications, and the '90s did so once again by popularizing e-mail and the Internet.

This is by no means a complete list of the communications arsenal made available to world media in the 20th century. I have mentioned nothing about the invention of the airplane and the jet, and, of course, the automobile, which have made travel, news gathering and dissemination so much faster and easier; the advances in photography, photojournalism and printing; the continuous improvements in the storage and retrieval of data, and the proliferation of databases.

The significance of this catalog is that all these innovations are today available in the remotest parts of the globe. They are being adopted worldwide at a faster and faster pace as the 20th century comes to a close.

As we face the 21st century, therefore, we find world media energized by the most astounding communications technology — gadgets that only science fiction writers were dreaming of at the turn of the 20th century. How has the technological revolution affected media ownership and financing, their appearance and content, their audience, and their relationships with their own and with foreign governments?

Ownership and Financing

The most conspicuous changes in the world media in the last decade of the 20th century have occurred in the former Soviet Union and its allied Communist countries. The disintegration of this vast empire has resulted in a complete revamping of its mass media systems. . . . Newspapers in Russia, which used to cost a quarter at the official rate of exchange, are much more expensive today — how much more expensive varies from day to day. With sky-high inflation, no paper publishes its price. [Rising prices have] affected

newspaper and magazine readership. Before the dissolution of the Communist empire, the circulations of the four major national newspapers were between eight and ten million each. *Pravda,* the Communist party paper, today has a circulation of less than 200,000, and for a time its survival hung in the balance. A Greek businessman holds a 55 percent interest in this 72-year-old paper. Many of its staffers have quit and its archives and other properties are being sold.

Trud, no longer the labor union paper, now claims a circulation of 1.5 million. Similarly, *Izvestia,* the voice of the Soviet government, has dropped in sales to about half a million. The former Communist youth paper, *Komsomolskaya Pravda,* still boasts a relatively high readership of about two million.

Newspapers in Russia are finding it hard to make ends meet. During 1993, the Russian government allocated 11 billion rubles (some sources say 111 billion) to support newspapers and magazines. In the last half of 1994, 64 billion rubles were made available for subsidies, with a commission made up of journalists, politicians and government officials determining which publications are to receive aid. Priority is being given to the "universally recognized" periodicals. (Since the ruble went from .9 rubles to the dollar under Soviet rule to 2,000 rubles to the dollar in June 1994 and almost 4,000 in October 1994, these figures have only symbolic meaning.)

But the press in Russia and the former Communist countries are not alone in experiencing difficulties. In 1993, the French government donated 200 million francs as emergency aid to its newspapers, and the publishing conglomerate, Hachette, has been absorbing the mounting losses from French television. In most developing countries, where newspapers generally are unable to cover their publishing expenses through the sale of advertising space, governments step in with subsidies. Of course, almost invariably, support goes to the papers favored by the government.

Newspapers generally cannot support themselves solely through street sales and subscriptions. Marshall Field's New York paper, *PM,* tried it in the 1940s and failed. In fact, newspapers have been known to engage in price wars to increase their circulations so that they can charge more for advertising space. The *Times* of London and the *Sun,* two of Rupert Murdoch's newspapers, lowered their price from 25 to 20 pence in 1993. The London *Daily Mirror* responded by cutting its price from 27 to 10 pence. Circulations went up for these newspapers, according to *The New York Times.*

Advertising revenue is the answer, but it is not always easy to come by. Even in developed countries, the amount of advertising is a function of economic fluctuations and as in France in recent years, the press may fall on hard times when the economy is sluggish. Of course, the drop in newspaper circulations in France is part of a worldwide trend that includes the United States. Daily circulations in the U.S. were the lowest in 1993 (the most recent figures available) since 1960, dropping steadily from their peak in 1984.

Economic factors create the greatest diversities in the world's media. Countries where the media have a commercial base through advertising have a bold press that can stand up to government and even to individual businesses. In countries where the press has no capital base but is dependent on the government for its revenues, newsprint, equipment, access to information and the license to publish, mass media cannot serve as a watchdog over government or public and private institutions. In such countries, the press is viewed as a rival source of authority.

Even when the march of events have in recent years forced Communist and Third World governments to relinquish their stranglehold on the press, there is a reluctance to let go completely. The Russian parliament, for example, still feels it has the right to dictate to journalists the content of the media, according to a July 1994 article in *Izvestia.*

The parliament also has been planning to publish a national magazine and has set up its own television station to make sure its point of view gets to the public. Although, as mentioned, an impartial commission is supposed to allocate subsidies to needy media, editors successfully appeal to the President and the Prime Minister to intercede in their behalf.

Some Russians have raised the question of the inconsistency of government subsidies and press freedom. They would rather have a complete separation of mass media and government, with the government buying time and space from the media. On the other hand, many Russians are more bothered when commercial, financial and industrial groups finance the media than when the government does. Business interests are just not trusted in the former Communist states.

Meanwhile, journalists are being harassed and threatened in many former Communist and Third World countries. In October 1994, an investigative reporter in Moscow, who was looking into military corruption, was killed by a bomb placed in his briefcase. Violence, threats and jail sentences are also common against journalists in some Latin American, Asian and African countries.

Media Types

Another way of categorizing the media is whether their purpose is mainly to make a profit for their owners or mainly to give their owners power. A third type of medium supports a cause, such as a religious organization, an ethnic or sexual orientation group, or some other demographic interest. Very few media exist purely for the good of the community, although one might say that PBS (the Public Broadcasting Service in the U.S.) probably has such a function.

Power-seeking media (whether they are controlled by the government, a church, political party, labor union, business or wealthy individual) give the public what is "good for it," which almost invariably turns out to be what is good for the group or individual controlling the medium. Such media are seldom permitted to publish anything that is contrary to the controller's interests. On the other hand, since commercial media must make a profit, their content is generally limited to what the public is willing to pay for.

In the developed world, which comprises mostly North America, Western Europe, Japan, Australia, New Zealand, South Africa, and some of the countries on the Pacific rim, media are largely of the profit-seeking, commercially supported type. The media in many of the countries in the former Soviet sphere of influence, in Latin America, and in some African and Asian countries are attempting to establish themselves as profit-making, independent entities. This is especially true of printed media. Many are actively seeking advertising revenue. In Russia, for example, *Izvestia* started accepting ads in 1988 and by 1994 had begun to turn a profit. However, in countries where journalists' wages are low, as they are in former Communist and Third World countries, the temptation is great to accept bribes for publishing or refraining from publishing a story. And in some Latin American countries, journalists earn commissions on ads they solicit from the government departments they cover.

In order to become economically viable, *Izvestia* has had to close down most of its 42 foreign bureaus. By early 1994 it had only eight left. U.S. television networks, too, have had to cut back their foreign news bureaus. They try to cover all of Western Europe from a single base, generally London. Similarly, in many developing countries, cost-cutting has forced the media to reduce their staffs, which means less coverage of local news and more dependence on wire service and syndicated news. Of course, the larger the number of subscribers to a news service, the less it costs each individual subscriber. But clearly, depending on news services means there are fewer people who decide what is news, and

these people tend to come from five powerful countries.

While most countries have their own national news agencies, they can't afford to keep a correspondent in more than a few of the major world capitals. They buy the rest of the world's news from the Big Five international news services that have dominated the world's news media almost throughout the 20th century. The Associated Press of the U.S. and Reuters of Great Britain have been operating throughout the century. The French news agency, Agence France Presse, which succeeded Havas after World War II, was the first of the news services, having been founded in 1832, and is still very active. The Russian, for a time Soviet, agency, TASS, is now ITAR, and China's New China News Agency (Hsinhua) has pushed its way to global prominence in recent years, replacing America's second news service, United Press International, which went into bankruptcy in 1986.

In the meantime, media empires are being built by Rupert Murdoch of Australia, Hachette of France, Giancarlo Parretti of Italy, Time-Warner of the U.S., and Bertelsmann of Germany. These "lords of the global village," as media critic Ben Bagdikian calls them, "exert a homogenizing power over ideas, culture and commerce that affects populations larger than any in history. Neither Caesar, nor Hitler, Franklin Roosevelt nor any Pope, has commanded as much power to shape information on which so many people depend to make decisions. The media empires include newspapers, magazines, radio and television stations, book publishing and distribution outlets, audio and video tapes, data bases and syndicated news services."

To this must be added the incomparable impact of CNN's global television news service. Its importance became obvious at the outbreak of the Gulf War in 1991, which it covered as no wars have ever been covered before and which was watched simultaneously by all parties to the conflict. The power of TV in general and CNN is particular is unquestionable. Its coverage of starving children in Somalia resulted in massive economic and later military aid being sent by the U.S. and other countries. And it was the picture of a dead American soldier being dragged through the streets of Mogadishu that forced the U.S. government to withdraw its troops.

CNN has become an important channel for communicating with ambassadors abroad and in the conduct of diplomacy. A U.S. policy maker, for example, told the *Washington Post* that his first consideration on hearing about the attempted coup against President Gorbachev in 1991 was not how to send instructions by the usual electronic mail to U.S. diplomats abroad. To let them know how the State Department reacted to the news, his first thought was how to get a statement to CNN that would shape the response of all the allies. Through CNN, he thought, the message would also get to Yeltsin.

Global Impact

Mass produced news has its pros and cons. On the one hand, exposure to the same news and entertainment creates a sense of community. The world becomes part of a global village, sharing triumphs such as the conquest of space or the wedding of a charming prince and princess, and disasters, such as wars, an earthquake, people starving or being massacred. One cannot overemphasize the importance of common experiences through joint spectatorship and the bonding effect of language.

English is fast becoming a global language because of the sheer universality of English-language entertainment, news programs, English-based technology, databases, and commercial goods and services. International airline pilots and ship's captains must know English to earn their licenses. To get ahead in international commerce and politics, one must have a good working knowledge of English.

On the other hand, many people are concerned about the potential loss of their cultural identity. They speak of "cultural imperialism," "dependence" and "electronic colonialism," since mass produced entertainment and news are presented mostly from the viewpoint of wealthy, developed countries, with their values as the guiding principle. Constant exposure to such communication raises the expectations, and also the frustrations, of less developed or wealthy peoples.

Media Content

In an earlier edition of *Media/Reader*, I pointed out that if you were to take a trip around the world, you would be struck by how similar newspapers and magazines look everywhere, how familiar television is and radio programs sound, even if the languages are unintelligible. That is still true — if anything, truer than it has ever been.

At the same time, the last decade of the 20th century finds the printed media losing out to the electronic or broadcast media. Newspaper circulations have been dropping everywhere, while television has been taking over as the principal source of news and entertainment in an ever increasing number of countries. In the United States, for example, 50 percent of the population say they get all their news from television and two-thirds say they get most of it from TV.

Since American news values tend to focus on conflict and problems rather than on solutions and resolutions, and in the light of the powerful influence of U.S. technology on world media, what has been the effect of American journalism on the content of the press in other countries? First, one should emphasize that by no means do all developed countries have the same news values as the U.S. Observers, for example, noted that at a recent economic summit in Japan, the Japanese media focused on consensus and avoided criticizing leaders, while U.S. media focused on conflict.

Secondly, European journalism—especially in French- and German-speaking countries and in what was once in the Soviet sphere of influence—literary style, erudition, authority and polish are still valued over reporting skills. But having said that, there appears to be a growing tendency worldwide to present more facts and less polemics and propaganda. In trying to appeal to as large an audience as possible in the effort to become solvent, media are forced to tone down their advocacy of partisan opinions. Presenting the facts "objectively" makes fewer enemies among readers and advertisers, as the American press has found. Of course, there also is more sensationalism in the world's press than there used to be because the media have discovered that sensationalizing coverage attracts a larger audience.

If there are important differences in the content of the world's press, they are due in part to the different emphasis that is placed on the individual versus the collective in determining news values. These range all the way from the strong individualism of Americans to the deep-rooted collectivism of, say, the Chinese. News is viewed in terms of the individual or the collective, and it varies in treatment and content in different parts of the world. While this is changing because of the trend toward centralized news gathering, English-speaking countries tend to be the most individualistic and Asian countries, especially the former and present Communist countries, are probably the most collective in outlook.

Press Freedom and Responsibility

Press diversity also lies in how different countries and cultures view the concept of press freedom. In Western countries it is generally viewed as a constraint on government, which cannot arbitrarily limit the right of people to speak out on any subject they like. Present and former Communist countries feel that this is an empty right. A more important consideration, people in these countries say, is whether they have the means to speak out, which the rich have in far greater measure then the poor.

Besides the freedom to speak and write, there is the question of responsibility. Who is responsible and to whom? The American belief is that both the press and the government are responsible to the people. The market is the barometer of whether the press is acting responsibly, according to this view. Also the press represents the people vis-à-vis the government. In the former Communist countries and many parts of the developing world on the other hand, the doctrine is that it is the government that represents the people and the press has no greater rights than the people.

Finally, countries differ in their view of the right to privacy. In the United States, the individual has the highest right to privacy, organized groups are next, with public officials having the least right to privacy. Many countries reverse this order.

Twentieth century technology and the ease of access and communication are rapidly changing the world. This will not remove competition and conflict; on the contrary, physical and psychological proximity may increase competitiveness and discord, at least in certain situations. But it also opens up the opportunity for understanding, friendship and cooperation. The village, whether global or parochial, has never been a model of constant and permanent goodwill. But it has the potential for greater understanding and common effort.

"World Media at Century's End," by L. John Martin. Article written for this text.

PERSPECTIVE 16-2

Regulated Speech

In 1988, Canada banned all billboard, print, and broadcast advertising for cigarettes. The Tobacco Products Control Act was part of a larger strategy to reduce smoking, especially among young people. The implications of the ad ban, and the results, are discussed in this article by Andrew Wolfson from the Louisville *Courier-Journal*.

Consider:

1. While the Tobacco Products Control Act banned billboard, print, and broadcast advertising for cigarettes, some types of promotional activities are still allowed. What are they?

2. How has the ad ban changed the way tobacco manufacturers market their products in Canada, according to Wolfson?

3. Do you think a similar ad ban would be successful in the United States? Why? Why not?

Canada's Ad Ban Puts Cigarettes Out of Sight

Andrew Wolfson

You notice it first at the airport, which is smoke-free, of course. There are billboards for Buick Regals and Tony Roma Ribs, but no advertising for cigarettes.

Ditto for Winnipeg's daily newspapers and for Canadian magazines like *Maclean's*.

What you see — or don't see — is the fruit of the Tobacco Products Control Act, which banned billboard, print, and broadcast advertising for cigarettes.

Enacted in 1988 as part of a broad strategy to reduce smoking, the sweeping legislation aims to protect the health of all Canadians and especially shield young people from inducements to smoke.

Even its staunchest supporters say the ban is weakened by a major loophole and that Canadians are still bombarded by advertising from the United States.

But health and government officials, and everyday Manitobans, say the ban has stripped smoking of some of its allure by eliminating image ads that depict smokers as sexy, successful, macho and athletic.

"They can't show a race car driver leaning against his Ferrari smoking a cigarette with two beautiful women draped all over him," said Dr. Richard Stanwick, a pediatrician who is Winnipeg's city health officer.

The ban's impact is still debated, but a 1992 British government study found that consumption had fallen 4 percent more than would have been expected from other anti-smoking measures.

If the measure reduced smoking deaths proportionately, anti-smoking groups say it would save the lives of four Canadians daily; similar results in the United States would save 46 lives a day.

The British study also found that advertising bans send a powerful health message to smokers — that their government truly believes smoking is dangerous. The fact that tobacco advertising is allowed at all may suggest that smoking "cannot truly have dangerous effects or the government would ban it," the report said.

The Canadian Tobacco Manufacturers' Council insists the ban has had little or no impact on smoking rates; the group's president, Rob Parker, cites figures that he says show the rate of decline has actually slowed the ban's enactment.

Canada's three major cigarette makers — like their American counterparts — say advertising is designed to instill brand loyalty or encourage smokers of competing brands to switch. After a 14-month trial in Quebec, a judge agreed, advertising increased consumption. An appellate court reinstated the ban anyway, and the case will be argued in November [1994] before Canada's Supreme Court.*

Even if cigarette makers don't set out to attract new smokers, the British study said it is quite possible that advertising recruits some anyway — and that they will most likely be teenagers.

In Manitoba, veteran smokers who have tried to quit say that passing up cigarettes is easier without constant messages that smoking is fun and relaxing. "I still get yearnings, and the less exposure the better," said Rick

Kramble, 40, a park ranger who last year quit a pack-a-day habit.

Still, Manitobans say they are inevitably exposed to cigarette advertising in American magazines. "I see ads with women smoking Kool in my mother's magazines," said Spencer Borland, 16, an occasional smoker. "And they look cool."

The ban's supporters also concede that memories of ad images may not fade for a generation. "If you banned all cigarette advertising in the U.S. today, people tomorrow would still know who the Marlboro man is, and they still would know a year from now," said David Sweanor, senior counsel for Canada's Non-Smokers' Rights Association.

The widest breach in Canada's advertising ban is an exemption that allows manufacturers to sponsor sporting and cultural events. The law allows sponsorships in corporate names only, but health groups say tobacco companies have flouted the spirit of the law by incorporating their brand names into shell companies that sponsor events.

For instance, Imperial Tobacco — the sister company of Louisville's Brown & Williamson Tobacco Corp. — created Player's Ltd. Racing, after its leading brand. With the same colors and lettering as on a Player's cigarette pack, "Player's Ltd. Racing" adorns the scoreboard at Winnipeg Stadium, home of the Blue Bombers pro football team, and is featured on billboards depicting hot racing cars.

The effort appears to have paid off on smokers such as 19-year-old Todd Trumback, who said he started smoking Player's Lights after seeing a Player's racing car at a Winnipeg shopping mall. "It was kind of cool seeing a fast car painted all blue, like a Player's pack," he said.

Manufacturers say the sponsorship ads — which cannot show cigarettes or smokers — aren't aimed at children. But the Canadian Council on Smoking and Health says that Player's ads are posted at stadiums across Canada and that ads for "Matinee Ltd.

Fashion Foundation," which tout an Imperial brand popular among women, were placed on Ottawa transit buses that carry 100,000 school children a day.

Parker, the president of the manufacturers' group, says that sponsorships help sustain art and athletics in Canada and that manufacturers obey the law.

Industry analyst Jacques Kavafian of Montreal's Levesque Beauvien said the ban has made it harder for companies to introduce new brands but has had no impact on profits, which he said have been substantial in recent years.

Other businesses that lobbied fiercely against the ban also say it has had little adverse effect.

Canada's billboard industry quickly replaced $20 million in lost cigarette revenues with ads for food, soap, toothpaste and beer, said Robert Reaume, president of the Outdoor Advertising Association of Canada.

The country's ad agencies and media firms haven't suffered significantly either, said Suzanne Keeler, vice president of the Canadian Advertising Foundation. "There was concern . . . that if ads for this product are banned, it would lead to other bans." So far, that hasn't happened, she said.

Brian Segal, publisher of *Maclean's* and chairman of Magazines Canada, which represents the nation's 25 largest magazines, said the ban "wasn't calamitous."

Notwithstanding the tobacco industry's claims that the ban would trample on free speech, the British government study said it actually allows magazines once dependent on cigarette advertising to write more freely about smoking and health.

*Note: The advertising ban remained in place as of the June 1995 publication date deadline for *Media/Reader.*

Worldwide Audiences

In this article from the *Atlanta Constitution,* Charles Haddad details the challenges facing Turner Broadcasting's attempt to launch an international TV network. Turner Broadcasting, based in Atlanta, has expanded its audience by bringing American entertainment overseas. Global television, however, faces many cultural, economic, and technological barriers.

Consider:

1. List and explain the *economic* obstacles that Turner Broadcasting must overcome to establish a truly global television network, according to Haddad.

2. List and explain the *cultural* obstacles that Turner Broadcasting faces. List and explain the technological obstacles.

3. With so many obstacles, why is Turner willing to take the risks?

Entertaining the World from London:

Turner Broadcasting's Push: Millions of International TV Viewers Are at Stake, But the Going Isn't Easy

Charles Haddad

It's 2 P.M. and business executives stand on the curb outside the Hog's Head pub holding glasses of warm dark beer.

They look across the street into a window display of new televisions, which all show Fred Flintstone sliding down a dinosaur into his foot-pedaled car.

In unison, the businessmen raise their glasses of beer and shout, "Cheers."

While their taste in beer—when they drink it—may differ, Europeans share Americans' taste in popular entertainment. And that provides a tremendous opportunity for Atlanta-based Turner Broadcasting System Inc.

As owner of one of the world's largest libraries of TV cartoons and movies, no company is better positioned than Turner Broadcasting to slake a European thirst for mass TV entertainment. And doing so offers Turner Broadcasting's best opportunity for growth in coming years.

"We envision a series of networks that circle the globe," says Terence F. McGuirk, an executive vice president who is considered Turner Broadcasting's second-in-command. "We want to be in every TV market."

The company is well on its way to meeting that goal, but it will not be without cost.

[In 1993] it had a $40 million operating loss spent on starting and expanding new entertainment channels in Latin America and Europe. The company will roll out its entertainment programming in Asia [in October 1994].

Already, Turner Broadcasting's new international channels have attracted nearly 24 million viewers. International sales account for about 14 percent — or $300 million — of the company's total revenue of nearly $2 billion.

That's a good start, but company officials are the first to concede that they have a long way to go before their TNT and Cartoon Network channels become truly international.

The statistics are daunting. There are 860 million homes with televisions worldwide. Right now, Turner Broadcasting's entertainment programming is in less than 3 percent of those.

A Toe in the Water

"Compared to other American companies, like Coca-Cola Co., we have just stuck our toe in the international market," says William I. Grumbles, Jr., Turner Broadcasting's vice president for worldwide distribution.

Every one of Turner Broadcasting's international homes has been hard won. Because few foreign newspapers list Turner Broadcasting's shows, it's difficult for Europeans to know what's available.

In France, Turner Broadcasting has to start over from scratch because of a spat with government officials. The French feared Turner Broadcasting would swamp their TV market with U.S. shows, driving out indigenous programmers.

And in Germany, the company lost $19 million [in 1993] on a German-language news channel.

Turner Broadcasting gave up a 50 percent stake in what might become one of Russia's first networklike TV channels. Its Russian partner, uncomfortable with Turner Broad-

casting's large stake, asked the company to bow out. The company agreed because of the risk factor.

Turner Broadcasting's top executives are unshaken by these setbacks. They never expected international expansion to be easy. The effort, however, has been classic Turner.

"Historically, we've tried to be ahead of the curve," says McGuirk. "We try to get into markets before others."

And that means spending a lot of money upfront and forgoing a quick profit. "I see ourselves turning the corner in three to five years," says Ross Portugeis, an executive vice president leading entertainment's international expansion.

In essence, the company's entertainment channels are riding on the coattails of CNN, the 24-hour news channel Turner Broadcasting took worldwide in 1985.

[In 1994], CNN is proving the long-term value of international expansion. After years of losses, the international arm, CNNI, has become highly profitable. It's expected to earn between $50 million and $60 million on $113 million in revenue, says W. Thomas Johnson, the executive vice president heading CNN. Four years ago [in 1990], CNNI lost $3.12 million on revenue of $13.6 million.

Turner Broadcasting's entertainment channels, however, face a different challenge from that of CNN. The news channel needed only the small international audience that spoke English and was interested in world affairs.

"CNN captures only .001 percent of the world ad market," says Robert Ross, president of Turner International Ltd., which sells and markets the company's channels outside the United States.

In contrast, Ross explains, entertainment programming won't succeed without a broad advertising base and a mass audience.

At first glance, selling Europeans American entertainment seems a breeze. American culture is everywhere in Europe.

London's subways are covered in imitation American gang graffiti. The "Flintstones" movie is selling out across the continent. And German bookstores carry "Von Winde Wermecht" ("Gone With the Wind").

First impressions are deceptive, though. In Germany, one of the most popular TV shows is something called "Literary Quartet" — something that wouldn't even show up in American ratings. "Literary Quartet" features a panel of book critics discussing literature.

Humor is also different. Turner Broadcasting's most popular cartoon in Europe is "Richie Rich," about a kindhearted rich kid. The show has almost no U.S. following.

The Scandinavians like Richie because no one gets hit in the head every few minutes. "We were an assault on the brains of the Scandinavians when we first launched," says Finn Arnesen, TNT/Cartoon's associate director of programming. "We had to cut out some violent scenes and slow down the pace for them."

Language Barriers

While English is widely spoken among the elite, that is not true among the majority of Europeans. Yet this is exactly the audience Turner Broadcasting is trying to reach.

"It would be foolish to think that, when a Frenchman or German goes home at night, he wants to watch entertainment in anything other than his own language," says Mark Rudolph, managing director of Turner International's London office.

Turner Broadcasting is not the only programmer vying for the European market. Every major company, from NBC to the Atlanta-based Weather Channel, is trying to sell its shows overseas.

"The competition is among U.S. companies — not against local channels," says Ross. Among the competitors are such well-known U.S. programmers as Nickelodeon, MTV and HBO.

American programmers are fighting over a much smaller pie than in the United States, where TV ad sales total about $22 billion annually. Outside the United States, TV ad sales total $21 billion a year, with $20 billion of that in Western Europe.

But there is greater opportunity for subscriber growth.

While still growing, the U.S. cable TV market has slowed sharply from the unprecedented surge of the 1970s and 1980s.

With Turner Broadcasting's top channels attracting 60 million-plus subscribers, "We've saturated the [U.S.] market," says Robe Thalman, senior vice president of Turner International Network Sales.

Turner Broadcasting is going international at a time of rapid change in world TV markets. Longtime government control of television is giving way to private ownership. That in turn has triggered a boom in the demand for programming.

Few entertainment companies have more programming than Turner Broadcasting. It controls a library of 3,400 movies and 3,500 half-hour cartoons.

The company can offer its library through an already vast distribution, marketing and sales organization. Ross' international division has more than 200 employees in 11 different places. The London office alone includes 15 different nationalities.

"We can expand our franchises at little incremental cost," says McGuirk.

While needing a lot of viewers, Turner Broadcasting doesn't need them all from one place. Instead, the company is trying to get a 2 percent market share from a hundred different markets.

"We don't need a 14 rating in Sri Lanka or an 8 in Germany," says Ross. "A little bit from here and a little bit from there will make us successful."

Nowhere is that strategy more evident than in Europe, where Turner Broadcasting is now putting most of its resources. [In 1993] the company launched the TNT/Cartoon network, a 24-hour channel that features cartoons during the day and movies at night. The fare differs little from Turner Broadcasting's TNT and Cartoon Network cable channels.

TNT/Cartoon has headquarters in a fashionable but rundown London neighborhood. Its headquarters is beside an old canal that hundreds of years ago was the international trade highway in northern Europe.

[In 1994], TNT/Cartoon ships its product out via satellite and cable wire. The product consists of American movies and cartoons processed for European tastes.

Stopping the Clobbering

While not a factory, TNT/Cartoon is factory-like. Instead of looms, workers use Macintosh computers. They make Porky Pig speak Swedish and stop Tom from clobbering Jerry too much.

From a corner wall, a giant black and white photo of Chairman Ted smiles down benevolently.

Turner has good reason to smile. So far, Europeans appear to like what his entertainment processing factory is beaming out. An independent survey recently commissioned by the company showed Turner's movies and cartoons are favorites among those who receive them.

"In France, we like to say that the most popular channel in Europe is the French-speaking TNT/Cartoon," says Thierry Mielo, former adviser to the French minister of communications.

Europeans may like TNT/Cartoon, but many of them have a hard time getting it. Imagine if every U.S. state were a separate country, each with its own language, telecommunications laws and own way of receiving TV shows. That's what much of Europe and the former Soviet Union are like today.

In France, for example, only 161,000 people have cable TV. Germany, however, has wired nearly 40 percent of its homes with cable.

Different technologies in different countries have required Turner Broadcasting to learn how to ship its programming via any means possible, including cable, satellite and over-the-air broadcast.

Transmission, though, is the least of Turner Broadcasting's distribution problems.

In Germany, for example, the company must show its cartoons only in English, which is not widely spoken. The German rights to these cartoons were sold years ago.

Worse yet, commercial TV as Americans know it is young and unsteady in Germany. There's only one profitable commercial channel, RTL Plus. The same is true across Europe.

In France, for example, government officials fear U.S. television will drown out French shows. They wanted Turner Broadcasting to guarantee up to 50 percent of its shows were French. The company balked.

Former French Communications Minister Alain Carignon said he would monitor Turner Broadcasting's channel. Soon after, Turner executive Rudolph was quoted in a French newspaper attacking Carignon.

Rudolph denied the quote, but the damage was done. The French government slowed Turner Broadcasting's entry to a crawl. "We've had to start all over again in France," says Grumbles. [In 1994], the company has only 178,000 of France's 20 million-plus TV viewers.

Turner Broadcasting is trying to make amends. It created Turner Production SA, which will provide Euro-French programming in France. Its seven-member board includes three Frenchmen, including a nephew of former French leader Charles de Gaulle.

"Cultural Imperialism"

"France is not unique," says Grumbles. "Cultural imperialism is an issue in many countries and it has to be dealt with."

Many Europeans agree. The continent seems to be of two minds when it comes to U.S. television.

"It's garbage," says Lars Bergman, a Swedish student at Berlin University. "American television is ruining the minds of our children and drowning out Europe's grand artistic tradition."

Bergman holds forth at an outdoor pub in east Berlin. He's surrounded by other students, who nod and applaud.

Yet moments later, the students — from Holland, Denmark and Germany — fondly reminisce about growing up with the "Flintstones."

"Yabba-dabba-doo," Bergman shouts, and the pub explodes in knowing laughter.

"Entertaining the World from London: Turner Broadcasting's Push: Millions of International TV Viewers Are at Stake, But the Going Isn't Easy," by Charles Haddad, *Atlanta Constitution*, September 11, 1994. Dow//Quest Story ID: 0000356023DC. Reprinted with permission from *The Atlanta Journal* and *The Atlanta Constitution*.

Journalists and the Government

In this article, written in 1990, John R. MacArthur describes the attitude about Western journalistic values he confronted on a visit to Uganda. MacArthur, publisher of *Harper's* magazine, found that the greatest criticism was that Westerners tend to treat Ugandans with "neocolonial condescension," judging the country according to Western ideals.

Consider:

1. How do the journalistic values that MacArthur describes in Uganda differ from Western values? Which values seem to work best for Uganda?

2. Do you agree with Englishman William Pike, who told MacArthur, "You're having the evolution of press freedom here. I don't think you can go from complete dictatorship and terror to pure democracy overnight." Why? Why not?

3. How does government control of broadcast signals affect what is broadcast? How do the media adapt to changing governments, according to MacArthur?

Slouching Toward Freedom in Uganda

John R. MacArthur

Toward the end of my week-long stay in Uganda [in the fall of 1990], a ferocious storm swept away the equatorial torpor that had enveloped Kampala since my arrival, announcing the start of the rainy season. Near my hotel the wind ripped an enormous branch off a tree, and later I learned that a young boy had been killed by falling debris at his grammar school.

Untouched by the storm was a nearby construction crane. Nothing odd about that,

I thought, given the state of modern technology. Except that this crane has been standing in the same empty pit for more than 15 years, awaiting materials that will never arrive and surveying an economy so collapsed that no one can afford to remove it.

Amid such ruinous poverty — Uganda's annual per capita income is $282 — it seemed ungracious to carp about government censorship and the harassment of journalists, which was the purpose of my visit on behalf of the

Committee to Protect Journalists (CPJ). Surely a country that has endured the hideously violent regimes of Idi Amin and Milton Obote and now suffers from an AIDS epidemic of terrifying proportions should for a time be spared the earnest entreaties of free-press activists. Uganda, after all, has been relatively peaceful [since 1986] under President Yoweri Museveni's vaguely socialist National Resistance Movement (NRM).

And in some ways the press in Uganda, though ragged in appearance, is freer and livelier than in neighboring Kenya, where the one-party government of President Daniel Arap Moi brooks less criticism than Museveni's single-party state.

Yet, to some of the Africans I've met, there are more annoying things one can do than protest the censorship and imprisonment of journalists in disabled nations like Uganda. The greater sin committed by Western visitors is neocolonial condescension: "Your country," goes the *mzungu* (white person) cliché, "is too primitive (illiterate, unstable, tribally divided, poor, corrupt, pathetic, etc.) to enjoy the fruits of liberty." As the exiled Kenyan dissident Gibson Kamau Kuria told a gathering in New York [in the] summer [of 1990], "The British treat us like children, and the Americans feel too sorry for us to treat us like adults."

These days, the talk of Kampala's popular Speke Hotel cafe remains the government's seemingly endless vendetta against three journalists who dared ask impertinent questions of visiting Zambian President Kenneth Kaunda at a press conference in Entebbe in January 1990. Hussein Abdi Hassan, a stringer for the BBC's Kiswahili service, wondered aloud about the failure of the Zambian authorities to charge one of Kaunda's sons with the murder of a 20-year-old woman, said to be a girlfriend who quarreled with the son, Kambarage, over his impending marriage to another woman. (He has since been charged.) Festo Ebongu of the government's own newspaper, *New Vision,*

wanted to know how Kaunda's anti-apartheid rhetoric squared with Zambia's business ties to South Africa. And Alfred Okware of *Newsdesk* magazine asked whether it wasn't time for the aging Kaunda to let a younger man take over.

Outraged by the boldness of his national press corps, Museveni had the reporters prosecuted and detained under a colonial-era defamation law designed to protect visiting dignitaries from unpleasantness. However, a magistrate and then a high-court judge dismissed the charges, in part on the grounds that the law refers to published defamation. Thus, the cases appeared to be dying natural deaths — the journalists were all free on bail or police bond — when my CPJ colleague, Kim Brice, and I asked Uganda's attorney general, George W. Kanyeihamba, about press censorship.

We expected polite assurances that we had no cause to question the impartiality of the legal system. To our surprise, Kanyeihamba announced the government's intention to appeal the latest dismissal.

"We are not interested in punishing these journalists," he said with a smile. "But it's imperative that we reestablish the rule of law." Conviction could result in prison sentences of three years.

With faint irony Kanyeihamba explained that the chief magistrate, Hensley Okalebo, had perhaps acted out of ignorance when he dismissed the charges against Okware and Ebongu because "he might have been missing certain volumes of the Ugandan penal code." Against the shabby backdrop of the attorney general's office, and given the obvious paucity of texts in his own law library, this theory almost seemed plausible. But then I remembered that Okalebo had been promptly transferred "upcountry" after the dismissal.

As we left, Kanyeihamba offered his card, with apologies, for he hadn't one that identified him as a government official. A business card with the name of his farm would have to do. Uganda, I was reminded, lacks virtually everything.

Our encounter with the nation's top legal officer might seem slightly comical if it weren't for the chilling effect the prosecutions have had on what passes for the opposition press. Incredibly, the *Weekly Topic* manages to function as the nation's most independent, effective and professional paper, even though it's owned by two government ministers — including the minister of information — and a former minister. Time and again, when I expressed astonishment at this arrangement, people of every political stripe would say that the *Topic* really *was* fairly responsible and that its owners viewed it as a business investment best not tampered with.

But *Topic*'s journalists still have to tread lightly, as evidenced by the frantic killing of a story last September. The editors were planning to run a brief item on the Zambian government's decision in May to amend the mandatory death penalty for murderers, granting judges discretion in sentencing based on the "social class" of the convict. The piece was slated for the front page under the headline "Zambia's new murder laws for the rich" and strongly suggested that the only purpose of the change was to protect Kambarage Kaunda.

This was tough stuff, given the government's response the last time the press disturbed Kaunda. But the night the issue was to close, and after most of the staff had gone home, word filtered to the newsroom that Kaunda was scheduled to arrive in Entebbe the next day for a meeting of the Organization of African Unity, now chaired by Museveni. The most senior editor who could be reached (few Ugandans have working phones) rushed to the plant to stop the press and found a truck loaded with freshly printing newspapers preparing to leave. The delivery was aborted in time to avert the likely jailing of several staff members. A silly filler about elephants was substituted, and the paper put back on press. When one of *Topic*'s

owners found out about the offending article, he demanded the firing of Richard Tebere, an assistant night editor who was on duty at the time. But after the entire staff threatened to resign in protest, management settled for a brief suspension.

Sometimes the president himself gives reporters helpful reminders of their limits. One of them told me that during a visit by Nigerian President Ibrahim Babangida in late September [1990] — shortly after the execution of 27 alleged coup plotters in Lagos — Museveni warned journalists not to repeat their performance with Kaunda.

"If you want to ask embarrassing questions," he reportedly said, "buy a ticket to Lagos and ask them there."

This was not your typical Amnesty International horror story, and compared with Amin, who reportedly killed people he dreamed about, Museveni is a paragon of restraint. No one is keener to promote this point of view than William Pike, the Englishman who edits the government's *New Vision*. My curiosity about Pike had been growing as I heard one journalist after another assail or praise him. Either Pike was a neo-colonial freebooter or he was the crusading friend of the revolution who had brought professional standards to Ugandan journalism.

Tall, bearded and brimming with rationalizations, Pike is a study in contradictions: white editor of a black newspaper; "progressive" journalist required to espouse the government line in editorials, no matter how absurd or reactionary; an egalitarian who manages his staff with evident but possibly unconscious condescension.

Our interview took place at the Lido Beach, a decrepit cafe near the Entebbe airport on the shore of Lake Victoria. To enter we had to pass through a swarm of lake flies so thick you had to take care not to swallow one. Pike and his American wife, Catherine Watson, were tired after a long flight from London but friendly enough and quite forthcoming. Accompanying us was

New Vision Associate Editor Perez Owori, Pike's chief aide.

We took a table outdoors, and for the first time on my trip I found myself appreciating the beauty of Uganda. A warm wind had whipped up whitecaps on the lake, and I was temporarily able to forget the country's oppressive shabbiness. To my great relief I would be leaving that afternoon and was very much in the mood to be seduced by Pike's explications. Perhaps, also, I was acquiring the sense of superiority the British, and later the Americans, cultivated to keep out the strangeness of primitive surroundings. Here at last was someone who could explain things in terms I would understand.

I'm afraid this was colonial parody at best. Pike's view of Uganda did little to relieve my discomfort. He had the humorless, distracted air of an ideologue, rarely looking at the person he was addressing, and I'm not sure he realized how incongruous his positions sounded.

Pike met Museveni in 1984, when he was reporting in Africa for London-based *South Magazine*. He later predicted the NRM's eventual triumph over the government of Major General Tito Okello. The NRM, grateful for the advance publicity, asked Pike to revive the moribund government daily, renamed *New Vision*. Pike took over in May 1986 and put out the first edition on a used Soviet press, which may explain the somewhat muddy look of the paper today.

Pike said he accepted the post for reasons of "solidarity" with the NRM and because he'd always wanted to return to Africa. Born in Tanzania in 1952, he moved with his family to England when he was seven.

"It's hard to get a proper job in Africa," he remarked, and editing *New Vision* was a proper job. "They [the NRM] just wanted a newspaper that was accurate and objective and in accordance with NRM principles. They wanted it progressive, anti-contra for example, and anti-corruption. They thought I might have a better perspective as an outsider."

I asked how this was possible given any government's tendency to cover up its mistakes and corruption. No such problem, said Pike. *New Vision* was an "independent" enterprise that received no subsidy from the government.

After four years in business, *New Vision* was still exposing corruption, Pike told me. Witness the lead story of that day's paper: "Minister linked to shady chimps deal." The story questioned the propriety of an unlicensed exchange of four Ugandan chimpanzees for a pair of Soviet tigers arranged by the deputy minister of tourism and wildlife, Wilson Nadiope.

To James Namakajo, president of the Uganda Journalists Association (UJA), Pike is nothing but "a paid agent of the government" who's in it for the money. According to Namakajo, who is publisher of *Africa Speaks* magazine, Pike gets £12,000 (about $20,000) a year paid into a U.K. account and an additional £9,600 in Ugandan currency, as well as a free car, house and plane tickets to and from London.

But Pike isn't just a mercenary like Amin's British apologist Bob Astles, Namakajo told me. "He's from a top public school in England. He used to be very nice and modest: Now he's become very pompous."

Pike didn't seem to take Namakajo's insults very seriously. He claims he receives only £7,000 a year "plus living expenses" and with a wave of his hand dismissed his antagonist as having once been in the employ of the CIA. (Like many press critics in Uganda, Namakajo, a successful businessman, has no lack of critics himself. His credibility isn't helped by the fact that the East African Journalists Association, which he also heads, has asked the government for rent-free office space in Kampala.)

Pike's and Namakajo's mutual antipathy erupted into a shouting match at the infamous Kaunda press conference, and for once in Uganda two versions of the same story more or less matched. Namakajo had in-sisted that Kaunda answer the question about stepping down in favor of a younger man *after* Museveni had intervened to protect Kaunda.

Kaunda reportedly replied, "People who think democracy is only for young people have cobwebs in their heads."

To Pike Namakajo's persistence went too far. "He publicly contradicted Museveni," he said. "It just can't work like that. The coun-try's not used to a free press. I said [to Na-makajo] 'if you continue to be so arrogant you'll get the press in trouble.' We started shouting at each other."

Pike said the president didn't prosecute Namakajo as he did the other journalists "for P.R. reasons." Cynics I spoke to said Musev-eni leaves the UJA president alone because Namakajo is in the pay of the government, a charge Namakajo denies. This is interesting and perhaps revealing given Namakajo's own cynical view of Museveni and Pike. Accord-ing to Namakajo, "Museveni will say to peo-ple, 'Everyone in Uganda is corrupt. What do you want me to do? If I made you a minister tomorrow, you'd be the same.'"

But it wasn't the ambiguity of Pike's rhetoric that interested me so much as its rad-ical relativism. The interview was almost over when I asked him about charges that *New Vision* soft-pedaled National Resistance Army (NRA) killings of civilians while exag-gerating guerrilla atrocities.

With chilling candor, he replied, "Maybe it's true that we soft-pedaled NRA atrocities. This is just tactical. But the information [about atrocities] *is* in the paper."

What about the defamation cases against the three journalists, including his own reporter?

"It *is* a trumped- up charge. They're [the government] just being pigheaded. The attorney general thought he'd gain favor with the president. But you know, there was no freedom of the press during the colonial period."

How did he feel about cases like that of Francis Odida, the former publisher of *Sun-day Review,* a now-defunct Kampala weekly, who spent seven months in notorious Luzira prison on charges of sedition and treason? Odida's articles had criticized the govern-ment's slaughter of poorly armed followers of Alice Lakwena, a messianic revolutionary leader whose Holy Spirit Mobile Force was routed in 1987.

"You do get upset in the short term," said Pike. "But there's no point in getting upset about just one thing like press freedom [when there are so many other problems]."

Well, in the short term, what did Pike do to help people like Odida or Festo Ebongu, a *New Vision* reporter jailed for 10 days in an eight-by-eight-foot cell with 25 other prisoners?

"Of course, we lobby behind the scenes," he said. "I'm pretty confident that Festo will be cleared, although Festo and Alfred [Ok-ware] are discriminated against for ethnic reasons because they're easterners and Abdi [Hassan] because he's ethnically Somali." (At press time, it did appear that the three prose-cutions would at last be dropped.)

Was he willing to place the editorial weight of *New Vision* behind efforts to free journalists or political prisoners?

"We run the Amnesty International press releases," he said, but "we have to follow the government line in editorials. It would be ab-surd for the government to publish a newspa-per that contradicted its policies."

I was becoming thoroughly confused by now, but Pike wasn't finished. He turned to the topic of press freedom and revolution in general.

"You're having the evolution of press freedom here," he explained. "It's a political struggle. We have to establish the boundaries and rights of the press. I don't think you can go from complete dictatorship and terror to pure democracy overnight." Evidently not. In December [1990] Pike fired a reporter who learned, to the government's embarrassment, that thousands of soldiers suffering from AIDS had been discharged with large "pensions."

It was time to go, but I wanted to know why the BBC had used Pike's wife, Catherine Watson, to profile Museveni after his election as OAU chairman. Given Pike's ties to the government, wasn't there a conflict of interest?

"That assumes William and I agree on everything," she said with annoyance. "The British aren't as uptight about these things. *The Christian Science Monitor* killed a piece I wrote because they thought there was such a conflict."

Our party broke up, and I decided to tour Entebbe until it was time for my plane to leave. A taxi driver in the beat-up old Toyota showed me the sights: the unkempt botanical garden where, Pike told me, the first Tarzan movie was filmed and monkeys still leap from tree to tree; the yacht club, where British expatriates were said to congregate (we couldn't get past the gate); and the old Entebbe airport, where the Israelis humiliated Amin and a crippled DC8 lies beached like something out of an apocalyptic Hollywood film.

At the new airport I paid the driver with thick wads of nearly worthless Ugandan shillings plus a few dollars and passed through five security checks to the cobwebbed departure lounge. If you sit still long enough, you find yourself flicking off spiders.

Except for the duty-free items for sale, nothing seemed to have changed in the waiting room since the airport was built in 1975, including the faded Sabena poster and a surreal herd of stuffed hippos, impalas and zebras.

Is there any hope for William Pike's hazy new vision of Uganda? I wondered. I recalled a visit with Faustin Misavnu, the director of programming for the Uganda Broadcasting Corporation. Several civil wars had taken their toll on UBC headquarters, whose poorly lit corridors, crumbling walkways and dangling electrical wires typified Kampala's public buildings. Soft-spoken and gentle, Misavnu had survived eight years in his job, through several violent changes of government. He carefully removed a well-worn UBC brochure from a locked cabinet, unwrapped its plastic cover and handed it to me. Printed in 1977, it was the most up-to-date history of the UBC available — and Misavnu's only copy.

He told me and my CPJ colleague that the soap opera "Another Life," produced by the U.S. Christian Broadcasting Network, was the most popular show in Uganda, and we chatted for a while about the difficulty of broadcasting on behalf of a "grudgingly helpful" government.

How had he escaped death? I asked. Why hadn't a trigger-happy guerrilla with show business ambitions taken a shot at him?

"The soldiers know that TV and radio people are better alive than dead," he replied. "Someone has to run the equipment."

And when the guerrillas are preparing to seize the broadcast tower, what does the news announcer say five minutes before the inevitable occurs?

"You put out the government line up to the last minute."

And five minutes after that?

Misavnu smiled wanly.

"Then you put out the new government line."

"Slouching Toward Freedom in Uganda," by John R. MacArthur, *Washington Journalism Review,* Vol. 13, No. 4, May 1991, pp. 35–38. Used with permission of *Washington Journalism Review.*

Opportunities in New Markets

Public Relations Journal reports that great opportunities for public relations companies are emerging in Latin America. In the following article, Jeffrey Sharlach presents a rundown of the growing potential for PR firms in Mexico, Argentina, Brazil, Chile, and Venezuela.

Consider:

1. Why is the growing trend toward "privatization" such an opportunity for public relations companies, according to Sharlach?

2. What role will the American media play in these new markets?

3. List the social and cultural factors that will influence the market for public relations in each of these five countries, according to Sharlach.

A New Era in Latin America: Free Markets Force Changes in Five Key Nations (Mexico, Argentina, Brazil, Chile, and Venezuela)

Jeffrey Sharlach

A new generation of leaders is taking hold of the political and business reins in Latin America. That means new public relations opportunities, both south of the Rio Grande and here in the United States. "Privatization" is the big word on everyone's lips from Mexico City down to Tierra del Fuego at the southern tip of Argentina, creating increased demand for business communications. The bulk of this growing demand is coming from companies that have had little, if any, contact with the media or the public in the past.

As free market economies become the rule rather than the exception in Latin America, the need for public relations services will grow at a faster pace than nearly any other area in the world today. "There's no question that Latin America will be an important focus of the world's multinational companies for marketing goods and services in the '90s," said Robert Siegmann, president of Latin American Marketing Communications, a two-year-old firm in New York which specializes in communications to and from Central and South America.

Poverty, however, is still an issue in this developing part of the world. Of the total population of 480 million, some 196 million people are classified as living in poverty, according to the United Nations. But organizations like the Inter-American Development Bank are joining forces with the United Nations Development Program (UNDP) and other government and business leaders to address the poverty issue and to make sure that the sweeping economic reforms being implemented in the region reach down to the impoverished.

Change Presents Opportunities

Privatization and free trade mean that companies which previously had no competition or never had to worry about their corporate reputations suddenly have to be concerned with what people think.

However, traditional media — newspapers and magazines — still don't reach the masses in many Latin American countries. "As a result you see increased interest in community relations and sponsorship activities that reach these people," Siegmann said. For instance, Pepsi-Cola spent millions of dollars to send pop star Michael Jackson on an eight-city tour of Latin American countries to promote its soft drinks, the New York Times reported in April [,1993].

Like everything else, the media landscape is changing rapidly too. For example, although terrorism has isolated Peru's business community from much of the world in recent years, satellite dishes and cable television bring foreign programming on dozens of channels from the United States and the rest of the world directly into the homes and offices of the educated and influential who live in Lima and its affluent suburbs. Even in the less economically developed countries of the region, electronic media is able to easily penetrate national boundaries. Satellite dishes, for example, currently sell in Brazil at a rate of 25,000 per month.

NBC and Fox are two U.S. television giants that have already announced plans to establish Latin American television networks.

MTV Latin America is reportedly gearing up for a launch in October [1993] with separate Spanish-language programming and regionally supported advertising. And MTV Brazil, which is getting ready to celebrate its third anniversary, now reaches nearly eight million households.

On the print side, a separate Latin American edition of *Fortune* magazine just hit the newsstands, joining English-language editions of *Time, Newsweek* and *Business Week* in the region. Although the circulations of these publications are small throughout Latin America, the audiences tend to be highly educated influentials and business people, making them important media targets for many public relations programs. Spanish translations of popular U.S. magazines are also available.

Future Looks Bright

Despite setbacks, Latin America's future looks bright. The trends toward privatization and democratic rule will not be reversed, most experts agree. Population estimates indicate that Latin America will represent a market of more than 500 million people by the year 2005.

And the increasingly unregulated print and broadcast media are gearing up to meet the huge future demands for information. Supplemented by the growth in new regional networks and communications media, that should create virtually limitless opportunities for public relations initiatives in a part of the world eager to hear what companies have to say.

Not a Single Market

It's just as tough to look at Latin America as a single market as it is to view Western Europe that way, regardless of the much-touted "1992" trade reforms across the Atlantic. "You're still dealing with different people, in many cases isolated from one another, with very different cultures, economies and politics," noted Flavio Valsani, former head of the Brazilian Public Relations Society and president of LVBA Comunicacao in Sao Paulo, one of Brazil's largest public relations firms.

Although there's not a country in Latin America that's not being impacted by sweeping economic and political reforms, most businesses tend to focus on five countries: Mexico, Argentina, Brazil, Chile and Venezuela. Here's a look at the business opportunities available in these countries.

Mexico

The closest Latin American neighbor to the United States, Mexico is the focus of much of the international business community's interest and was an early expansion market for U.S.-based multinationals. General Electric first began selling products in Mexico in 1896. Gillette has been a key player in the region for more than 60 years. And 3M, Dow Chemical and Procter & Gamble are all familiar names in Mexico. Mexican shoppers are starting to leave the traditional neighborhood merchants behind and head off to nearby Wal-Mart, Sears, Kmart and J.C. Penney stores.

Easy transportation links to the Southwestern United States and the pending North American Free Trade Agreement (NAFTA) mean tremendous opportunities for U.S.-Mexico trade. Eventually, it could mean the end of all existing restrictions on foreign ownership of banks, insurance companies, and securities firms in Mexico.

NAFTA will create a free-trade area which includes the United States, Canada and Mexico, making it the world's largest open market. In addition to eliminating trade barriers in agriculture, manufacturing and services among the three countries, NAFTA will also remove most import restrictions and more effectively protect intellectual property rights.

As currently drafted, NAFTA marks the first time in U.S. trade policy that a comprehensive trade agreement directly addresses environmental concerns, a development that should increase the need for savvy environmental communicators.

Beyond NAFTA, the individual Latin American countries are taking important steps to reduce or abolish the barriers that inhibit and restrict trade or investment among themselves. Roger Bensinger, president of Communications Interamericanas, one of Mexico City's oldest and largest public relations firms, has enjoyed impressive business growth [from September 1992 to September 1993]. "Mexico is now part of the global business environment, so it's essential to provide clients here with cost-effective communications programs reaching their target audiences," Bensinger said. "There's tremendous interest in the sort of strategic positioning, image management, and product support programs that were virtually unheard of here several years back."

Argentina

In many ways, Argentina has set the example for economic reform which has been followed by many other countries in Latin America. Government intervention in the private business sector has been sharply reduced under the government of President Carlos Saul Menem. State-owned companies have been privatized at a rapid rate and a legislative reform package, currently in its fifth year of implementation, has curtailed government subsidies to most industries.

Now privately owned, these companies are reaching out to investors and the general public using traditional public relations techniques. "Today, companies are very concerned about the public reputation of their products, services and image," said Mariel Joly, who heads Promocion Periodistica in Buenos Aires. Although the bulk of the public relations activity in Argentina tends to be marketing support, in recent years there has been considerable growth in the public affairs area, particularly in crisis and issues management. "Many of the newly privatized companies suffer from poor corporate images which they want to improve," said Joly.

Major multinationals have long been present in Argentina, but recently stepped-up investment means new opportunities. Exxon, for example, has just bid about $75 million to take over the previously state-run natural gas distribution system. Ford recently completed construction of an automobile parts assembly plant. And not long ago, Japan's NEC entered into a major telecommunications joint venture with Perez Companc, one of the country's largest industrial groups.

Argentina's labor movement, representing more than one-third of the national work force by some estimates, is a strong political and economic power that must be handled through effective employee and community relations programs. Although some of the U.S.-headquartered multinationals have exported employee and community affairs programs to their South American operations, local companies are not creating additional demand for programs that address their workers and communities.

Brazil

Brazil's huge population of nearly 160 million people (the sixth largest in the world) has nurtured the growth of a well-developed public relations industry. Many of the major international firms have long been represented in Brazil, considered to be the world's tenth-largest market. President Fernando Collor de Mello was forced out of office at the end of 1992 following an impeachment vote. But his successor, Itamar Franco, has indicated that he will continue many of the free-market reforms that Collor instituted to curb inflation.

The political changes, however, have not stopped multinational investment. Rhone-Poulenc is investing some $80 million to expand its chemical/fiber operations and is joining with Amoco, Hoechst, Akzo and other manufacturers to mount a countrywide public relations program to support the use of polyester, similar to the multimillion dollar public relations campaign run for many years by the Polyester Council in the United States.

Luiz Straunard Pimentel, director of marketing at Amoco do Brasil in San Paulo, says this is one of the first times that competing companies in Brazil have pooled their efforts in a joint campaign to enhance the image of a product. "I am confident that the good results of this program will inspire more companies operating in Brazil to support communications programs such as those which have run successfully elsewhere in the world," Pimentel said.

Chile

While Brazil's large population base at least provides the potential for self-sufficiency, Chile — with only 13 million people — has had to look outside of its own borders for economic growth. Although the groundwork had been laid by the military governments of the '70s and '80s, it was the switch to full democratic rule just three years ago (in March 1990) that opened the way for the huge success of Chile in the world community.

Today, Chile is often referred to as "The Switzerland of Latin America," for its concentration of banking and investment activities. Chilean business leaders have been fanning out to their Latin American neighbors, selling their services to other newly privatized industries seeking to compete effectively in the world marketplace.

[In 1992], Chile signed a free-trade agreement with Mexico. Chile was also one of the first countries in Latin America to sign an agreement in principle for the framework of a trade and investment pact with the United States.

Venezuela

Proximity to U.S. ports, vast oil reserves and open markets have helped Venezuela to develop one of the top performing economies in Latin America. But political instability following two coup attempts [in 1992], the president's resignation under threat of impeachment, and the resulting downturn in foreign investment have recently hindered economic progress.

Venezuela was a founding member of OPEC and until [1992's] coup attempts, had a history of political and economic stability that provided a strong infrastructure for development.

Now government and private efforts are under way to diversify and lessen the country's dependence on oil exports.

Tips for Doing Public Relations in Latin America

1. Work with local people who know the market and the media in the country you want to reach.

2. Use indigenous translators. Don't assume that someone in your office who speaks and writes Spanish learned in the United States, Spain or another Latin American country can communicate error-free in other countries. Materials must be sensitive to cultural differences and subtle linguistic changes.

3. Although the traditional afternoon siesta and mañana mentality are fast-disappearing as Latin America competes in the world marketplace, this is still a part of the world where people slow down to enjoy life. Try to understand this. Don't plan to rush out of a lunch meeting after an hour for your next appointment; your hosts may not have gotten around to opening their menus yet.

4. Be sure you have a concrete assignment, with budgets and deadlines confirmed in writing, before you start work. It can be easy to misinterpret Latin Americans' warmth and enthusiasm for a "go-ahead" when the deal really must be approved by layers of bureaucracy.

5. Keep an eye on business opportunities. Many people in Latin America are overflowing with optimism and enthusiasm. They believe this is their decade and that Latin America in the '90s will be the success story that Asia was in the '80s.

Advertising in Asia

This article describes the efforts of J. Walter Thompson (JWT), one of the world's largest advertising agencies, to establish a presence in Asia. To succeed, says Noreen O'Leary, the agency had to overcome many cultural, social, and political barriers.

Consider:

1. In the case study example of the creation of the International Wool Secretariat's logo, why did this marketing attempt fail? What could have made it succeed?

2. Why is consistency so important in the success of global advertising, according to Alan Fairnington?

3. List three barriers to developing a successful advertising campaign in Asia, and describe how JWT overcame these obstacles.

Playing the Asia Card

Noreen O'Leary

In 1986, J. Walter Thompson set out to introduce the concept of brands to China. JWT launched a major ad campaign promoting the International Wool Secretariat's three-spiral wool logo, one of the first international corporate symbols marketed to the Chinese people. The pitch was successful, alright. Within two years, the Woolmark logo has higher recall than Coca Cola, and all over China manufacturers began stamping the wool logo on everything — plastics, leather, even polyester.

"They didn't understand the meaning of the symbol obviously. But they knew it meant quality," laughs Grace Atkinson, JWT chairman of Greater China/Korea. "Before, people in China didn't even know what a brand was. They couldn't name a bar of soap. But once the big multinationals came in and talked about brands, the Chinese caught on quickly. They began to know Pierre Cardin and Yves St. Laurent. Suddenly, labels and brands became very important to them." From the bustling streets of Shanghai — where men often leave brand labels on the outside of their suits — to the sleepy tea-and-rice growing towns of rural China, consumers not only differentiate among brands these days, they demand them.

When Westerners think about the potential of Asia, it's usually in boxcar numbers — the hundreds of millions of TVs and washing machines yet to be sold in countries like China. But the human face of Asia's modern assimilation is far more subtle. Thanks in large part to De Beers, for instance, 85% of Japanese brides now wear a diamond ring — a new expression of love in a culture accustomed to arranged marriages. In China, consumers are increasingly filling their tea cups with java, making Nescafe the No. 1 coffee brand. Perhaps the most improbable sign of change comes from Vietnam, where [in May 1994] John Denver kicks off a concert tour, playing to crowds in the Hanoi Opera House.

For J. Walter Thompson, its long and continuous investment in the region has positioned it to cash in on that change. "Timing is absolutely critical," says Alan Fairnington, the president of JWT Asia Pacific, who oversees 43 offices in 24 cities. "We got into Korea too early and lost $3 million a year. At the same time, you can't afford to be late."

The timing seems just right for JWT these days. In 1993, JWT Asia Pacific accounted for 17% of the agency network's $876 million worldwide revenue. [In 1994] that contribution is expected to grow to 20%, with the region's offices boasting higher profit margins than their European counterparts. While other agencies like McCann-Erickson and Saatchi & Saatchi have individual market strongholds in Asia, JWT's offices rank among the top three in China, Hong Kong, Indonesia, Taiwan, Singapore, the Philippines, Pakistan, Vietnam and Sri Lanka. In the semi-closed markets of Japan and South Korea, Thompson is listed among the top three foreign agencies as well. JWT once was the biggest agency in Australia and New Zealand, where it set up shop in 1929 to service General Motors. It had slipped badly in recent years, but under Peter Steigrad's new leadership, the offices have moved back up, from 12th place to seventh in the market.

"Consistency has been absolutely critical to our success," says Fairnington, a 46-year-old Brit who first arrived in the region in 1980 to take over JWT's Malaysia office.

"As clients move more towards global advertising, they want to feel as if they're dealing with the same agency around the world. We either own or operate all of our offices here. With affiliates, clients complain, 'They don't speak my language, they don't understand my brand.' We realized that in the early '80s and set out to make JWT the best agency in every market."

Fairnington certainly knows his way around the diverse parts of the Pacific Rim. [In 1993] he spent 230 days out of his Hong Kong headquarters, tending to clients that range from such glittering names as De Beers to the mundane likes of Lux soap. The peripatetic pace helped JWT add $178 million to its Asia Pacific billings [in 1993], a gain of 26%. And 1994 is off to a strong start. Among JWT's wins [in 1994] are the national airlines in Philippines and Sri Lanka, San Miguel beer in Hong Kong and Foster's breweries in China.

"This area is extremely critical to us and to our clients," says Peter Schweitzer, president/chief operating officer JWT Worldwide. "It's the fastest-growing region, and the pace of change in many countries is unbelievable. It's like where the pioneers in our industry were at the turn of the century."

If Asia has become synonymous with marketing opportunity, the reality of implementing those efforts are far more complex in a region with the world's richest countries and its poorest. JWT divides it into four levels of consumer development: affluent markets (Japan, Hong Kong and Singapore); growth markets (Taiwan and South Korea); emerging markets (Thailand, Malaysia, Philippines, Indonesia) and untapped markets (China, India, Vietnam).

The more mature, affluent economies, with wealthy and well-educated consumers, are similar to those in the U.S., with their taste for Western goods and quality products. The "growth markets" of Taiwan and South Korea are spawning a middle class hungry for household items and leisure-time diversions;

by the end of the [decade], some 20–30% of their households should have incomes of more than US$30,000. Emerging countries still are held back by low spending power, but promise a significant future: They have large youth populations that are rapidly changing consumption behavior. (By the year 2000, the Asia/Pacific region will gain 80 million consumers aged 20–39, while the U.S. and Europe will show declines in that demographic.) The most long-term prospects are the giant landscapes of China and India, with hundreds of millions of poor, uneducated consumers — most of them aspiring to emulate their neighbors.

The range of markets and needs in Asia has long attracted JWT clients like Unilever and Nestle, which can sell their packaged goods and consumer staples across most countries and classes. They have been followed by other multinationals on JWT's roster, such as Ford, Kodak and Citibank, who are offering more sophisticated products or services. JWT now has the region's largest direct marketing operation, for instance, driven by Citibank's plunge into credit cards, retail banking and financial services. JWT also handles some of the region's largest local advertisers, like Hong Kong Telecom, Singapore Telecom and the Australian Travel Commission.

Perhaps most surprising is the marketing prowess of De Beers, which has become JWT Asia Pacific's third-largest client. JWT, which claims to have created the "engagement ring" concept for De Beers in Japan, says Asia now accounts for six of the 10 biggest markets for diamonds. The agency is even working for De Beers in China and Vietnam.

"Asia Pacific has become the most important part of the world for De Beers," says Marc Capra, JWT De Beers regional account director in Hong Kong. "The potential out here is incredible, especially since ownership is still low. You have fantastic cultures with a history of jewelry, places like Indonesia and Thailand. There are such young populations out here and, of course, status symbols are very important to people with new money."

In fact, De Beers has developed market strategies unique to the region. The South African mining consortium has targeted young Asian women with a pitch for jewelry made from lower-grade diamonds. Women are responding, not only as a way to flash their new financial status, but also as a sign of modernity. (Their mothers wore only gold.) In a mature market like Japan, JWT's ads encourage women to buy diamonds for themselves, as a sign of their increased self-confidence and importance in society. In China, De Beers' ads simply teach them about diamonds as an enduring symbol of marriage. One spot shows a couple, from childhood through teenage years to their wedding, graduating from flowers to a diamond ring as a gift.

"In the Asia Pacific area, there's a great preoccupation with luxury brands and logos in general," says JWT worldwide new business director Brian Johnson. "People see it as a fast badge of success. There's a good market there for Rolex, cognacs, fine liquors." A recent study of Chinese consumers found that Rolex was the most recognized brand of watch — even though Rolex does not advertise in China.

No country in the region captures marketers' imagination like China, with its 1.2 billion consumers and their pent-up demands. The Mao suit is being replaced by Dior; "to be rich is glorious," as chairman Deng Xiaoping recently crowed. "Assimilation in China has accelerated unbelievably," notes Atkinson, whose family fled the mainland in 1948 for Hong Kong; she returned after growing up in the U.S. and joining Thompson in the mid-'70s. "There is a lot of product leapfrogging. You have a country of no phones going to cellular; a country with no typewriters moving straight to computers. People have gone from washing their hair with a bar of soap to using four-in-one shampoo/conditioning products."

The standard Western impression of China is fading, she says, as its economy gains strength. "The masses in China are not so poor. Housing, medical care, food, even personal care products are provided by employers, so a lot of people are saving 30–50% of their salaries, which are rising. Some people even save 60%."

For marketers, tapping into that buying power isn't limited to new products or constricted by existing rivals. "In the West it could take years for a company to establish a shampoo brand, but in Asia it can take off right away," says Johnson.

With huge populations like those in China and India, it's easy to see how sales can expand dramatically. The share potential is staggering. Consider telephones: Only 1–2% of Chinese households have one currently. Hooking up just another 1–2% of the country adds 12 million new phones. Even ordinary retail statistics take on larger-than-life dimensions. On an average weekday in Shanghai, 400,000 people visit its First Department Store.

The power of such numbers is magnified by the region's Confucian ideals, which value hard work, savings and reputation. "'Face' is an important concept over here. You should always look respectful, good, rich," says Sattar Khan, a JWT regional client account director in Singapore.

JWT client Warner Lambert, for instance, wouldn't sell Asians much Listerine if the marketer told them outright that mouthwash was good for them. Instead, Listerine woos them with promises of confidence and social poise.

Kahn, who was head of JWT Asia/Pacific's strategic planning in 1990–91, says that while some traditions remain, many past impediments to commercial change are gone. "Religion used to be a barrier. But money has transcended religion." And unlike Europe, Asia's political ideologies seem not to get in the way of productivity and entrepreneurship.

"The difference between Asia and Eastern Europe is that Eastern Europe has some fundamental economic problems as those countries move from communism to capitalism," says JWT new business exec Johnson. "Consider the hold of Stalinism in Europe and the number of years people have lived with cradle-to-grave support from the state. Despite its politics, the Asia Pacific region has always had a fierce capitalistic work ethic. There's more of a tradition of hard work, aggressiveness and affluence."

Not that politics is an inconsequential factor for multinationals doing business in Asia. The Chinese government's crackdown after the Tiananmen Square protests scared off many marketers in 1989. The current specter of North Korea's arms buildup also serves as a sober reminder of regional tensions. No one knows fully what to expect when Hong Kong, the region's banking and trading center, is absorbed into mainland China in 1997.

Even some of the region's biggest boosters are cautious in their predictions. "If political systems don't evolve fast enough to keep up with economic progress, things could get out of balance and you might see political leaders pull back," says Atkinson.

The 52-year-old Shanghai native has bridged JWT's two worlds in the region. She lived in the U.S. for 20 years, earning her college degree and becoming fluent in Western culture. And she has spent 18 years working for JWT Asia Pacific, establishing regional offices in countries like Indonesia. Her current office in Hong Kong is designed according to the Chinese practice of fung shui, which holds that certain objects and their positioning in interiors can ward off misfortune. JWT has a fung shui expert on retainer; he visits Atkinson's office three or four times a year and is consulted before important presentations. (A lute placed in her office is meant to bring harmony and serenity; frogs on her window sill are to "help capture money from the sea.")

Such traditional customs are married to Western-style business practices. Under Fairnington, who became JWT's area director for South and East Asia in 1988 and assumed responsibility for the entire region four years later, the agency has prospered, becoming the fastest-growing part of the agency network. Since 1988, JWT Asia Pacific billings have increased 130%, or 15% on an annualized basis, compared to the 4.5% annual gain eked out by the company's U.S. operations. Billings jumped from $370 million in 1988 to $873 million in 1993, and the upward trend shows no sign of slowing.

"The success and principles of JWT in this part of the world are largely driven by Alan," says Peter Steigrad, JWT area director of Australia and New Zealand. Fairnington, who first worked for JWT in Toronto, made the Malaysia office No. 1 in its market in three years, then built up JWT's newly acquired Hong Kong shop into the leading firm there. He also established JWT divisions in China and Taiwan before taking on the top regional posts.

Along the way, Fairnington stressed the importance of having up-to-date practices and production values in place. "JWT has really distinguished itself with its media expertise here," says Atkinson. "Early on Alan saw that media could give us a cutting edge. We've established media systems that do post-buy analysis."

Even without such elaborate research data bases, agency investment in the region can be considerable. In densely populated Hong Kong, for instance, commercial rents for a modest office can run up to $25,000 a month. Poor countries like Vietnam, where America's trade embargo was just lifted [in 1993], can nonetheless come at a stiff price because of the lack of commercial infrastructure.

In addition, the cost of recruiting management talent in the Asia Pacific, both locals and ex-pats [ex-patriots], is high. JWT has one of the most rigorous training programs in the region, which has yielded good results.

The majority of senior staff were developed within the agency, and only two of its offices have foreign managers. "Executive costs can be so expensive here," says Fairnington. "It pays to get a good local manager."

That extensive local know-how has paid off in dealing with government red tape associated with restrictions that limit foreign business ownership. JWT is one of the few international agencies to have wholly-owned offices in Korea and Japan, where its 38-year-old office was started before ownership limitations were implemented. In countries like Indonesia, where foreign companies aren't allowed to have equity in local concerns, JWT has resorted to some novel business practices. The agency operates an Indonesian-owned firm, called Ad Force, as a JWT office and pays the local owner 2.5% of income.

Local governments have also gotten in the way of regional media development. But that bureaucrat's stranglehold on broadcast outlets is coming to an end. "Media in Asia is changing faster than anywhere else in the world. It's the last frontier," says Sue Johns, JWT's executive media director for Hong Kong and China. "We're seeing the free-up of government control. Cable is making inroads. When everything was government owned, it was a seller's market, and you couldn't get into quality programming."

In some cases, JWT clients — which in countries like China are the biggest purchaser of airtime — couldn't get into any programs, quality or otherwise. "These governments didn't care about profit and loss and rates were kept artificially low," says Fairnington. "In places like Korea, the government charged the same rate for 4 P.M. as they did for 8 P.M. It was so hard to get time because anyone could get on the air. You'd be competing with the local shopkeeper for time."

With Rupert Murdoch's takeover and expansion of Star TV, . . . the startup of dozens of private TV channels in Asia, and the birth of a professional cable industry, media opportunities are opening up to meet advertiser demand. Agencies like JWT can leverage their clients' considerable media clout, although measurement remains a problem in several countries. "We have good quantitative research, we have people meters," says Johns. "It's the qualitative research that's lacking."

That will surely come, as a consumer consciousness takes hold, reinforced by modern programming and advertising.

"Countries like China have gone too far down the road," says Atkinson. "People have had a taste of spending money and making their own choices. There's no turning back."

"Playing the Asia Card," by Noreen O'Leary, *Adweek Eastern Edition,* May 2, 1994. Dow//Quest Story ID: 0000400827ZF. © 1994 *Adweek,* L.P. Reprinted with permission from *Adweek.*

INDEX